Critical Gerontology Comes of Age

Critical Gerontology Comes of Age reflects on how baby boomers, caretakers, and health professionals are perceiving and adapting to historical, social, political, and cultural changes that call into question prior assumptions about aging and life progression. Through an exploration of earlier and later-life stages and the dynamic changes in intergenerational relations, chapter authors reexamine the research, methods, and scope of critical gerontology, a multidisciplinary field that speaks to the experiences of life in the 21st century. Topics include Medicare, privatization of home care, incarceration, outreach to LGTBQ elders, migration, and chronic illness. Grounded in innovative research and case studies, this volume reflects multiple perspectives and is accessible to lay readers, advanced undergraduates and graduate students, and professionals in many fields.

Chris Wellin, PhD, is an associate professor of sociology and coordinator of gerontology programs at Illinois State University. In addition to publishing articles in numerous professional journals, Dr. Wellin was commissioned by a Committee of the National Academy of Sciences (NAS) in 2008 to review and assess ethnographic research on direct caregiving for older and/or disabled people. He served from 2009 to 2011 as chair of the Division on Youth, Aging, and the Life Course in the Society for the Study of Social Problems.

Critical Gerontology Comes of Age

*Advances in Research and Theory
for a New Century*

Edited by
Chris Wellin

Routledge
Taylor & Francis Group
NEW YORK AND LONDON

First published 2018
by Routledge
711 Third Avenue, New York, NY 10017

and by Routledge
2 Park Square, Milton Park, Abingdon, Oxon, OX14 4RN

Routledge is an imprint of the Taylor & Francis Group, an informa business

© 2018 Taylor & Francis

The right of Chris Wellin to be identified as the author of the editorial
material, and of the authors for their individual chapters, has been
asserted in accordance with sections 77 and 78 of the Copyright,
Designs and Patents Act 1988.

All rights reserved. No part of this book may be reprinted or reproduced
or utilised in any form or by any electronic, mechanical, or other means,
now known or hereafter invented, including photocopying and recording,
or in any information storage or retrieval system, without permission in
writing from the publishers.

Trademark notice: Product or corporate names may be trademarks or
registered trademarks, and are used only for identification and
explanation without intent to infringe.

Library of Congress Cataloging-in-Publication Data
Names: Wellin, Christopher, editor.
Title: Critical gerontology comes of age : advances in research and theory for
a new century / edited by Chris Wellin.
Description: First Edition. | New York : Routledge, 2018.
Identifiers: LCCN 2017057708 | ISBN 9781138630277 (hardcover : alk. paper) |
ISBN 9781138630284 (pbk. : alk. paper) | ISBN 9781315209371 (e-book)
Subjects: LCSH: Gerontology. | Social gerontology. | Aging—Social aspects. |
Older people—Care. | Older transsexuals—Care.
Classification: LCC HQ1061 .C694 2018 | DDC 305.26—dc23LC record available
at https://lccn.loc.gov/2017057708

ISBN: 978-1-138-63027-7 (hbk)
ISBN: 978-1-138-63028-4 (pbk)
ISBN: 978-1-315-20937-1 (ebk)

Typeset in Minion
by Florence Production Ltd, Stoodleigh, Devon, UK

Contents

About the Contributors   vii
Acknowledgments   x

1   **Introductory Chapter: The Need for, and Fruits of, a Current Critical Gerontology**   1
Chris Wellin

2   **A First-Generation Critic Comes of Age Revisited: Reflections of a Critical Gerontologist**   19
Carroll L. Estes

3   **Critical Questions for Critical Gerontology (and Critical Gerontologists)**   35
Harry R. Moody and Jennifer R. Sasser

4   **Qualifying the Aging Enterprise: Micro- and Meso-Level Studies in Human Service Organizations**   46
Gale Miller and Alexandra Crampton

5   **Who are You in *Medicare and You*? Examining *This* Second Person**   62
Timothy Diamond

vi *Contents*

6 Who Rules Home Care? The Impacts of Privatization on
Profitability, Cost, and Quality 79
William Cabin

7 Challenges and Achievements Regarding Outreach to
Lesbian, Gay, Bisexual, and Transgender Elders: Perspectives
from Nursing 92
Marcena Gabrielson

8 Paid Caregiving for Older Adults with Serious or Chronic
Illness: Ethnographic Perspectives, Evidence, and Implications
for Training 112
Chris Wellin

9 Silver Alert: Societal Aging, Dementia, and Framing a Social
Problem 134
Gina Petonito and Glenn W. Muschert

10 Aging in Places 151
Stacy Torres

11 Meanings of Age and Aging among Older, Incarcerated
Women: Implications for Adaptation and Policy Reform 164
Leah M. Janssen

12 How Thinking about Children from a Global Perspective
Can Fortify Social Gerontology 193
Maria Schmeeckle

13 Lost in the "Big World"?: Korean College Students Coming of
Age in the United States 208
Kirsten Younghee Song

14 Migration and Gendered Webs of Obligation: Caring for my
Elderly Puerto Rican Mother in a Transnational Context 225
Maura I. Toro-Morn

Index 243

About the Contributors

William (Bill) Cabin (PhD, City University of New York) is assistant professor of social work at Temple University. In addition to aging, his interests include home health care, palliative care, and hospice care.

Alexandra Crampton (MSW, PhD, University of Michigan) is an associate professor in the Department of Social and Cultural Sciences, Marquette University. She earned her MSW and a joint PhD in anthropology and social work from the University of Michigan. Her research interests are in social interventions for populations identified as vulnerable due to age (i.e., children and older adults) and in the use of alternative dispute resolution as one such social intervention.

Timothy Diamond (PhD, Ohio State University) is at work on a book about health care as a right. He is the author of *Making Gray Gold: Narratives of Nursing Home Care*, and lives in Colorado.

Carroll L. Estes (PhD, University of California, San Diego) is professor emerita at the University of California, San Francisco (UCSF), and the founding director of the Institution for Health & Aging at UCSF. Estes, who in 2014 was awarded the University of California Medal, the university's highest recognition, has authored, co-authored, or co-edited twenty-four books.

Marcena Gabrielson (RN, PhD, University of Iowa) was awarded a John A. Hartford Fellowship and taught at Illinois State University and Milliken University. She is currently balancing teaching with advanced training in clinical nursing.

viii *About the Contributors*

Leah M. Janssen (MGS, Miami University) is a doctoral student in social gerontology at Miami University and Scripps Gerontology Center. She directed personal and professional development programs for older adults and single mothers in central Wyoming and northern Kentucky. Her research focuses on whole-person growth and development, recognizing the importance of social and relational intelligence in gerontology.

Gale Miller (PhD, University of Kansas) is emeritus professor of sociology in the Department of Social and Cultural Sciences, Marquette University. He has long-standing research interests in the sociology of troubles and social problems, social theory and institutions.

Harry R. Moody (PhD, Columbia University) is retired vice president of academic affairs for the American Association of Retired Persons (AARP),. He is currently visiting professor at Tohoku University in Japan, and distinguished visiting scholar at Fielding Graduate University. He previously served as executive director of the Brookdale Center on Aging at Hunter College and chairman of the board of Elderhostel (now Road Scholar).

Glenn W. Muschert (PhD, University of Colorado at Boulder) is professor of sociology and social justice studies at Miami University, Oxford, Ohio. His areas of scholarly interest are in digital sociology, technologies of social control, and the sociology of social problems.

Gina Petonito (PhD, Syracuse University) is an associate professor in the Social and Behavioral Sciences Program at Miami University Regionals. She is also affiliated with the Sociology and Gerontology Program at Miami University, Oxford. Her main research area is the social construction of the other centering on race and ethnic categorization. Most recently, she has focused on the ways claims makers construct surveillance practices of elders as forms of caring, rather than forms of control.

Jennifer (Jenny) Sasser (PhD, Oregon State University) is an educational gerontologist, transdisciplinary scholar, and community activist. She has been working in the field of gerontology for more than half her life, beginning as a nursing assistant and aging advocate. She served as chair of the Department of Human Sciences and founding director of Gerontology at Marylhurst University, in Portland, Oregon, from 1999 to 2015.

Maria Schmeeckle (PhD, University of Southern California) is associate professor of sociology in the Department of Sociology and Anthropology at Illinois State University. Her areas of interest include children and childhood, marriage and family relationships, global and transnational sociology, intersectionality, aging, and the life course.

Kirsten Younghee Song (PhD, Rutgers University) is a visiting assistant professor at the Department of Sociology and Anthropology in West Virginia University. Her research has focused on transnationalism, international migration, culture, identity, life course, and adulthood transition.

Maura I. Toro-Morn (PhD, Loyola University of Chicago) is professor of sociology and director of Latin American and Latino/a Studies at Illinois State University. As a scholar in the fields of immigration and sociology, she has always been curious about why people move, how, and what are the consequences of their movements; thus, she has devoted much of her career to studying migration in global perspective.

Stacy Torres (PhD, New York University) is assistant professor of sociology in the Department of Sociology, University at Albany, SUNY. Her areas of interest include gender, family, health, urban communities, qualitative methodology, aging, and the life course.

Chris Wellin (PhD, Northwestern University) is associate professor of sociology and coordinator of gerontology programs in the Department of Sociology and Anthropology, Illinois State University. In addition to aging and the life course, his interests include the study of occupations and careers and qualitative research methods.

Acknowledgments

This book is the culmination of three decades' experience in the field of aging—first as a paid caregiver, later as a student, researcher, teacher, and collaborator with diverse community agencies and advocates. I am filled with gratitude for the insight, support, and collegiality of many people and institutions along the way. As an undergraduate in the sociology program at the University of Wisconsin, Milwaukee, I had the exceptionally wise and devoted mentorship of Dale Jaffe, a fine teacher, and later co-author, whose commitment to creative and policy-relevant research have guided me throughout my career. Eleanor Miller in that program provided a lucid and challenging introduction to the study of gender, and theoretical analysis more generally. As a graduate student at Northwestern University, I was fortunate to work with Art Stinchcombe, Charles Ragin, Roberto Fernandez, Christopher Jencks, Michael Burawoy (a visiting scholar), and, especially, Howie Becker, who has remained a vital friend and resource in the years since, as he has for so many. All shaped my thinking in indelible ways. Carroll Estes supported my selection for a post-doctoral position in the Institute for Health & Aging at the University of California, San Francisco, funded through the National Institute on Aging and the Agency for Healthcare Research and Quality. This experience allowed me to become better informed about health services research and, gradually, to better integrate my questions and method-ological approach in areas of scholarship and policy analysis which had not typically featured interpretive studies. I hope that this volume contributes to even stronger linkages between policy studies and qualitative inquiry. I owe special appreciation to Arlie Hochschild and Barrie Thorne, who, as co-directors of the Center for Working Families at the University of California, Berkeley (an interdisciplinary research center, funded by the Alfred P. Sloan Foundation), created and nurtured a warm and vibrant working group centered on "cultures of care. " This group, along with the *Carework Network* affiliated with the American Sociological Association and the Society for the Study of Social Problems (SSSP), was essential in bringing together a diverse group of scholars who had often struggled to locate our questions and aspirations in traditional disciplinary subfields. In later years, the SSSP has continued to be an essential professional association in sustaining my career. As chair of the Division on Youth, Aging and the Life Course of the SSSP, I was able to contribute to the program of the annual meetings (from 2009 to 2011), which in turn fostered personal and scholarly connections that made this book possible. My colleagues in the Department of Sociology and Anthropology, and in kindred programs that enrich the gerontology program at Illinois State University, have maintained the highest standards of collegiality and humanity. Professor Caroline Mallory, then a faculty member in the Mennonite College of Nursing, was particularly generous and skillful in helping me plan and receive funding for an interdisciplinary conference, sponsored by the ISU School of Social Work, an event that informed the agenda of this book. Madonna Harrington Meyer showed important early support for this project, and helped greatly to refine the original prospectus. I thank Elsevier who granted permission to publish a revised version of an article by Carroll Estes, which first appeared in the *Journal of Aging Studies*, and the National Academy of Sciences, which commissioned a report that, in revised form, appears as Chapter 8 in this volume. Other scholars in the field who, directly or indirectly, have enriched my understanding and helped to sustain my career include Bernard Beck. Toni Calasanti, Dale Dannefer, Marj DeVault, Tim Diamond, Jaber Gubrium, Jon Hendricks, Gale Miller, Leonard Schatzman, Robert Weiss, and Judy Wittner. I celebrate the work and legacy of Barbara Myerhoff, whose spirit animates the book, and, more personally, the unwavering love, strength, and support of Valerie Wellin, whose intellect and editorial skill were essential in completing the project. To my father, Edward—a fine scholar, teacher, mentor, and person—I dedicate this book.

CHAPTER **1**

Introductory Chapter: The Need for, and Fruits of, a Current Critical Gerontology

Chris Wellin

Introduction

The academic study of aging has flourished in recent decades, along with the growth in the older population of the United States and other developed nations. This demographic process, dramatic in itself, is accompanied by equally far-reaching changes in the meanings, timing, and sequence of social roles and transitions that have organized the life course for decades, certainly since the mid-twentieth century.

Among the key issues that have arisen in the United States and other aging societies are: impacts of greater longevity and disability on family ties and living arrangements; new residential forms and policies that depart from the institutional bias of the past (e.g., assisted living and home- and community-based services, as an alternative to nursing home placement); strains in public policies that historically assumed caregiving to be a family responsibility, primarily borne by women; new forms of community—both place-based and virtual—that are distinctive to the baby boomer cohorts; and whether/how these patterns differ by race, social class, gender, and ethnicity in an increasingly diverse society. There is clearly a need for attention to how these forces are remaking intergenerational ties, and for careful observation and description of how people, in diverse contexts and with varying resources, are adapting.

Rather than isolate later life, or older adults, as focal concerns—which was often true of earlier generations of scholarship (e.g., see Hendricks, 1992)—we now see how longer life trajectories, family formation, intergenerational ties, political agendas, and personal identity and role expectations are all being called urgently into question. In response to these dynamics, academic programs, research, professional practice, advocacy, and commercial interests within social gerontology have all proliferated (Wellin, 2010).

As a theoretical framework, more than a theory, per se, the *life course perspective* is the most encompassing and interdisciplinary explanatory map for understanding the interplay between social structures, history, and human lives. In a concise summary, Quadagno (2018) defines the framework as "an approach to aging

1

2   Chris Wellin

that emphasizes the interaction of historical events, individual decisions and opportunities, and the effect of early life experiences in determining later life outcomes" (pp. 26–27). Foundational concepts in the social-behavioral sciences— social roles and role transitions, kinship and social support, stratification, health status, occupational and other careers, welfare state policy—are placed in dynamic motion in ways that reveal their interrelationships and historical particularity, in light of the life course perspective. In addition, the framework enables one to resolve apparent dilemmas that have persistently inhibited understanding within social inquiry, specifically: how to reconcile agency and structure in exploring social life, a tension that, in other terms, frames a reductive debate between micro- and macroscopic levels of analysis (e.g., Alexander, 1988, pp. 87–88). Life course perspectives help transcend these constraints and (to quote a book title from a prominent scholar) advance the understanding of *Lives in Time and Place* (Settersten, 1999). In all, there has been enormous and varied growth in the scholarship on aging, propelled by life course thinking, especially over the past four decades.

However, there are several reasons why a contemporary collection of writings on aging and the life course is especially useful now. First, most of the published research now available was conceived and conducted before the implications of the large "baby boomer" cohorts of the post-World War II period could be visible, much less analyzed or understood. This diverse group, numbering some eighty million, has transformed the demographic structure of the United States, in which the older population, defined as those older than 60 years, will soon constitute 20% of the total. Within a period of one human life span, from the early twentieth to the early twenty-first centuries, the percentage of elders in the United States has at least quadrupled. This has presented both bracing challenges and opportunities to which cultural norms, social policies, and established institutions are struggling to adapt.

It is important to note that earlier perspectives in gerontology rightly decried ageism—the negative stereotyping of older people, abetted by the increasingly age-segregated nature of modern society—but tended to exaggerate differences or variation *between* older and younger cohorts. However, as Dannefer (1987) and others have shown both theoretically and empirically, older cohorts are the *most* diverse and heterogeneous in the population. This pattern, rooted in social class, historical change, and people's biographical choices and priorities, is evident across the topical areas that have characterized the study of aging for decades: family life, employment and retirement, economic fortunes, religiosity, health, and even death and dying. Moreover, the maturation of a global economic and political order, which is now the focus of intense political debate in the United States, United Kingdom, and elsewhere, is implicated, along with a turn toward neoliberal social policy (Hasenfeld & Garrow, 2012), with levels of social inequality not seen in nearly a century. *How are such conditions reverberating in the lives and aging experiences of people today?*

We believe that such dynamic change calls for inductive, contextualized, and historically sensitive accounts, rather than attempts to discern what is typical,

Current Critical Gerontology 3

normative, or in keeping with older, quasi-causal models. Our approach found support in an earlier, lucid review of theory in gerontology:

> . . . we call for future theoretical directions which concretely analyze the social contexts of aging. By social context we do not mean the kind of analysis commonly done by age-stratification and life course researchers, which merely examines statistical comparisons of select cohort demographics. Our concern, rather, is with social *experience*, the fluid and dynamic features of social context.
>
> (Passuth & Bengston, 1996, p. 25 [emphasis in original])

The authors go on to advocate for a marriage, so to speak, between macro-oriented, structural awareness and fine-grained study of language and action, social phenomenology. This methodological emphasis, on qualitative/interpretive approaches, is evident in these pages.

A second feature of this volume is the explicit influence of *critical gerontology* perspectives. Never static, this stance invites ongoing scrutiny of the assumptions, concepts, topics, stakeholders, and consequences of what might be termed "established" gerontology. In the next section, I sketch the major thrust of a political economy perspective on aging and the aged, which is perhaps the most visible strain in critical gerontology, certainly in the academic presentation of the field. The emphasis on political economy, however, is but one part of the broader spectrum of critical gerontology. Moody (quoted in Bengston, Burgess, & Parrott, 1997, p. S83) identified four goals that have characterized this approach, which are: (1) *to theorize subjective and interpretive dimensions of aging*; (2) *to focus not on technical advancement but on praxis, defined as action or involvement in practical change (such as public policy)*; (3) *to link academics and practitioners through praxis*; and (4) *to produce emancipatory knowledge*. These goals, even when implicit, animate contributing authors, and buttress this book. The same goals underlie the diversity of writing strategies and voices authors use and, at times, justify longer or less conventional presentations than are typical of academic journals or conference presentations. A shared commitment among authors is to aim for the widest accessibility, both within and beyond academic circles, in an effort to fulfill Mills' (1959, p. 3) promise that social inquiry might shed light on the connections between biography and history and reveal the forces impelling "seemingly impersonal changes in the very structure of continent-side societies."

Internal Debates and Policy Analysis in Critical Gerontology

As editor, I never conceived this book in terms of pre-determined or proposed sections or topical foci within critical gerontology. Such a strategy would not be in keeping with the spirit of innovation we seek to embody and, in any case, would only have led to insoluble disputes about which topics to include or how to justify the choice of sections. Instead, through experience in teaching and reading, along with networks forged through professional associations, I sought out contributors

4   *Chris Wellin*

who are breaking new ground and who have sustained their engagement with areas of interest throughout their careers, or in multiple roles in their careers. As the collection took shape, topical connections and complementary arguments emerged.

After briefly elaborating on the diversity of critical gerontology, I will point to ways in which the current collection represents innovation and synthesis in critical aging studies. Though internally diverse and even contested (Bengston et al., 1997), critical gerontology places aging and related issues in historical and cultural contexts. For some scholars in this tradition (e.g., Estes, 1979), the status of older people, collectively and across sub-groups, is most powerfully explained in reference to the *political economy* at particular historical periods, and the resultant power relations, cultural/media imagery, and macro-level policies that shape access to roles (such as in employment or retirement) and economic resources.

In the United States, a nation whose history has reflected exceptional resistance toward welfare state expansion as compared with those of other advanced countries, federal policy regarding older adults has been anomalous: the two obvious and contrary cases—Social Security in 1935 and Medicare three decades later—define older people, in part, as a *deserving* constituency. These policies, eligibility for which is based on chronological age, might instead have been based on *need* (Neugarten, 1982), and this idea fuels an ongoing controversy. That said, critical gerontologists have shared an enduring tension regarding whether to view such policies as benevolent entitlements for a "good" old age or, alternatively, as mechanisms that ultimately consign older people to a status of *structured dependence* and vulnerability in late- or post-capitalist societies.

In this volume, contributors Estes, Moody and Sasser, Diamond, and Cabin engage and elaborate on this strand of critical aging studies, from diverse philosophical, political, and methodological stances. Specifically, Estes and Moody, in dialogic fashion, aim to define and celebrate critical gerontology, though they differ on such issues as how to square the approach with current political alignments in the United States, which differ by age, and whether there is a benign or even constructive role for private, market-based responses to challenges that aging poses, both individually and collectively.

Estes' chapter sets the tone for the book, both in terms of substance and voice. She pairs a richly candid and personal account of her career, as a pioneering gerontologist and builder of a research center, with a declaration of the kinds of knowledge and praxis she has aspired to enhance through the decades. Her career reveals the trade-offs, for example, between constructing policy-relevant scholarship and advocacy (shaped by specialized discourse and by the range of possible policy options at given political moments) and her desire to engage in a more broadly engaged *public sociology* (see Burawoy, 2004).

Diamond, drawing on the distinctive tradition of institutional ethnography (see DeVault, 1999), examines the text of a public manual on Medicare, as well as narrative material from various public settings, in order to challenge widely held premises regarding the nature and quality of coverage. This is a novel if not heretical project, given the strong public support for Medicare and current threats by the newly installed Trump administration radically to alter major welfare state policies (especially Social Security Disability and Medicaid expansion, under the Affordable Care Act) in the proposed (FY) 2018 budget. Cabin, drawing on extensive experience in health care administration and related research, examines the expansion of home health care, questioning how and to what extent non-profit and proprietary ownership shape the quality of care. Cabin's contribution reflects the rather specialized language and analysis of formal policy that, even among critical scholars, has shaped the field.

Engaging the "Aging Network" and the Domains of Occupational/Professional Practice

Indeed, from its origins, gerontology has had a strong focus on application and policy, which in earlier decades strongly reflected a *problem-centered* orientation—one that assumed and emphasized losses and decline in later life (Katz, 1996). In her book, *The Aging Enterprise*, Estes (1979, pp. 16–30) was among the first to advance an explicit critique of the "services strategy," that expanded sharply, especially after the passage in 1965 of the *Older Americans Act* (OAA). While the spirit and text of the OAA strike readers as quasi-utopian in these austere times for federal funding, Estes and others argue that the "aging network," and the "helping professionals" that provide such services, tends to *individualize and pathologize* the persistent problems facing substantial groups of older people (and, equally, people with disabilities). As such, this approach, which Morgan and Kunkel (2007, pp. 298–299) discuss as "compassionate ageism," tends to obscure and diffuse attention from what many critical scholars see as the political, economic, and professional exploitation that reproduces such inequalities— poverty, inadequate or unaffordable housing, social and geographic isolation—over the decades, even during periods when service provision has expanded. For Biggs, Hendricks, and Lowenstein (2003, p. 2), "*Aging Enterprise* is an apt example of critique building to a novel and antithetical understanding of the growth in services for older adults. It is suggested, from Estes' view, that the ostensive development of services to meet a growing need, in reality disguises the exploitation of new markets and the consolidation of new forms of professional power." This paradox, I can attest, complicates the teaching of gerontology from a critical angle, since a great many motivated and professionally oriented students, drawn to courses on aging, are committed to the very fields, such as social work and allied health, which are targets of the critique. How, then, can we reconcile the quasi-cynical indictment of the services strategy while allowing for more inductive and affirmative arguments regarding the motives and achievements of those in the helping and policy professions?

Indeed, even those who subscribe to macro-level, critical approaches might acknowledge and investigate how, in practice, intermediate/meso-level institutions and interactions contribute to shaping experiences and identities, linked to age. More recent scholars and advocates are more likely to document the humane or even potentially empowering impacts of clinical and human services, rejecting

6   Chris Wellin

what some regard as nihilistic tendencies, for example, in warnings about the *biomedicalization* of aging (Estes & Binney, 1989). Though vital and provocative, arguments framed at this level of analysis limit, in effect if not by intent, inquiry into the motives and contradictions of those within the "aging network" and related fields, as well as their contributions to the quality of life for people facing the burdens of advanced age or disability.

Perhaps another reason why there has been relatively scant qualitative or experiential research on the helping professions is that, as Pithouse (1987) asserted, fields such as social casework are "invisible," by virtue of the ethical and organizational constraints surrounding detailed inquiry into what are, after all, encounters involving vulnerable people facing fateful circumstances. Still, in what I regard as an exciting and pertinent development, scholars such as the medical anthropologist Cheryl Mattingly (1998) have brought narrative analysis into our understanding of clinical encounters and, in turn, into processes of healing and rehabilitation that are ever more important in our age of chronic illness and increased longevity.

> "Narrative," she argues, "not only functions as a form of talk; it also serves as an aesthetic and moral form underlying clinical action. That is, therapists and patients not only tell stories; sometimes they create story-like structures through their interactions. Furthermore, this effort at story-making, which I will refer to as *therapeutic emplotment*, is integral to the healing power of this practice."
> (emphasis in original, p. 2)

In principle, the open-ended quality of human service interactions has long been acknowledged, even by those, such as Estes (1979), who have called the efficacy of the aging network into question. She writes that the symbolic interactionist perspective, "argues that it is possible for the interactional context and process (the environment, the persons, and encounters in it) to significantly affect the kind of aging process a person will experience" (1979, p. 9). We hold a somewhat fluid, constructionist view, seeking to mesh macro-level and interactionist theory in tracing how social views of age or disability are typified and routinized within policies and institutions and, often, internalized by those who are reliant on programs and services. Nonetheless, more inductive and detailed investigations of human service and medical encounters have been slow to appear or more fully to inform critical gerontology—a gap that we seek to address in this book.

In this connection, Miller and Crampton address the broad domain of ethnography in/of human service institutions, offering a meta-analysis of themes and implications, rooted in their respective and lengthy experiences of immersion in programs that serve clients across the age spectrum. They document how "seemingly personal life experiences are socially organized and given meaning in diverse institutional contexts." The value of fine-grained, ethnographic attention to the local practices and staff discretion that mediate the impact and, potentially, justice of human service interventions was articulated decades ago by Lipsky (1980) and others. Miller and Crampton revisit and expand on this vital theme.

Current Critical Gerontology 7

In turn, Gabrielson, a nurse-scholar, addresses how her field—defined by its distinctive commitment to patient advocacy and community support—is seeking to enhance outreach to LGBTQ elders, a community that, in the past, was neglected, if not stigmatized, within the health care system. My own chapter on direct care workers (such as certified nursing assistants [CNAs] and home health aides) draws on first-hand experience and research, as well as on a thematic review of earlier literature, to define and document the skillful quality of direct care work. This account is a counterpoint to conventional economic and policy discourse, which tends to equate skill with formal training and credentials, and which has accepted and reproduced culturally embedded assumptions about gender, race/ethnicity, and caring which continue to undermine the public appreciation of or compensation for the work (see Cancian & Oliker, 2000). Inasmuch as direct care work (including that for children, as well as for those who are aged or disabled) represents the largest and fastest-growing sector of the service economy in the United States, the stakes for all concerned could not be higher. This chapter also exemplifies the fact that while much policy analysis and evaluation research have been dominated by positivist approaches and quantitative strategies, narrative approaches and meta-analysis can also have an impact, especially if/when conventional framings and data sources show diminishing returns (Wellin, 2007).

"Places" as Contexts for the Study of Aging

Earlier I alluded to the value of anchoring the study of aging in discrete contexts, *places*, which one can define in myriad ways—cultural, institutional, historical, communitarian. The study of aging and places—environmental gerontology—is in itself a rich subfield (e.g., Rowles & Bernard, 2013). Several authors frame their contributions in connection with places, ranging from the metaphorical (an idealized sense of "home" and safety) to the brutally material (aging behind bars).

An implied backdrop to these studies is the often unexamined concept of *aging in place*, which Quadagno (2018, pp. 198–199) and others discuss as containing the ideal of continuity and independence, tied to remaining in one's own home. This ideal is often untenable, either because a reduction in mobility can render the home restrictive (unless modifications are possible) or because residents lack the energy or resources to maintain or sell their homes. In any case, rates of home-ownership are highest among older people, in the United States, and many equate this, for good or ill, with middle-class status: "home" and "place" are deeply symbolic, entwined with history, social status, and identity.

Drawing from the constructionist approach to social problems, Petonito and Muschert trace the policy phenomenon of "Silver Alerts," centered on missing elders which, they argue, emerged "on the coattails," so to speak, of the earlier "Amber Alerts" which focused on the location of missing children. *Silver Alerts* reflect and seek to address looming concerns about missing elders, disoriented to place and rendered vulnerable and less than fully adult, by virtue of dementia. After reviewing the constructionist approach to social problems (see Best, 1995), the authors argue that despite the compassionate framing of the issue, this policy

8   *Chris Wellin*

"solution" denies older people a voice or sense of agency, in essence infantilizing them in the process, ostensibly, of bestowing a kind of protection—a paradox of "care and control."

Torres extends the theme of aging "in places," in two ways: first, by reviewing and integrating insights from earlier ethnographic studies, and second, by pointing to the innovations and adaptations elders make, when compelled to find new places. Her ethnographic project explored the impact of gentrification in greater New York City and, she discovered, the significance of a local bakery in providing a "gathering spot," ". . . a bubbling hub of neighborhood life, the center of an invisible world of older people hiding in plain sight." Complementing recent research (e.g., Klinenberg, 2012) documenting the rise of solitary living among more affluent elders in the United States and abroad, Torres exposes and extends meanings of place in aging studies, as a fulcrum for understanding identity, community, and adaptation.

Janssen offers a penetrating view into the meanings of age and aging among incarcerated women. Moving beyond the harrowing and pervasive accounts of mass incarceration in the United States over recent decades (e.g., Carson, 2014), her in-depth interview project provides subjective and narrative texture that is rare in the literature. Informants' accounts give shape to the meanings of time, biographical themes, and strategies of survival behind bars, and insights into how programming with prisons could be reformed and redesigned, better to meet the needs of aging or disabled women inmates. This population has been triply silenced—by virtue of their criminal sanction, and by their age and gender. Though the targeting of young African-American men within the criminal justice system has been vividly documented, Janssen offers a different and vital window into what is a fast-aging prison population. Though not expressly framed as a narrative study, she finds the power and resources of narrative, as a source of both personal resilience and directions for policy reform, much as Gubrium (1993) did in his illuminating study of residents' perceptions of and adaptations to life in nursing homes.

The Expanding Scope, Challenges, and Intergenerational Nature of Life Course Transitions

Earlier in the Introduction section, I touched on the nature and promise of life course perspectives and inquiry. The ascendance of the life course perspective in recent decades, despite its internal diversity, has encouraged and allowed us to understand *lives* in a more holistic way. The promise of what a leading scholar calls "developmental science" is to reject the fragmentation of inquiry, rooted in the multiple methods and theoretical orientations that have informed social research on aging, and move toward more contextualized, person-centered understanding. Specifically, we seek "a synthesis of the central concepts, propositions, and methods related to human development, one that bridges scholarship in different disciplines and on different life periods" (Settersten, 1999, p. 2). Certainly, one of the most powerful influences on how lives unfold is history,

Current Critical Gerontology 9

which, through the flow of birth cohorts (Mannheim, 1952; Ryder, 1965), connects individual biographies to the welter of larger events and conditions—economic, political, and cultural—that shape but do not determine, life trajectories. Like swimmers in the ocean, we ride the waves that propel some toward social opportunity and mobility, even as they break upon others. In the study of aging, this dynamic brings the productive tension between structure and agency, endemic in the human sciences, into vivid relief. In turning to topics and projects that have absorbed their careers, the contributors to this book orient their discussions to particular historical conditions that have been consequential, for good or ill, for how we navigate the aging process.

The life course framework is essentially ahistorical—neither assuming nor celebrating particular historical conditions or trajectories. Nonetheless, given our commitment to contemporary dynamics, it is important to spell out significant ways in which the twenty-first century life course is shaping life choices and trajectories. These changes, widely acknowledged and documented across kindred fields concerned with aging and adaptation, frame the inductive arguments that authors develop. The post-World War II period saw the institutionalization, for most, of what Riley and Riley (1994) termed the "age differentiated life course," characterized by a sequential and normative focus on roles in education, work, and then "leisure" or retirement, in advanced industrial societies. This pattern, which seemed natural and robust for those coming of age between the late 1940s and the 1970s, was firmly rooted in the state and federal policies. The G.I. Bill vastly increased access to higher education; federal home loans and rising productivity and real wages expanded the American middle class; and the same "social contract" (Rubin, 1996), enforced by strong labor union density, helped to provide supplementary pensions that made secure retirement possible, even for many with limited formal education.

This mid-twentieth century phenomenon—and its impact on the trajectory of so many lives and the expansion of the middle class in the United States—has left vivid traces in my own life. My father, Edward, is a first-generation American, born to Russian-Jewish parents who had fled the Ukraine in 1910 or so. Passing through Ellis Island, they embarked on a difficult life in Worcester, Massachusetts: my grandfather, a blacksmith and tool maker, struggled with employment through much of the 1930s, and my father, born in 1917, was compelled to work to help support the family. His plan, if not ambition, in his early twenties, was to complete training as a machinist in a local textile factory and secure a stable job as a skilled tradesman. World War II, for all its devastation, proved to be a catalyst in his life when, having survived the conflict, he was encouraged to attend college on the G.I. Bill. In that era, the benefit extended to private, as well as public, universities, and he ultimately completed a doctorate in anthropology and sustained a career in the then-nascent field of medical anthropology (e.g., Wellin, 1998, 1955). This historical roller-coaster—defined by harsh adversity, followed by a tide of upward and sustained mobility—is central to the narrative concerning what some journalists have celebrated as the *greatest* generation (Brokaw, 1998). In the decades following World War II, this historical/cultural narrative has shaped—even if not

10   *Chris Wellin*

always consciously—the ways in which many in the United States came to perceive and assess their own biographies. After all, there was evidence of widespread mobility and expanded opportunity, despite the glaring inequalities that remain.

Despite these gains, there were always inherent gaps and problems with the age-differentiated model/ideal, which have only become more sharply apparent in the global, post-industrial economic order in which we live today. Among the problems are the increased premium on formal and extended educational careers, to achieve middle-class status (despite yawning inequalities that persist in educational access and attainment); less stable employment arrangements and careers, which were visible even before the Great Recession of a decade ago; and the assumption that later life is non-productive (centered on "leisure"), which fueled ageism and undercut the sense of civic engagement among older people, and played into debates about generational equity.

Riley and Riley, in their discussion in 1994, argued for a need to move toward a more *age-integrated* life course model, allowing greater flexibility for people to move between educational, work, and other roles throughout their lives. Family, gender, and caregiving roles were largely absent from this analysis, an omission that has since been addressed in a vibrant stream of scholarship that integrates feminist and political economy/policy perspectives (Meyer, 2000.) In short, more by necessity than choice, we now see convulsions in life plans that reveal the obsolescence of the earlier, more "orderly" model. As Heinz (2003) demonstrated, ours is now a far more *contingent* life course, in which the risks and uncertainties of entering "full adulthood " and building family and community careers fall much more heavily on individuals at every stage. These changes have injected tension and instability into the meta-narratives of culture and identity that, for many, had come to seem natural in prior decades. As McAdams (1993, pp. 11–12) argued, a powerful strand of identity is coming to know oneself by

> . . . creating a heroic story of the self . . . What is a personal myth? First and foremost, it is a special kind of story that each of us naturally constructs to bring together the different parts of ourselves and our lives into a purposeful and convincing whole . . . A personal myth is an act of imagination that is a patterned integration of our remembered past, perceived present, and anticipated future.

The convulsive changes in the twenty-first century life course in many advanced nations, intensified in the United States by the results of the 2016 election, constitute a jarring breach in the assumptions and expectations by which—even if implicitly—many have navigated their lives. Becker (1997), in her book, *Disrupted Lives*, wrote that

> People's efforts to create linkages with the past during times of disruptive changes—whether societal, such as those caused by a revolution, or individual, such as the onset of illness—have been readily observed. People maintain

Current Critical Gerontology   11

continuity with the past amid the facts of change by interpreting current events so they are understood as part of a tradition.

(p. 4)

This ongoing process of reconciliation is, in good part, a *narrative* process, in which we place events and choices in time, seeking to discern the potential and limits of human *agency* to heal the breach; in this sense, there is substantial overlap between the power and efficacy of historical/cultural narratives, and individual ones, such as clinical counselors, seek to excavate via therapy (Polkinghorne, 1988). The promise is that one can *re-story* events, such that they become more coherent and morally acceptable. Social researchers on aging are certainly implicated in this process, and the concluding chapters in this volume reflect and expand on this theme. Like our informants, those who investigate aging are continuously *constructing the life course* (Holstein & Gubrium, 2000).

Schmeeckle offers both an intellectual memoir, recounting the development of her interests, training, and agenda as a sociologist, and a detailed appeal for gerontology to expand the study of the life course—to earlier life stages including childhood, and to global patterns and connections. Her initial interest, in the diverse and contested nature of family ties, drew her to examine children more directly, including their rights (or lack thereof); comparative status and well-being, internationally; and the extant state of law and policy which, at least potentially, advances social justice for children. In an especially poignant question, she asks us to consider the untold numbers of *missing elders,* those in so many stressed nations for whom reaching adulthood itself is fraught with risk.

Song, in her ethnographic study of life perspectives and strategies of Korean university students in the United States, draws from and expands on the timely theme of *prolonged adolescence,* or alternatively, *delayed adulthood.* This has become an enormously troubling and visible issue (e.g., Settersten & Ray, 2010), and not only in the United States. Other nations in Western Europe are also facing very high rates of unemployment (even for the most educated youth), stalled progress for young people seeking to establish independent homes or families, and high levels of student debt. These stresses combine and compound their sense that adulthood, as their parents or grandparents perceived it, is, not to strain our earlier oceanic metaphor, a receding horizon that they may not be able to reach until their thirties, if then. The informants in Song's account are highly motivated, worldly and, to be sure, sophisticated and accomplished. Multilingual, they reveal a new kind of subjectivity, quite different from that which we assumed to be the case in earlier iterations of research on immigration, based on models of *assimilation.* Rather than being anchored in national, cultural, or temporal matrices, their identities seem to be as fluid and contextual as is their use of language (code-switching) in their hectic routines. Dutiful toward parents and compliant with a rather vague obligation to prepare for life in "the big world, " their lives on campus and in their communities are, by contrast, rather limited and ascetic, certainly lacking the kind of exploration, autonomy, or rebellion that one assumes from stereotypes of American college students. In their social gatherings, nested

12   *Chris Wellin*

within a larger church community in central New Jersey, Song's informants make visible a kind of liminal young adulthood and community that one assumes must be present in virtually any large college or university. In the spirit of praxis and sensitivity to policy, Song concludes with some thoughts on how colleges, as institutions, might better support and integrate such students.

In the final chapter, Toro-Morn draws on the approach of auto-ethnography, to recount a saga of transnational caregiving—spanning boundaries of nation, culture, gender, and social class—involving her mother's final years. A native of Puerto Rico, the author frames the account in the context of a modernization project within her home country; of traditional gendered expectations regarding care within the family; and, finally, of hard-won experience that she filters through a sophisticated gender lens. For example, she argues that while accounts of immigration, based on men, reveal ways in which the transition may enable them more effectively to "do gender" (West & Zimmerman, 1987) and masculinity (despite the obvious tribulations immigration imposes), the same odyssey may conflict with women's ability to integrate their traditional and newly acquired roles and aspirations. Moreover, this analysis complements others, which have documented transnational care chains involving women from the developing world, providing care for more affluent "first world" women (Hochschild & Ehrenreich, 2002). Toro-Morn's account is equally revealing about the hidden dilemmas and costs—typically seen as private troubles—that roil the lives of those who have achieved our shared hope of "upward mobility" (see Roberts & Rosenwald, 2001). Given the inevitable and existential nature of mortality, it is fitting to conclude the book with a meditation on how, despite the breadth and velocity of social change, we labor to honor intergenerational commitments.

Final Thoughts on Narrative and Personal Biographies in Critical Gerontology

Thus, contributors to the book present topics, questions, and findings in ways that speak to current social conditions and debates. Critical gerontology resists codification or consensus, in terms of theoretical or methodological approaches, but insists upon ongoing reflection and critique of how, by whom, and with what moral or political stances age and aging are rendered problematic.

Introducing readers to a contemporary group of chapters on critical gerontology leads one to reflect on the range of voices and stances that are increasingly animating this area of inquiry. An especially welcome turn, in my view, is, as noted, toward *narrative* gerontology, which is equally relevant for scholars, recounting their careers, as for understanding others' lives (e.g., Kenyon, Ruth, & Mader, 1999). Estes' early chapter exemplifies this commitment. After all, it would be difficult to refute Hendricks' (1992) point that, "As social scientists, we study the structure and process of our 'subjects" behavior. Is it not legitimate to study our own behavior as well?" (p. 31). This insight echoes earlier critiques, such as that by Gouldner (1970, pp. 46–49), who argued for the need to reject "theory" or theorizing as disembodied practices, carried out by detached social scientists.

Current Critical Gerontology 13

Instead, he called attention to the *infrastructure* of social theory—made up of the sentiments, experiences, and quasi-political stances of those involved, who carry out their work against the backdrop of powerful, though implicit, perceptions of the nature and justice of their society, at particular historical moments.

Taken too far, this call to "personalize" inquiry could be inhibiting or somehow seen as self-indulgent, whether from positivist or post-positivist quarters. But today, one sees more co-existence, between such personal awareness and candor (what many term *reflexivity*) and diverse kinds of scholarship, teaching, and advocacy (see Glassner & Hertz, 2003). I concur with Krieger (1985), who argued that we need to honor our experience but, also, move *beyond subjectivity*, using the self and biography as vehicles for understanding social processes that are distinctive, in our lives, but not unique to us.

The narrative stance (rooted in the larger tradition of social constructionism) calls for particularity over broad generalization, for attention to context and agency over deterministic schemes of analysis. Narratives engage and reflect *time*, in its historical, organizational, and biographical dimensions, and they allow for, if not insist on, greater subjective and emotional candor than has been typical in positivistic studies. Myerhoff (1978), an exceptionally insightful figure in this tradition, did much to exemplify and promote narrative approaches in her book, *Number our Days*. Centering on a community of older, Eastern European Jews in Venice, California, Myerhoff's work displays the transcultural need for people to tell, to witness, to ritualize the fateful events and achievements of their lives—especially dramatic given that her informants, born early in the twentieth century, were survivors of the Holocaust. Though the events and accounts in this book are far less dramatic, Myerhoff's ethos has informed the project from the outset.

Such a stance is not narrowly subjective but, rather, mines experience for insight into social life and social change, anchored by an explicitly comparative turn of mind. Though characteristically interpretive (often ethnographic), this approach is open to diverse sources and methods of inquiry. As stated by Gubrium and Holstein (1999), in a precis of constructionist and narrative approaches in aging studies: "conceptualization on the part of the researcher is less a matter of theorizing than it is an effort to formulate analytic or sensitizing vocabularies that make the social world visible on its own terms" (p. 291). This goal does not at all reject theoretical development but leads to a more inductive, nuanced, comparative, historically specific exploration and understanding of aging (see also Hendricks, 1996). Ultimately, the contributions speak to new realities and possibilities in the early twenty-first century, without any presumption that they are either representative or comprehensive in this regard.

One topical connection that I was not successful in including in the book is to the burgeoning area of disability studies (Albrecht, Seelman, & Bury, 2001). Many of the fears and challenges ascribed to later life are, on reflection, revealed to be rooted in disability and chronic illness, rather than to aging, per se. The trans-disciplinary field of disability studies offers some of the most exciting and important insights for critical gerontology, and many scholars (e.g., Priestley, 2003) have

14   *Chris Wellin*

turned to explicit investigation of how the experience of, and management of, disability intersects with particular life course periods and, also, with gender (Gerschick, 2000).

Of course, this dialectical approach to linking *social structures* and *human lives* is venerable, even if the specific trends, questions, and implications are newer. Nearly three decades ago, Riley (1988a) edited a collection (to which we owe a great debt) bearing that title; it was paired with a second volume (Riley 1988b) containing what Robert K. Merton termed "sociological biographies" by celebrated scholars. These rich essays traced the emergence of social gerontology as a sub-discipline in the decades following World War II. Through the eyes of such influential scholars as Bernice Neugarten, we learn how the Committee on Human Development at the University of Chicago flourished even during the pre-war years. By the mid-1970s, with the establishment of the National Institute of Aging and several independent academic programs nationwide, there was a critical mass of activity, across kindred fields. Neugarten (1988b) writes, "During that 20-year period, some 80 Ph.D.s graduated from our special program, almost all of whom are now in university faculties around the country, teaching and carrying out research, with some . . . administering multidisciplinary gerontology centers" (p. 94). More recently, research centers that foster multidisciplinary research and dense professional and policy networks were established, such as the *Institute for Health & Aging*, at the University of California, San Francisco, founded by Carroll Estes. These teachers and scholars, in a resonant and apt cliché, are the mothers and fathers of our contributors, the giants on whose shoulders we stand; many of their names will appear in the acknowledgments as well as prominently in the citations.

In my own case, life experience certainly shaped the interests and agenda that have unfolded over the past 30 years. As a non-traditional student, starting college in my late twenties, I was avidly interested in the nature and trade-offs of age-role transitions, including those that, as in my case, were "disorderly" or "off-time" (George, 1993). Seeking to make sense of employment in an elder care setting, I was drawn to the Chicago School of Sociology—in particular to the comparative and detailed case studies of occupations and careers that Everett Hughes and others fostered in that program (see Barley, 1989). The intellectual appeal of this approach, for me, combined with a more pressing, practical set of questions that grew out of my role as a paid caregiver in a group home setting (among the first in the nascent "group home" movement) for older women diagnosed with dementia (e.g., Jaffe & Wellin, 2008; Wellin & Jaffe, 2004). I puzzled over the social/interactional nature of identity and memory, and how both were mediated by mundane, quasi-medical institutional categories and interactions. Such questions seemed to me equally relevant to understanding work roles and occupational careers, as to the study of aging, more narrowly.

Parallel assumptions and questions were equally prominent in the work of sociologists who shaped my thinking, but who are not generally associated with gerontology, such as Erving Goffman and Howard S. Becker. Becker (1970a, 1970b), who would have known Neugarten and others at the Committee on

Current Critical Gerontology 15

Human Development at Chicago and, later, at Northwestern, where I studied, published papers such as "Personal Change and Adult Life " and "The Self and Adult Socialization," which are as illuminating and relevant as ever and helped (through reference to his empirical studies of school teachers, medical students, jazz musicians, and others) to sustain a rich tradition of field research into occupational socialization and careers. This strand, or lineage, in the earlier development of research on aging, identity, and institutional timetables and contingencies has not always been linked to the development of gerontology, per se. However, this strand emerges as important in this collection and reinforces my message that critical gerontology has strong and deep roots in approaches that have long shaped the study of lives. That connection is certainly strong regarding the Chicago School of Sociology, informed as it was by symbolic interactionism, the study of careers (to which Goffman [1961] imbued a sharper subjective and moral dimension), and attention to how institutions and role-transitions shape one's sense of identity over time (see Barley, 1989; Hughes, 1984). Pointing out this continuity in my own concerns and aspirations is certainly not to imply any rigid or consensual agreement among those who would claim to be critical gerontologists, including the contributors to this book. What we offer, then, is a contemporary and (we believe) conceptually coherent cross-section of scholarship, reflecting the range of current topics and questions that we see as important for a broad readership.

A final word to the audiences of the book, including students—whether doing advanced undergraduate work or graduate study—as well as practitioners. It is true that readers will find little direct reference to pedagogy in these pages. However, virtually all of the contributors to the book are long-time and devoted teachers, and our ideas and modes of presentation have been honed through and informed by years of classroom experience and collaboration with community partners, involved in internships, advocacy, and action research. We hope the volume will be a touchstone for students, teachers, advocates, policymakers, and interested readers who share our desire to make sense of and engage both challenges and prospects regarding age and aging in a new century.

References

Albrecht, G.L., Seelman, K.D., & Bury, M. (Eds.). (2001). *Handbook of disability studies.* Thousand Oaks, CA: Sage.

Alexander, J.C. (1988). The new theoretical movement. In N.J. Smelser (Ed.), *Handbook of sociology* (pp. 77–101). Newbury Park, CA: Sage.

Barley, S.R. (1989). Careers, identities, and institutions: The legacy of the Chicago School of Sociology. In M.B. Arthur, D.T. Hall, & B.S. Lawrence (Eds.), *Handbook of career theory* (pp. 41–65). New York: Cambridge University Press.

Becker, G. (1997). *Disrupted lives.* Berkeley, CA: University of California Press.

Becker, H.S. (1970a). Personal change in adult life. In H.S. Becker (Ed.), *Sociological work: Method and substance* (pp. 275–288). New Brunswick, NJ: Transaction Books.

Becker, H.S. (1970b). The self and adult socialization. In H.S. Becker (Ed.), *Sociological work: Method and substance* (pp. 289–303). New Brunswick, NJ: Transaction Books.

16　Chris Wellin

Bengston, V.L., Burgess, E.O., & Parrott, T.M. (1997). Theory, explanation, and a third generation of theoretical development in social gerontology. *Journal of Gerontology: Social Sciences*, 52B(2), S72–S88.

Best, J. (1995). Constructionism in context. In J. Best (Ed.), *Images of issues* (2nd ed., pp. 337–354). Hawthorne, NY: Aldine de Gruyter.

Biggs, S., Hendricks, J., & Lowenstein, A. (2003). The need for theory in gerontology. In S. Biggs, A. Lowenstein, & J. Hendricks (Eds.), *The need for theory; Critical approaches to gerontology* (pp. 1–12). Amityville, NY: Baywood.

Brokaw, T. (1998). *The greatest generation.* New York: Random House.

Burawoy, M. (2004). ASA Presidential address: For public sociology. *American Sociological Review*, 70(1), 4–28.

Cancian, F.M., & Oliker, S.J. (2000). *Caring and gender.* Thousand Oaks, CA: Pine Forge Press.

Carson, E.A. (2014). Prisoners in 2013. *U.S. Department of Justice: Bureau of Justice Statistics.* 32 pages. Washington, DC.

Dannefer, D. (1987). Aging as intracohort differentiation: Accentuation, the Matthew effect, and the life course. *Sociological Forum*, 2, 211–236.

DeVault, M.L. (1999). Institutional ethnography: A strategy for feminist inquiry. In M.L. DeVault (Ed.), *Liberating method: Feminism and social research* (pp. 46–54). Philadelphia, PA: Temple University Press.

Estes, C.L. (1979). *The aging enterprise.* San Francisco, CA: Josey-Bass.

Estes, C.L., & Binney, E.A. (1989). The bio-medicalization of aging: Dangers and dilemmas. *The Gerontologist*, 29(5), 587–596.

George, L.K. (1993). Sociological perspectives on life transitions. *Annual Review of Sociology*, 19, 353–373.

Gerschick, T.J. (2000). Toward a theory of disability and gender. *Signs*, 14(4), 1263–1268.

Glassner, B., & Hertz, R. (Eds). (2003). *Our studies, ourselves.* New York: Oxford University Press.

Goffman, E. (1961). *Asylums.* New York: Doubleday.

Gouldner, A. W. (1970). *The coming crisis of western sociology.* New York: Basic Books.

Gubrium, J.F. (1993). *Speaking of life: Horizons of meaning for nursing home residents.* Hawthorne, NY: Aldine de Gruyter.

Gubrium, J.F., & Holstein, J.A. (1999). Constructionist perspectives on aging. In V.L. Bengston & K.W. Schaie (Eds.), *Handbook of theories of aging* (pp. 287–305). New York: Springer.

Hasenfeld, Y., & Garrow, E.E. (2012). Nonprofit human services organizations and advocacy in a neoliberal welfare state. *Social Service Review*, 86(2), 295–322.

Heinz, W.R. (2003). From work trajectories to negotiated careers. In J.T. Mortimer & M.J. Shanahan (Eds.), *Handbook of the life course* (pp. 185–204). New York: Springer.

Hendricks, J. (1992). Generations and the generation of theory in social gerontology. *International Journal of Aging and Human Development*, 35(1), 31–47.

Hendricks, J. (1996). Qualitative research: Contributions and advances. In R. Binstock & L. George (Eds.), *Handbook of aging and the social sciences* (4th ed., pp. 52–72). San Diego, CA: Academic Press.

Hochschild, A.R., & Ehrenreich, B. (2002). Introduction. In A.R. Hochschild & B. Ehrenreich (Eds.), *Global woman: Nannies, maids, and sex workers in the new economy* (pp. 1–13). New York: Henry Holt.

Holstein, J.A., & Gubrium, J.F. (2000). *Constructing the life course* (2nd ed.). Lanham, MD: General Hall.

Current Critical Gerontology 17

Hughes, E.C. (1984). *The sociological eye*. New Brunswick, NJ: Transaction Books.

Jaffe, D., & C. Wellin. (2008). June's troubled transition: Adjustment to residential care for older adults with dementia. *Care Management Journals*, 9(3), 128–137.

Katz, S. (1996). *Disciplining old age*. Charlottesville, VA: University Press of Virginia.

Kenyon, G.M., Ruth, J.E., & Mader, W. (1999). Elements of a narrative gerontology. In V.L. Bengston & K.W. Schaie (Eds.), *Handbook of theories of aging* (pp. 40–58). New York: Springer.

Klinenberg, E. (2012). *Going solo*. New York: Penguin Press.

Krieger, S. (1985). Beyond "subjectivity": The use of the self in social science. *Qualitative Sociology*, 8, 309–324.

Lipsky, M. (1980). *Street level bureaucracy: Dilemmas of the individual in public services*. New York: Russell Sage Foundation.

McAdams, D. (1993). *Stories we live by*. New York: William Morrow.

Mannheim, K. (1952). The problem of generations. In K. Mannheim (Ed.), *Essays on the sociology of knowledge*, (276–322). London: Oxford University Press.

Mattingly, C. (1998). *Healing dramas and clinical plots: The narrative structure of experience*. New York: Cambridge University Press.

Meyer, M.H. (Ed.). (2000). *Carework: Gender, labor, and the welfare state*. New York: Routledge.

Mills, C.W. (1959). *The sociological imagination*. New York: Oxford University Press.

Morgan, L.A., & Kunkel, S.R. (2007). *Aging, society, and the life course* (3rd ed.). New York: Springer.

Myerhoff, B. (1978). *Number our days*. New York: Touchstone.

Neugarten, B.L. (Ed.). (1982). *Age or need: Public policies for older people*. Beverly Hills, CA: Sage.

Neugarten, B.L. (1988). The aging society and my academic life. In M.W. Riley (Ed.), *Sociological lives* (pp. 91–106). Newbury Park, CA: Sage.

Passuth, P.M., & Bengston, V.L. (1996). Sociological theories of aging: Current perspectives and future directions. In J. Quadagno & D. Street (Eds.), *Aging for the twenty-first century* (pp. 12–30). New York: St. Martin's Press.

Pithouse, A. (1987). *Social work: The social organisation of an invisible trade*. Aldershot, UK: Gower.

Polkinghorne, D.E. (1988). *Narrative knowing and the human sciences*. Albany, NY: SUNY Press.

Priestley, M. (2003). *Disability: A life course approach*. Malden, MA: Polity.

Quadagno, J. (2018). *Aging and the life course* (7th ed.). New York: McGraw-Hill.

Riley, M.W. (Ed.). (1988a). *Social structure & human lives: Social change and the life course* (Vol. 1). Newbury Park, CA: Sage.

Riley, M.W. (Ed.). (1988b). *Sociological lives: Social change and the life course* (Vol. 2). Newbury Park, CA: Sage.

Riley, M.W., & Riley, J.W. (1994). Age integration and the lives of older people. *The Gerontologist*, 34, 110–115.

Roberts, J.S., & Rosenwald, G.C. (2001). Ever upward and no turning back: Social mobility and identity formation among first-generation college students. In D.P. McAdams, R. Josselson, & A. Lieblich (Eds.), *Turns in the road: Narrative studies of lives in transition* (pp. 91–120). Washington, DC: American Psychological Association.

Rowles, G.D., & Bernard, M. (Eds.). (2013). *Environmental gerontology: Making meaningful places in old age*. New York: Springer.

Rubin, B.A. (1996). *Shifts in the social contract*. Thousand Oaks, CA: Pine Forge Press.

18 Chris Wellin

Ryder, N.B. (1965). The cohort as a concept in the study of social change. *American Sociological Review*, 30(6), 843–861.

Settersten, R.A. (1999). *Lives in time and place.* Amityville, NY: Baywood.

Settersten, R.A., & Ray, B.A. (2010). *Not quite adults.* New York: Bantam Books.

Wellin, C. (2007). Narrative interviewing: Process and benefits in teaching about aging and the life course. *Gerontology & Geriatrics Education*, 28(1), 79–99.

Wellin, C. (2010). Growing pains in the sociology of aging and the life course: A review of recent textbooks. *Teaching Sociology*, 38(4), 373–382.

Wellin, C., & Jaffe, D.J. (2004, August). In search of personal care: Challenges to identity support in residential care for elders with cognitive illness. *Journal of Aging Studies*, 18(3), 275–295.

Wellin, E. (1955). Water boiling in a Peruvian town. In B.D. Paul (Ed.), *Health, culture, and community* (pp. 71–103). New York: Russell Sage Foundation.

Wellin, E. (1998). Theoretical orientations in medical anthropology: Continuity and change over the past half-century. In S.V. Sjaak & A. Rienks (Eds.), *The art of medical anthropology: Readings* (pp. 10–22). The Netherlands: Het Spinhuis.

West, C., & Zimmerman, D.H. (1987). Doing gender. *Gender and Society*, 1(2), 125–151.

CHAPTER 2

A First-Generation Critic Comes of Age Revisited: Reflections of a Critical Gerontologist

Carroll L. Estes

Revised and updated from an article in the Journal of Aging Studies, *22, 120–131 (2008), with permission from Elsevier*

The Sociology of Knowledge: Sentiments, Domain Assumptions, and Reflexivity

The Coming Crisis in Western Sociology is Alvin Gouldner's (1970) "historically informed critique of sociology as a theory and as a social institution" (p. 12). His "sociology of sociology" contained a blistering critique of structural functionalism (then the dominant theory of American Sociology) where he highlights the conservative potential of sociology and contrasts it with the opposite—the liberative potential of different theoretical systems. He studies not only social theory but also the theorist, featuring the iconic American sociologist, Talcott Parsons. In so doing, Gouldner (1970) contests the value-free debate and asks,

> In short, what are the social and political consequences of the intellectual system under examination? Do they liberate or repress . . . ? Do they bind men into the social world that now exists, or do they enable men to transcend it? Any and every statement about the social world, as well as the methodologies by which it is reached, has consequences that may be viewed quite apart from its intellectual validity.
>
> (p. 12)

Gouldner (1970) criticizes sociologists for their devaluation of "other meanings and consequences of theories and . . . refusing to take responsibility for them even though they exist" (p. 13):

> The extrication of the liberative potential of Academic Sociology is not to be accomplished by research alone. It will also require action and criticism, efforts to change the social world and efforts to change social science, both of which are profoundly interconnected, if for no other reason than that social science is a *part* of the social world as well as a *conception* of it.
>
> (p. 13)

20   *Carroll L. Estes*

This point has been well argued and advanced subsequently by feminist, race, and other scholars in epistemological critiques of mainstream positivist methods, including the sexist and racist ways of knowing that privilege the white male experience (see Acker, 1988, 1992, 2000; Collins, 1990; Feagin, 2006; Harding, 1996; Katz, 2001–2002; McCarthy, 1996; Omi & Winant, 1994, 2015; Powell, 2006; Ray, 2003; Smith 1990, 2005).

Gouldner's critique invokes multilevel analyses at the macro-historical and institutional levels of the state, the university, and the individual—that is, how "men" (yes, this was my sociology) work as teachers and researchers and within "an intellectual community with a received occupational culture, where they pursue careers, livelihoods, material ambitions, [and] intellectual ambitions," including the "standpoints" and "intellectual products that are created" (p. 14). For Gouldner, the task of social theory is to provide meanings to the universe as it "maps" the world of social objects. Gouldner's plea is to critically analyze the assumptions, values, and the potentially liberative and repressive elements of different theories. He advances the radical notion that social theorists "believe out of need" just as do the human subjects of sociological inquiry. Therefore, "sociologists must surrender the human but elitist assumption that others believe out of need whereas they believe because of the dictates of logic and reason." Indeed, the scientific method and belief that sociology must be "value free" "is not simply a logic but also a morality; . . . the ideology of a . . . social movement . . . a . . . kind of reform—of sociology itself" (Gouldner, 1970, pp. 25–26). He blasts the sociologist's keeping "two sets of books, one for the study of 'laymen' and the other when he [she] thinks about himself [/herself]" (Gouldner, 1970, p. 55).

As Gouldner sees it, social theory, empirical work, and the advances in Academic Sociology have two bases: the extra-technical and the technical. The *extra-technical* is the "personal reality" and "structure of sentiments" of the theorist and scholar that are situated in the lived experience in her socio-historical "moment" and the *technical* is based on empirical, methodological, and theoretical advances of the discipline to which the scholar is exposed.

Extra-Technical Sources: Personal Realities

The extra-technical is relevant since "Articulate social theory . . . is in part an extrusion from, and develops in interaction with, the theorist's tacit domain assumptions" (Gouldner, 1970, p. 34). This section locates my scholarship in a sketch of key life events in my "social surround" and "personal reality." Much more than mere "context," my early childhood as a Southern girl in a patriarchal family set me up for wrenching personal and professional conflicts and struggles that have shaped my intellectual career. Who am I? What can I be as a woman, wife, mother, scholar, citizen (Agency), as I am mindful of the surrounding, "given" seemingly obdurate, institutionalized social structure, gender norms, and expectations?

My Mom was 12 years old when women got the vote. I was early in my grad school education during her first reading of Betty Friedan's (1963) *The Feminine*

Mystique, which—in Mom—unleashed a torrent of anger. (Coming full circle, decade's later I had the privilege of meeting and working with Betty Friedan on women and Social Security.)

I witnessed Mom's pain in confronting a *double bind*. She was a Wonder Woman with a master's degree from Columbia University, who could do anything: be a selfless Mom and wife, a nationally and internationally published mystery writer, a mathematician, seamstress, artist, stock analyst. Yet, she was a woman blocked by a virtual red stop sign. That sign was the distillation of what she learned she was "allowed" (and not allowed) to do and be as a Southern white woman. Her daily lament was, "It's a man's world." I grieve even today that so much of my Mother's vitality and enormous talent were suffocated by the structural impediments, internalized oppression, and rage that she swallowed daily.

Anguish over the deeply personal and destructive consequences of my Mother's situation initiated my earliest feminist consciousness. I understood the dearth of Mom's real "choices" within the existing structure of power and gender hierarchies and the patriarchal thought structure (even as a privileged white woman) that operated both inside and outside my home. The consequences of larger social forces and prejudices were obvious in the unending familial expectations and obligations that not only controlled Mom's every moment but also quite probably would control mine. I was passionate about wanting to stop the blatant unfairness of it—to fix it. But how? Mom's survival outlet, first, was reading murder mysteries, then writing her own. Although her recognition as an author in the vaunted Doubleday Crime Club infuriated Dad, she showed me that writing books was both do-able and possibly "safe." Speaking out definitely was *not* safe. The "wrinkle" was that, although Mom did write three mysteries, Dad grew angrier with the gathering acclaim of each one, finally giving Mom an ultimatum to quit writing or else. She quit writing. I then began to comprehend that I could find myself in the same alarming position of not being able to do or be what I wanted. Writing a book, or whatever else, might not be safe after all.

My Dad, an attorney, later US Federal Judge and "strict constructionist," was vocal on issues of fairness and justice as he understood them within his Southern white male privilege. Dad and the home routines sent plenty of mixed messages: I felt pressures to excel in school, to go to the best university, and to earn a graduate degree after college to acquire enough "cultural capital" to raise my children. Later, on reflection, I was puzzled and miffed that I was expected to work hard and do all of the same things as my brother until finishing college. Then the proscription was that marriage and family would be my sole endeavor.

This was reinforced when Dad explicitly said that I could not go to law school because I would "never get a job." (I was considering it after acing a Stanford law course.) The double standard was obvious since my brother, a law graduate, was then about to clerk for Mr. Justice Tom Clark of the US Supreme Court! What I "heard" was that Dad would (or could) not help me, and that I would be denied equal law clerking and work opportunities, should I choose such a path. It was infuriating, competing for my parents' approval as a daughter against my male sibling. I was disadvantaged in both the dream department and the options

22   Carroll L. Estes

department. Should I think beyond the prescribed Pink "box," I would have to do it with one (or two) hands tied behind my back.

Another significant influence was living in the South during a period of intense racial segregation, separate drinking fountains for "coloreds," poll taxes and literacy tests to vote, and servants in my home. Systemic racism (Feagin, 2006) was so pervasive and so big, when my Dad, the US District Judge, ordered school integration in Dallas, backing the Supreme Court's ruling on Brown versus The Board of Education, he was "hung in effigy," and burning crosses dotted school yards. I was afraid, and ashamed. My later experiences of the civil rights movement and my residing in the North, the South, and the West would give me opportunities to learn more.

My leaving Texas for college in California was pivotal. Skipping forward a decade (from my 1958 Stanford graduation to 1968), the biggest event of my life was and is the birth of my only child, my daughter, Duskie. In the delivery room when we had our baby girl, my emotions flooded, immediate and intense. I was both overwhelmed with joy and gripped by sadness. My grief was about the hardships that my baby would endure as a girl. I knew I could not protect her from that. During her infancy, I would rock Duskie to sleep singing, "We Shall Overcome."

I was afraid for Duskie and for me. I did not want her to suffer the woman thing; the sex-object thing. I wanted her to do and be anything she wanted without limits. And I wanted to avoid the trap of giving her a mother who did not have a Self. That would be a mom who did not have a core or a center, one who might disappear into exhausting self-sacrifice and bitterness, maybe even insanity. My life's struggle was fully engaged at that moment. The sleepless nights with a crying baby provided my first inkling of the meaning of the endless work ahead.

Since then, my journey has been steeped in the caring and anguish of a mother who could not do it all: days and nights chock-full of driven, fractionated overwork, matched by mournful regrets about my failures and choices as a mother and human being. My marriage was plagued by infuriating gender inequality in our baby care. I was doing quadruple time as a mother, wife, teaching at the local state college (40 miles away), and working on my own doctoral studies. Several years later, with my PhD and academic faculty position tenured, I was a single mom and sole breadwinner. Three books offered solace and a deeper layer of feminist consciousness: Jessica Benjamin's *The Bonds of Love* (1988), Anne Crittenden's *The Price of Motherhood* (2001), and Judith Warner's *Perfect Madness: Motherhood in the Age of Anxiety* (2005). I learned that I am not crazy after all.

Having never had a female professor or academic mentor anywhere in my college or graduate education, it was my great fortune to encounter two remarkable older women (crones) who were the essence of such possibilities: Maggie Kuhn, co-founder of The Gray Panthers, and Tish Sommers, co-founder of Displaced Homemakers and The Older Women's League. Both women understood what they were living for and what they were fighting for (Huckle, 1991; Kuhn, 1978). Each transcended the self-censorship and self-abnegation that were still suffocating me. With each, I witnessed a social movement in the making and a courageous

Reflections of a Critical Gerontologist 23

and relentless woman in the vanguard. These two women taught me more about the real meaning of Agency than all of my academic training ever has. Praxis and possibility were the adventure of their everyday life worlds. Neither woman would permit me to remain the verbally mute female I was. My voice grew bolder and my writing more critical. Nevertheless, becoming an academic witness to injustice in the halls of power and official authority was (and still is) scary. It also was chancy for my university career.

Maggie Kuhn's mentorship and words were transformational. "Go to the root of the problem." "Do your homework." "Go to The Top." "Speak your mind, even though your voice shakes." "Everything is connected." It was crystal clear to Maggie that the problems of the old and the solutions to them are *indivisible* from those of the young. My sense of the world was also inspired by my invaluable mentor and policy advisor, Robert M. Ball, the legendary Social Security Commissioner who served under three presidents (Kennedy, Johnson, and Nixon). "We are all in this together" (Ball, 1989).

Bridging the personal, extra-technical and the technical, two other biographical events profoundly shaped my family life and policy perspective. First, my Dad's federal courthouse office was next door to the office of Texas Congressman George Mahon, then Chairman of the all-powerful House Appropriations Committee. In 1977, Dad arranged a joint meeting with Mr. Mahon and me to discuss federal appropriations for the newly established National Institute on Aging. This opening changed my life; I was catapulted into the interpersonal communications orbit of lead Hill staffers dealing with the US Budget. Second and most significant, in 1980, I married a physician who served twice in the nation's top health policy post (Assistant Secretary for Health) under Presidents Lyndon Johnson and Bill Clinton. My husband was an invaluable source of support and guide who demystified health policy and the byzantine politics of Medicare and Medicaid, unveiling the deep money pockets within them.

Technical Sources—Disciplinary and Interdisciplinary

My academic work is profoundly influenced by my early immersion in social and philosophical thought acquired during undergraduate and graduate days at four universities: Stanford University (1955–1958); the University of California, Berkeley (1960–1961); Southern Methodist University (SMU) (1962–1963); and the University of California, San Diego (UCSD) (1969–1972). In my own research and teaching jobs along the way, I learned from and collaborated with faculty and students at Brandeis University and Simmons College (1963–1967) and San Diego State University (1967–1971). I benefitted from guided course readings of original texts of social theorists including Max Weber, Emile Durkheim, Karl Marx, George Herbert Mead, Herbert Blumer, Talcott Parsons, C. Wright Mills, Alvin Gouldner, and Randall Collins.

My MA thesis at SMU on the power structure of Dallas (Estes-Thometz, 1963) became my touchstone in understanding power structures in local and state government. My Brandeis University job immediately following SMU exposed

24   Carroll L. Estes

me to Franklin D Roosevelt's New Deal and social welfare; the War on Poverty; medical insurance; and for the first time, gerontology. My sights were directed toward all levels of state action: Roxbury MA, the state of Massachusetts, and the federal government.

Lucky enough to be in my twenties during the 1960s and on college campuses, my consciousness was blown by reading, witnessing, and marching in emerging social movements around Vietnam, feminism, civil rights and race, and integrated neighborhoods and housing. While in PhD study nearly a decade later, UCSD was a hot-house of radical empiricism and ontological critiques of positivism and deductive research and the dominant sociological theory, structural functionalism. The new rage was ethnomethodology (Cicourel), grounded theory (Glaser and Strauss), and the social construction of reality (Berger and Luckmann). My PhD methods courses were taught as *theory* as well as *resistance* to established techniques of inquiry. Over the next decades as a faculty scholar, I read from Frankfurt school, post-modernists, and critical thinkers and practitioners.

Post-PhD as UCSF faculty, sabbaticals offered needed energies at the London School of Economics; the Sorbonne in Paris; the University of California, Santa Cruz; and Washington, DC. I have always been comfortable in multidisciplinary-friendly and inter-disciplinary sites, in which discourse spanned not only sociology but also anthropology, social work, economics, public health, nursing, medicine, political science, public policy, and law.

I believe that perhaps my strongest original contribution is to have developed and bridged two somewhat disparate theoretical paradigms, which I then brought into the nascent field of research on social policy and aging. These are: the Macro and Micro perspectives, respectively building on the macro Conflict and Critical Theory *and* the micro Social Constructionist Theory (Symbolic Interactionist Interpretive tradition). As a medical sociologist, much of my research has been on technical aspects of aging programs and politics in the Meso institutional and organizational levels of policy, the professions, medical entities, and experts. As a Weberian and critical scholar, my focus has embraced the organizational, political, and socio-cultural processes and forces in and of the State and the policy and politics that is imagined, contested, produced, and implemented through various levels of the state. As an interactionist, I have examined the contested social construction(s) of social problems (e.g., old age and aging) that are the subject of the debates, agendas, and battles in policy and politics on multiple geo-political levels. I have examined these in terms of their effects on self-esteem, personal-control, and relations to empowerment or disempowerment of older persons and other vulnerable groups and communities. Utilizing both the conflict and the constructionist theoretical lenses, my analyses examine (1) the power struggles and disparate rewards (win or lose) of disparate definitions of "the problem" and proscriptions of the solutions, while studying (2) the ongoing conflicts (symbolic and material) that reside in the power dynamics of class, status, race, ethnicity, age, gender, and ability and (3) the effects of these on the older persons as individuals and in diverse communities. My theoretical and empirical approach (Conflict Theory) is distinctly *oppositional* to the structural functionalist

Reflections of a Critical Gerontologist 25

(Consensus Theory) that accepts the State in the traditional pluralist rendering, as a "neutral" arbitrator of competing interests—in which the State functions through accommodative relations between the citizen (universal white male) and members of society.

The political economy of aging and constructionist perspective in *The Aging Enterprise* (1979) reflect the core framework that I have built upon in studying: (1) the aging enterprise and the medical industrial complex; (2) crisis, austerity, and aging; (3) the legitimacy issues confronting and contradicting relations between and among various elements of the State, capital, and democracy; and (4) the distributive (and discriminatory) effects of policy and practice according to race, class, gender, sexuality, ethnicity, (dis)ability, age, generation, and nation/ immigration—and their intersectionalities.

Mapping the Division of Sociological Labor and My Career

As a critical scholar and organic intellectual, I am committed, both scientifically and normatively, to identifying and working to eradicate oppression in all forms and faces. This is a *subaltern* perspective, historically contentious in the academy. Michael Burawoy (2005) identifies four types of sociological knowledge, which are: (1) professional sociology, (2) policy sociology, (3) critical sociology, and (4) public sociology. Although any work may contribute to more than one of these ideal types or alternate over time, "the sociological field of power" is one in which the relations of power and dominance support the "more or less stable hierarchy of antagonistic knowledges." There is:

> a ruling coalition of professional and policy sociology and a subaltern mutuality of critical and public sociology. This pattern of domination derives from the embeddedness of the discipline in a wider constellation of power and interests. In our society, power and money speak louder than values and influence. In the U.S., capitalism is especially raw with a public sphere that is not only weak but overrun by armies of experts and a plethora of media.
>
> (Burawoy, 2005, p. 18)

Public sociology and critical sociology are *subaltern*, meaning subordinate, marginalized, in lower status. Significantly, however, public sociology is the *conscience* of policy sociology, while critical sociology is the *conscience* of professional sociology (Burawoy, 2005). Burawoy (2005) warns of the "growing gap between the sociological ethos and the world we study" (p. 4), asking, "For whom and for what do we pursue our discipline?" This echoes my own perspective, as I wrote 25 years ago with colleagues:

> Academic gerontology is in danger of "selling its soul" to mindless theory-less positivism without retaining or regenerating the reflexivity that is essential to the resurgence of the "gerontological imagination."
>
> (Estes, Binney, & Culbertson, 1992, p. 60)

26   *Carroll L. Estes*

Most of my published research may be categorized as policy sociology/gerontology, while my later work has focused on extending the political economy of aging and critical sociology/gerontology. The bulk of my funded research has been on the effects of particular programs of the Older Americans Act, and on Medicare and Medicaid policy on the elderly and the services they receive. With colleagues, I pioneered in developing the methodologies for fifty state and hundreds of community policymaker studies in aging and health services. One of our innovations is the design and implementation of elite telephone surveys of policymakers, administrators, and advocates that were paired with detailed coding and content analyses of policy and regulatory documents.

A Confession. Engaging in all four types of knowledge building, I have "lived" the tension and antagonisms of critical and public sociology *against* professional and policy sociology. There were and are relentless pressures to be "mainstream," necessitating daily, and murky, risk analyses of potential costs and benefits, especially given my added liabilities of being female and committed to *praxis.* More significantly, the subaltern nature of the critical and policy knowledges, coupled with highly consequential considerations of funding and tenure that reward professional and policy sociology, *blocked* new pathways that often diverted my focus, as I imposed my own self-censorship, stunting both the development of my critical thinking, voice, and written word. I have lived the triple life of being a mother, and, simultaneously juggling intellectual schizophrenia, alternating between being the academic professional and policy sociologist who got tenured, funded, advanced, and built a research institute while simultaneously *suppressing* the critical and public scholarship that most called to me. In many instances,

Table 2.1 Selected Work by Primary Type of Knowledge

Professional Sociology/Gerontology	**Policy Sociology/Gerontology**
The Decision Makers: The Power Structure of Dallas (1963)	*Austerity & Aging: Shifting Governmental Responsibility for the Elderly* (Estes, Newcomer, & Associates, 1983)
The Aging Enterprise: A Critical Examination of Social Policies and Services for the Aged (1979)	*Long Term Care of the Elderly: Public Policy Issues* (Harrington, et al. 1985)
"Constructions of Reality" (1980)	*The Long Term Care Crisis: Elders Trapped in the No Care Zone* (Estes, Swan, & Associates, 1993)
Critical Sociology/Gerontology	**Public Sociology/Gerontology**
Political Economy, Health & Aging (Estes, Gerard, Zones, & Swan, 1984)	"Social Security Privatization and Older Women: A Feminist Political Economy Perspective" (Estes, 2004)
Social Policy & Aging: A Critical Perspective (2001)	*Breaking the Social Security Glass Ceiling* (Estes, O'Neill, & Hartmann, 2012)
Social Theory, Social Policy & Ageing (Estes, Biggs, & Phillipson, 2003/2009)	"Older U.S. Women's Economic Security, Health, and Empowerment" (2017)
"Critical Feminist Perspectives, Aging & Social Policy" (2005)	*Critical Aging Policy: A–Z.* (Estes with DiCarlo, 2018, forthcoming)
"Crises and Old Age Policy" (Estes, 2011)	

Reflections of a Critical Gerontologist   27

I was complicit in averting a critical eye, rendering myself mute and disappointed in my silence. Reflectively and in the present, my anguish is compounded by my *lack* as a fractionated mother for my dearest and only child, Duskie Lynn Estes.

From Professional Sociology to Critical Sociology

From my first paper in aging (Schooler & Estes, 1966) forward, I have sought to understand the human and policy implications of social policy within theoretical sensibilities.

The socially constructed "problems" of aging and their policy remedies are examined in relation to: (1) the capacity of strategically located agents and interests to define the problem and to press their views into public consciousness and law (i.e., the exercise of power and ideology) and (2) the objective facts of the situation (e.g., demographic and distributional patterns). Note the order here: power and ideology, first, and objective facts, second (Estes, 1979).

Ideology consists of "systematically distorted accounts of reality which attempt to conceal and legitimate asymmetrical power relations . . . [that reflect] social interests, conflicts, and contradictions . . . expressed in thought, and how they are produced and reproduced in systems of domination" (Bottomore, 1983, p. 183). Gramsci's (1971) concept of "ideological hegemony" refers to the ruling or dominant ideas of any historical period that may explain the divergence between people's ideas and their economic conditions. His pivotal insight is that ideas may have the weight of material force, explaining consent of the people (acquiescence) without overt coercion or repression. Power struggles over ideology reflect the dominant social relations and interlocking systems of oppression of gender, race and ethnic status, and social class (Collins, 1990; Estes & Associates, 2001, pp. 17–18). We know that the effects of each are singly and in combinations, intersectional and cumulative across the life course (Crystal & Shea, 1990; Dannefer, 2003).

Presently, the reigning ideologies of neo-liberalism, individualism, and the market, in conjunction with apocalyptic demography (Robertson, 1999) are being jointly advanced by and for political and economic gains of global financial capital (Estes & Phillipson, 2002). Blatant ageism, sexism, racism, ableism, and nativism are major vehicles being used by capital and the United States under multiple guises to privatize welfare states and shift state resources to private and military markets around the globe, as well as tax cuts and avoidance for the wealthy and their corporations. Ageism we experience as the prejudice, vilification, fear, and portrayal of older adults as insane people and vultures preying on their families, communities, and the society that elders produced and built up over generations (Butler, 1963; International Longevity Center, USA, 2006). One goal is to "*responsibilize* a new senior citizenry to care for itself" (Katz, 2003, p. 26).

Specifically, much of my research has focused on the processes of privatization, commodification, rationalization, informalization of caring work, globalization, and discrimination via specific health and aging policy decisions and debates. The role and relations of the gendered and raced State in social policy are fore-grounded (Estes, 2011). I argue that discourses, ideologies, and framing are integral

28   *Carroll L. Estes*

to the relationship between meaning and action in the context of education, activism, and policy.

Given that *the realization of Agency is foundational to public sociology and public gerontology*, serious attention needs to be given to its promise and limits. *Framing is core to exercising Agency.* Lakoff is correct that, "Framing itself is an action" (Lakoff & Rockridge Institute, 2006, p. 25), and "Reframing *is* social change" (Lakoff, 2004). Frames are a study of persuasion as the way into the consciousness of the American psyche. My attention to the import of Agency is consistent with my long-standing view that, "both self and society are . . . capable of creating new alternatives" (Estes, 1979) and that "situational events and interactional opportunities" for Agency occur within the context of "structural constraints that limit the range of possible interactions . . . reinforcing certain lines of action while barring others" (Estes, 1981, p. 400).

I am persuaded by Randall Collins' (2004) "radical micro-sociological" advance in the study of interaction ritual chains and their pivotal role in social movements, and the expressions of Agency therein. I am keenly appreciative of Durkheim's, Goffman's, and Collins' work on rituals, co-presence, and solidarity as cornerstones of understanding the processes of social integration AND conflicts engaging social change. Agency is all about processes of social change that move power relations that embed power structures and conflictual relations going forward.

A Critic Comes of Age: From Critical Sociology to Public Gerontology

Now in my own Third Age, my work has quickened in critical and public sociology and gerontology.

My personal objective is to more fully become an organic intellectual (Gramsci, 1971). Contrasted with traditional intellectuals, organic intellectuals work with and through grassroots, various publics, their medium and media, working directly of and on the ground (and cyberspace) to establish or reestablish a new hegemony. A new hegemony occurs when there is widespread consent for political and social reforms (Macey, 2000). In a sense, all people are intellectuals on the ground; it is organic intellectuals who openly connect, speak, and identify with and work with and on behalf of the oppressed, the injured, the subjugated. There are formidable difficulties in transforming the "pessimism of the intellect" into the "optimism of the will" (Sassoon, 2000) as one participates in a grounded, radical re-thinking designed to produce social change. Pierre Bourdieu makes the point:

> The ethnosociologist is a sort of organic intellectual of humankind who, as a collective agent, can contribute to denaturalizing and defatalizing existence by putting her competency at the service of a universalism rooted in the understanding of particularisms.
> (Cited in Wacquant, 2004; see Burawoy, 2005, p. 24, fn 10)

My public gerontology aims to advance knowledge, public understanding, and collective action concerning what is at stake in the most significant policy struggles

Reflections of a Critical Gerontologist   29

of my lifetime—the deeply financed and politically powerful commitment to destroy Social Security, Medicare, Medicaid, and the Affordable Care Act, and with that, the eradication of social insurance and the brutal individualization of risk in the United States and elsewhere around the globe.

One of my intellectual tasks has been to locate the State and capital at the center of the study of aging politics and policy as they affect the everyday lives of the aging. I call attention to use of the imprecise, blurred, abstract concepts of "context" that serves as a "wastebasket" predictor variable somewhere exogenous out yonder. Remaining illusive, the concept may impede or elude specification that would problematize the analysis of larger and smaller institutions of capitalist practices and processes. The commitment to a critical perspective requires "taking it big," meaning the study and measurement of large institutional processes and structures within which our life chances are constructed (and constrained) as we age over the life span. Such work must necessarily embrace global and green politics, economics, and culture. Ideologies must be interrogated as cultural products as well. Advances in research and theory of Cumulative Advantage/Disadvantage and the challenges of gene-environment research cry out for a location bigger that individual lives and collective communities. The bandwidth of our sciences and practice must stretch.

Enduring themes draw from a large and critical welfare state literature. Over the past three decades, my work has sought to delineate the crisis tendencies at the levels of the state, capital, democracy, and the individual. Through it I call attention to social processes at multiple meso- and macro-levels of organization and power network structures including the State and global financialization, rationalization, privatization, and informalization and cross migration in chains of caring across generations, long-term care, and related trends in aging network service collaborations. Global, state, and local Pension schemes, their politics, economics and welfare state restructuring are required subjects and objects of investigation.

My work is continuing efforts to explicate the dominant forces and processes of the construction and expression of ideology, power, domination, oppression, and resistance. Critical scholarship is required to track, unmask, and unpack the details of their evolving role and effects on the existential and material consequences for aging persons and for social policy. Of profound concern and significance is the degradation of "the social" and the efforts to undo democracy down to the core of the franchise, the very right to vote.

My theoretical commitment is toward the promise of a *Critical Realism of Old Age and Aging*. It requires the micro-, meso-, and macro analytic mappings of power, the state, capital, and the peoples confronting oppression through the material, political, cultural, and personal injuries of social exclusion and deprivation. Critical Realism (CR) attempts to discern new (and fake) knowledges in the quest "to discard old interpretations, hopes and expectations" and to offer "a fundamentally new orientation whenever 'reality' appears to demand it . . . [It] is concerned with questions about socio-political values and the criteria of progress"

30   Carroll L. Estes

(Offe, 1985, p. 90). Our focus is opening up the disjunctures, disruptions, and unravelling (and binding) social processes and structures that pervade our daily existence. In aging, for example, the CR lens could widen across the life course, to the identification of toxic triggers of psychological, biological, and neighborhood stress that produce maternal depression and alteration of fetal and infant development trajectory related to health and illness (Bhaskar & Hartwig, 2010, p. 261). This is a familiar element of the now-trending gene-environment work that is bridging scholarship on the life course and big longitudinal data. A continuing challenge for the political economy of aging is to hold fast to the benefits of *Taking it Big* in the deepest sociological sense, crossing lots and reaching beyond today's "received theories" and methods.

Emancipatory Knowledges and Critical Pedagogy

Emancipatory knowledges demand reflexivity in thinking and speaking out about regimes of truth (and untruth), sensitive to critical, feminist, race, ethnic, class, ability, age, and generation lenses. Critical pedagogy obligates education, research, and praxis in the *pursuit of possibility and social transformation.*

Presently in my late seventies, I am mindful of the urgency and broader message for social scientists and gerontologists of two insights. The first is Dorothy Smith's (1990) warning of the danger of a social science that is captured by and envisioned through the "relations of ruling" and the blinkers of gendered, raced, and classed (elite) knowledges and epistemologies. The second is Gramsci's urgent calling us to the vital role of organic intellectuals.

A touchstone for critical gerontology, rendered urgent in the present Trump era, is the unflinching investigation of discourses of domination and resistance (Bourdieu, 1998); the rise, meaning, and expansion (as well as contraction) of social movements; and the power conflicts and corporeal struggles within and across them. Emancipatory pedagogies (Freire, 1970) are essential pathways out of the potential dead-end cul-de-sac for social justice and democracy.

For critical and public gerontologists, bell hooks models *Teaching to Transgress: Education as the Practice of Freedom.* Engaged pedagogy is a form of progressive, holistic education in which teachers teach and are themselves committed to self-actualization. The theory is one of "liberatory practice." Hooks' (1994) commitment to "a life of the mind" is, in her words, a "counter-hegemonic act" that enables her to "enact . . . a revolutionary pedagogy of resistance that [is] profoundly anticolonial" (p. 2).

As a critical sociologist committed to the political economy of aging, public sociology, and public gerontology, one thing is certain: there is serious harm, profound suffering, and an urgency of human needs which motivate us to study, write, speak, organize, and labor on the ground. Our quest is to effect steps toward social justice in the lives of the children, the youth, the middle aged, the old and aging especially for those subservient by virtue of class, race, ethnicity, gender, ability, and nationality. Democracy is in peril. The US welfare state is becoming the precariat state (Estes & DiCarlo, 2017). Unacceptable egregious inequality and human suffering amid our abundance denigrate America's moral values in the public interest of social responsibility, democracy, and the fundamental right to have rights.

My energies are focused on forwarding and expanding awareness, knowledges, and action to protect and advance "The Social" and our democracy. My cause is, ultimately, for my daughter, Duskie, and my granddaughters, Brydie and Mackenzie, and for all generations present and future. Albert Camus (1951) describes it well: "Real generosity toward the future consists in giving all to what is present."

In my every day and *every night* life (credit to Dorothy Smith), I seek to realize my own Agency as fully as possible in the body, mind, and spirit of a committed feminist organic intellectual. In so doing, my hope and intention is to realize what Adrienne Rich (1995, 1997) counsels: "The most important thing one woman can do for another is to illuminate and expand her sense of actual possibilities."

Acknowledgments

The author gratefully acknowledges the thoughtful review and contributions of Chris Wellin in the preparation of this chapter and his vision in conceptualizing and bringing this volume to fruition. The author is indebted to Ruth Ray for her contribution to the original version of this chapter (JAS, 2008) in addition to multiple academic colleagues, students, and post-docs with whom the author has had the privilege to author and co-author publications (see references).

References

Acker, J. (1988). Class, gender and the relations of distribution. *Signs*, 13, 473–493.

Acker, J. (1992). From sex roles to gendered institutions. *Contemporary Sociology*, 21 (5), 565–569.

Acker, J. (2000). Rewriting class, race, and gender: Problems in feminist rethinking. In M.M. Ferree, J. Lorber, & B.B. Hess (Eds.), *Revisioning gender* (pp. 44–69). Walnut Creek, CA: Alta Mira Press.

Ball, R., & Bethell, T. (1989). *Because we're all in this together*. Washington, DC: Families USA Foundation.

Benjamin, J. (1988). *The bonds of love*. New York: Pantheon.

Bhaskar, R., & Hartwig, M. (2010). *The formation of critical realism: A personal perspective*. New York: Routledge.

Bottomore, T.B. (1983). *A dictionary of Marxist thought*. Cambridge, MA: Harvard University Press.

Bourdieu, P. (1998). *Acts of resistance: Against the tyranny of the market*. New York: New Press.

Burawoy, M. (2005). A call for public sociology. In D. Clawson, R. Zussman, J. Misra, N. Gerstel, R. Stokes, & R.L. Anderton (Eds.), *Public sociology* (pp. 4–28). Berkeley, CA: University of California Press.

32   Carroll L. Estes

Butler, R. (1963). The life review: An interpretation of reminiscence in the aged. *Psychiatry*, 26, 65–76.

Camus, A. (1991). *The rebel: An essay on man in revolt.* New York: Vintage.

Collins, P.H. (1990). *Black feminist thought: Knowledge, consciousness, and the politics of empowerment.* Boston, MA: Unwin–Hyman.

Collins, R. (2004). *Interaction ritual chains.* Princeton, NJ: Princeton.

Crittenden, A. (2001). *The price of motherhood: Why the most important job in the world is still the least valued.* New York: Henry Holt.

Crystal, S., & Shea, D. (1990). Cumulative advantage, cumulative disadvantage, and inequality among elderly people. *The Gerontologist*, 30(4), 437–443.

Dannefer, D. (2003). Cumulative advantage/disadvantage and the life course. *Journal of Gerontology*, 58B, S327–S337.

Estes Thometz, C. (1963). *The decision-makers: The power structure of Dallas.* Dallas, TX: SMU Press.

Estes, C.L. (1979). *The aging enterprise: A critical examination of programs and services for the elderly.* San Francisco, CA: Jossey-Bass.

Estes, C.L. (1980). Constructions of reality. *Journal of Social Issues*, 36(2), 117–132.

Estes, C.L. (1981). The social construction of reality: A framework for inquiry. In P.R. Lee, N.B. Ramsay, & I. Red (Eds.), *The nation's health* (pp. 395–402). San Francisco, CA: Boyd & Fraser.

Estes, C.L. (2004). Social Security privatization and older women: A feminist political economy perspective. *Journal of Aging Studies*, 18(1), 9–26.

Estes, C.L. (2011). Crises and old age policy. In R. Settersten & J. Angel (Eds.), *Handbook of sociology of aging* (pp. 297–320). New York: Springer.

Estes, C.L. (2017). Older U.S. Women's economic security, health, and empowerment. In S. Dworkin (Ed.), *Women's empowerment and global health* pp. 232–250. Berkeley, CA: University of California Press.

Estes, C.L., & Associates. (2001). *Social policy and aging: A critical perspective.* Thousand Oaks, CA: Sage.

Estes, C.L., Biggs, S., & Phillipson, C. (2003/2009). *Social theory, social policy and ageing: A critical introduction.* London: Open University Press, US: McGraw-Hill.

Estes, C.L., Binney, E.A., & Culbertson, R.A. (1992). The gerontological imagination: Social influences on the development of gerontology, 1945–present. *The International Journal of Aging and Human Development*, 35(1), 49–65.

Estes, C.L., with DiCarlo, N. (2018, forthcoming). *Critical aging policy: A to Z.* New York: Routledge.

Estes, C.L., Gerard, L., Zones, J.S., & Swan, J. (1984). *Political economy, health, and aging.* Boston, MA: Little Brown.

Estes, C.L., Newcomer, R.J., & Associates. (1983). *Austerity and aging: Shifting governmental responsibility for the elderly.* Beverly Hills, CA: Sage.

Estes, C.L., & Phillipson, C. (2002). The globalization of capital, the welfare state, and old age policy. *International Journal of Health Services*, 32, 279–297.

Estes, C.L., Swan, J.H., & Associates. (1993). *The long term care crisis: Elders trapped in the no care zone.* Newbury Park, CA: Sage.

Estes, C.L., O'Neill, T., & Hartmann, H. (2012). Breaking the Social Security glass ceiling: A proposal to modernize women's benefits. Washington, DC: The National Committee to Preserve Social Security and Medicare Foundation, the National Organization of Women Foundation, and the Institute for Women's Policy Research.

Feagin, J.R. (2006). *Systemic racism: A theory of oppression.* New York: Routledge.

Reflections of a Critical Gerontologist   33

Freire, P. (1970). *Pedagogy of the oppressed.* New York: Herder & Herder.

Friedan, B. (1963). *The feminine mystique.* Portland: Powell's Book.

Gouldner, A. (1970). *The coming crisis of western sociology.* New York: Basic Books.

Gramsci, A. (1971). *Prison notebooks* (Q. Hoarc & G. Nowell Smith, Eds., Trans.). London: Lawrence and Wishart.

Harding, S. (1996). Standpoint epistemology (a feminist version): How social disadvantage creates epistemic advantage. In S.P. Turner (Ed.), *Social theory and sociology: The classics and beyond* (pp. 146–160). Cambridge, MA: Blackwell.

Harrington, C., Newcomer, R.J. & Estes, C.L. & Associates (1985). *Long-term care of the elderly: Public policy issues.* Beverly Hills, CA: Sage.

Hooks, B. (1994). *Teaching to transgress: Education as the practice of freedom.* New York: Routledge.

Huckle, P. (1991). *Tish Sommers, Activist.* Knoxville, TN: University of Tennessee Press.

International Longevity Center, USA. (2006). *Ageism in America.* New York: ILC–USA.

Katz, S. (2001–2002). Growing older without aging? Positive aging, anti-aging and anti-ageism. *Generations*, 25(4), 27–32.

Katz, S. (2003). Critical gerontological theory: Intellectual fieldwork and the nomadic life of ideas. In S. Biggs, A. Lowenstein, & J. Hendricks (Eds.), *The need for theory: Social gerontology for the 21st century* (pp.15–31). Amityville, NY: Baywood Press.

Kuhn, M. (1978). Open letter. *The Gerontologist*, 18, 422–424.

Lakoff, G. (2004/2014). *Don't think of an elephant: Know the debate and frame your argument.* Chelsea,VT: Chelsea Green.

Lakoff, G., & Rockridge Institute. (2006). *Thinking points.* New York: Farrar, Straus and Giroux.

McCarthy, E.D. (1996). *Knowledge as culture: The new sociology of knowledge.* New York: Routledge.

Macey, D. (2000). *Dictionary of critical theory.* New York: Penguin Book.

Offe, C. (1985). *Disorganized capitalism: contemporary transformations of work and politics.* Cambridge, MA: MIT Press.

Omi, M., & Winant, H. (1994). *Racial formation in the United States: From the 1960s to the 1990s.* New York: Routledge.

Omi, M., & Winant, H. (2015). *Racial formation in the United States* (3rd ed.). New York: Routledge.

Powell, J. (2006). *Social theory and aging.* New York: Rowman & Littlefield.

Ray, R. (2003). The perils and possibilities of theory. In S. Biggs, A. Lowenstein, & J. Hendricks (Eds.), in *The Need for Theory* (pp. 33–44). Amityville, NY: Baywood.

Rich, A. (1979). *On lies secrets, and silence.* New York: Norton.

Rich, A. (1995). *Of woman born: motherhood as experience and institution.* New York: WW Norton and Company.

Robertson, A. (1999). Beyond apocalyptic demography: Toward a moral economy of interdependence. In M. Minkler & C.L. Estes (Eds.), *Critical gerontology: Perspectives from political and moral economy* (pp. 75–90). Amityville, NY: Baywood.

Sassoon, A.S. (2000). *Gramsci and contemporary politics: Beyond pessimism of the intellect.* New York: Routledge.

Schooler, K., & Estes, C. (1966). *Differences between current gerontological theories.* Vienna, Austria: International Congress of Gerontology.

Smith, D. (1990). *The conceptual practices of power: A feminist sociology of knowledge.* Boston, MA: Northeastern University Press.

34   *Carroll L. Estes*

Smith, D. (2005). *Institutional ethnography: A sociology for people.* New York: Alta Mira Press.

Wacquant, L. (2004). Following Bourdieu into the field. *Ethnography,* 5(4), 387–414.

Warner, J. (2005). *The perfect madness: Motherhood in the age of anxiety.* New York: Riverhead Books.

CHAPTER 3

Critical Questions for Critical Gerontology (and Critical Gerontologists)

Harry R. Moody and Jennifer R. Sasser

Preamble

Over recent decades, Critical Gerontology has emerged as a distinctive voice and analytic framework for challenging power and injustice in an aging society. Critical Gerontologists ask troublesome questions about ideology, control, and the ways in which knowledge is constructed (and by whom). Above all, they have called for a deeper approach to theory-work and praxis around the wild, emergent, and complex phenomena of adult aging, especially as we travel into the farthest reaches of the life course (Biggs, Hendricks, & Lowenstein, 2003; Sasser, 2014). But Critical Gerontologists need to deepen our commitment to asking troublesome questions by posing these same questions to themselves. We need to interrogate received opinions that are too easily accepted—commonly known as "group think"—by advocates and academic specialists. Those of us aligned with the "thought space" of Critical Gerontology, to borrow Katz's phrase (2003), would do well to engage in ongoing critical reflection about why we believe what we believe and why we do what we do. In other words, we need to turn the lens of Critical Gerontology back upon ourselves, as Ray (2008) entreats us to do, by asking:

> What have I been doing all these years and why? What motivates—even compels—my research and theorizing? How has my personal life shaped and been shaped by my work in gerontology? How has my sense of the field, and myself in it, changed over time? What do I celebrate—and regret—about my scholarly life and the progress of critical gerontology overall? What do I see as the central issues for critical gerontologists in the future?
>
> (p. 97)

In the conversation that follows, our intent is to engage some of those troublesome questions that are essential to ask so that we might foster the flourishing of Critical Gerontology—and the flourishing of Critical Gerontologists as we grow older.

What Are We Thinking in the Critical Gerontology "Thought Space"?

Critical Gerontology has been inspired by hostility to commodification and rationalization, rejection of forms of instrumental domination that prevent freedom in later life, whether that domination originates in government bureaucracy or in the marketplace. As well, Critical Gerontology critiques the positivist paradigm as the dominant approach to research on and about aging, later life, and older persons. Critical Gerontology remains an indispensable perspective guiding theory, research, and praxis, helping us imagine a future for aging—and older persons—which is different from the past (Vincent, Phillipson, & Downs, 2006). Individual and collective reflection through the Critical Gerontology prism can help us recover a more vigorous "sense of the possible," or to use the terms of Castoriadis (1998), a "social imaginary" so needed to counter the pessimism and ageism that remain widespread (Applewhite, 2016).

In practice, Critical Gerontology has often been allied with a critical perspective known as the political economy of aging (Walker & Foster, 2014). At the same time, Critical Gerontology also includes the domain of cultural critique that has relatively little to say about political economy: for example, the critique of ageism or attention to the role of culture and the humanities in positive human development. Critical Gerontology might be best thought of as a "meta" framework in that it provides a grounding from which to ask and pursue answers to questions about the most complex aspects of our travels through the life course as human beings, and the contexts in which we are situated; it is not about the "content" of the research, theory, or praxis, per se, but about a life-wide critical and emancipatory sensibility and process for inquiry and action. There are voices who have brought together these different intertwined streams and have also considered different levels of analysis: the individual, inter-personal, national, global, and the cross-national dimensions of all the sorts of questions Critical Gerontologists might ask (Baars, Dannefer, Phillipson, & Walker, 2016; Edmonson, 2015). Political economy, cultural critique, and global inquiry are all indispensable elements of Critical Gerontology.

The Political Economy Stream

In this essay, we foreground the political economy stream of Critical Gerontology while keeping the other streams visible in the background. The political economy approach to Critical Gerontology displays a deep and persistent hostility to market economics and its influence on aging policy, particularly health care (Armstrong, Armstrong, & Coburn, 2001). Above all, it offers a critique of neoliberalism and globalization: for instance, the shift to defined contribution pension plans and the prevalence of immigrant labor in long-term care. That critique is welcome because these trends are too easily taken for granted and normalized in the absence of critical reflection. Even if we accept this critique as a starting point, we are still left with the following fundamental questions: Must all services for an aging population

Questions for Critical Gerontology 37

be provided under government control? Is there any place for market economies consistent with the perspective of Critical Gerontology?

More specifically, are there forms of market economics in aging which do not result in commodification, or what Habermas termed "the colonization of the life world" (Habermas, 1984/1987)? Can the market, under specific conditions, lead to values and practices we could describe as emancipatory for older adults and later life (Gilleard & Higgs, 2000)? These questions are not often asked by professional and academic specialists in the strangely named "field of aging." In practice, it is usually assumed that the market is the problem and government is the solution. But questions need to be asked, and asking such questions is part of what it means to be "critical" about Gerontology as well as "critical" about "Critical Gerontology" (and to engage in critical reflection and praxis as a Critical Gerontologist). Whether as cause, or consequence, it is a fact that at national meetings for practitioners in what Carroll Estes (1979) called *The Aging Enterprise*, most of the participants come from professions or institutions in health care, higher education, social welfare, or government-provided services. It is hardly ever the case that one could even meet someone at those meetings from fields such as financial services, travel and hospitality, or private housing development. And when one does encounter professionals from such fields, they are often on the outside of action, not considered to be "official" gerontologists.

This strange absence is particularly striking because, along with health care, these same fields comprise so-called "Silver Industries" which are certain to grow in years to come (Kohlbacher & Herstatt, 2011). In the United States, with 10,000 Boomers turning 65 every day, one could not imagine a more promising marketplace. Why then should we assume that all markets are simply varieties of "neoliberalism?" Should we not be concerned if the most promising fields or industries are ignored, especially since these fields and industries represent opportunities in the United States, specifically potential jobs for gerontology students? Are we in academia paying attention to student loan debt and to the jobs of our students that would help them repay these loans? These are troublesome questions that deserve attention, but they are hardly ever asked in official settings (though it must be said that gerontology and allied programs at community colleges tend to foreground preparation for jobs, if not career development).

Another area where questions are not being asked concerns the politics of aging. Most practitioners and academic specialists in aging tend to be on the left side of the political spectrum, whether called "liberal" or "progressive" or some other term. In the United States, for example, it would be highly unusual to meet supporters of the Republican Party at a gerontology conference. That fact is self-evident to anyone who has been in the field for any length of time. This is not to say that there is not a diversity of political views among gerontologists; the issue is whether or not there is actually a welcoming and critical space in which a diversity of views can be expressed, especially those views which are outside the "aging enterprise norm."

But the political views of aging specialists, and of senior leadership in groups like the American Association of Retired Persons, or AARP, tend to be at variance with the views of older people as a group. We know this because older voters were the only adult group in the US population to definitively support the Republican candidate in the national elections of 2008 and 2012 (McCain and Romney). Older voters are known to turn out at consistently higher rates than voters in other age-groups, which partly explains the Republican successes in 2010 and 2014. The disjunction between political views of elites, such as aging specialists, and the views of the citizenry is a pattern that became strikingly evident in the 2016 US presidential election. Trump won the election, capturing a majority of older voters, in contrast to younger voters. But the Aging Enterprise has its elites also, and in this case, the center of gravity of the liberal or progressive views of academic gerontologists is distinctly at variance with political views held by a majority of older voters. This topic demands discussion by gerontologists, a discussion that has yet to be engaged in as widely and concertedly as it needs to be.

During the 2016 US presidential campaign, immigration turned out to be the highly controversial "flash point" for the public. Ironically, immigration was actually declining at the time that public opinion turned decisively hostile to immigrants, foreclosing the possibility of any serious policy response to problems of illegal immigration. As well, older voters' concerns and anxiety about immigration proved an important element in the "Brexit" referendum of 2016 in the United Kingdon. The same pattern was evident in Europe, beginning in 2015, when a strong surge of public opinion turned hostile to immigrants from North Africa and the Middle East, during the largest refugee crisis since World War II. But we have seen similar trends in the US public opinion surveys by Pew as early as 2011, which showed that a majority of aging white Baby Boomers and other older generations looked on growing numbers of immigrants as a threat to American values and customs. Similar polls in 2015 showed that, in contrast to younger generations, older whites believe the country's culture and values are worse now than in the 1950s (Frey, 2017). This political demographic divide, and the gap between younger and older voters, has not received the attention it deserves in gerontology.

Immigration issues have major implications for the aging population, for at least two reasons: (1) immigrants, as a group, are younger and therefore, as part of the workforce, they make public pensions more sustainable and (2) immigrants, as a group, are likely to be a critical part of the labor force in health care and long-term care facilities. In the United States, as in Europe, more and more live in multicultural communities with diverse ethnic groups in the population, especially in cities. There has been a pronounced negative reaction—fear and worry—among some groups in the population, and older people and those in rural areas are among those who are worried the most and likely to be hostile to immigrants.

Older people, as a group, have spent their earlier adult lives as workers and contributors to social welfare programs, such as the US Social Security system and public pension programs in European countries. As a group, older people commonly feel that they "deserve" these "earned benefits." For the most part,

Questions for Critical Gerontology 39

political rhetoric encourages that feeling. But there are genuine problems of sustainability for public pension programs. In particular, in the United States, the aging of the Baby Boomers means that the proportion of the population older than 65 years is going from 14.5% to nearly 20% by the year 2030. Population aging, then, inevitably results in some increased fiscal pressure on pension programs. A declining worker-to-beneficiary ratio—the dependency ratio—will remain a flash point for political debate. The debate is inflamed because of what has already happened in some states like Illinois and Rhode Island, where promised pension benefits could not be provided because money to pay for benefits was not set aside by managers of the pension programs.

Analysts on all sides of the political spectrum agree that the US Social Security program is not currently funded in a way to make it sustainable after approximately 2034. Opponents of Social Security, along with many young people, mistakenly charge that this means that Social Security will be "bankrupt" by 2034, and charges of this kind reflect "apocalyptic demography" so vigorously, and properly, criticized by advocates for the aging (Gee & Gutman, 2000). The fact is that by 2034, Social Security will still be able to pay up to 80% of promised benefits. The Program is not, and will not be, bankrupt, and in fact enjoys enormous public support across the political spectrum. But there is no reason why fear of "apocalyptic demography" should make us turn away from the practical problem of making Social Security and Medicare sustainable over the long run. The sustainability of Medicare, for example, was improved by the *Affordable Care Act*. We should not allow right-wing opponents to adopt the rhetoric of sustainability of these programs. Nor should it be left to future generations of recipients to fix the problems that have long been familiar, problems that can actually be fixed relatively easily as we learned in the 1983 Social Security reforms (Moody, 2009).

We have argued elsewhere that Critical Gerontology has a vital role in emphasizing the ways in which all knowledge is socially constructed and historically contingent and is therefore susceptible to distortion by interests not openly admitted nor recognized. Critical Gerontology, then, is part of a wider enterprise of "ideology critique" long familiar to those advocating for social justice. But it is one thing to put forward a critique, to identify problems and failures. It is quite another to offer positive benchmarks for progress that give us hope. Critical Gerontologists must do both.

Paying Attention

Critical Gerontologists need to pay attention to elements sometimes neglected: namely, attention to positive aging and the domain of practice. Both these elements have always been part of the critical tradition that is based, even if implicitly, on a vision of human possibility in later life. The challenge we confront is how to expand this emancipatory ideal in a fashion that is more than merely utopian or imaginary. If we fail to do so, Critical Gerontology will remain, as Dannefer and colleagues say, in its "comfort zone" of criticism and speculation. Criticism remains

40 *Harry R. Moody and Jennifer R. Sasser*

"an essential and perennial task," but we need to go beyond "the comfort of the negative moment and its incompleteness" to identify elements of hope (Dannefer, Stein, Siders, & Patterson, 2008).

In recent decades, in the United States, Western Europe, and Japan, there have been movements of older adults themselves on behalf of what we may term "positive aging," essentially a tangible kind of practice built on a more hopeful image of later life. The best of these movements puts forward a viable alternative to prevailing institutional models. For example, in the field of long-term care, the Eden Alternative, and later the Greenhouse Project, have offered pioneering and yet very practical forms of support for older people with chronic conditions. In Elderhostel (now Road Scholar), adult educators have created the largest education-travel program in the world. Interestingly enough, Road Scholar operates as a market system, mediating supply and demand, but without a profit motive. It acts much as community banks or utilities exist to provide services analogous to a profit-making business but with different incentives.

Both the Eden Alternative and Road Scholar represent a kind of "practical utopianism" that offers hope for positive aging. Although few of us would choose to live in a nursing home, residents of facilities inspired by the Eden Alternative may find more freedom and fulfillment than they would as medicalized objects of instrumental control in conventional long-term care facilities. Road Scholars, more than 200,000 each year, are pursuing a form of freedom by engaging in lifelong learning and travel adventures, with thousands of possible programs to choose from. In this case, the marketplace offers possibilities for individual choice and growth on a scale not otherwise available. They represent examples of positive aging that deserve attention from Critical Gerontologists.

When elder participants in these New Aging Enterprise programs "vote with their feet," we cannot simply dismiss their responses through the marketplace as "false consciousness" (Pines, 1993). On the contrary, their participation itself has helped to foster and sustain the life-world manifest in their activities themselves. These "success stories" help us reflect on the dialectic of theory and practice in new ways and appreciate the diversity of possibilities for positive aging.

Part of this reflection will include a reappraisal of the role of the marketplace and business, just as the success of micro-capitalism has done in the economics of developing countries (Yunus, 2011). These ventures would suggest many ways in which they meet the profile defined by Jim Collins (2001) in *Good to Great* and match many of the criteria for what Hawken has called "natural capitalism" (Hawken, Lovins, & Lovins, 2000). For non-profits, as for business ventures, the key question is sustainability: Can the non-profit enterprise move beyond dependence on foundation grants or the enthusiasm of a founder to develop a dependable and durable income stream? An important factor here is whether the non-profit enterprise develops its fee-based revenue stream and operates in a "business-like" fashion while still remaining faithful to its non-profit mission.

Let us now turn our attention to another dimension of Critical Gerontology, namely the domain of culture. Gilleard and Higgs (2000) conclude their book,

The Cultures of Ageing, with these words: "... the aim of an increasingly commodified economy is to a maximize people's ability to spend at each and every point in their life course." What about poverty in later life? Their own solution to inequities in old age is for people earlier in the life course to have better jobs and therefore better retirement income. Gilleard and Higgs insist that they are trying merely to document this ever-advancing differentiation into commodified "cultures of ageing."

Resisting commodification is where cultural gerontology can make its contribution, and where it belongs as an integral part of Critical Gerontology (Katz, 2005; Twigg & Martin, 2015). Critical Gerontology, at its best, is dialectical: that is, an interrogation of categories of dualism that blind us to the complexities and contradictions of lived experience. Does aging mean loss or gain? The dualistic framing of this crucial question denies the inherent complexity of aging. The answer is both (and more, because there is stability, as well). We see these dualistic categories in our academic and popular discourse: structure and agency, modernity and tradition, youth and old age.

How do these dualities play out in the last stage of life? For example, what happens when individuals move from the (celebrated) "Third Age" into the (denigrated) "Fourth Age"? What of the duality between the "well-derly" and the "ill-derly," or between those with limited life expectancy (e.g., centenarians) and those who are terminally ill? Is aging a "disease" as some biogerontologists like Aubrey de Grey and Rae (2008) would argue? Perhaps the *dis-ease* in question is not in elders but in us, the observers, from all who are suffering from "hardening of the categories." Critical Gerontology asks us to interrogate these categories and dualisms both in our popular and in our academic discourses, to make the true complexity of lived experience not only visible but the focus of inquiry and practice.

But is advancing commodification the only foreseeable scenario for an aging society? The message from the New Aging Enterprises is quite different. New Aging Enterprises need not constitute endless "commodification," which Habermas has called "the colonization of the life-world" (Habermas, 1984/1987). Road Scholar, for example, is fundamentally a travel business but is hardly well described as a bundle of commodities, unless we want to claim that anything mediated by a market has ipso facto become a commodity. Indeed, the very term "commodity" tends to be a derogatory term, designating interchangeable items of diminishing price and value (e.g., computer chips). Indeed, New Aging Enterprises tend to embody the "Third-Ageism" and "project of the self" that Gilleard and Higgs find so attractive as part of the "cultural turn" celebrated in their books. But this cultural turn, and the primacy of agency, should not be equated with the marketplace, still less with commodification. We should be mindful here of the dialectic between social structure (the marketplace), on the one hand, and individual agency, on the other.

One important example of the primacy of agency is the role of older people themselves in finding their voice by narrating their own experience. Some

42 Harry R. Moody and Jennifer R. Sasser

prominent gerontologists, such as James Birren and Robert Butler, have been among the most vigorous in pressing this point. Butler originated the term "ageism" and also first developed the idea of "life review." Birren, after his retirement from founding the first major academic gerontology center in the United States, went on to pioneer an approach to "guided autobiography," which could be seen as an early impetus of the cultural turn in gerontology (Birren & Deutchman, 1991). The promise of "narrative gerontology" (De Madeiros, 2013; Kenyon, Bohlmeijer, & Randall, 2010) offers hope that academic gerontology can reclaim the voices of older persons that are too easily lost.

Despite the leadership of leaders like Birren and Butler, the practice of most professionals in the Aging Enterprise has been entirely different. The voices of age have been absent. It may seem strange, yet it is a fact that it is hardly ever possible to hear presenters at national meetings on aging speak from personal experience. It is nothing less than bizarre that, in professional and academic settings, it is almost impossible to find "experts" on aging who speak from lived experience of age. In fairness, a notable exception is the fact that the Gerontological Society of America commissioned a special journal issue in which older gerontologists were invited to speak from their personal experience of aging (Scheidt, 2017). Another exception was the special issue of *The Journal of Aging Studies* which featured biographical and autobiographical writing about the connection between personal experience and critical gerontology (Moody, 2008).

More than four decades ago, Carroll Estes wrote *The Aging Enterprise*, and she has since then been a unflinching advocate for older people and their needs. Her work has advanced Critical Gerontology in historic ways. But since 1979, a whole generation has passed and the conditions of aging have changed, which Gilleard and Higgs have documented in detail. Despite these changing conditions, poverty and disability have not disappeared, and Critical Gerontologists need to work on behalf of the most vulnerable. But this negative dimension is only part of the picture. Since 1979 new forms of human organization, whether business or non-profit, have developed to respond to the historical challenge and opportunities of population aging. Older people, as a group, have become more diverse in social, ethnic, and economic terms. Their diversity demands greater recognition by organizations and institutions that seek to serve their needs, whether in academe, government, business, or the non-profit sector.

Some of that diversity in aging can be met in the private marketplace, while public policy remains a bedrock for assuring security in health and adequate income. Despite its problems, the *Affordable Care Act* was a step in this direction, blending private and public initiatives. The argument proposed here is not that we should turn over all tasks to "privatization," as if business is the answer to all our problems. Instead, we need to learn from, and apply, the lessons exemplified by New Aging Enterprises (Moody, 2010). Some of these lessons apply to public policy as well as in the marketplace. For example, just as Federal Express has lessons for the government-run postal system, and private universities have lessons for public ones, so New Aging Enterprises can be a seedbed for new policies that help our public institutions respond to population aging. Similarly, we should

Questions for Critical Gerontology 43

look for lessons from Road Scholar in late-life learning or the Eden Alternative as we try to re-imagine long-term care provision.

The ideal of positive aging has implications for all institutions, whether public or private. It is not difficult to imagine a world where community colleges make low-cost late-life learning more available, or where the public aging network adopts health promotion more aggressively. Indeed, steps are already underway in this direction. In short, "public versus private"—yet another imagined duality— is a false choice. The domain of the "private" includes sustainable non-profit groups, whose employees are now nearly 10% of the entire US labor force. These non-profits have been vital agents in providing a critique for business as well as for government bureaucracies. What we face is the challenge in making all organizations more efficient, effective, and sustainable. Critical Gerontology should challenge all institutions to live up to their own values.

Concluding Thoughts

Critical Gerontology has not appeared in an historical vacuum. But, with rare exceptions, it has not always recognized its own historicity, nor acknowledged the relationship between the lived experience of gerontologists and the theories we have developed. That gap persists, in part, because the dominant academic culture of the humanities and human sciences promotes an ideal of objectivity that tries to distance us from whatever we study. The result is a distancing of academic discourse from the lived experience not just of old age but the human journey in all its rich and vexing complexity.

A similar process of distancing has been evident in the political sphere—Political developments in 2016, as shown by both Brexit in the United Kingdom and the election of Donald Trump in the United States. These shocking events revealed how far elite groups, including academics, have become distanced from the lived experience of people for whom they saw themselves as advocates. As discussed previously, in the United States, gerontologists are almost invariably on the left or liberal side of the political spectrum. Yet a clear majority of older voters favored Trump in the presidential election. Evidently, some voices were not heard or not understood. Whenever we lose the voices of age, we run the risk of developing a discourse that is distanced from and misunderstands the concerns of those we should be serving—even if as Critical Gerontologists we hold views different than those of whom we aspire to serve.

There are many today who criticize, often appropriately, the ways in which higher education has abandoned its own best traditions of liberal education and critical thinking. Critical Gerontology represents the perspective of critical reflection and praxis applied to adult aging. Critical Gerontology will, perhaps, continue to have its place in putting forth a vision for a more just and sustainable aging society. But Critical Gerontology—and Critical Gerontologists—can do this only if it—and we—ask troublesome questions and focus the keen reflection of Critical Gerontology back upon ourselves.

44 *Harry R. Moody and Jennifer R. Sasser*

References

Applewhite, A. (2016). *This chair rocks: A manifesto against ageism.* New York: Networked Books.

Armstrong, P., Armstrong, H., & Coburn, D. (2001). *Unhealthy times: Political economy perspectives on health and care.* New York: Oxford University Press.

Baars, J., Dannefer, D., Phillipson, C., & Walker, A. (Eds.). (2016). *Aging, globalization and inequality: The new critical gerontology.* New York: Routledge.

Biggs, S., Hendricks, J., & Lowenstein, A. (Eds.). (2003). *The need for theory: Critical approaches to social gerontology.* New York: Routledge.

Birren, J., & Deutchman, D. (1991). *Guiding autobiography groups for older adults: Exploring the fabric of life.* Baltimore, MD: Johns Hopkins University Press.

Castoriadis, C. (1998). *The imaginary institution of society.* Cambridge, MA: MIT Press.

Collins, J. (2001). *Good to great: Why some companies make the leap and others don't.* New York: Harper Collins.

Dannefer, D., Stein, P., Siders, R., & Patterson, R.S. (2008). Is that all there is? The concept of care and the dialectic of critique. *Journal of Aging Studies*, 22, 101–108.

De Medeiros, K. (2013). *Narrative gerontology in research and practice.* New York: Springer.

Edmonson, R. (2015). *Insight and wisdom: Meaning and practice across the life course.* Cambridge, UK: Polity Press.

Estes, C. (1979). *The aging enterprise: A critical examination of social policies and services for the aged.* San Francisco, CA: Jossey-Bass.

Frey, W. (February 10, 2017). *Trump's early actions will widen America's political demographic divide.* Washington, DC: Brookings Institution.

Gee, E., & Gutman, G. (Eds.). (2000). *The overselling of population ageing: Apocalyptic demography, intergenerational challenges, and social policy.* New York: Oxford University Press.

Gilleard, C.J., & Higgs, P. (2000). *Cultures of ageing: Self, citizen, and the body.* Saddle River, NJ: Prentice Hall.

de Grey, A., & Rae, M. (2008). *Ending aging: The rejuvenation breakthroughs that could reverse human aging in our lifetime.* New York: St. Martin's Griffin.

Habermas, J. (1984/1987). *The theory of communicative action (Vols. 1 and 2).* Boston, MA: Beacon.

Hawken, P., Lovins, A., & Lovins, H. (2000). *Natural capitalism: Creating the next industrial revolution.* Washington, DC: US Green Building Council.

Katz, S. (2003). Critical gerontological theory: Intellectual fieldwork and the nomadic life of Ideas. In S. Biggs, A. Lowenstein, & J. Hendricks (Eds.), *The need for theory: Critical approaches to social gerontology* (pp. 15–31). Amityville, NY: Baywood.

Katz, S. (2005). *Cultural aging: Life course, lifestyle, and senior worlds.* Toronto, ON: University of Toronto Press.

Kenyon, G., Bohlmeijer, E., & Randall, W. (Eds.). (2010). *Storying later life: Issues, investigations, and interventions in narrative gerontology.* New York: Oxford University Press.

Kohlbacher, F., & Herstatt, C. (Eds.) (2011). *The silver market phenomenon: Marketing and innovation in the aging society.* New York, NY: Springer.

Moody, H.R. (2008). The maturing of critical gerontology. *Journal of Aging Studies*, 22(2), 205–209.

Moody, H.R. (2009). Restoring confidence in social security: Our obligation to future generations. In C. Estes, L. Rogne, B. Hollister, B. Grossman, & E. Soloway (Eds.), *Social insurance and social justice* (pp. 279–291). New York: Springer.

Questions for Critical Gerontology   45

Moody, H.R. (2010). The new aging enterprise. In D. Dannefer & C. Phillipson (Eds.), *Handbook of social gerontology* (pp. 483–494). Thousand Oaks, CA: Sage.

Pines, C.L. (1993). *Ideology and false consciousness: Marx and his historical progenitors.* Albany, NY: SUNY.

Ray, R.E. (2008). Foreword: Coming of aging in critical gerontology. *Journal of Aging Studies,* 22, 97–100.

Sasser, J. (2014). *Transforming trauma: Enacting principles of critical gerontology in daily life.* Sage Open, (pp. 1–10).

Scheidt, R. (2017). The defense of my aging self: A report from the field. *The Gerontologist,* 57(1), 110–115.

Twigg, J., & Martin, W. (Eds.). (2015). *Routledge handbook of cultural gerontology.* New York: Routledge.

Vincent, J., Phillipson, C., & Downs, M. (Eds.). (2006). *The futures of old age.* Thousand Oaks, CA: Sage.

Walker, A., & Foster, L. (2014). *The political economy of ageing and later life: Critical perspectives.* Cheltenham, UK: Edward Elgar.

Yunus, M. (2011). *Building social business: The new kind of capitalism that serves humanity's most pressing needs.* Philadelphia. PA: Public Affairs.

CHAPTER **4**

Qualifying the Aging Enterprise: Micro- and Meso-Level Studies in Human Service Organizations

Gale Miller and Alexandra Crampton

Introduction

In this chapter, we examine the contributions of qualitative studies of human service institutions to critical gerontology. We draw from the macro-level critique of the aging enterprise as a "medical-industrial complex" that marginalizes older adults as frail, dependent, and vulnerable. The critique draws attention to dominant Western social welfare policy trends of the twentieth and early twenty-first centuries which have shaped the goals and operations of contemporary human service institutions (Baars, 1991; Minkler & Estes, 1999). Structurally focused and interactionally oriented qualitative studies have emerged within the same social environment, often yielding different conclusions about the power of institutions to shape the personal experiences and social realities of clients served through human service institutions.

Qualitative studies of human service institutions form a distinctive standpoint for engaging critical gerontology. The social activities of human services work are points of contact between macro-level social structures and people's lives. They are particularly useful in seeing how factors such as race, class, gender, age, and culture are implicated in the social interactions, decision-making, and client-processing activities of contemporary institutions (Carr, 2011; The, 2008; Watkins-Hayes, 2009). Qualitative studies of human service institutions also add new dimensions to literary and humanistic studies of people's biographies and lived experiences by exploring how seemingly personal life experiences are socially organized and given meaning in diverse institutional contexts (Gubrium, 1993; Laird, 1979; Miller, 1986, 2001).

Our use of research on micro and meso practices in human service organizations includes more than those organizations associated with the Aging Network. Specifically, we discuss studies of organizations that serve people defined as young and old based on chronological age (the major focus of critical gerontology) and based on personal characteristics that are presumed to indicate persons' levels of physical, cognitive and emotional competence, and maturity. The latter orientation to age is evident in criminal justice officials' deliberations about whether to refer chronologically young offenders to adult courts (Kupchick, 2006). In addition,

Qualifying the Aging Enterprise 47

Järvinen and Miller (2010, 2014) examined how staff members in the Copenhagen methadone treatment program socially constructed participants as old regardless of their chronological ages. As one staff member stated, "'Old' in this system doesn't mean old. The 'old' drug users here may very well be in their 30's or 40's" (Järvinen & Miller, 2014, p. 884).

We also attend to how human service professionals orient to younger and older clients as individuals and as part of families. Families, in turn, may be treated as part of intervention solutions directed at individual clients or as sources of clients' problems. Indeed, persons who might be defined as in need of social services in some institutional contexts may be cast as service-providing family members in other contexts. For example, child welfare cases can include grandparents in kinship care meetings, used to determine where to place a child and what changes are necessary for their return (Crampton, 2007). Miller (1997) analyzed children's shifting statuses in ecosystemic therapy sessions where "problem" children are sometimes recast as insightful messengers to their families by redefining their troublesome behavior as signals of more serious problems among all family members.

Using this broader scope to examine aging and human service work, we find that qualitative researchers are well positioned to observe the micro-political processes that pervade social interactions in human service institutions. The processes consist of the seemingly small and mundane ways that participants in human service settings define and pursue their interests in practical issues. Emerson and Messinger's (1977) analysis of the micro-political processes through which institutional officials negotiate clients' problems and assess available remedies to the problems is particularly useful. The processes involve socially constructing clients and others as kinds of people, sometimes in terms of age and life span development. Such social constructions concern clients' present circumstances and their future possibilities.

Qualitative studies of human service institutions orient to distinctive interpretive frameworks for conceptualizing age, aging, empowerment, dependence, and human rights (Crampton, 2013a). The frameworks include symbolic interaction, ethnomethodology, existential sociology, phenomenology, interpretive anthropology, auto-ethnography, and Foucaultian discourse analysis (Douglas, Adler, Adler, Fontana, Freeman, & Kotarba, 1980; Geertz, 1973; Phillips & Hardy, 2002). This chapter provides some examples of how these frameworks can be used in addressing critical gerontologists' interest in empowerment, dependence, and human rights.

We begin with the general political, economical, and cultural context within which critical gerontology emerged and has developed (eg., Estes, 1999). This context forms a backdrop for the development of numerous qualitative studies of human service institutions conducted by social scientists over the last 35 years. The following two sections discuss local practices as policy-making activities, and the usefulness of Foucaultian discourse studies, ethnomethodology, and conversation analysis in examining institutional discourses. The final two sections discuss the value of expanding critical gerontology to include qualitative studies

48   *Gale Miller and Alexandra Crampton*

of the socio-emotional economy, and how debates between structural and qualitative analysts offer a road into the future for critical gerontology.

Welfare State, Post-Welfarism, and Critical Gerontology

The welfare state has been an important focus in critical gerontology studies. *The Aging Enterprise* (Estes, 1979) was published at the end of two decades of welfare expansion. While enacted differently in different countries in the early twentieth century, the concept of the welfare state rests on a commitment to public assistance for at-risk populations. Advocates of the welfare state explain that public aid is needed because "the private market cannot on its own eliminate risks to economic security from unemployment, low wages, illness, disability and old age" (Battle & Torjman, 2001, p. 13).

The welfare state consists of a variety of social programs intended to alleviate suffering resulting from persistent social problems. The programs sustain people at all points in the life span—from cradle to grave. The programs most often associated with the welfare state are those that provide economic assistance to unemployed, underemployed, and unemployable persons, access to health care for the uninsured and housing for persons who would otherwise be homeless. We extend this vision to include those intended to integrate marginalized groups within the contemporary Western societies. They include programs that address the needs of young people, socialize immigrants, and treat persons addicted to alcohol and other drugs.

Hudson (1995) stated that the welfare state was based on four fundamental values: universalism (welfare programs are available to all persons at risk), adequacy (they provide sufficient support to sustain recipients' well-being), solidarity (they express the shared will of the society), and progressivity (persons with greater means should shoulder more of the costs of welfare than do other persons). These values formed the ethical foundation of the welfare state, which defined the relationship between citizens and their governments. Thus, they formed a rhetorical context for debates about the responsibilities of society to its at-risk members and vice versa. The debates turned on questions about who is entitled to public services, what counts as adequate support of those in need, and what sorts of responsibilities recipients of public assistance have toward their fellow citizens.

Political and practice challenges to the welfare state, which gained momentum in the 1980s through the present, come from two major shifts in the socioeconomic and political contexts of contemporary Western societies. The first is the emergence of a neoliberal ideology that updates *laissez-faireist* themes of the past. It emphasizes private market-based solutions to social problems, individual self-reliance, and local social support centered in family and community. This happens as "neoliberalism recasts the role of the welfare state by shifting responsibility from state to market and from the collective to the individual" (Hasenfeld & Garrrow, 2012). In this context, the aging enterprise of the state becomes the aging (and anti-aging) enterprise of private entrepreneurs (Moody, 2004–2005).

Qualifying the Aging Enterprise 49

The second challenge consists of several practical questions about the welfare state (Meier & Werding, 2010; Weiner & Tilly, 2002). For example, critics ask about the effectiveness of social welfare policies in addressing persistent social problems, as well as the programs' sustainability in an era of declining government revenue and expanding demand for social services. Others point to financial pressures associated with recent migration patterns and globalization (Oorschot, 2006; Razin & Sadka, 2005). Further, population aging is changing the dependency ratio of retirement-aged adults to working-age adults. Increasing numbers of older people has become a rationale for changing typical retirement ages, and reconsidering the implicit social contract of the welfare state (Crampton, 2013b).

Recent challenges to the welfare state express new orientations to social justice and entitlement. Questions are being raised about who should be entitled to public assistance; specifically, "What does it mean to be truly at risk?" and "Is simply being at risk sufficient grounds for aid?" Past definitions of adequate public support and recipients' responsibilities are also being challenged. While the answers given to these questions vary across contemporary Western societies and social programs, the questions highlight a growing skepticism toward welfare state values. This of course includes skepticism toward Social Security, the largest welfare program in the United States, and related programs in other countries. Older adults are increasingly encouraged to seek "active" and "successful" aging that allows them to remain productive across a longer life span. This discourse also justifies retraction of social welfare supports with an expectation of longer years of independence from government assistance.

Social scientists use a variety of terms in characterizing recent trends in welfare policies, such as post-welfarism (Morgan & Markovsky, 2003), do-it-yourself welfare state (Hyatt, 1997), and neoliberalism (Hasenfeld & Garrow, 2012). These trends are perhaps best captured in King Willem-Alexander's depiction of the Netherlands as an emergent participation society (*The Independent*, 2013). He explains that in the future, individuals will be expected to plan for hard times and provide for their own health, disability, and financial needs across the life span. Families and communities will also be asked to provide assistance to their members in need.

As with other Western countries, post-welfarism in the Netherlands involves the privatization of human service agencies and reductions in social services and service-providers. This contributes to a life course of contingency rather than progressive stages that social scientists described as normative (for white men) in the twentieth century (Heinz, 2003). A somewhat different pattern is evident in the global South where welfare state values and programs are being advanced in some developing countries (Crampton, 2013b). It is important to notice, however, the central role of international and national non-governmental organizations in fostering these developments. Thus, the contributions of government are minimized even as some welfare state programs are retained.

Critical gerontology is a useful framework for tracing the impact of post-welfare policies. For example, critical gerontologists have analyzed how intergenerational conflict is used to erode public responsibility to older adults, particularly in arguing

50   *Gale Miller and Alexandra Crampton*

for the privatization of Social Security. Estes (2008, p. 127) explained that older adults are constructed as "vultures preying on their families, communities and society." Moody (2007) has examined the shifting orientations to justice between older and younger generations from the 1960s onward. He describes a pattern of declining optimism about the sustainability of welfare state programs, a trend that justifies treating programs for older people as unfair, overly expensive, and risky entitlements.

Intergenerational conflict is encouraged as older adults are depicted as "greedy geezers" in competition with others. In politics, Moody (2007) notes a constitutional amendment considered by the German parliament to increase children's interests relative to the elderly by allowing children's parents to vote for them. His essay illustrates the usefulness of macro studies focused on the impact of overlapping ideological and fiscal policies on the life chances of persons at various points in the life span. His analysis reveals a post-welfare moral economy concerned with the sustainability of current policies in a world of risk, and involving new rhetorics for defining the moral obligations of older and younger people to each other.

Despite the strengths of critical gerontologists' macro-level analyses, this approach may overlook the nuances, complexities, and ambiguities that infuse everyday social activities as macro-level policies are realized in direct practice. Such analyses risk reducing human service professionals and clients to being captives of social policies by minimizing the situational contexts in which those policies are implemented. Qualitative analysis, on the other hand, orients to human agency as an important factor in shaping the impact of social policies on people's lives. While social structures may be organized to allow for differing degrees of local discretion, qualitative analysts note the continuing presence of agency in social interactions concerned with the provision of concrete social services to clients and the public. They also point to how organizations that presumably implement the same social policies do so in ways that facilitate different levels and types of agency by program participants (Weinberg, 2005). We elaborate on this them in the next section.

Social Policy as Local Practice

Concern for local context is central to qualitative studies of human service institutions. Qualitative researchers replace macro analysts' top-down approach, which stresses the impact of formal policies on people's life chances across the life span, with a bottom-up strategy emphasizing how social policies are defined in diverse social contexts. Locally defined social policies transform abstract formal policies into concrete practices that address the—often non-formalized—contingencies of particular social settings (Lipsky, 1980). Miller and Holstein (1989) conceptualized such policy-making as social problems work involving the application of general social problems categories and remedies to concrete situations and persons. They stated that in doing social problems work, institutional

Qualifying the Aging Enterprise 51

participants "produce and reproduce particular and distinctive instances of social problems" (Miller & Holstein, 1989, p. 6).

Cruikshank (1999) provided a useful example of how localized practices may give the appearance of being part of a unitary social policy. While in graduate school, she noticed a change in her neighborhood—garbage bins associated with local businesses were now being locked. She then searched for the source of this apparent policy. She inquired at local groceries and other stores, the company that owned the dumpsters, and workers at area food banks and soup kitchens. Cruikshank received a variety of explanations for why individual organizations were locking their garbage bins. Many seemed contradictory, overly localized, and unrelated to a unitary source for the apparent policy. After more thought, however, Cruikshank (1999) concluded:

> Either most were seriously deluded, and only one or two coinciding interests were in fact served, or I was deluded in thinking that a particular set of interests had to be served for an act of power like the lockup to occur. No common interest was articulated, only particular and local interests, yet collective action was taken.
>
> (p. 14)

This story reminds us of the value of conducting qualitative studies of patterns that appear to reflect unitary social interests. Patterns that are discernible from afar may mask the multiple and sometimes contradictory contingencies and discourses to which individuals and groups orient. Distanced policy analyses may also fail to notice how the social conditions within which seemingly straightforward social policies sometimes foster unintended consequences.

Qualitative studies detail how human service institutions are organized as "going concerns" (Hughes, 1971). Going concerns are interpretive frameworks for defining and responding to practical issues emergent in social interactions among institutional participants and between institutions and their environments. Hughes (1970, 1976) also analyzed human service institutions as sites for social dramas. They are contexts for micro-political negotiations in which macro-level institutional goals are defined and instrumentally realized, and power relations among institutional participants are socially constructed. This happens through participants' pursuit of shared and divergent social interests that sometimes produce collaboration and other times competition.

We may observe this process when members of organizations within the aging enterprise interact with others who do not construct older adults as frail, dependent, and vulnerable. Consider, for example, Crampton's (2007) study of interactions between elder advocates and mediators about whether older persons could participate directly in mediation. The mediators assumed that older persons were capable of advancing their interests in mediation (unless they had a dementia diagnosis). The advocates argued for including all older adults, preferably with an advocate. Crampton (2007, p. 189) inoted the ensuing social drama in a mediator

52   *Gale Miller and Alexandra Crampton*

response to her question about elder advocacy by defining it as, "assuming you know what is best for another and acting on that assumption."

Such dramas orient to a host of practical and ethical concerns, including defining what activities are most central to the institution's work, who should decide how work should be done, what counts as a proper attitude toward one's own and others' work activities, and when enough work has been done. We see the interconnections between practical and ethical concerns in The's (2008) ethnography of Park House, a private nursing home serving elderly people at advanced stages of Alzheimer's disease in the Netherlands. Official policy defines Park House as a resident-centered institution in which residents are treated as individuals possessing different abilities and needs. Alternatively, The (2008) described it as a world of scarcity, administrative crises, and low morale. She concluded that their workloads overwhelm caregivers.

> Carers often cannot do much more than get the residents out of bed and feed them. This is not just the case in Park House. According to one study, two thirds of nursing carers in the Netherlands have insufficient time to care for residents properly, and one in five carers admits to making residents wear 'incontinence gear'—a sort of nappy—because they don't have time to help them go to the toilet.
>
> (p. 13)

The picture of post-welfarism that emerges in The's study is a collage of people engaged in diverse, often disconnected and hurried, activities. Through these activities, staff members cope with an uncertain environment while making consequential decisions about residents' health statuses, needs, and entitlement to particular services. Staff member decisions made in the course of getting through the day form the de facto policies and ethics of Park House. Complicating this picture are times when staff members acted in resident-centered ways.

One such case involved Mrs Scharloo who refused to eat or drink anything after being placed at Park House by her family. Often staff members treated such refusal as evidence that residents were near death, in which case they did not force residents to eat or drink. In this case, however, they decided that Mrs Scharloo's problem was that she was angry about being forced into the nursing home without advance discussion. Christa, a staff member who took a special interest in Mrs Scharloo's situation, asked family members to rectify the problem that they created. It is significant that staff members' resident-centered response to Mrs Scharloo emerged as they continued to seek shortcuts in caring for other residents. Further, staff members' treatment of Mrs Scharloo was neither random nor a one-time occurrence. These exceptions direct attention to staff members' ongoing efforts to balance concerns for giving residents what they are entitled to and accepting the practical constraints of their work.

For Hughes, the staff members' choices are aspects of the going concerns of Park House. He adds that a major task of qualitative researchers is to notice and analyze the social conditions associated with participants' recurring and less frequent actions. In the context of care offered to older adults who are frail, dependent, or vulnerable to some degree, the flow of recurrent and less frequent actions is likely to fluctuate in part because the capacity and incapacity of older adults can change over time and be highly context-dependent (Jaffe & Wellin, 2008). Rather than presume all older adults are reduced through a biomedical construct of loss and disability, qualitative researchers examine how capacity is addressed as a going concern sorted out through social dramas among staff, clients, and family.

Hughes' approach to everyday life in social institutions highlights the interconnections of language, interpretation, and action in providing services to clients at differing points in the life span. This brings us back to Miller and Holstein's (1989) treatment of social problems as work. Social problems and policies directed to them are matters of continuous concern and action in human service institutions. This is why qualitative analysts treat social problems and policies as locally constructed social realities. We now turn to related perspectives also concerned with language and interpretation as aspects of the social construction of public policies and realities.

Institutional Discourses, Interactions, and Post-Welfarism

Foucault (1972, 1980) used the term *discourse* in analyzing the various shared ways of talking and writing which characterize different eras, societies, and institutions. Discourse involves both language and orientation because different ways of talking are also different ways of seeing social realities and acting within them. Discourses organize systems of meaning that include categories for sorting and vocabularies for naming aspects of people's experiences. Discourses also include preferred explanations for why and how the world is the way it is, and justifications of people's past and future actions. For Foucault, these aspects of discourse are conditions of possibility that encourage some ways of constructing social realities and discourage others.

Critical gerontologists and medical anthropologists have used Foucault to critique how institutional discourses construct older adults as frail, dependent, and vulnerable (Katz, 1996; Kaufman, 1994). However, the power of this discourse can also be negotiated and resisted. For example, older adults reduced to bed and body work through nursing home policies and practices are nevertheless able to claim personal identities by resisting staff efforts to treat them as objects of care (Paterniti, 2003). This is in part due to the looseness of discourse in which categories, theories, and justifications are sometimes inconsistent, and meanings emergent from their use may be ambiguous (Merry, 1990). Competing and parallel discourses may emerge in such a context as well. Consider Crampton's (2013b) study of a Ghanaian elder advocacy organization in which older persons were typically described as vulnerable and dependent. On one occasion, however, Crampton was warned of "crafty old persons" who leveraged the construction of older adults as needing help by taking resources they did not need.

54 *Gale Miller and Alexandra Crampton*

Thus, while people's senses of reality are influenced by the conditions of possibility encouraged by particular discourses, there is still room for interpretation and disagreement among persons participating in the same discourse or using competing discourses. Social interactions are major contexts of such interpretation and debate. This is one way of making sense of Park House staff members' interpretation of Mrs Scharloo's refusal to eat as evidence of a family problem, even as they continued to interpret other residents' seemingly similar actions as signs of impending death.

Further, participants in human service settings have multiple discourses available to them in describing their concerns and experiences. Qualitative studies of human service institutions show that different discourses are often preferred by institutional clients and staff members, respectively. Different discursive preferences also often distinguish staff members associated with different occupations and those positioned differently in institutional hierarchies. Thus, disagreement about meanings among participants in human service institutions are related to both internal inconsistencies in particular discourses, and differences in the discourses used by participants in orienting to practical issues. It is possible to overstate the extent of discursive disagreement, however, because participants in human service institutions are often knowledgeable about the discourses preferred by others and sometimes use them in making sense of issues.

Qualitative researchers—particularly ethnomethodologists and conversation analysts—have expanded Hughes' approach to language and social drama by examining the interpretive and interactional practices of institutional participants (Garfinkel, 1967; Sacks, 1992). The studies involve detailed analyses of how participants enter, contest, and shift among available discourses as they go about their everyday lives in human service settings (Miller, 1994). The studies also describe participants' artful moves in negotiating the meanings of discursive categories, theories about particular situations, and justifications for preferred actions. These emphases in ethnomethodology and conversation analysis cast social interactions as work sites within which social realities are talked into being (Heritage, 1984; Miller, 1990).

White's (2002) analysis of a clinical staff meeting about Sarah (a child suffering from health issues) illustrated how participants in human service settings artfully manage institutional discourses in addressing practical issues while casting themselves as ethical professionals. The meeting turned on whether the medical and social work staff ought to initiate child protection procedures. The physician began by using medical discourse to provide a treatment history and then shifted to psychosocial discourse to explain why weight gains achieved in hospital were lost once the child returned to family. The physician's terminology referenced language in legislation defining conditions justifying child protection. He then turned to Sarah's mother's worrisome behavior, but the social work team leader quickly directed the discussion back to the medical discourse by asking if Sarah's medical problems had been resolved. The physician stated that they had and returned to Sarah's mother's lack of "normal" parental feelings for her child. Next, the social worker described the purposes of case conferences. It was agreed that this case fit with those purposes. The meeting closed with the development of a plan for informing the parents of the need for child protection services.

There is a dominant discourse in this interaction, as seen in the preference for defining Sarah's problems as medical matters. It is significant that the social worker asks a question following the physician's shift to a psychosocial discourse. The social worker positions her question as a necessary step in taking up child protection. White highlights the significance of interactional processes in analyzing other similar meetings in which depictions of patients' medical problems as resolved were challenged, thereby cutting off opportunities to shift to psychosocial discourse. Such challenges point to how social interactions in human service settings are social dramas, as well as to the usefulness of detailed interactional analyses in revealing the micro-political processes that organize the dramas.

The staff meeting also illustrates how family is implicated in human service institutions. Here family is constructed as a focus of concern by noting changes in Sarah's body weight upon returning home from the hospital and assessing Sarah's mother's state-of-mind based on behaviors that the physician depicts as inappropriate. Questions about justice and entitlement are addressed in the interaction as staff members consider whether Sarah is suffering sufficient harm from her mother to justify placing her in a child protection program. The micro-political processes evident in this interaction represent local means for engaging post-welfare concerns about serving only those who are truly at risk. Such concerns have practical, moral, and emotional implications for service-providers and recipients in human service institutions. We now turn to the socio-emotional organization of such going concerns.

The Socio-Emotional Economy

Emotions are rarely examined in macro analyses, although virtually all of the socially significant events making up the life span are infused with emotions. These include birth and death, illness and recovery, employment and unemployment, marriage and divorce, and entering one's school years, graduation, and retirement. Emotions may be evident even in contexts, such as a court, in which professionals work hard to avoid them (Crampton, 2015). Qualitative studies document how emotions are a widespread concern in human service institutions serving people across the life span (Carr, 2011; Rundstedt, 2013). For example, The (2008) described the interrelated emotions of family members feeling guilty about placing loved ones in Park House, residents' feelings of abandonment by family members, and caregivers' responses to residents' and family members' disrespectful and racist actions toward them. She also discusses the emotional satisfactions that the caregivers cite in explaining why they remain in jobs that are physically and emotionally taxing and provide inadequate wages and few opportunities for advancement. Kolb (2014, p. 23) analyzed the latter orientation as moral wages, that is, feelings experienced by persons who define their work as "doing good."

56 *Gale Miller and Alexandra Crampton*

Studies of the socio-emotional economy show how emotions are aspects of social settings (Clark, 1997; Hochschild, 1983; Kolb, 2014). Within the socio-emotional economy, emotions are resources that are micro-politically managed in social interaction (Clark, 1997). The socio-emotional economy is also a moral economy because different social relationships involve different expectations about when and how particular emotions should be displayed. Clark (1997) noted that it is possible to ask for or offer too little and too much sympathy to others.

> The exchange logic a person considers appropriate and fair at any given moment depends on such factors as (1) the person's location in the societal subcultures and social statuses, (2) the other party's social location, (3) the resources they are exchanging, (4) the circumstances, and (5) the history of the relationship. Of course, the other party may have a different sense of which principle is appropriate.
>
> (p. 137)

Hughes (1971) analyzed the socio-emotional economy as a going concern involving both predictable and situationally variable forms of emotional expression. The drama of emotions centers in people's ongoing practical and ethical assessments of their rights and responsibilities within their mutual interactions. Put in the context of post-welfare policies, socio-emotional assessments in institutional interactions define who is entitled to personal considerations and particular human services. Further, the relevance of particular emotions and how they are assessed varies across institutional discourses. Returning to White's (2002) analysis of the staff meeting about Sarah, it is only when the physician shifts from the medical to the psychosocial discourse that Sarah's mother's lack of "natural" parenting emotions is raised.

Hochschild's (1983) analysis of emotional work points to a different aspect of the emotional dramas implicated in institutional interactions. Through their moment-to-moment emotional work, people work up feelings and emotional displays that they do not initially feel but which are expected in particular situations (Gubrium, 1989). Emotion work might be said to mirror ethnomethodologists' analyses of interpretive work involved in the social construction of realities. Further, while the conditions of possibility associated with particular settings may encourage some forms of emotion work, all institutional settings are susceptible to breaches of typical practice. Consider the case of Leontien, a caregiver at Park House, who responded to a resident (Mrs Grasberg) who spit at her by spitting back (The, 2008). Leontien's action breached typical institutional expectations for caregivers, and signaled her unwillingness or inability to do the emotion work needed to cast Mrs Grasberg's spitting as an impersonal and involuntary symptom of Mrs Grasberg's disease. We see the close connection between emotion and interpretive work in staff members' ensuing efforts to make sense of Leontien's behavior.

These qualitative studies of the socio-emotional economy challenge structurally oriented critical gerontologists to expand their orientations to political and moral

Qualifying the Aging Enterprise 57

economy to include interactional transactions involving emotions, identities, and other intersubjectivities. A useful starting point involves examining the unspoken aspects of critical gerontologists' claims and values. For example, analyses of structured dependence implicitly point to a limited range of interpersonal relations and socio-emotional orientations that foster dependence. A more comprehensive critical gerontology would analyze how marginalized age groups' dependence is mystified, denied, or mitigated in institutional interactions. An example is seen in Jaffe and Wellin's case study of a woman in a dementia care residence who resists, negotiates, and reinterprets construction of her otherwise "spoiled identity" (Jaffe & Wellin, 2008). Socio-emotional implications can be an important part of critically examining such concepts as ageism, empowerment, and intergenerational interdependence and solidarity.

These studies might be extended to consider how structural variables such as race, gender, class, and age are also social identities involving socio-emotional orientations. Watkins-Hayes (2009) analyzed how such variables are aspects of human service workers' professional identities, orientations to clients, and interpretations of social policies. There is a sense in which race, class, and gender are discourses within which human service workers "assess and reassess their boundaries, goals, motives, and investments to actively decide just what function they will serve with a particular client in a particular moment" (Watkins-Hayes, 2009, p. 33). Critical gerontologists might consider how human service workers' professional identities are sources of resistance and change within post-welfarism.

These possibilities suggest how qualitative analysis might inform the development of macro studies within critical gerontology. It is important to note, however, that our point is not to blend critical gerontology with qualitative approaches; rather, it is to suggest one direction for further development of critical gerontology. We see little long-term value in glossing the differences between structural and qualitative critical gerontology. We conclude by elaborating on this point.

Difference as a Road to the Future

We have examined the relationship between structurally oriented and qualitative approaches to critical gerontology in this chapter. We see the strengths of the relationship as lying in how they are linked symbiotically. Challenges and insights emerge as structural and qualitative critical gerontologists explore their differences while continuing to pursue their respective agendas. To use Burke's (1984) language, they are counterstatements to each other that call attention to that which is overlooked and marginalized in the other approach. The differences between the structural and qualitative approaches are particularly important in discussions about globalization, diversity, human rights, the third age, and the distinction between existential and contingent aspects of age and aging (Carr & Komp, 2011; Crampton, 2013c; Settersten and Trauten, 2009; Townsend, 2007). These issues are points of contestation about the extent to which global structures consist of many local settings to which formal social policies are made to fit, or, whether it is possible to define universal human rights or differentiate inherent

58 Gale Miller and Alexandra Crampton

and inevitable aspects of aging from those that are humanly constructed and changeable.

Other debates between structural and qualitative critical gerontologists might focus on questions about the social organization of diversity. For example, is it sufficient to define diversity in terms of cultural differences between societies or differences between racial, gendered, class-based, and age groups? Here, qualitative critical gerontologists are likely to point to the diversity of life circumstances, discursive preferences, and interactional styles within cultural groups that are often said to represent a few shared interests. Put differently, how is diversity locally organized and achieved? Similar conversations might take place around questions about the third age as a time of productive civic engagement (Minkler and Holstein, 2008). Qualitative researchers are particularly well positioned to reveal the Western cultural limitations of critiques of civic engagement by describing the many ways in which older people living in other cultural contexts are active and productive participants in their extended families and local communities. Further, such descriptions are useful in seeing the limits of post-welfarist social policies shaping age and aging on the international stage.

In sum, our symbiotic orientation treats critical gerontology as an internally diverse and emergent context for studying age and aging. Structural, qualitative, and other critical gerontologists challenge each other to refine and expand their analytic horizons while resisting the impulse to integrate and homogenize their methods and perspectives. This is both the strength of critical gerontology and a road into its future.

Acknowledgments

The authors would like to thank the many research respondents who have made our empirical studies possible. In addition, funding for Dr Crampton's research on elder mediation in Ghana and the United States was provided by the University of Michigan School of Social Work, Department of Anthropology, and International Institute, pre-doctoral fellowship through the National Institute on Aging #AG00017, the Hartford Foundation of New York City & the Program on Negotiation at Harvard Law School. Funding for Dr Crampton's research on family court in the United States has been done by the College of Arts and Sciences and the Center for Peacemaking at Marquette University.

References

Baars, J. (1991). The challenge of critical gerontology: The problem of social constitution. *Journal of Aging Studies*, 5(3), 219–243.

Battle, K., & Torjman, S. (2001). *The post-welfare state in Canada: Income-testing and inclusion.* Toronto, ON: Caledon Institute of Social Policy.

Burke, K. (1984). *Permanence and change: An anatomy of purpose* (3rd ed.). Berkeley, CA: University of California Press.

Carr, D., & Komp, K. (2011). *Gerontology in the era of the third age: Implications and next steps.* New York: Springer.

Qualifying the Aging Enterprise   59

Carr, E.S. (2011). *Scripting addiction: The politics of therapeutic talk and American sobriety.* Princeton, NJ: Princeton University Press.

Clark, C. (1997). *Misery and company: Sympathy in everyday life.* Chicago, IL: University of Chicago Press.

Crampton, A. (2013a). Elder mediation in theory and practice. *Journal of Gerontological Social Work,* 56(5), 423–437.

Crampton, A. (2013b). Population aging as the social body in representation and real life. *Anthropology & Aging Quarterly,* 34(3), 100–112.

Crampton, A. (2013c). No peace in the house. *Anthropology & Aging Quarterly,* 34(2), 199–212.

Crampton, A. (2015). Ethnographic refusal as research method. *Qualitative Social Work,* 14(3), 453–470.

Crampton, A.L. (2007). *Negotiating old age, mediation, and elder advocacy in the social life of helping.* Unpublished doctoral dissertation. University of Michigan, Ann Arbor, MI.

Cruikshank, B. (1999). *The will to empower: Democratic citizens and other subjects.* Ithaca, NY: Cornell University Press.

Douglas, J.D., Adler, P.A., Adler, P., Fontana, A., Freeman, C.R., & Kotarba, J.A. (Eds.). (1980). *Introduction to the sociologies of everyday life.* Boston, MA: Allyn and Bacon.

Emerson, R.M., & Messinger, S.L. (1977). The micro-politics of trouble. *Social Problems,* 25(2), 121–135.

Estes, C.L. (1979). *The aging enterprise: A critical examination of social policies and services for the aged* (1st ed.). San Francisco, CA: Jossey-Bass.

Estes, C.L. (1999). Critical gerontology and the new political economy of aging. In M. Minkler & C.L. Estes (Eds.), *Critical gerontology: Perspectives from political and moral economy* (pp. 17–36). Amityville, New York: Baywood.

Estes, C.L. (2008). A first generation critic comes of age: Reflections on a critical gerontologist. *Journal of Aging Studies,* 22(special issue), 120–131.

Foucault, M. (1972). *The archaeology of knowledge* (A.M.S. Smith, Trans.). New York: Harper & Row.

Foucault, M. (1980). *Power/Knowledge: Selected interviews and other writings 1972–1977* (L.M. Colin Gordon, J. Mepham, & K. Soper, Trans.). New York: Pantheon Books.

Garfinkel, H. (1967). *Studies in ethnomethodology.* Englewood Cliffs, NJ: Prentice-Hall.

Geertz, C. (1973). *The interpretation of cultures.* New York: Basic Books.

Gubrium, J.F. (1989). Emotion work and emotive discourse in the Alzheimer's disease experience. *Current Perspectives on Aging and the Life Cycle,* 3, 243–268.

Gubrium, J.F. (1993). Voice and context in a new gerontology. In T.R. Cole, W.A. Achenbaum, P.L. Jakobi, & R. Kastenbaum (Eds.), *Voices and visions of aging: Toward a critical gerontology* (pp. 46–64). New York: Springer.

Hasenfeld, Y., & Garrow, E.E. (2012). Human-service organizations, social rights, and advocacy in a neoliberal state. *Social Services Review,* 86(2), 295–322.

Heinz, W.R. (2003). From work trajectories to negotiated careers: The contingent work life course. In J.T. Mortimer & M.J. Shanahan (Eds.), *Handbook of the life course* (pp. 185–204). New York: Kluwer Academic/Plenum.

Heritage, J. (1984). *Garfinkel and ethnomethodology.* Cambridge: Polity Press.

Hochschild, A.R. (1983). *The managed heart: Commercialization of human feeling.* Berkeley, CA: University of California Press.

Hudson, R.B. (1995). The evolution of the welfare state: Shifting rights and responsibilities for the old. *International Social Security Review,* 48, 3–17.

60 Gale Miller and Alexandra Crampton

Hughes, E.C. (1970). The humble and the proud: The comparative study of occupations. *The Sociological Quarterly*, 11(2), 417–427.

Hughes, E.C. (1971). Going concerns: The study of American institutions. In E.C. Hughes (Ed.), *The sociological eye: Selected papers* (pp. 52–64). Chicago, IL: Aldine Atherton.

Hughes, E.C. (1976). The social drama of work. *Mid-American Review of Sociology*, 1(1), 1–8.

Hyatt, S.B. (1997). Poverty in a 'post-welfare' landscape. In C. Shore & S. Wright (Eds.), *Anthropology of policy: Critical perspectives on governance and power* (pp. 217–238). New York: Routledge.

Jaffe, D.J., & Wellin, C. (2008). June's troubled transition: Adjustment to residential care for older adults with dementia. *Care Management Journals*, 9(3), 128–137.

Järvinen, M., & Miller, G. (2010). Methadone maintenance as last resort: A social phenomenology of a drug policy. *Sociological Forum*, 25(4), 804–823.

Järvinen, M., & Miller, G. (2014). Selections of reality: Applying Burke's dramatism to a harm reduction program. *International Journal of Drug Policy*, 25(2), 879–887.

Katz, S. (1996). *Disciplining old age: The formation of gerontological knowledge*. Charlottesville, VA: University of Virginia Press.

Kaufman, S. (1994). Old age, disease, and the discourse of risk: Geriatric assessment in U.S. health care. *Medical Anthropology Quarterly, New Series*, 8(4), 430–447.

Kolb, K.H. (2014). *Moral wages: The emotional dilemmas of victim advocacy and counseling*. Berkeley, CA: University of California Press.

Kupchik, A. (2006). *Judging juveniles: Prosecuting adolescents in adult and juvenile courts*. New York: New York University Press.

Laird, C. (1979). *Limbo*. Novato, CA: Chandler Sharp Publishing.

Lipsky, M. (1980). *Street-level bureaucracy: Dilemmas of the individual in public services*. New York: Russell Sage Foundation.

Meier, V., & Werding, M. (2010). Ageing and the welfare state: Securing sustainability. *Oxford Review of Economic Policy*, 26, 655–673.

Merry, S.E. (1990). *Getting justice and getting even: Legal consciousness among working-class Americans*. Chicago, IL: University of Chicago Press.

Miller, G. (1986). Unemployment as a dramaturgical problem: Teaching impression management in a work incentive program. *The Sociological Quarterly*, 27(4), 479–494.

Miller, G. (1990). Work as reality maintaining activity: Interactional aspects of occupational and professional work. *Current Research on Occupations and Professions*, 5, 163–183.

Miller, G. (1994). Toward ethnographies of institutional discourse: Proposal and suggestions. *Journal of Contemporary Ethnography*, 23(3), 280–306.

Miller, G. (1997). *Becoming miracle workers: Language and meaning in brief therapy*. New Brunswick, NJ: Transaction Publishers.

Miller, G. (2001). Changing the subject: Self-construction in brief therapy. In J.F. Gubrium & J.A. Holstein (Eds.), *Institutional selves: Troubled identities in a postmodern world* (pp. 64–83). New York: Oxford University Press.

Miller, G., & Holstein, J.A. (1989). On the sociology of social problems. In J.A. Holstein & G. Miller (Eds.), *Perspectives on social problems* (Vol. 1, pp. 1–18). Greenwich, CT: JAI Press.

Minkler, M., & Estes, C.L. (1999). *Critical gerontology: Perspectives from political and moral economy*. Amityville, NY: Baywood Publishing Company.

Minkler, M., & Holstein, M.B. (2008). From civil rights to . . . civic engagement. Concerns of two older critical gerontologists about a "new social movement" and what it portends. *Journal of Aging Studies*, 22, 196–204.

Moody, H.R. (2004–2005). Silver industries and the new aging enterprise. *Generations*, 28(4), 75–78.

Moody, H.R. (2007). Justice between generations: The recent history of an idea. In M. Bernard & T. Scarf (Eds.), *Critical perspectives on ageing societies* (pp. 125–138). Bristol, UK: The Policy Press.

Morgan, S., & Maskovsky, J. (2003). The Anthropology of welfare 'reform': New perspectives on US urban poverty in the post-welfare era. *Annual Review of Anthropology*, 32, 315–346.

Oorschot, W.V. (2006). The Dutch welfare state: Recent trends and challenges in historical perspective. *European Journal of Social Security*, 8(1), 57–76.

Paterniti, D. (2003). Claiming identity in a nursing home. In J.F. Gubrium & J.A. Holstein (Eds.), *Ways of aging* (pp. 58–74). New York: John Wiley & Sons.

Phillips, N., & Hardy, C. (2002). *Discourse analysis: Investigating processes of social construction*. Thousand Oaks, CA: Sage.

Razin, A., & Sadka, E. (2005). *The decline of the welfare state: Demography and globalization*. Boston, MA: MIT Press.

Rundstedt, C. (2013). Pain and nurses' emotion work in a paediatric clinic: Treatment procedures and nurse-child alignments. *Communication & Medicine*, 10(1), 51–61.

Sacks, H. (1992). *Lectures on conversation: Volumes I & II*. Oxford, UK: Blackwell.

Settersten, R.A., & Trauten, M. (2009). The new terrain of old age: Hallmarks, freedom and risks. In V. Bengston, D. Gans, N. Putney, & M. Silverstein (Eds.), *Handbook of aging* (2 ed., pp. 455–470). New York: Springer.

The, A.-M. (2008). *In death's waiting room: Living and dying with dementia in a multicultural society*. Amsterdam, the Netherlands: University of Amsterdam Press.

The Independent. (2013). *Dutch King Willem-Alexander declares the end of the welfare state*. Retrieved September 17, 2016 from www.independent.co.uk/news/world/europe/dutch-king-willem-alexander-declares-the-end-of-the-welfare-state-8822421.html.

Townsend, P. (2007). Using human rights to defeat ageism: Dealing with policy-induced 'structured dependence'. In M. Bernard & T. Scarf (Eds.), *Critical perspectives on ageing societies* (pp. 27–44). Bristol, UK: The Policy Press.

Watkins-Hayes, C. (2009). *The new welfare bureaucrats: Entanglements of race, class, and policy reform*. Chicago, IL: University of Chicago Press.

Weinberg, D.W. (2005). *Of others inside: Insanity, addiction and belonging in America*. Philadelphia, PA: Temple University Press.

White, S. (2002). Accomplishing 'the case' in paediatrics and child health: medicine and morality in inter-professional talk. *Sociology of Health and Illness*, 24(4), 409–435.

Wiener, J.M., & Tilly, J. (2002). Population ageing in the United States of America: implications for public programmes. *International Journal of Epidemiology*, 31(4), 776–781.

CHAPTER 5

Who Are You in *Medicare and You?*
Examining *This* Second Person

Timothy Diamond

Eligibility, fr. Latin, eligibilis, selectible; "fit or proper to be chosen"
(Webster's, 2001, p. 632)

Experienced Situations

Susan insisted we go. "You can't miss it!" exclaimed the Director of Research at California State University, Los Angeles, to me, the new gerontologist on faculty. So over we drove on a clear-aired Sunday to a massive old church on Wilshire Boulevard. A bit late, we ushered ourselves into a rear pew, from which we gazed over a church filled with elderly women and men. Active, agitated participants, their heads bobbed up and down like a sea of frothing white caps, waves intermittently interrupted by fists raised in affirmation of the speaker at the pulpit. "Down with Medicare!" she declared, "Up with health care for all!" "Right on," agreed the audience with hoots and hollers. The diminutive octogenarian at the microphone knew well how to arouse a crowd. She had been doing it for years as leader of the Gray Panthers. It was the early 1990s. The speaker was Maggie Kuhn (1984).

Over the years, I have delighted in sharing that magic moment with gerontology students, like passing along an ancestral gem. It was an important event conceptually as well, for it called Medicare itself into question. In Medicare's five decades of existence, that position has been rare.

Nonetheless, Medicare makes an exciting topic to teach, able to stimulate students of all ages. They soon find out that it touches their lives no matter what their age or circumstances. Intense discussions can arise in trying to decode its complexities. And so it went for years, as I taught and learned about Medicare. It went fairly smoothly during those day and evening classes. It was in the middle of the night that my troubles began.

That is when the ghosts began to visit. I have heard them over and over, always the same voices, a chorus of fifteen or so. These are people I have known, in classes and out, whose lives did not fit into the appropriate categories. For now, I just want to get their comments off my chest; as yet, they are not offered as data or representative of anything larger than ordinary twists and turns. But I am using

Who are You in Medicare and You? 63

this chapter to make sense out of them. I am unsure of the ontological status of ghosts in gerontology theory. Rational scientists, of course, are inclined to dismiss them. So I introduce them not as ghosts (even though they haunt) but as voices from the past:

"If you want to know how I spend my nights," Joyce confided in our seminar, "it's worrying about my father. He's on Medicare and going broke paying for drugs."

Pauline, 86, also a student, waved her red, white and blue card, and instructed us all, "Sure, it helps. But don't get me wrong, I don't see a dime. It costs me money."

Laura's grandmother "uses her pension to pay her supplemental premium."

Medicare beneficiary Bob "needed a part-time job to pay for the co-pays." During one conversation he slapped his enrollment card on the table, made an obscene gesture with his arm, and declared, "That Medicare is killing us."

Helen's father "got most of his care from Medicare, but he and my mom don't have any money, so (husband) Paul and I have to pay for a lot of their medical stuff."

Paul's father, Casey, "had to keep working at the dairy even though it wasn't good for his bronchitis. He was old enough for Medicare, but my mother wasn't, and she was the sick one."

Fred didn't qualify for Medicare because during his working years he "didn't pay into Social Security. When I was younger they told me I wouldn't need it."

Herb, 61, lost his long-time job, where he had paid insurance premiums and Medicare deductions for years. He was too young to enroll in Medicare. Before he could get interim coverage he had a heart attack. There he lay in his hospital bed. "I owe $50,000. I guess the insurance companies sure got a bargain when they got me."

Susan, 51, "worked for Simpsons for 30 years until they closed. Now I don't have health insurance. I've been on my feet all my life and I'm getting tired. I don't want to get old, I just want to get old enough for Medicare."

Ellie lived in a nursing home. "How are you getting along?" I asked. "I feel like I'm being punished," she fired back." Trying to change the subject, I probed, "So what do you think of Medicare?" "Well, you better have insurance!" She had some but not enough.

64   *Timothy Diamond*

Fern was also a nursing home resident. Once, while working as a nursing assistant on her floor, I had occasion to notice an expensive fur coat in her closet. I inquired, "Wow, where did this come from?" Her answer was, "I've managed to hold on to it even though I had to switch nursing homes. For a while I was on Medicare. Then my time ran out" (Diamond, 2006).

Judi, caring for her 94 year old father at home, lamented that, "Just last week he got so confused that he cancelled the Part D policy; he didn't know what he was doing. Why, if he had a medical crisis, we'd have to sell the house. I don't know how anyone gets along without someone like me. Still, I feel like I'm in a cage."

Barrie didn't know "where we'd be if my husband hadn't bought that supplementary policy for my mother." Flailing her arms, "I'm still trying to figure out what Medicare covers and what it doesn't."

Linda was "trying to work through the maze. I'm left dangling waiting for Medicare's decision about my mother. I'm going nuts with it all."

Kathleen, caregiver for a younger disabled person, felt "sorry for old people who have to read all this stuff. It's hard enough if you can see."

Norm, 81, former college president, mentally as sharp as ever, waved his arm in dismay when I asked, "What do you think of Medicare?" "Oh, all that stuff is in a box in my closet. I can't understand any of it."

In class we always started with stories like these to ground the group in lived experiences. Whatever they were, good, bad, indifferent, we tried to make sense out of them by matching them to what was taught in the official texts. We approached these texts with confidence, sure that they would explain how such varied experiences might come about. Stories are qualitative data, open to interpretation. By contrast, *Medicare and You*, the official text, is widely accessible, reproducible, and generalizable. It provides the paper's "hard" empirical data.

Reading the Official Text

This booklet is published annually and distributed to all Medicare enrollees (available online in full text at Medicare.gov). The 2018 edition is 139 pages. It has a glossy cover with a collage of six snapshots: ethnically diverse older enrollees, one with a caregiver, and one younger woman using a wheelchair. They are all smiling.

Prior to the Table of Contents and an Index, the first sentence cautions that "Medicare health plans and prescription drug plans can make changes each year— things like cost, coverage, and which providers and pharmacies are in their networks" (p. 6). Medicare is defined as "health insurance for people 65 and over,

Who are You in Medicare and You? 65

people under 65 with certain disabilities, and people of any age with End Stage Renal Disease (p. 15)."

This guide has twelve sections. The first explains the different parts of Medicare: Part A for hospitals, Part B for doctors and outpatient services, Part C (Medicare Advantage, which are private plans that combine A and B), Part D for prescriptions and Medigap (supplementary insurance plans that augment Medicare). Section 2 begins the explanations of costs to the enrollee.

Section 3 alphabetically describes Medicare's covered services. Over the course of thirty-two pages, it lists a specific array of covered goods and services, with the introductory note that "copayments, coinsurance or deductibles may apply for each service listed on the following pages (p. 30)."

Sections 4 and 5 compare Original Medicare, managed by the federal government, with the Medicare Advantage programs managed by insurance companies. Section 6 elaborates on the supplementary insurance policies (Medigap). Section 7 describes how Part D (prescription drug coverage) works. Section 8 lists websites that offer possible discounts for low-income applicants.

Section 9 concerns rights, appeals, and fraud. Section 10 tells how to get more information online. Section 11 contains Definitions. The final section, Section 12, charts comparisons of health and drug plans in an enrollee's local area.

Four terms appear with regularity and frame much of the discussion: "*premium,* the periodic payment to Medicare, an insurance company or a health care plan or prescription drug coverage; *deductible,* the amount you must pay for health care or prescriptions before Original Medicare, your prescription drug plan, or your other insurance begins to pay; *copayment,* the amount you may be required to pay as your share of the cost for a medical service or supply . . . usually a set amount; *coinsurance,* an amount you may be required to pay as your share of the cost of services after you pay any deductibles . . . usually a percentage (pp. 125–128)."

Medicare's Social World

In the official text, the authors of *Medicare and You* do the explaining; they describe what the program "is" and how it works. Similarly, the supporting literature and documentation reinforce this narrative. In classes, we mined a variety of publications in addition to *Medicare and You,* including insurance manuals, popular literature, newspaper reports, and Evidence of Coverage and Summary of Benefits forms. All of these texts explain in their own ways the intricacies of the program. They all participate in the same inter-textual conversation, using the same vocabulary (Smith, 1999; Weston, 1996). Together they constitute the conventional discourse of what Medicare "is."

For the remainder of this chapter that "is" is not taken for granted. I put quotes around it, noting that to declare an "is" is to posit an assertion, and already to make ontological presumptions. Here I attempt an ontological inversion, asking of Medicare not to do the explaining but to be explained; the explanans becomes the explanandum (Hempel, 1948).

66   *Timothy Diamond*

The point is to highlight certain dimensions of social life which are written into these texts, but remain unacknowledged. The official explanations of what Medicare "is" themselves have sociological and philosophical foundations. What is Medicare's "story," and who is this You within it? What is Medicare's writing of the social (Smith, 1999)?

Among multiple dimensions of social life forming these foundations, I note seven in particular: eligibility, expense, time, place, bodies, personal relationships, and language.

1) *Eligibility*. Although the official text asserts that Medicare is "for persons over 65 and those with certain disabilities," such a claim is not sociologically precise. The program is open to those who belong to those categories—as a necessary but not sufficient condition to be chosen. Eligibility comes through some connection to the workplace and proper participation in Social Security. Those unable to demonstrate appropriate qualifying criteria either pay more (Part A premium, approximately $500 per month) or are eliminated. Persons with disabilities must continually prove with medical certification that they cannot participate in the labor force—ever (Paletta, 2011).

Once chosen, one becomes an enrollee, joining an institution of a sort, with its own contracts, hierarchy and language, all of which are explained in the official text and in insurance plans. There one finds the rules of membership.

2) *Expense*. The primary required activity of membership is that You attend properly to premiums, deductibles, co-pays, coinsurances. The official text itemizes, page after page, the percentages of what You will pay for each. It does not add them up. A sketch of the cumulative beneficiary outlay is shown in Figure 5.1.

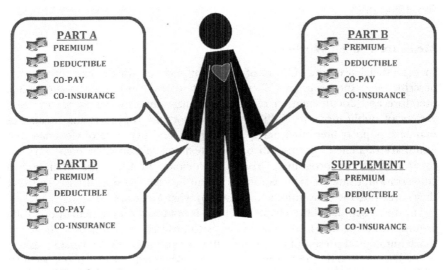

Figure 5.1 Beneficiary Payouts

Who are You in Medicare and You? 67

To pay is the essence of this You. Other characteristics, like personal or dependents' medical needs or desires, history or circumstances, are rendered accidental, indeed not mentioned. Stated differently, if You do not pay, You have no place on these pages.

Underneath the Official Text's discussion of Your pay-out, called "cost-sharing," is a *financially resourced* You. How or whether you can afford these expenses is not under discussion, save for a note on possible discounts for low-income applicants. This You is a universalized, all-equal-at-the-starting-gate, market-ready consumer.

3) *Time.* Time is of the essence; this You is enveloped in time. It is there at the outset with specification of open enrollment periods, and it permeates participation in this institution: payment deadlines, benefit periods, contract time, time-in-workplace, short/long term care, waiting periods, waiting for approval, expirations, lifetime benefit periods, reserve days, penalties for lateness, cut-offs. Rules of time take up a portion of every page of the booklet; they are constitutive of this narrative. Without explanation for why they exist, firm timelines are there on the pages. Their time.

4) *Place.* Similarly, You are put in place. The place is a hospital, clinic, or office, where Medicare coverage begins and ends. These places are themselves encased in corporate webs of affiliation, networks and service areas, which carry their own rules and geographic boundaries. Among the other place markers, "Medicare generally doesn't cover health care while you're traveling outside the U.S. (p. 57)." It is thus a localizing program. The best way to participate as a fit and proper member is to stay in place, in country, in network, in home.

Home, too, takes a strict turn when Medicare enters in the form of home health. It does so with rules of place, most notably that you cannot leave ("You must be homebound" [p. 48]). Roberto, a home health aide, told about the professor he was looking after "until he got caught going to a lecture. Medicare says you can't leave your house. So my agency dropped him." The reasoning is that if one can leave, home health care is not needed. The result is a variation on the theme of house arrest.

5) *Bodies.* In the official texts, you have a very specific body. Pages 29–60 of *Medicare and You* list what is covered. They list body parts, specific services, and prescribed timetables (e.g., Colonoscopy screening is covered "once every 120 months" [p. 41]). An enrollee must read the text to understand Medicare's conception of his or her body and what parts are legitimated for service or intervention. You are required to search through their pre-fabricated conceptions and calendars to find yourself; what you find is your body folded into textual categories where it may or may not fit (Church, 1995). Dorothy Smith once wryly noted this kind of active reading as "an out of body experience" (Smith, 1999). There is an eligible body part here, a pre-timed procedure there. Bodies are arrayed like a Picasso painting, disjointed and disarticulated: their version of your body.

68 *Timothy Diamond*

There are body parts here and body parts missing. "Some of the items and services Medicare does not cover include: most dental care, eye examinations, dentures, hearing aids, and long-term care, cosmetic surgery and acupuncture" (p. 59).

6) *Personal Relationships.* Within these texts, You are cast into a specific social nexus. That is, there is no social nexus. You are alone. Spousal, familial, friendship connections find no place in this social ontology. (e.g., "A Medigap policy covers only one person; spouses must buy separate policies (p. 81)"). Every person is an island here; this is a social organization of individual entities, contractees. You are transported out of situated, relational connections and circumstances, textually transformed into a social monad.

A wife gets sick but she's too young, a friend in the next nursing home bed runs out of time, a lover comes down with the wrong disease, a brother has to get a part-time job to pay for co-pays, a grandmother spends her pension on premiums. And You, even if fitting nicely into these pages, can do nothing for them. This rendition of the social world does not reflect reality as much as a peculiar contortion of it.

7) *Language.* You are told how to speak. The basic terms are contained in the glossary. An exercise in knowing is contained therein. There is where you learn their language and how to read your body into it. There is where the basic terms of pay-out and covered body parts are defined, and where you learn how to communicate using them.

The language contains and prescribes social relations as well. Beyond terms alone, there is a grammar in these pages. Who speaks and who is spoken to, who the actor and who the acted-upon. It is a language of authority and clear conveyance of who is in charge (e.g., terms of payment, time, place, body, appeal). As well, inside the language there is an implicit relation, encapsulated best in the core term "benefits." The term contains a benefactor and a beneficiary, a giver, and a receiver.

Starting in Standpoints

Another line of analysis, beginning with a different cast of characters, leads in a different direction. The people who spoke from situated experiences at the beginning of this chapter also offer standpoints from which to examine Medicare. Here "standpoint" is not about finding out what persons of a certain grouping "know," nor what any of them "thinks." Here we take their comments as ground notes, starting points from which to build knowledge, from which to proceed on the trails they invite. These speakers initiate a line of reasoning, an alternative way of knowing "You" (Campbell, 1998; Smith, 2005; Wellin, 2006).

1) "I don't see a dime. It costs me money." Pauline's comment begins a line of inquiry. Before meeting her I used to teach that the elderly "get" Medicare. Buried in this notion was the image that the billions of dollars that circulate under Medicare somehow go to beneficiaries. After Pauline's explanation, it

Who are You in Medicare and You? 69

never again seemed that simple. With potentially sixteen sources of outlay, as Figure 5.1 displays, "cost-sharing" is spending. Regarding financial resources, Medicare does not *go to*, it *extracts from* beneficiaries.

2) "He was old enough, but she wasn't, and she was the sick one." The excluded and the denied came up against the rules and the rules won out. They were too young, or could not fit into a category or a timetable or body part, or payment deadline. The frozen categories turned out to be thin ice that could not bear the weight of their needs, and they fell through. They are the other side of eligibility.

Herb, Fred, and Susan all spoke from that other side. They had an insider's knowledge of being left out, itself an exercise in knowing, as one learns rejection from Medicare, and its many possible reasons. Exclusion is not mysterious; it is there to be discerned between the lines of the official text.

3) "I feel like I'm being punished." At the end of the Medicare road, there is a beyond—a *post* Medicare. Ellie and Fern both had to stay in nursing homes longer than Medicare permitted. They lived out their Medicare time and then were erased from the ranks of the chosen. Then they had to exhaust personal resources to qualify for Medicaid, after which they became too poor to move anywhere, and they became locked into place. It makes sense that Ellie felt she was being punished (Diamond, 2006).

4) "I'm going nuts with it all." The caregiver who appeared on the cover of *Medicare and You* was never seen or heard from inside again, except as a website referral. Nor do caregivers get a listing in the glossary. They are produced textually as not there.

But long before Medicare gets activated in medical settings, she has already been at work, with the feeding, bathing, dressing, and driving it took to produce the you prior to the You of the official text, readied to participate as a proper enrollee (DiIorio, 1989; Ungerson, 2000). Before that, she has tended to the paperwork, paid bills, met premiums, chosen plans, fetched prescriptions, made the appointments, met the enrollment deadlines, learned the rules and the language— all the while looking after not just her person-in-care, but looking after Medicare as well. Were it not for caregivers' work, beneficiaries would be piling up and spilling through the doors of the clinics and offices and hospitals where the program begins and ends, and where it presupposes and builds upon the unpaid labor of family or personal caregivers, Medicare's hidden others.

These standpoints yield not only their own points of departure for knowledge building but, taken together, they dislodge Medicare from its Archimedean pivot point, disrupting it from "truth," if not from authority (Acker, Barry, & Essenweld, 1983). This objective position also carries its own narrative of how the Medicare production process works.

Proceeding from situated, embodied outsiders, Medicare becomes destabilized *as* knowledge. These standpoints lead to yet one more: Medicare itself can be understood as having a standpoint of its own. From their points of departure, Medicare can be seen as an exercise in knowing, with its own social imaginary, cast of characters, lexicon and rules about who is in charge and who is written in and written out, who speaks, and who is silent.

Medicare as a Production Process

Medicare is a production process in the sense that it is put together by humans every day, continually brought into being in material and relational contexts (Griffith & Smith, 2005; Sharma, 2015).

Within its objective/objectified position, an orthodox teaching prevails, identifiable in the official texts. There is a set of actors, called stakeholders, who operate within a sphere of exchange. Except for consumers, they are formal organizations, public and private. Here is the conventional array of active movers and shakers (clockwise): consumers, government, hospitals (long- and short-term), insurance companies, doctors, pharmaceuticals. These components, in conventional discourse, produce Medicare (Figure 5.2).

Products

How can anyone not celebrate Medicare's existence? Who would dare to wish that it did not exist? Who would not argue and struggle to keep it alive for ourselves and the next generations?

These rhetorical questions contain their own answers. In its 50 years of existence, Medicare has enjoyed widespread popularity and, except for right-wing elements

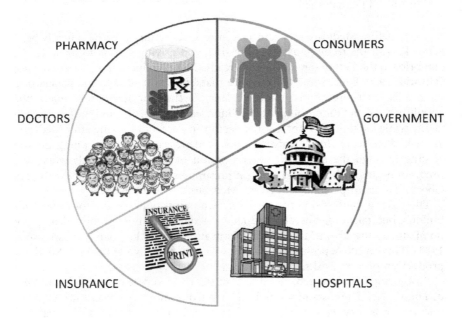

Figure 5.2 Conventional Stakeholders

that would abandon it and leave nothing in its wake, has been roundly supported; the only lively political debate has concerned whether to expand or contract it, and how to replenish the Trust Fund.

What "is" Medicare? It is security and safety, a thrill to get accepted into and have that card drop in the mailbox. It is eagerly anticipated by persons still too young, like Susan and Judi. It is greatly appreciated by beneficiary and caregiver when it pays a percentage of the huge medical prices.

It offers services and products, listed specifically, for which it partially pays providers and organizations. Medicare has proven an effective way to promote profit in the medical industries that serve its designated populations (Calasanti & Slevin, 2001; Estes et al., 2001).

Where does the money go? Matthews and McGinty (2010) offered an organizational breakdown, using 2009 data. While the amounts have increased over the years, the recipient organizations and their proportions have not. Part A, hospital insurance, mostly goes for hospital inpatient care ($134 billion). Managed care organizations take the second largest chunk ($59.4 billion). Skilled nursing facilities follow ($26.3 billion), while hospice care ($12.1 billion) and home health organizations consume the remainder.

Regarding Part B, medical insurance, physicians on fee schedule earned the most ($62.5 billion), followed by managed care facilities ($53.4 billion). Outpatient hospital charges consumed $27.2 billion, while home health organizations took in $11.3 billion. Medical equipment ($8.1 billion) and lab tests ($8.0 billion) completed the Part B expenditures. Part D, the drug benefit program, cost the program $60 billion.

This official distribution of the recipients does not incorporate insurance companies, which mediate all sectors of this program, directing their income to services, salaries, and administration and profit.

To learn about Medicare from the official texts is to appreciate the unimaginable burden of US medical costs, which presumably without Medicare patients and their families would have to bear. Such a situation by definition would plunge the elderly and disabled population, and the whole economy, into chaos. So some of these financial burdens are relieved for eligible enrollees, who are up to date on premiums and whose needs match the services offered (Lalli, 2016; Neugarten, 1982).

There is a widespread apprehension that Medicare will not be sustained in the future. Personally and collectively people fear losing it. "It's the best we've got." "It's better than nothing." "It's better than relying on private insurance." Comments like these reflect an acceptance of this privatized program as the US version of public health care. Here to stay; inviolable, the law of the land, a hegemonic grip on Medicare-as-good.

There is a problem here, a potential totalizing, a precluding of oppositional discourse. In the absence of lively debate about whether it should exist at all, open inquiry is closed off. In many circles, it would be heresy to speak out for its demise.

Therefore, to open this nearly closed door, I pose two questions: One, what is the opposite of Medicare and two, what is Medicare not? The paralyzing fear that

72   Timothy Diamond

grips the American citizenry is what would happen in its absence. Calamity would ensue: black holes of bills and bankruptcies, untreated pain and disease, weeping and gnashing of teeth—even if teeth, never having been covered in the first place, were already gnashing.

But what is its opposite in the other direction? One possibility is a far more comprehensive and less expensive program. And a recognition that Medicare is not a publicly funded, tax-based universal coverage. It is and has been since its inception a compromise on that issue, and an impediment toward its development.

By-Products

To learn about this production process from the people who opened this chapter is to discern that along with products these arrangements generate by-products. These negative consequences are discoverable through following the trails these standpoints revealed as we tried to weave their dilemmas into the official texts. These speakers point to at least four toxic consequences:

1) *Impoverishment.* For all enrollees, Medicare is a financial expense. For those with sparse resources, it can be impoverishing, as with Joyce lamenting her father going broke paying for drugs, and Bob claiming with words and gestures "That Medicare is killing us," and Laura's grandmother paying her supplement with her pension. These actual payers, with actual wallets and fixed incomes, potentially paying into sixteen streams of "cost-share," did not fit into the universalized, resourced You of the official text. They experienced Medicare as a poverty-making program.

   This depletion process is erased in the official texts, replaced by the universal You, transcendent of resources, poised to cost-share. Medicare can make its enrollees poor, and enrollees (or anyone) reading the texts will never read about its built-in downward spiral.

2) *Exclusion and Denial.* Eligibility breeds exclusion. This production process includes the creation of the Unchosen. Both "people 65 and over" and "people under 65 with certain disabilities" become over-generalized categories, misnomers in effect (Emerson, 1983; Thorne, 2006). Too young, too sick for too long, too poor to pay—some of the reasons for older persons to fall off the rolls of inclusion; while for persons with disabilities younger than 65 years inability to prove that one can never work is a widespread differentiation between application and acceptance (Gill, Ingman, & Campbell, 1991). Exclusion is implicit in eligibility. The ineligible are erased from the text . . . not that, as actual human beings, they go away.

3) *Abandonment.* On this consequence, nursing home residents, especially really long-termers, are the most articulate. Medicare covers nursing home care, but for a limited time. "You'd better have insurance," Ellie warned, though hers had expired. As Fern instructed, then one goes to a "spend down" phase, exhausting all personal resources, ("not my fur coat!") hopefully to become eligible for Medicaid, after "my Medicare time ran out."

The official text defines the program as "for people 65 and over ..." It does not encompass those in need of long-term care for years, too old, too frail for Medicare. They become, like the ineligible, absented from these pages. We who are not where they are—yet—owe them a debt of gratitude for their truly long-term standpoint, from which we can learn about the results of a program that erases their existence.

4) *Isolation.* Here we call on caregivers to introduce the isolation that characterizes their work in the absence of any publicly supported help, with their work not even noted in the official texts. They learn to carry on in the absence of pay, Social Security, health insurance, sick days, occupational classification, codification of tasks, and even vocabulary with which to speak about it. Unable to leave the house, private help being too expensive, Judi's feeling "like I'm in a cage," and Linda's "going nuts with it all" contain a sensible caregivers' logic of their own (Abel, 1990; Armstrong & Armstrong, 2004; Fisher & Tronto, 1990).

Experiential knowledge yielded identification of these by-products (Brush, 1999; Campbell, 1998; Haraway, 1988; Ray, 2000). This identification is not possible through reading only the official texts; by-products are not to be found there, no caregiver "trying to work through the maze," or father "going broke paying for drugs." A reader cannot confront these dilemmas by way of the official texts. Within this discourse, the objective standpoint, these by-products become unnoticed and unknown, if unintended, consequences.

By contrast, the method of investigation I have used, institutional ethnography, began with actual people and attended to the text(s) they point toward. In turn, the text is scrutinized in other than its own terms (Eastwood, 2005; Luken & Vaughan, 2003; Mueller, 1985). The procedure opened the way to the discovery of by-products and then led to the inevitable conclusion that they must happen. They are intrinsic to this production process. The text tells you so. As the speakers revealed the by-products, the text revealed their source, from whence they are produced. Like unchosen is to chosen, like closed is to open, the sources are within the rules that separate the in from the out, the eligible from the ineligible. The categories, once dislodged from their imputed objectivity, revealed not just what the official texts contained but what they did not, and who they did not.

A New You: Toward an Alternative Image of Production

When not bounded by the official text, a new image can be conjured which not only identifies but begins from the positions of these marginalized persons. It casts them as co-producers in the production process.

To begin from the standpoints of beneficiaries-made-poor, the unchosen and the denied, the abandoned and the isolated—is to extend the range of activities beyond that contained in the objective story of how Medicare works. These active, co-producers have shown themselves to be vital to the ongoing viability of the program. If any of these agents stopped contributing as they do, Medicare's wheels would grind more slowly; they all participate in keeping them turning.

Beneficiaries, who paid in via deductions every paycheck of their working lives, continue to provide integral financial contributions in these relations of production. They help the government subsidize the medical industries (Figures 5.2 and 5.3). Conceptualized into the language of recipients, they who "don't see a dime" are crucial contributors.

The ineligible and the denied, in being rejected, provide savings for the program. Cast away, they must turn to the workplace for survival, where they and their employers continue to contribute Medicare premiums through deductions. Meanwhile, they mark out the categories of exclusion. From their standpoint, they teach how easy it is to not be accepted, or to fall off. They point out and embody the pitfalls inherent in a program designed for selectibles.

The abandoned sit in the back wards of Medicaid nursing homes, apparently idle, but every minute enabling the transfer of funds over their heads, and without whom there would be no transfer, and no profit. Ellie and Fern provide human mediums in the government to corporate exchanges. Not that they see a dime either; there they sit, silently, actively generating revenue.

Caregivers coordinate the vast uncoordinated needs of their charges (Griffith & Smith, 2005). Medicare writes its social as if caregivers did not exist. It is Medicare that could not exist if it were not for caregivers. Only by making them appear as non-existent can Medicare operate as it does, while it is wholly dependent on their before-and-after Medicare unpaid and unnamed labor. Caregivers teach about a generation trapped in indentured servitude. Left alone by their government, while contributing billions of dollars of savings to it, they are "forced to care" (Glenn, 2010).

With the addition of these post-objective standpoints, grounded in flesh and blood situations and context, a broader understanding of the motor of the Medicare machine comes into focus. Revisited, the Medicare production process

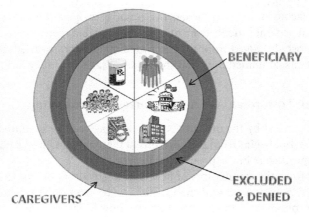

Figure 5.3 The Medicare Production Process Revisited

includes the monetary contributions and unacknowledged labor that has to occur before the stakeholders in the inner circle can begin to mobilize.

This relational image breaks the boundaries of the conventional paradigm by incorporating the labor and financial contributions of those in the outer circles (Fisher & Tronto, 1990). Studying Medicare as lived experience (ethnographic gerontology) opens up avenues for how to change or dissolve it by starting from outer circles and moving inward.

This alternative view of the production process inspires nothing less than the mandate for a new You. To imagine such an inversion does not require far-fetched fantasy. An image can congeal directly from these data.

You could start with a whole intact body, and enter into medical care from its wants and needs, enmeshed in intimate connections with other people, whose care means as much to you as your own.

You could be free to come and go in time and place, to escape house arrest (like a retired professor not afraid of getting caught going to a lecture); free to leave the country, for example, or network or service area or state, free to seek an expert opinion from a different medical practice or philosophy.

You could be free to speak a language of needs and desires and financial capabilities, with a vocabulary even a former college president could understand, a lexicon less mired in terminology about how much you owe, and speak not just for oneself and one's nuclear family, but for others, like Herb, lifelong contributor who fell through the cracks of time and from whom the "insurance companies sure got a bargain."

You could be free to look ahead at the generations to follow, to imagine liberating them from this financial drain, and rules of time and place and bodies and relations, and transforming the constrictive and authoritarian "giver-taker" language of benefits and benefactors into a new glossary.

So looking back and collecting these speakers' comments, it turns out that they were not ghosts at all. They were ordinary Americans who went through their working lives paying their Medicare deductions, "not wanting to get old, just old enough for Medicare," believing that it was "health insurance for people 65 and over and people under 65 with certain disabilities . . ." Certain disabilities, indeed, and now as we have learned from them, certain persons and body parts and time frames and places as well.

From this analytical lens, I conclude that the best hope for the future will come from the dispossessed. They offer a starting point from their situations and the foresight that such twists and turns are doomed to be repeated by members of future generations. To all these marginalized persons we owe a debt. Together they deliver a new perspective for Medicare analysis. They give us the gift of fear. If these built-in by-products continue to be reproduced, generation after generation, they cannot be cleaned up without shutting down their source and seeking its total transformation (Estes, 2001; Estes, Linkins, & Binney, 1996). We have the marginalized and dispossessed to thank for giving us the fear not that Medicare will not be here in the future, but that it will be.

76 Timothy Diamond

If the United States is to evolve toward more humane arrangements for the delivery of health services, we will need to move *beyond* Medicare. Given the weak and damaging sociological and philosophical foundations upon which it is built—its intrinsic exclusions and denials; its restrictions on time, place, and bodies; its monadic You; its resource drain and pauperizing potential—Medicare is incompatible with a goal of universal coverage. Such a perspective on this incompatibility is not new; it has been advanced in the past. It was at the heart of the message Maggie Kuhn delivered back in that church ("Down with Medicare. Up with health care for all!"), with that chanting congregation of white hairs urging her on. In the health care settings they called for, no one's access to health care will be dependent on proving eligibility. There, everyone will be a fit and proper member of the chosen people.

Acknowledgments

Thanks to Kathryn Church and Mary Diamond for their insightful reading and to Sherry Williamson for her assistance in creating the figures.

References

Abel, E.K. (1990). Family care of the frail elderly. In E.K. Abel & M.K. Nelson (Eds.), *Circles of care: work and Identity in women's lives* (pp. 65–91). Albany, NY: State University Press of New York.

Acker, J., Barry, K., & Essenweld, J. (1983). Objectivity and truth: Problems in doing feminist research. In J.A. Cook & M.M. Fonow (Eds.), *Beyond methodology: Feminist scholarship and lived research* (pp. 133–53). Bloomington, IN: University of Indiana Press.

Armstrong, P., & Armstrong, H. (2004). Thinking it through: Women, work and caring in the new millennium. In K.R. Grant, et al. (Eds.), *Caring for/caring about: Women, home care, and unpaid caregiving* (pp. 5–40). Aurora, Ontario: Garamond Press.

Brush, P. (1999). The influence of social movements on articulation of race and gender in black women's autobiographies. *Gender and Society*, 13(1), 120–137.

Calasanti, T.M., & Slevin, K.F. (2001). *Gender, social inequalities and aging.* Walnut Creek, CA: Alta Mira Press.

Campbell, M.L. (1998). Institutional ethnography and experience as data. *Qualitative Sociology*, 21(1), 55–73.

Church, K.L. (1995). *Forbidden narratives: Critical autobiography as social science.* Amsterdam, the Netherlands: Gordon and Breach.

Diamond, T. (2006). "Where did you get the fur coat, Fern?": Participant observation in institutional ethnography. In D.E. Smith (Ed.), *Institutional ethnography as practice* (pp. 45–63). Lanham, MD: Rowman and Littlefield.

DiIorio, J.A. (1989). Feminism, gender and the ethnographic study of sport. *Arena Review*, 13(1), 49–60.

Eastwood, L.E. (2005). *The social organization of policy: An institutional ethnography of UN forest deliberations.* New York: Routledge.

Emerson, R.M. (1983). Holistic effects in social control decision-making. *Law and Society Review*, 17, 427–455.

Estes, C.L., and Associates. (2001). *Social policy and aging: A critical perspective.* Thousand Oaks, CA: Sage.

Estes, C.L., Linkins, K.W., & Binney, E.A. (1996). The political economy of aging. In R.H. Binstock & L.K. George (Eds.), *Handbook of aging and the social sciences* (pp. 346–361). San Diego, CA: Academic Press.

Fisher, B., & Tronto, J. (1990). Toward a feminist theory of caring. In E.K. Abel & M.K. Nelson (Eds.), *Circles of care: Work and identity in women's lives* (pp. 35–62). Albany, NY: State University Press of New York.

Gill, D.G., Ingman, S.R., & Campbell, J. (1991). Health care provision and distributive justice: End-stage renal disease and the elderly in Britain and America. *Social Science and Medicine,* 32(5), 565–577.

Glenn, E.N. (2010). *Forced to care: Coercion and caregiving in America.* Cambridge, MA: Harvard University Press.

Griffith, A., & Smith, D.E. (2005). *Mothering for schooling.* New York: Routledge/Falmer.

Haraway, D. (1988). Situated knowledges: The science question in feminism and the privilege of partial perspective. *Feminist Studies,* 4(3), 575–601.

Hempel, C.G. (1948). Studies in the logic of explanation. *Philosophy of Science,* 20, 135–175.

Kuhn, M. (1984). Challenge to a new age. In M. Minkler & C.L. Estes (Eds.), *Readings in the political economy of aging* (pp. 7–9). Farmingdale, NY: Baywood.

Lalli, F. (2016). *Your best health care now.* New York: Touchstone.

Luken, P.C., & Vaughan, S. (2003). Living alone in old age: Institutionalized discourse and women's knowledge. *Sociological Quarterly,* 44, 109–131.

Mathews, A.W., & McGinty, T. (2010). Physician panel prescribes the fees paid by Medicare. *Wall Street Journal,* CCLVI (October 27), 1, A-16.

Medicare and You 2018 . (2017). *CMS Product No. 10050–09.* Baltimore, MD.: Centers for Medicare and Medicaid Services.

Mueller, A. (1995). Beginning in the standpoint of women: An investigation of the gap between cholas and "women of Peru." In M.L. Campbell & A. Manicom (Eds.), *Knowledge, experience, and ruling relations: Studies in the social organization of knowledge* (pp. 96–107). Toronto, ON: University of Toronto Press.

Neugarten, B. (Ed.). (1982). *Age or need? Public policies for older people.* Beverly Hills, CA: Sage.

Paletta, D. (2011). Disability payments slow as managers chase targets. *Wall Street Journal,* CCLIX (September 30), A4.

Ray, R. (2000). *Beyond nostalgia: Aging and life-story writing.* Charlottesville, VA: Univeristy of Virginia Press.

Sharma, K. (2015). Governing difficult knowledge: The Canadian museum and its publics. *Review of Education, Pedagogy and Cultural Studies,* 37(2/3), 184–206.

Smith, D.E. (1999). The ruling relations. In D.E. Smith (Ed.), *Writing the social: Critique, theory and investigations* (pp. 73–95). Toronto, ON: University of Toronto Press.

Smith, D.E. (2005). *Institutional ethnography: A sociology for people.* Latham, MD: Rowman and Littlefield.

Thorne, B. (2006). How can feminist sociology sustain its critical edge? *Social Problems,* 53(4), 473–478.

Webster's new unabridged dictionary. (2001). Jess Stein (Ed.) New York: Random House, p. 632.

78 *Timothy Diamond*

Wellin, C. (2006). Scrutinizing familial care in consumer-directed long-term care programs: Implications for theory and research. In S.R. Kunkel & V. Wellin (Eds.), *Consumer voice and choice in long-term care* (pp. 195–220). New York: Springer.

Weston, K. (1996). *Render me, gender me.* New York: Columbia University Press.

Ungerson, C. (2000). Cash in care. In M.H. Meyer (Ed.), *Care work: Gender, class and the welfare state* (pp. 68–88). New York: Routledge.

CHAPTER **6**

Who Rules Home Care? The Impacts of Privatization on Profitability, Cost, and Quality

William Cabin

Introduction and Chapter Overview

It was January 1983. I was in Washington, DC, for the first time in my life, about to start an exciting new job. I was the first Director of Regulatory Affairs and Research for the newly formed National Association for Home Care (NAHC), later to be named National Association for Home Care and Hospice. I was only the fourth employee in what would become a large national trade association for home care and hospice providers. I was coming to the job with enthusiasm, having become somewhat familiar with the hope and promise of home care from my experience as a nursing home regulator in New York State.

In less than 2 years, I had become a major, successful advocate for nursing home reform. I was assistant welfare inspector general for nursing homes, heading a unit that field audited some of the state's largest Medicaid nursing homes which had only had their annual cost reports and reimbursement verified by a "desk audit" by the state. The desk audit process was done by bureaucrats in Albany, reviewing the submitted cost reports without requiring supporting documentation (i.e., checks, invoices, bills) to verify that the transactions reported on the cost report were actually real, not fictitious. Two of our field audits were of the first and second largest Medicaid nursing homes in the state (both in New York City), resulting in discovery of major fraud and garnering major media attention. We found that patient care Medicaid funds were being used for activities such as paying the college tuition of a bookkeeper at the nursing home; payments for cars, boats, and costly paintings; political campaign contributions; and lucrative consulting contracts to family members and friends in excess of Medicaid guidelines. Patient care was being replaced by greed and the desire for personal power as the driving force in operating nursing homes.

As a result of the investigations, I became involved with New York Secretary of State-designate Mario Cuomo's preparation of a nursing home reform report which resulted in creation of a Moreland Act Commission to reform the state's Medicaid nursing home reimbursement system and a new position of deputy attorney general for Health and Social Services. I worked with the new

80   *William Cabin*

deputy attorney general for several months, helping prepare several cases for successful prosecution.

It was exciting! And now I was excited to help further develop the antidote to nursing homes, namely home care. I became familiar with home care as an alternative to nursing homes through my contact with members of the US Senate Aging Committee staff who were simultaneously working on similar nursing home investigations nationally. There seemed some evidence that home care cost less than institutional care and overwhelming evidence that most Medicare beneficiaries lived at home and preferred their care at home. Patient care was the clear priority in home care, not profit or personal gain. Home care was delivered by voluntary organizations (Visiting Nurse Associations) and local government in the tradition of public health nursing. The first home care program was created by Lillian Wald at the Henry Street Settlement in the early 1900s, eventually becoming the Visiting Nurse Service of New York. That tradition continued with the advent of Medicare and Medicaid with for-profits being banned from participation in Medicare home health in the original legislation, resulting in 92% of all Medicare-certified home health agencies (HHAs) being either voluntary associations or government agencies (National Association for Home Care and Hospice, 2011).

There were other factors expected to accelerate the growth of home care over hospital- and facility-based care, the foremost of which was the aging boom. There were numerous studies and books about the current and future growth of the aging population (Butler, 1985), their mobility assistance and medical needs, and the clear preference of the aging population for receiving care at home (Estes, 1979). In addition, Medicare home health reimbursement was based on a fee-for-service payment for all goods and services that were documented as medically necessary and associated administrative costs.

So, in 1983, it looked like these would be exciting times in home care. However, the glow of the home care revolution faded relatively quickly. I left NAHC in 1986, spending the next 17 years as an executive operating home care agencies and hospices. By the time I left home care and began my graduate work in social work and public health in 2003, there had been massive changes that raised questions about the cost increase and quality decrease in home care. As a result, my doctoral and post-doctoral work focused in large part on studying the transformation of Medicare home health from its public health nursing roots to a nearly $20 billion annual profit-driven industry dominated by for-profit agencies. The remainder of this chapter recounts my journey in studying the home care transformation, through a literature review and conducting two studies, and its implications.

Background and Significance of the Problem

Studies of hospitals, health maintenances organizations, nursing homes, hospices, and dialysis providers have found that proprietary ownership (ownership by a for-profit company) may be associated with poor care and, for hospitals, higher costs (Aaronson, Zinn, & Rosko, 1994; Carlson, Gallo, & Bradley, 2004; Devereaux, Choi, et al., 2002; Devereaux et al., 2004; Devereaux, Schünemann,

Who Rules Home Care? 81

et al., 2002; Harrington, Woolhandler, Mullan, Carrillo, & Himmelstein, 2001; Himmelstein, Woolhandler, Hellander, Wolfe, 1999; Woolhandler, Campbell, & Himmelstein, 2003; Woolhandler & Himmelstein, 1997, 2004). However, research is limited on the ownership issue as regards Medicare-certified HHAs.

Proprietary ownership of HHAs merits attention for several reasons. First, home health expenditures have grown by 123% since the creation of the Medicare home health prospective payment system (PPS) in October 2000, from $8.5 billion in 2000 to $19 billion in 2010, according to the Medicare Payment Advisory Commission (Medicare Payment Advisory Commission, 2012). Proprietary ownership of HHAs has grown rapidly to 62% of all agencies (and 88% of all freestanding agencies), up from 40% in 2000 (National Association for Home Care and Hospice, 2011). Medicare HHAs have garnered significant profits under PPS, averaging 19.4% of revenues across all agencies in 2010, the second highest profit rate among all Medicare provider types (Medicare Payment Advisory Commission, 2012). Proprietary HHAs' profit margins are 20.7%, about 35% higher than non-profits', raising concerns that resources are not being deployed optimally for patients' needs (Medicare Payment Advisory Commission, 2012). Home health also is important because it is one of the two major drivers of geographic variance in overall Medicare service utilization (Reschovsky, Ghosh, Stewart, & Chollet, 2012). Finally, a 2011 analysis by the Senate Finance Committee suggested that some proprietary agencies have gamed PPS to increase profitability, possibly using fraudulent techniques (Senate Committee on Finance, 2011).

Research on the relationship between home health cost, quality of care, and ownership type has been limited because of multiple changes and the lack of a national set of quality measures for much of the Medicare program. Prior to 2000, there was no mandated national assessment form to gather quality data. Investor ownership was not an issue until the Omnibus Budget Reconciliation Act of 1980 removed the statutory prohibition against proprietary ownership of Medicare-certified HHAs (Vladeck, 1997). Even after 1980, mandated quality measures were absent. Beginning in 1972, reimbursement was cost-based, like much of Medicare, with agencies allowed to receive reimbursement up to a lesser-of-aggregate-cost-or-charges annual amount (General Accounting Office, 1992). In 1982, Congress allowed hospital and other facility-based HHAs to legally add-on facility overhead costs to their HHA (General Accounting Office, 1992). The system became so costly that Congress severely restricted home health reimbursement with a new Interim Payment System (IPS) under the Balanced Budget Act of 1997 (BBA), resulting in 10% of HHAs closing and declines in Medicare home health utilization and spending (Levit, Smith, Cowan, Lazenby, Sensenig, & Catlin, 2001; McCall, Petersons, Moore, & Korb, 2003; Murkofsky, Phillips, McCarthy, Davis, & Hamel, 2003).

The BBA also mandated a new Medicare home health PPS to replace the interim IPS. The stated goal of PPS was to decrease costs and improve quality of care (Medicare Payment Advisory Commission, 2006; Outcome Concept Systems, 2004). PPS took effect in October 2000, instituting a managed-care risk-based model using home health resource groups (HHRGs) to reimburse agencies for

82   *William Cabin*

each 60-day episode. The per episode payments were flat amounts paid to the HHA based on the HHRG classification of the episode, regardless of the actual type and number of home care visits provided. If the HHA kept its costs below the HHRG payments, they could make a profit; if not, they could lose money. This managed-care risk model, based on the private health insurance managed-care concept, began in Medicare in the 1980s with the Medicare inpatient hospital diagnosis-related groups (DRGs) and spread quickly to all other Medicare provider types. In the wake of the managed-care revolution, alarms were sounded by many aging and health care experts that the results were actually decreasing quality; creating shorter inpatient stays and earlier, sometimes medically questionable, discharges; increasing burdens on patients and their caregivers; and placing increased workloads and pressures on nursing home and home care providers (Cabin, 2010; Estes, 1992; Harrington & Estes, 1997). These warnings were ignored and Medicare home health PPS proceeded.

PPS has 153 HHRGs based on seventeen elements from Outcome and Assessment Information Set (OASIS)—a national home health assessment instrument (Medicare Payment Advisory Commission, 2012). Much like the earlier DRGs for Medicare inpatient care, the provider took the risk for costs (per episode) being above or below the reimbursement rate, creating potential for profit or loss. HHAs began using OASIS in 1999. Beginning in 2003, the Centers for Medicare and Medicaid Services (CMS), used ten OASIS-based elements to create a nationally mandated set of quality indicators in the publicly available Home Health Compare (HHC) database and website (Centers for Medicare and Medicaid Services, 2012). The number of OASIS-based elements included in HHC expanded several times and the public quality database currently uses twenty-three elements. HHC quality scores are updated quarterly, reflecting the prior 12 months of data. Consumers are encouraged to comparison shop HHC in their geographic area to compare agencies' quality scores in selecting a provider for themselves, a family member, or a friend.

The Literature

There has been limited research on home health cost and quality and no studies on the relationship between ownership type, cost, profitability, and quality. Rosenau and Linder (2001) conducted a systematic review of peer-reviewed articles on pre-PPS Medicare home health performance differences, including cost and quality, between for-profit and non-profit HHAs. The search covered the pre-PPS era from 1980 to 2000 and found only six articles, with no data collected on the topic since 1991 and no peer-reviewed journal articles after 1995. They concluded that comparative performance of for-profit and non-profit HHAs "is one of the most understudied areas of health care provider services in the U.S. today" and "is a research priority urgently in need of attention" (Rosenau & Linder, 2001, p. 47).

Literature reviews indicate that PPS-era (i.e., post-2000) research has been limited on the relationships between ownership type, cost, and quality (Christman,

2011; Dey, Johnson, Pajerowski, Tanamor, & Ward, 2011). These reviews used PubMed, Academic Search Premier, and targeted PubMed with the following MeSH search terms: home care agencies/economics; prospective payment system economics; home care services/cost; home care services/profitability; home care services/quality; home care services/cost of services; home care services/utilization; home care services/therapy cost; home health expenditures; home health care/ Medicare expenditures; ownership status/home health; home health care/cost of services; home health care/quality of services; and home health care utilization. The literature reviews covered period from January 1, 1960 till December 31, 2010. The search was replicated for this study for the period of January 1, 2011 to October 31, 2014.

Mukamel, Fortinsky, White, Harrington, White, & Ngo-Metzger (2014) examined Medicare-certified HHA cost structure based on ownership-type 10 years after PPS implementation. They found that for-profits tended to be newer than non-profits and have higher average costs per patient but lower costs per visit. No other variables were addressed in the study. Jung, Shea, and Warner (2010) examined the association between selected agency characteristics, including ownership type, and changes in seven HHC quality indicators from 2003 to 2007. They found that while for-profits started with higher scores than non-profits in 2003, non-profits improved over time, with better performances than for-profits in 2007 on all seven measures. They did not address cost-by-ownership type, focuses only on seven of twenty-three HHC indicators, and provides no aggregate quality measure analyses, though it does have a large sample size. Decker (2011) had a small sample ($n = 510$) and linked ownership status to only one quality outcome, risk of an episode ending in hospitalization; it found that for-profit status was associated with a greater risk of hospitalization. Haldiman and Tzeng (2010) used 12 HHC measures retrieved in May 2009 for a sample of 505 Michigan HHAs, finding statistically significant differences between for-profits and non-profits on six measures, with for-profits performing better on five of the six measures.

MedPac has looked at average home health quality and found "quality measures appear to be steady for home health care on most measures" (Medicare Payment Advisory Commission, 2012, p. 223). However, steady is not impressive. Home health performance has not displayed significant increases on most functional measures since 2007 and has not improved on the two adverse event measures (emergent care use and hospitalization) since 2004. One older MedPac analysis from 2004 to 2011 found a few significant percentage increases for improvements in functional measures: walking (36–55%), transferring (50–53%), bathing (59–64%), medication management (37–46%), and pain management (59–66%). In another MedPac analysis, emergent care use, where a lower score is better, which was 21% in 2004 and 22% in 2010, and relatively stable each year in between. Hospitalization (how often home health patients had to be admitted to the hospital), where a lower score is better, was similar at 28% in 2004 and 29% in 2010, also relatively stable in between (Medicare Payment Advisory Commission, 2011, 2012). The hospitalization rate is important because of the high Medicare

84 *William Cabin*

costs of re-hospitalizations and Medicare's efforts to control such cost (Jencks, Williams, & Coleman, 2009; Stone & Hoffman, 2010).

Home health PPS quality data has been available on one database (Medicare HHC) since fall 2003, with cost and personnel data available on another (Medicare Home Health cost reports [CR]), a separation that obstructs the analysis of the relationship between agency cost-related and quality variables. This separation may account for why no previous studies have included data on both quality and costs.

The New Studies

In 2011, my colleagues and I assembled a merged database using data from both the national Medicare HHC quality database and the 2010 Medicare home health cost reports. The 2011 HHC data included twenty-two individual home health quality indicators and five aggregate indicators that the CMS compute from combinations of individual indicators (see Table 6.1 for a list of indicators). The CR database provided cost and revenue figures from the cost reports filed by Medicare-certified HHAs.

Determining whether the type of HHA ownership plays a significant role in agency operations was the fundamental goal of the study. Because the focus of the

Table 6.1 Summary of Second Study Variables

Variable		Regression Coefficient	
Independent (Predictor)	*Dependent (n)*	*Ownership Type*	*Significance of Increase in R)[1]*
A. Structural/environmental			
1. Years of certification	Quality (5,168)	.055	.076ns
	Cost (5,168)	.163	.188>
	Profitability (5,167)	.070	.078ns
2. HHAs in state	Quality (5,560)	.091	.151>
	Cost (5,560)	.163	.234>
	Profitability (5,559)	.070	.086>
3. Non-profits as % of total HHAs in state	Quality (5,560)	.091	.091ns
	Cost (5,560)	.163	.180>
	Profitability (5,559)	.070	.072 ns
B. Service delivery			
1. Therapy visits (PT+OT) as % of total patient visits	Quality (5,428)	.088	.097>
	Cost (5,428)	.164	.401>
	Profitability (5,427)	.074	.113>
C. Therapy volume			
1. Therapy visits/patient	Quality (5,428)	.088	.097**
	Cost (5,428)	.217	.305>
	Profitability (5,427)	.074	.088>

[1]Statistical significance = increase in R^2; F: .05*, .01**, .001>

Who Rules Home Care? 85

study was a comparison of proprietary versus non-profit agencies, all other relatively small ownership categories were excluded (i.e., agencies owned by a local government, those owned by a state or county government, and those whose ownership was categorized as "other" or "mixed").

Key findings from that study were that compared to non-profits, for-profit agencies scored slightly but significantly worse on overall quality indicator, notably on the clinically important outcome *avoidance of hospitalization*; had higher costs per patient ($4,827 vs. $4,075); were more profitable (15.0 vs 6.4%); and had administrative costs.

The findings "raise concerns about whether for-profit agencies should continue to be eligible for Medicare payments and about the efficiency of Medicare's market-oriented, risk-based home care payment system" (Cabin, Himmelstein, Siman, & Woolhandler, 2014, p. 1460).

In 2014, I conducted a study to determine whether the previously demonstrated significance of ownership type (proprietary vs. non-profit) could be enhanced by the inclusion of five new independent variables that have the potential to significantly influence HHA quality, costs, and profitability. The five new variables were: years of agency certification; number of HHAs in the state; non-profits as a percentage of HHAs in the state; therapy visits—physical and occupational therapy—as a percentage of total patient visits; and number of therapy visits per patient. Linear multiple regression models were used to test the relationships.

Findings

Table 6.1 summarizes statistically significant results of multiple regression analyses. In summary, the second study found that: (1) variables in two of the three new categories were significant predictors of HHA quality and/or cost; (2) for two of the variables (*number of HHAs in the state* and *therapy visits as a percentage of total patient visits*), the observed relationship is a significant improvement over the model using only ownership type; and (3) none of the new variables are significantly related to profitability. As in the first study, compared to non-profits, proprietary agencies had lower overall quality and higher costs per patient. Proprietaries also had more visits per patient, with therapy visits accounting for a larger share of those visits. Taken together, the two studies are consistent in the significant differences found between proprietary and non-profit HHAs.

Research Strengths and Limitations

The major strength of the two new studies is that they addressed a significant research gap in the literature by effectively creating a unique merged database—one that maximized valid HHA financial and quality information. The sample size is large and multiple steps have been taken to make the final database sample representative of the national HHA population, including use of trimming and sensitivity analysis to address potential cost report inaccuracies (due to agency report submissions with typographical, decimal point, and computational errors).

86   *William Cabin*

The database is limited by the exclusion of small agencies in the original Medicare Cost Report database and facility-based agencies. The database also has a limited number of clinical variables and does not include other clinical variables from OASIS, such as primary and secondary diagnoses; questions related to Activities of Daily Living (ADLs) and Instrumental ADL (IADLs); mental health status; and more questions on other clinical conditions such as diabetes, wound, and urinary tract infections, among others. These variables are not in the Medicare cost report database. They are in the OASIS database. At this point, it is not known whether such OASIS clinical variables may be available in aggregate to match the cost report and HHC time periods. Future research should explore with the Research Data Assistance Center, a CMS contractor, the availability of OASIS national clinical data and the potential integration of the OASIS results into the existing merged database.

Discussion and Implications

The Payment Model

Even with the methodological limitations, the evidence seems overwhelming that managed care Medicare home health PPS has failed to achieve its goals of reduced government costs and increased quality of care for beneficiaries. There seems to be more than a reasonable amount of data supporting the adverse economic and patient care effects of maintaining the current for-profit-based risk-based system, at least in Medicare home health. There are several alternative policies worth further exploration. At least one source (Cabin et al., 2014) has suggested returning to the pre-1980 Congressional prohibition on for-profit participation in Medicare home health. However, such a proposal may have some significant potential legal obstacles (Dombi, 2015) and does not address the PPS managed-care profit-driven payment model, namely the profit motive would remain even without for-profit agencies.

One alternative payment model would be returning to some form of pre-PPS cost-based reimbursement. Such a model would reimburse HHAs based on reasonable costs related to medically necessary patient care with some type of annual cap on payment. The upside of such a model is that it explicitly prohibits profit; the downside is that there is no evidence from past use that it would control costs better and improve quality than PPS.

Another option is to maintain PPS but include a reinvigorated emphasis on quality by including payment for chronic care, including psychosocial interventions, instead of Medicare home health's historic limitation to acute care. This would include expanded coverage and reimbursement for conditions such as Multiple Sclerosis, Parkinson's Disease, Alzheimer's disease, and other types of dementia, diabetes, cardiovascular disease, respiratory disease and other conditions, including caregiver support. The cost and quality benefits of Medicare home health coverage of chronic care was raised by several presenters at a recent Institute of Medicine meeting on the future of home care (Institute of Medicine, 2014).

In addition, at least one study (Rosati et al., 2013) indicates that Medicare PPS' failure to factor complex chronic care cases with multiple co-morbidities into the reimbursement formula financially penalizes HHAs (at least non-profits). The PPS system has ignored complex chronic care cases that require significant nursing and home health aides. Instead, PPS has been driven by level of combined physical, speech, and occupational therapy use. HHRGs meeting the highest therapy utilization thresholds receive the highest reimbursement (Medicare Payment Advisory Commission, 2015).

Furthermore, a 2013 settlement in the *Jimmo* case stated Medicare home health coverage and eligibility determinations should be based on a *need* standard instead of the historic acute care-oriented *improvement* standard. CMS signed a settlement agreement acknowledging the *need* standard, but explicitly stated it was not modifying any eligibility, coverage, or reimbursement criteria to expand need to chronic care (Center for Medicare Advocacy, 2014; United States Department of Health and Human Services, 2014).

The Quality Issue

The payment model may affect quality. The two studies' findings indicate that the for-profit agencies, which cost more and make more profit, have lower overall quality. Regardless of any actual or proposed change to the payment model, the measurement and evaluation of Medicare home health quality is ripe for reform. As noted from MedPac studies earlier in this chapter, improvements in the existing HHC quality indicators have been limited, if not stagnant in some categories, including a high discharge to hospitalization rate. Improving quality can be addressed by altering the payment model or by altering the measurement and use of quality measures given the existing OASIS system.

As noted above, payment for chronic care offers the opportunity to decrease re-hospitalization rates and improve patient functional and clinical limitations. The current HHC measures reflect a narrow focus on only twenty-two process and outcome measures and do not include relevant measures such as changes in depression, anxiety, and agitation levels; and improvement in blood sugar control, diabetics' ability to do self-care, urinary tract infections, continence, ability to dress, and ability to feed. HHC has no measures on IADLs, which include managing finances, handling transportation (driving or navigating public transit), shopping, meal preparation, using the telephone and other communication devices, and ability to do housework and basic home maintenance. HHC also has limited pre-post measures of a variety of mental health conditions and no measures of improvement in caregiver capacities, caregiver burden, or suitability and safety of the home environment.

Beyond Medicare Home Health

The evidence from the Medicare home health program should also prompt concern for other Medicare provider types displaying similar patterns, such as Medicare

88   *William Cabin*

hospices and nursing homes. Medicare imposed a managed care model on nursing homes in July 1998. Currently 70% of Medicare nursing homes are for-profit, with a 2012 profit margin of 16.1% compared to 5.4% for non-profits (Medicare Payment Advisory Commission, 2014). There also should be concern for the Medicaid program, which had more than 74% of its enrollees in managed care plans as of 2011 and is the focus of expansion under the Affordable Care Act (Medicare Payment Advisory Commission 2014).

Medicare imposed a managed-care model on hospice in creating the Hospice Medicare Benefit (HMB) in 1982 (Gage et al., 2000; Luft & Greenlick, 1996; Medicare Payment Advisory Commission 2014; Mor & Kidder, 1985). Unlike Medicare HHAs, hospitals, and nursing homes, Medicare has not created a standardized, national, publicly available quality outcomes database for Medicare hospices, thus limiting research on comparative quality outcome effectiveness of Medicare hospices.

Medicare hospice expenditures have risen sharply since HMB's inception, from $205 million in 1989 to $13.8 billion in 2011 (Brumley, Enguidanos, & Cherin, 2003; Brumley & Hillary, 2002; Gage et al., 1999). Investor ownership of HHAs has grown rapidly, with for-profits more than tripling their growth between 2000 and 2011, resulting in for-profits accounting for 57% of all Medicare hospices in 2011 compared to 30% in 2000 (Medicare Payment Advisory Commission, 2014). This represents a significant shift in hospice ownership, which was dominated by non-profits pre-HMB and in the early years of HMB. In 1995, for example, non-profits represented 72% of all Medicare-certified hospices compared to 43% in 2011. Medicare hospices have garnered significant profits averaging 7.5% of revenues across all agencies in 2010. However, proprietary agencies' average annual profit margins far exceed non-profits, with for-profits' 2010 average profit margin at 12.4% compared to 3.2% for non-profits (Medicare Payment Advisory Commission, 2014). At the same time, there is some evidence that for-profit hospices are more costly than non-profits. In 2010, for example, the average cost of a Medicare hospice beneficiary who died while on hospice was $13,130 compared to $10,990 for those in a non-profit—a $2,140 per beneficiary or 15% difference (Medicare Payment Advisory Commission, 2014).

Conclusion

The Affordable Care Act (ACA) put an emphasis on prevention and more effective treatment of chronic care conditions. Significant latitude was given to states to use waiver programs, including Medical Homes, and to encourage providers to use alternative delivery systems, such as Accountable Care Organizations to reduce cost and improve quality. To date, there is limited mixed evidence of the success of these alternatives. What the ACA did not do is address the failures of the risk-based, profit-driven model by changing eligibility, coverage, reimbursement, or quality measurement requirements in Medicare home health to expand the use and quality of home-based care for the many elderly with one or more chronic conditions. The Medicare program, often criticized by Congress for cost concerns,

Who Rules Home Care? 89

continues headed in the wrong direction, with Congress paying no attention to evidence that seriously challenges the worthiness of the risk-based models and for-profit dominance. Without appropriate action, too many seniors may remain with significant and costly unmet needs in the "no care zone" (Estes, 1992).

References

Aaronson, W.E., Zinn, J.S., & Rosko, M.D. (1994). Do for-profit and not-for-profit nursing homes behave differently? *Gerontologist*, 34(6), 775–786.

Brumley, R.D., Enguidanos, S., & Cherin, D.A. (2003). Effectiveness of a home-based palliative care program for end-of-life. *Journal of Palliative Medicine*, 5(6), 715–724.

Brumley, R.D., & Hillary, K. (2002). *The tri-central palliative care program toolkit.* Oakland, CA: Kaiser Permanente.

Butler, R.N. (1985). *Why survive? Being old in America.* Baltimore, MD: Johns Hopkins University Press.

Cabin, W.D. (2010). *Phantoms of home care: Alzheimer's disease patients as victims of Medicare's designed neglect.* Saarbrucken, Germany: Lambert Publishing.

Cabin, W., Himmelstein, D.U., Siman, M.L., & Woolhandler, S. (2014). For-profit Medicare home health agencies' costs appear higher and quality appears lower compared to nonprofit agencies. *Health Affairs*, 33(8), 1460–1465.

Center for Medicare Advocacy. (2014). *New home health regulations: Improvement is not required to obtain coverage.* Retrieved September 10, 2014, from www.medicare advocacy.org.

Centers for Medicare and Medicaid Services. *Home health quality initiative.* Retrieved June 5, 2012, from www.cms.gov/Medicare/Quality-Initiatives-Patient-Assessment-Instrumenta/HomeHealthQaulityInits/index.html

Christman, E. (2011). Phone interview by William Cabin with Evan Christman, MedPac Senior Policy Analyst for Home Health Care. October 16, 2011.

Decker, F.H. (2011). Profit status of home health care agencies and the risk of hospitalization. *Population Health Management*, 14(4), 199–204.

Devereaux, P.J., Choi, P.T.L., Lacchetti, C., Weaver, B., Schünemann, H.J., Haines, T., et al. (2002). A systematic review and meta-analysis of studies comparing mortality rates of private for-profit and private not-for-profit hospitals. *Canadian Medical Association Journal*, 166(11), 1399–1406.

Devereaux, P.J., Heels-Ansdell, D., Lacchetti, C., Haines, T., Burns, K.E.A., Cook, D.J., et al. (2004). Payments for care at private for-profit and private not-for-profit hospitals: A systematic review and meta-analysis. *Canadian Medical Association Journal*, 170(12), 1817–1824.

Devereaux, P.J., Schünemann, H.J., Ravindran, N., Bhandari, M., Garg, A.X., Choi, P.T.L, et al. (2002). Comparison of mortality between private for-profit and private not-for-profit hemodialysis centers: A systematic review and meta-analysis. *Journal of the American Medical Association*, 288(19), 2449–2457.

Dey, J.G., Johnson, M., Pajerowski, W., Tanamor, M., & Ward, A. (2011). *Home health study report (HHSM-500–2010–00072C): Literature review.* Washington, DC: L&M Policy Research.

Dombi, W. (2015). Phone interview by William Cabin with William Dombi, Vice President for Law, National Association for Home Care and Hospice. January 5, 2015.

Estes, C.L. (1979). *The aging enterprise: A critical examination of social policies and services for the aged.* San Francisco, CA: Jossey-Bass.

90   *William Cabin*

Estes, C.L. (1992). *The long term care crisis: Elders trapped in the no-care zone.* Newbury Park, CA: Sage.

Gage, B., Miller, S.C., Coppola, K., Harvell, J., Laliberte, L., Mor, V., & Teno, J. (2000). *Important questions for hospice in the next century.* Washington, DC: U.S. Department of Health and Human Services (Office of Disability, Aging and Long-Term Care Policy).

General Accounting Office. (1992). *Medicare: Rationale for higher payment for hospital-based home health agencies.* Washington, DC: General Accounting Office.

Haldiman, K.L., & Tzeng, H.M. (2010). A comparison of quality measures between for-profit and nonprofit Medicare-certified home health agencies in Michigan. *Home Health Care Services Quarterly, 29*(2), 75–90.

Harrington, C., & Estes, C.L. (1997). *Health policy and nursing: Crises and reform in the U.S. health care delivery system.* Burlington, MA: Jones & Bartlett.

Harrington, C., Woolhandler, S., Mullan, J., Carrillo, H., & Himmelstein, D.U. (2001). Does investor ownership of nursing homes compromise the quality of care? *American Journal of Public Health, 91*(9), 1452–1455.

Himmelstein, D.U., Woolhandler, S., Hellander, I., & Wolfe, S.M. (1999). Quality of care in investor-owned vs. not-for-profit HMOs. *Journal of the American Medical Association, 282*(2), 159–163.

Institute of Medicine. (2014). The future of home health care—a workshop, September 30, 2014. Retrieved November 6, 2014, from www.iom.edu/. . ./FutureHomeHealthCare/2014-SEP.

Jencks, S.F., Williams, M.V., & Coleman, E.A. (2009). Rehospitalizations among patients in the Medicare fee-for-service program. *New England Journal of Medicine, 360*(14), 1418–1428.

Jung, K., Shea, D., & Warner, C. (2010). Agency characteristics and changes in home health quality after home health compare. *Journal of Aging and Health, 22*(4), 454–476.

Levit, K., Smith, C., Cowan, C., Lazenby, H., Sensenig, A., & Catlin, A. (2003). Trends in U.S. health care spending. *Health Affairs (Millwood), 22*(1), 154–164.

Luft, H.S., & Greenlick, M.S. (1996). The contribution of group-and-staff HMOs to American medicine. *Milbank Quarterly, 4,* 445–467.

McCall, N., Petersons, A., Moore, S., & Korb, J. (2003). Utilization of home health services before and after the balanced budget act of 1997: What were the initial effects? *Health Services Research, 38*(1 Pt. 1), 85–106.

Medicare Payment Advisory Commission. (2006). *Report to the Congress: Medicare increasing the value of Medicare.* Washington, DC: Medicare Payment Advisory Commission.

Medicare Payment Advisory Commission. (2011). *Report to the Congress: Medicare payment policy.* Washington, DC: Medicare Payment Advisory Commission.

Medicare Payment Advisory Commission. (2012). *Report to the Congress: Medicare payment policy.* Washington, DC: Medicare Payment Advisory Commission.

Medicare Payment Advisory Commission. (2014). *Report to the Congress: Medicare payment policy.* Washington, DC: Medicare Payment Advisory Commission.

Medicare Payment Advisory Commission. (2015). *Home health care payment services payment system* (updated October 2014). Washington, DC: Medicare Payment Advisory Commission.

Mor, V. & Kidder, D. (1985). Cost savings in hospice: Final results of the national hospice study. *Health Services Research, 4,* 407–421.

Mukamel, D.B., Fortinsky, R.H., White, A., Harrington, C., White, L.M., & Ngo-Metzger, Q. (2014). The policy implications of the cost structure of home health agencies. *Medicare*

Who Rules Home Care? 91

and Medicaid Research Review, 4 (1), E1–E21. Retrieved June 12, 2014, from www.cms. gov/mmrr/Downloads/MMRR2014_004_01_a03.pdf.

Murkofsky, R.L., Phillips, R.S., McCarthy, E.P., Davis, R.B., & Hamel, M.B. (2003). Length of stay in home care before and after the 1997 Balanced Budget Act. *Journal of the American Medical Association,* 289(21), 2841–2848.

National Hospice and Palliative Care Organization. (2004). *Hospice costs Medicare less and patients often live longer new research shows.* January 10–11.

Outcome Concept Systems. (2004). *The effect of the prospective payment system on home health quality of care: A study conducted by Outcome Concept Systems, Inc. for the Medicare Payment Advisory Commission.* Washington, DC: Medicare Payment Advisory Commission.

Reschovsky, J.D., Ghosh, A., Stewart, K.A., & Chollet, D.J. (2012). Durable medical equipment and home health among the largest contributors to area variations in use of Medicare services. *Health Affairs (Millwood),* 31(5), 956–964.

Rosati, R.J., Russell, D., Peng, T., Brickner, C., Kurowski, D., Christopher, M.A., & Sheehan, K.M. (2013). Medicare home health payment reform may jeopardize access for clinically complex and socially vulnerable patients. *Health Affairs,* 33(6), 946–956.

Rosenau, P.V., & Linder, S.H. (2001). The comparative performance of for-profit and nonprofit home health care services in the U.S. *Home Health Care Services Quarterly,* 20(2), 47–59.

Senate Committee on Finance. (2011). *Staff report on home health and the Medicare therapy threshold.* Washington, DC: Senate.

Stone, J., & Hoffman, G.J. (2010). *Medicare hospital readmissions: Issues, policy options and PPACA.* Washington, DC: Congressional Research Service.

United States Department of Health and Human Services. (2014). *MLN Matters Number: MM8458 Revised: Manual updates to clarify skilled nursing facility, inpatient rehabilitation facility, home health and outpatient coverage pursuant to Jimmo v. Sebellus.* Baltimore, MD: U.S. Department of Health and Human Services.

Vladeck, B.C. (1997). *Testimony on Medicare payment for home health agency and skilled nursing facility services* [Internet]. Washington, DC: Department of Health and Human Services. Retrieved June 12, 2014, from www.hhs.gov/asl/testify/t960723a.html.

Woolhandler, S., Campbell, T., & Himmelstein, D.U. (2003). Costs of health care administration in the United States and Canada. *New England Journal of Medicine,* 349(8), 768–775.

Woolhandler, S., & Himmelstein, D.U. (1997). Costs of care and administration at for-profit and other hospitals in the United States. *New England Journal of Medicine,* 336(11), 769–774.

Woolhandler, S., & Himmelstein, D.U. (2004). The high costs of for-profit care. *Canadian Medical Association Journal,* 170(12), 1814–1815.

CHAPTER 7

Challenges and Achievements Regarding Outreach to Lesbian, Gay, Bisexual, and Transgender Elders: Perspectives from Nursing

Marcena Gabrielson

Introduction

"This is a no brainer," the consultant replied, "You're going to study old lesbians!" Early in my career as a non-tenure track professor, the college of nursing I worked for received a grant to develop a doctoral program through collaboration with the University of Iowa. The focus of our doctoral program was to be gerontological nursing. Very early in the development of the program, a research consultant was brought in to meet with faculty members in order to identify suitable individual programs of research. Now, when I sought a master's degree in nursing, it was for the singular purpose of becoming a nursing educator. I remember my meeting with the consultant as if it were yesterday. As soon as I shut the door behind me, she wasted no time in asking me "What are you interested in?" to which I replied "education and teaching." "That won't do" she responded, "there is no chance of obtaining any major external funding for that!" She then asked me questions about myself and patient populations I was interested in. One thing I shared with her was that I was a lesbian. She asked me to tell her what I knew about lesbian health. I explained that I was aware that lesbians have higher rates of alcohol abuse and smoking compared to heterosexual women and that they often avoid health care due to fears of discrimination. I shared my belief that for a variety of reasons, lesbians were a vulnerable population and I suspected that early health behaviors and lifelong coping with all of the issues that go along with being a sexual minority might put them at higher risk for poor health outcomes as they age. So the declaration was made: "You're going to study old lesbians!"

Being a good team player, and as an individual in love with education, I soon volunteered to be the first student to enroll in the collaborative doctoral program with the University of Iowa and had the privilege of receiving a pre-doctoral fellowship from the John A. Hartford Foundation to study older LGBT health. As I immersed myself in the little research there was on the subject at the time, my interest in older lesbians was reinforced by the proposition that they are triply vulnerable as older adults, women, and a sexual minority (Kehoe, 1988).

Outreach to LGBT Elders 93

I completed a dissertation about older lesbians from which I discovered that "family of choice" (networks of created family that, for lesbians, largely consists of other lesbian friends) were a critical social support that had a huge impact on older lesbian health. I also discovered that nursing research regarding LGBT older adults was, and continues to be, sadly limited. The limited evidence base contributes to an uninformed nursing faculty across the United States who neglect coverage of LGBT health in nursing education, thereby continually perpetuating a nursing workforce that lacks the knowledge to adequately care for their LGBT patients. With this understanding, in order to make a significant contribution to the health of older adults, my research mission continues to be the health of LGBT elders.

In this chapter, I will introduce the reader to data from my dissertation—a qualitative study using narrative analysis of interviews with ten older lesbians (aged 55 and above), who have made a financial commitment to live in a continuous care retirement center specializing in lesbian, gay, bisexual and transgender (LGBT) care (Gabrielson, 2009). That work reinforced my concerns about service needs for older LGBT adults, as well as their many health issues and challenges. I will present those issues and challenges through a conceptual framework that reveals areas for possible intervention, particularly from a nursing perspective. I will discuss challenges in terms of nursing education, care, and research responsibilities regarding LGBT seniors. I will identify achievements in outreach to older LGBT adults by discussing exemplary programs across the United States that nursing and all providers can learn from. Finally, I will provide a summary with suggested implications for both nursing and other providers and investigators in terms of future care and research directions regarding LGBT elder health.

The Importance of Social Support for Older LGBT Adults: Reinforcement from my Dissertation Research

My dissertation research focused on older lesbians because they are an invisible, and therefore vulnerable, population. The invisibility that lesbians experience is associated with decreased social inclusion, resource availability, and health care access (Saunders, 1999). Lesbians older than 60 years often focus their social lives around friend networks. They commonly limit biologic family connections and avoid health and support service-providers for fear of experiencing discrimination (Goldberg, Sickler, & Dibble, 2005; Kehoe, 1988). Fear of discrimination reinforces social seclusion, placing lesbian elders at high risk for neglected health issues and subsequent poor health outcomes. Considering that the health care community has historically been a heterosexist social institution (Sullivan, 2004), an older lesbian's fear of mistreatment by providers is not surprising. It is important to note that while past research has recognized an increased risk for mental health issues among lesbians (Diamant & Wold, 2003; Koh & Ross, 2006), a significant mediator in that is social support (Oetjen & Rothblum, 2000).

94 *Marcena Gabrielson*

One of my dissertation participants described the importance of social support from their "family of choice" in this way:

> I think we kind of look out for one another in a different way being a minority and in just being there for each other. I know that we certainly feel like there's a community. For my 60th birthday, I went on a trip with my partner. Twenty eight people came along. I have this wonderful family of friends willing to spend the money and come. That is what I think is so wonderful. The support when my partner was in the hospital. I had 15 women sitting in the waiting room. They didn't know what to do with us! That happened with every one of the surgeries. I mean, it's like, everybody was there. It is different than what I experienced in the straight world. I don't think folks expect non-blood relatives to rally around each other.

Another expressed fears of losing their support network and not knowing who then would provide care to them:

> As a person growing older, I can see where I can do less, and I forget more, and, you know, that's a concern. The less mobile you become, maybe the less connected you become with this great support network of people. Who's going to help me out if there are important decisions to be made? We've always helped each other with that.

The greatest fear of one participant was having to potentially rely on senior services at some point in the future. She described it in this way:

> I think that the idea of growing old and ending up in a senior residence home or a skilled nursing home with a whole bunch of straight people is a concern. I mean, there's a chance you wouldn't even be in the same room together (with your partner). Those things could happen. That, to me, would be just awful. One of the fears is ending up someplace where I can't be me, I have to watch what I say, I have to watch what I do, I can't be me. I want to be someplace where I can be me. I want to be with people that are comfortable. I want to be comfortable. And I don't mean physically comfortable, I mean emotionally comfortable. Physically comfortable you can pay for. Emotionally comfortable you can't.

All of my dissertation participants were concerned that they would experience homophobia in senior services and were very concerned about it. As one stated, "I don't want to deal with homophobia." She emphasized the collective effects of aging, frailty in old age, and discrimination, saying "I think when you're older, racism, ageism, homophobia, sexism, all wound you much deeper than when you're younger. If I ever get to a point where I can't fight my own battles, I just can't see myself being in a place where I'm left to the whims of other people's discriminations."

Health Issues and Challenges among LGBT Seniors

The women in my dissertation were all aged 55 or older and most experienced being gay during a time period when it was considered a mental illness. It was not until 1973 that homosexuality was removed from the *Diagnostic and Statistical Manual of Mental Disorders*. Prior to that time, if you were homosexual, you were considered mentally ill. In the powerful documentary, "Gen Silent" (Maddux, 2010), many of the older LGBT participants described early knowledge of gays and lesbians being sent to mental institutions for shock treatments and anti-homosexual "therapies." Development of effective services for LGBT elders must stem from understanding the history of oppression and discrimination that this sub-group of older adults has had to endure. Providers must reach out to them from that understanding because they will not necessarily be forthcoming with us about their background, concerns, and needs.

The LGBT population experience significant health risks and concerns, as well as, care and access disparities when compared to the heterosexual population in the United States (Institute of Medicine [IOM], 2011). This is particularly true for older LGBT adults who, compared to heterosexual seniors, are more likely to age single, live alone, and have no children to provide support to them, creating social disadvantages that are determinants of health disparities (Cahill, South, & Spade, 2000).

The current one to three million LGBT Americans older than 65 years are expected to at least double by 2030 (Cahill et al., 2000). Healthy People 2020 adopted a specific goal to "Improve the health, safety, and well-being of LGBT individuals" and specifically emphasizes the need to increase the focus on older LGBT adults (United States Department of Health and Human Services [USDHHS], 2011). To best explicate how nurses should approach the health and care challenges of LGBT elders, I will first present theoretical underpinnings of a "nursing perspective."

What Nursing Is and How Nurses Know: Theoretical Integrations

To describe a nursing perspective regarding older LGBT adult health, I should first distinguish how the nursing focus is unique from medicine and what is considered nursing knowledge. To begin with, nursing significantly differs from medicine in its primary focus. A nurse's concentration is not in the diagnosis and cure of illness. The nurse's attention is directed toward the wholeness of the individual in attending to prevention of or response to illness, while considering environ-mental contexts. This requires further explanation through describing what we consider to be nursing knowledge.

In 1978, Barbara Carper conducted landmark work in which she examined early nursing literature and identified four fundamental and long-standing patterns of nursing knowledge. These patterns included "empirical knowledge," which she described as the overall science of nursing and "ethical knowledge," which

96 Marcena Gabrielson

comprises the moral imperative in nursing care. She also described "personal knowledge" as involving the nurse's self-knowledge and knowledge of others in relationship. Through understanding self and others, the nurse applies a "therapeutic use of self" to assist individuals in either prevention of or response to illness. Finally, Carper described "aesthetic knowledge," which she identified as the art of nursing. Aesthetic knowledge involves understanding the meaning of situations and bringing forth the correct mix of internal and external resources to assist individuals in moving toward the most positive health outcomes (Carper, 1978). Carper's work was invaluable in that it acknowledged the value of additional nursing knowledge extending beyond empirical knowledge. Unfortunately, empirical knowledge continues to be overrated within nursing and this, in my opinion, has much to do with why there is little research conducted by nursing scientists about older LGBT adults. This neglect contributes to superficial, and in some cases, possibly inaccurate, nursing education about the population. This fosters a nursing workforce that is not culturally competent to address the needs of and care for the LGBT population. This is a critical challenge for nursing that must be addressed if we are to effectively care for older LGBT adults (Eliason, Dibble, & DeJoseph, 2010; Gabrielson, 2011; Lim & Bernstein, 2012).

Chinn and Kramer (2008) affirmed a fifth area of nursing knowledge, "emancipatory knowledge." Emancipatory knowledge involves an awareness of injustice and a questioning of social problems that contribute to poor health outcomes among populations. In the application of emancipatory knowledge, a nurse reflects on social inequities that contribute to poor health outcomes among populations and takes action to address them. This chapter can be considered an application of nursing emancipatory knowledge, for here, I am describing social inequities that limit older LGBT adult health potential, circumstances that create and sustain those conditions, what is required by nurses and others to change the current conditions for LGBT seniors, and what nurses and others need to do in order to mitigate the current status quo (Chinn & Kramer, 2011).

In providing equitable care to patient populations such as LGBT elders, nurses need to integrate all the areas of nursing knowledge in what is known as praxis (Chinn & Kramer, 2011). Nursing praxis involves reflection and action, particularly in cooperation with key informants and advocates for the specific patient population of interest. When groups of people collectively share their insights and experiences, imaginings become symbiotic and possibilities for change multiply. The cycle of praxis and the emancipatory changes it produces are ongoing processes (p. 7). I propose that nursing's general neglect of the older LGBT population is due to a lack of praxis. In other words, nurses have not been integrating all of the areas of nursing knowledge to address the social determinants that contribute to poor health outcomes among LGBT seniors. In particular, nursing care of older LGBT adults has involved a disregard for applying emancipatory knowing, and the actions that it requires. Giving attention to emancipatory knowing, and integrating the breadth of nursing knowledge and subsequent praxis, are the major challenges for nursing at this time to address and prevent poor health outcomes among the LGBT elders. I next propose a conceptual framework not only for understanding a pathway to poor health outcomes among the older LGBT population, but also the multiple points at which nurses can apply emancipatory knowing in praxis to address inequities that impact older LGBT health and attend to their health care challenges and needs.

A Conceptual Framework for Understanding Older LGBT Health

Concepts from the Social Determinants of Health Theory (Marmot, 2006) and Minority Stress Theory (Meyer, 2003) can help providers understand older LGBT health issues and challenges. There are four concepts in these theories that describe how health outcomes of LGBT elders can be influenced. These concepts are Societal Exclusion, Socioeconomic Status (SES), Sexual Minority Stress, and Social Support. This theoretical foundation can provide a focus for education, care, and research (Figure 7.1)

Societal exclusion is the experience of being treated as less than equal in society and involves the stigmatization and discrimination that isolate minorities from the dominant culture. The isolation creates social disadvantage and affects access to resources and support from society. The greater the length of time that individuals live in societal exclusion, the more likely they are to have a range of negative health outcomes (Wilkinson & Marmot, 2003). SES (education and income level) is long known to impact health and is one of the most significant components of the Social Determinants of Health Theory. *Sexual Minority Stress* suggests that social disadvantage does not lead directly to poor health but creates a stress experience accruing over time that results in long-term health problems. Sexual minority stressors include those external (stress of rejection, stigmatization,

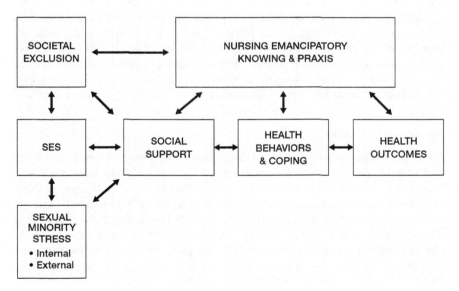

Figure 7.1 A Conceptual Framework for Understanding Older LGBT Health

98   *Marcena Gabrielson*

and discrimination) and internal (stress of hiding one's identity, anxiety about potential discrimination, and negative feelings about self as part of the minority group) (Meyer, 2003). My conceptual framework depicts that societal exclusion, SES, and sexual minority stress have an impact on health behaviors and health outcomes among older LGBT adults, but that social support can moderate their impact. Further, it elucidates that nursing emancipatory knowing and subsequent praxis can impact older LGBT health outcomes at multiple points.

Societal Exclusion

Societal exclusion is a serious challenge for older LGBT adults, a group yet to experience the full rights of the dominant heterosexual majority in the United States. Not possessing the full rights of and therefore perceiving oneself and group as less than equal and isolated from the dominant culture affects health behaviors and outcomes. Societal exclusion is more than simply a generic stressor, but a serious threat to perceptions of safety and well-being (MacDonald & Leary, 2005). The threat of unsafe social others can lead to avoidance of sources of assistance in times of need (e.g., avoiding health care and support services). Such avoidance contributes to negative health outcomes among societally excluded individuals. Societal exclusion results in a chronic psychological threat with physical effects like what we experience when anticipating a physical threat (MacDonald, Kingsbury, & Shaw, 2005). Eisenberger, Lieberman, and Williams (2003) found that psychological pain is experienced as pain in the same brain region that detects and experiences physical pain. This shared neural network likely shares the same evolutionary path. Much as we detect threats to survival from physical dangers, we detect threat from lack of societal inclusion (Eisenberger & Lieberman, 2005). Notably, the social pain of societal exclusion experienced by LGBT seniors is chronic and re-experienced. Past physical pain is not relived, while evidence suggests that social pain from societal exclusion is relived (Chen et al., 2008). LGBT elders are particularly vulnerable to increasing societal exclusion as their "family of choice" dwindles and their role/position in society is reduced through aging. That vulnerability may be intensified if a LGBT elder faces a lower SES.

Socioeconomic Status

SES is a consistent predictor of poor health outcomes. There is extensive evidence that individuals with lower SES experience poorer health than individuals with higher SES (Godley & McLaren, 2010; Haas, 2008). SES health disparities widen over the life course as a result of the cumulative impact of increased risk exposure and limited protective resources (Phelan, Link, & Tehranifar, 2010; Seabrook & Avison, 2012). Dupre (2008) identified that lower education levels lead to higher risk for hypertension, determining that the pathway from low education to high blood pressure was mediated by an increased tendency for individuals with lower education to smoke, drink alcohol, and be overweight over their lifetimes compared to those with higher education. Additionally, compared to their lower

SES counterparts, individuals with higher SES enjoy more social capital (Seabrook & Avison, 2012), resulting in greater resources to support personal "agency" to engage in health-promoting behaviors (Thoits, 2006). A psychological stress-related pathway has been proposed to explain health disparities relating to life experiences among people in lower SES strata (Dohrenwend, 2000; (Marmot, 2004). Research suggests that objective and subjective experiences of chronic economic adversity, insecurity about the future, and discouragements of those with low SES combined with their underlying awareness of low social position fosters emotional, behavioral, and physiologic responses to stress that increase health risk (Singh-Manoux, Adler, & Marmot, 2003; Singh-Manoux, Marmot, & Adler, 2005). As postulated, the stress experienced from low SES creates a pathway to poor health outcomes that is determined by behavioral and environmental factors interacting over the life course to influence individual risk trajectories (McEwen & Gianaros, 2010). Older LGBT adults with a lower SES are thus particularly challenged. If SES stressors are compounded by sexual minority stress, the consequential negative responses to stress are amplified and the likelihood of negative health behaviors and outcomes increased.

Sexual Minority Stress

Sexual minority stress has been a chronic challenge for LGBT elders and a significant factor in negative health behaviors and outcomes among them. Chronic activation of the brain's stress networks produces a generalized anxiety that can trigger stress response behaviors (McEwen, 2006) such as smoking and alcohol use. One aspect of sexual minority stress is internalized homophobia (defined as directing societal negative attitudes toward self [Meyer, 2003]). Internal homo-phobia has a direct influence on substance abuse among the LGBT population (Mendoza-Denton, Downey, Purdie, Davis, & Pietrzak, 2002; Lehavot & Simoni, 2011). Sexual minority stress is differentiated from societal exclusion and SES as a contributor to health behaviors and outcomes because it involves stigma-based rejection sensitivity as identified with comparable groups (Mendoza-Denton et al., 2002). Sensitivity to potential rejection based on sexual minority status is a predictor of poor health outcomes (Hatzenbuehler, Nolen-Hoeksema, & Erickson, 2008). One problematic outcome of expectations of rejection is avoidance of health services. If an older LGBT adult avoids health-promoting services and does not seek sufficient treatment for existing conditions, tragic health outcomes can result. Meyer (2003) delineated the four processes of sexual minority stress as prejudice experiences, discrimination expectations, internal homophobia, and concealment of sexual orientation.

Homosexuality can be concealed and its stigma potentially avoided through hiding one's sexual identity. However, while concealment may seem to protect in the short term, there are numerous chronic consequences of hiding sexual minority identity that affect levels of stress. Mental health outcomes (which influence physical health outcomes) of sexual minority concealment include hyper vigilance, threat of discovery, and social isolation (Pachankis, Goldfried, & Ramrattan,

100   Marcena Gabrielson

2008). Social support could be the key factor in coping with the seemingly insurmountable number of challenges experienced by LGBT seniors. I postulate that social support is a significant moderator in health behaviors, risks, and outcomes among the older LGBT population.

Social Support

As mentioned previously, LGBT elders must often rely on trusted friends, not biological and/or socially accepted kinships, to create their social support (Gabrielson & Holston, 2014). Trust strengthens social bonds through the expectation that others will remain obligated and will fulfill their obligations over time (Blau, 1964). Those LGBT seniors with a history of rejection, strained familial relationships, and/or childlessness may have limited, if any, trust in receiving sufficient aging support (Gabrielson, 2011a). Chosen family networks, aka "families of choice," are an essential feature of LGBT life (Comerford, Henson-Stroud, Sionainn, & Wheeler, 2004). These "families of choice" are constructed from friends, most often other LGBT people, and are a preferred source of support for them (Gabrielson, 2011b). LGBT elders experience a tragic conundrum, however. At a time when their preferred source of support is needed more than ever, their connection with and size of their "family of choice" may dwindle as a natural result of aging. The utility of positive support relationships has been evaluated by examining the association between allostatic load (cumulative biological risk) and cumulative relationship experiences and support (Seeman, Singer, Ryff, Love, & Levy-Storms, 2002). Positive cumulative relationship experiences and support were associated with lower allostatic load in adults older than 50 years, suggesting that social support may affect a range of biological systems and health outcomes in aging. There is a need for interventions that will effectively increase support that positively influences elders' health (Lubben & Gironda, 2003), particularly for vulnerable groups like the older LGBT population. We are challenged by the need to increase research exponentially if we are to identify and develop targeted and equitable services for LGBT elders that they can trust to be culturally acceptable, accessible, and free of discrimination and rejection. Reducing negative health behaviors, risks, and outcomes among older LGBT adults is contingent upon the development of such services.

Challenges Regarding Health Behaviors and Risks among LGBT Elders

The LGBT population has characteristic health risks that can affect their aging. For example, they exhibit higher rates of smoking (Gruskin, Greenwood, Matevia, Pollack, Bye, & Albright, 2007) as well as substance abuse and mental illness (Hughes & Eliason, 2002; McCabe, Bostwick, Hughes, West, & Boyd, 2010; McCabe, Hughes, Bostwick, West, & Boyd, 2009) compared to the heterosexual population. Additionally, lesbians exhibit higher rates of obesity (Yancey, Cochran, Corliss, & Mays, 2003) and lower birth rates (Johnson, Jackson, Arnette,

& Koffman, 2005; O'Hanlan, Dibble, Hagan, & Davids, 2004) in comparison to heterosexual women. High rates of obesity and lower birth rates among lesbians, and higher rates of smoking, substance abuse, and mental illness overall, increase the LGBT population's risk for a wide range of chronic diseases as they age (O' Hanlan et al., 2004), creating potential health disparities for them in aging. Further, many LGBT seniors have experienced stigma, discrimination, and victimization across the life course (IOM, 2011). More LGBT than heterosexual people do not seek, or delay, care when they need it (LGBT Movement Advancement Project and Services and Advocacy for Gay, Lesbian, Bisexual and Transgender Elders [SAGE] are only now emerging in many locales). LGBT people attribute their avoidance of care to the rejection/discrimination they fear and expect from providers (IOM, 2011; Johnson et al., 2005; O'Hanlan et al., 2004). Their fears are substantiated by common experiences of homophobia, discrimination, and mistreatment in aging care (Johnson et al., 2005). Many who have been open about their sexuality for most of their lives refuse to conceal their identity in order to secure assistance from providers (Cahill & South, 2002; Gabrielson, 2011) and as a result do not get the care they need, potentially furthering already poor health (Cahill & South, 2002; Lesbian and Gay Aging Issues Network, American Society on Aging [LGAIN, ASA], 2010). Fredriksen-Goldsen et al. (2011) discovered that in their sample of 2,560 LGBT adults aged 50 and above, almost one in four participants believed their overall health to be poor. The history of and current discrimination experienced by lesbian, gay and bisexual people with chronic illness has been found to result in significant psychological distress, leading to poor outcomes in terms of mental and physical health (Fredriksen-Goldsen, Kim, Barkan, Muraco, & Hoy-Ellis, 2013). LGBT elders fear being doubly discriminated against for being both older and LGBT. They sense vulnerability with health care providers, and feel socially disadvantaged and challenged (LGAIN, ASA, 2010).

Health Outcomes

Social disadvantage and health interact across the life course (Blane, 2006). Chronic health conditions can develop from cumulative effects of damaging physical and social environments (Ben-Shlomo & Kuh, 2002). A study, using data from the Women's Health Initiative, comparing younger and older non-heterosexual women on health risks such as the higher prevalence rates of obesity, smoking, and substance abuse discovered that these health risks do not decrease with aging, despite higher socioeconomic levels and increased resources of the older sample, suggesting that older lesbians have unmet needs that require better and more targeted intervention from providers (Valanis, Bowen, Bassford, Whitlock, Charney, & Carter, 2000). The interaction of health risk, social disadvantage, and a damaging health care environment perpetuate vulnerability to poor health outcomes among LGBT elders. Older LGBT adults, regardless of if they are open or closeted about their sexuality, may experience more debilitating conditions due to previous distrust and avoidance of health care. These factors are compounded by the poor investigation of the social determinants of their health outcomes.

102 *Marcena Gabrielson*

Without an adequate support system, LGBT elders must unfortunately decide between either turning to or rejecting potentially dangerous environments for care and support (Cahill, Ellen, & Tobias, 2002). Either scenario could result in poor health outcomes, depending on variables rendering certain groups more vulnerable. According to Cahill et al. (2000), as LGBT people grow older and rely more on public programs and services for care and assistance, they may have less independence from heterosexist institutions. The fear of experiencing discrimination can reinforce social isolation, placing people at higher risk for self-neglect, decreased long-term quality of life, and increased mortality risk (p. 17). LGBT elders are a largely invisible population due to both self-imposed social isolation and being disregarded as a group by investigators. This has furthered their marginalization and has rendered them an invisible population to health care providers. This has resulted in unresponsive, uninformed, and likely inequitable care provision to this vulnerable group. Poor health outcomes of LGBT elders could be decreased if an evidence base were established for services that specifically address their unique needs during the aging process. For example, Dibble and Roberts (2003) reported an increase in preventive health behaviors such as having mammograms, performing self-breast exams, and accessing pelvic examinations by older lesbians when offered a lesbian-specific educational program on preventive cancer screening led by a lesbian physician. This finding suggests that targeted interventions could potentially increase positive health behaviors among the older LGBT population (E78). The challenge to providers is clear and yet there are few who provide health and support services specific for LGBT seniors or even have established policies against homophobia. Because social determinants of LGBT elder health outcomes have not been explored, but risk behaviors have been identified, we have a largely uneducated health care work force who may blame LGBT people for the health disparities they experience. In other words, they may consider sexual identity to be the risk factor, rather than the social stigma and disadvantage their LGBT patients are challenged with (Eliason et al., 2010). The outcomes of this individual focus in health care are culturally incongruent services that both exclude and discriminate against LGBT people and a system that maintains rather than challenges and changes, their health disparities (p. 207).

The Challenge for Nursing Education

For nurses to integrate ideal "nursing" knowledge regarding the health and care needs of older LGBT adults, and to apply emancipatory knowing in praxis regarding LGBT elders, it is essential for nursing educators to achieve competency in teaching LGBT health. Providing nursing students with the knowledge and skills necessary to deliver culturally competent care to the LGBT population in our communities requires an informed and competent nursing faculty across programs. Nursing students are graduating without the competence to provide equitable/quality care to the LGBT population. This is a critical time in which nursing programs are challenged, based in emancipatory knowing and nursing praxis, to create change in this area. The mandates are clear. A report from the

IOM (2011) identified health, access, and care disparities among the LGBT compared to heterosexual population. This led Healthy People 2020 guidelines to include a specific goal to "Improve the health, safety, and well-being of LGBT individuals" (USDHHS, 2011). Further, the Healthy People guidelines emphasize that LGBT elder health needs more attention by both investigators and providers. The IOM report on and subsequent Healthy People 2020 inclusion of LGBT health are a few of the greatest achievements we have seen to date regarding an acknowledgement of LGBT elders and their needs. Finally, The Joint Commission recommends that US hospitals work to create a more welcoming, safe, and inclusive environment to contribute to health care quality for the LGBT population and their families (Joint Commission, 2011). The challenge is clear and the time is now. Nurse scientists need to give this neglected population concious attention immediately so that we can better equip a currently underinformed US nursing faculty. Nursing faculty require the information that increased research can offer if they are to achieve the competence necessary to provide both adequate and accurate education regarding LGBT health to nursing students across the country. The neglect of LGBT health content across nursing curricula in the Unites States is the likely consequence of a prevalent heterosexist culture within nursing education (Brennan, Walsh, Barnsteiner, de Leon Siantz, Cotter, & Everett, 2012; Eliason et al., 2010). Nursing faculty who neglect coverage of LGBT health may not be doing so because of disinterest, but most likely do so because they are just not thinking about it (heteronormative culture). If nursing faculty have thought about including LGBT content but choose not to, it may be because they feel they lack the knowledge base to comfortably teach LGBT health issues. Whatever the reason for the lack of LGBT health content across nursing curricula, our neglect of the LGBT population in nursing education perpetuates the populations' invisibility, limits students' potential to provide high-quality culturally competent care, and potentially maintains identified care and health disparities among the LGBT compared to the heterosexual population. The impact of this on LGBT elders is significant.

The Challenge for Nursing Research

To confront the LGBT health and care inequities identified by the IOM (2011) and address the Health People 2020 goal to "Improve the health, safety, and well-being of LGBT individuals" (USDHHS, 2011), nurse investigators must consider the population through emancipatory knowing and engage in a research agenda using nursing praxis.

An important research priority identified within the IOM report (2011) is advancing health inequities research. However, focusing on health inequities alone is not enough for nursing investigators. For nurse researchers to exercise their emancipatory knowing and engage in nursing praxis through research, a social ecological perspective, identifying the many social factors that influence group and individual behavior (Bradford and Mayer, 2007) must be applied to their work. Applying a conceptual framework to their research like the one I have

104 *Marcena Gabrielson*

provided in this chapter would be helpful for future nursing investigators. Further examining the social determinants that impact LGBT elder health behaviors and outcomes is our challenge. Where sources and variables of positive influence are identified, intervention studies should be designed that use and test them. In all future research on LGBT elders, efforts must be made to obtain large and diversified samples. Investigators should make serious attempts to create protected databases of potential study subjects who are willing to have their contact information shared with other investigators for potential inclusion in additional research. Investigators should seek to share such databases of potential participants with other researchers. This level of cooperation between investigators would expedite further research.

Nursing Care Challenges

One significant way that nurses and other helping professionals can apply emancipatory knowing is through simply seeking to create a welcoming care environment for their older LGBT patients. This can be provided not only through having an open and welcoming attitude as a nurse but also advocating for LGBT staff education trainings, the posting of signs about being inclusive, and the development of specific policies regarding LGBT patients. Word spreads through even the smallest LGBT community when it is made clear to them and they have experienced that a provider is LGBT friendly. Whether or not these measures are in place, nurses have the responsibility to convey support to and acceptance for their LGBT patients. They also need to demonstrate that they do not carry a heterosexist assumption that all patients are heterosexual. Simply stating to a patient that not all people consider biological relatives to be family and asking who they consider to be family is a great start. Nurses can also ask their patients if they have a specific individual they can rely on the most for support. If the patient says yes, the nurse has the opportunity to convey that they are not heterosexist or biased, by simply asking if that person is a relative, a partner of the same or opposite sex, or a friend, and if they would like to include that person in their care.

Nurses are challenged with increasing their own care competency regarding LGBT elders. A simple place to start is the National Resource Center on LGBT Aging (www.lgbtagingcenter.org), sponsored by the organization, Services and Advocacy for Gay, Lesbian, Bisexual and Transgender Elders (SAGE). The National Resource Center is another important achievement in addressing the health and care needs of LGBT elders. It is an online depository for most everything about and concerning LGBT elders. The "center" offers several different trainings on LGBT elders as well as online resources and a directory of resources at the state level. Further, the resource center offers a guidebook for providers to develop inclusive and culturally competent service to LGBT elders (www.n4a.org/files/programs/resources-lgbt-elders/InclusiveServicesGuide2012.pdf). Another great source from which nurses and organizations can obtain training about LGBT elders is The Nurses HEALE Project. Sponsored by the Howard Brown Health

Center in Chicago, Illinois, The Nurses HEALE Project is a cultural competency educational program, funded by a HRSA grant, to provide training on LGBT elders to medical professionals (www.nursesheale.org/).

Once nurses are culturally competent in LGBT elder health, they can engage in nursing praxis by attempting to address health-related social challenges faced by the elder LGBT population in their communities. Using the state-level resources provided by the National Resource Center for LGBT Aging, nurses can explore current programs being offered to provide support to LGBT elders in their state and make contacts to identify regional and local organizations that they could become involved in. Nurses can contact Area Agencies on Aging within their communities to see what the support programs and resources are, if any, for LGBT elders in their areas. Where no support programs and resources are available, nurses can engage in praxis by identifying and bringing together key stakeholders to develop outreach support programs and services for LGBT elders in their community. Contacting local grass roots LGBT organizations to discuss the needs of LGBT elders in their community and how their organizations might provide outreach may be necessary. Center Link (www.lgbtcenters.org) is an organization to help individuals find LGBT community centers across the United States. This may be helpful for nurses trying to find local and regional grassroots organizations where no formal resources for LGBT elders are set up in their communities. Through our emancipatory knowing, we, as nurses, understand that, after a life course of discrimination experiences, many LGBT elders have significant fears and may not seek assistance. In all likelihood, through emancipatory knowing and engagement in praxis, the nurse will likely have to seek out LGBT elders and search for LGBT organizations. Nurses should expect having to initiate dialogue about LGBT elder needs in their communities and having to work with and through caring others (especially members of the LGBT community) to create support programs and services that LGBT elders in their communities would trust and use. Through our understanding that the "family of choice" is a social support that LGBT people identify as critical to their health and well-being, involvement of members of the LGBT community will be a key component in nursing praxis regarding LGBT older adults.

Achievements in Outreach to Older LGBT Adults—Exemplary Programs

There have been some noteworthy achievements in outreach to LGBT elders in the last several years. One early program is SAGE. SAGE was created in New York City in 1978 by a group of activists who recognized that LGBT seniors did not have the network of support needed to age with a sense of well-being. SAGE has created several innovative programs of outreach to LGBT elders over the years that are still in existence today, including the nation's first friendly visitor program for LGBT elders, a support group for older adults with HIV/AIDS, municipally funded caregiver respite program, and, an LGBT Senior Center. Today SAGE has twenty-three affiliate sites in larger urban areas within seventeen states and

106 Marcena Gabrielson

the District of Columbia, providing services, programs, and support for older LGBT adults in communities across the country. As mentioned previously, SAGE sponsored the creation of The National Resource Center on LGBT Aging. SAGE also leads the National LGBT Aging Roundtable, a consortium of fifty organizations across the United States that is dedicated to improving overall quality of life for LGBT older adults (sageusa.org).

In Chicago, Illinois, the Center on Halsted (a SAGE affiliate) provides many support services for LGBT elders through their Senior Programs. One of their more innovative programs is their Home Sharing Program, established in 2010. The first program of its kind, the Center on Halsted's Home Sharing Program, pairs LGBT elders with younger LGBT renters who share their home. The renters assist their older roommates with general household and support tasks in exchange for reduced rent. This groundbreaking program helps offset the social disadvantages and challenges faced by LGBT elders.

Open House in San Francisco, California, supports LGBT seniors in overcoming the social disadvantages and challenges they face in aging by providing safe and affordable housing, direct care services, community programs, and provider training. Their safe and affordable housing program is noteworthy as other LGBT retirement communities that have been developed are largely unaffordable for the majority of the older LGBT population. The comprehensiveness of Open House's services is remarkable. In addition to their support services, every month, Open House offers an array of social activities for LGBT elders in the San Francisco Bay area, including exercise programs, support groups and grief counseling, health workshops, and more (http://openhouse-sf.org).

The Fenway Institute in Boston, Massachusetts, is a LGBT community health center. Fenway sponsors the LGBT Aging Project, a non-profit organization dedicated to the advocacy of older LGBT adults. The LGBT Aging Project offers community seminars for providers, cultural competency training and consultation to providers, an LGBT elder speakers' bureau, bereavement and caregiver support groups, classes on healthy aging, LGBT community meals, and a host of social events for LGBT elders (www.lgbtagingproject.org). Another innovative program of outreach to LGBT elders in the Boston area is the Stonewall Communities Lifelong Learning Institute, the first post retirement learning program in the United States to be created by and delivered to LGBT elders. The Stonewall Communities Lifelong Learning Institute provides stimulating opportunities of growth for LGBT seniors through study groups, speaker panels, workshops, and presentations (www.stonewallcommunities.org).

The reader will note that all of the exemplar programs of outreach I have mentioned are located in large urban areas. The problem and challenge are that LGBT elders are living everywhere, including in moderately sized cities, small towns, and rural settings. In these areas, LGBT senior services, like the ones mentioned, are basically non-existent. The challenge for providers is that there are large numbers of LGBT elders who are isolated and not receiving the services and social support they desperately need. Nurses working from emancipatory knowing and engaging in praxis are challenged to take action through finding and

Outreach to LGBT Elders   107

working with caring others in smaller settings to develop, promote, and provide needed support services to the older LGBT population, like the exemplar programs mentioned.

Summary

In this chapter, I have noted some outstanding achievements that have occurred regarding LGBT elder visibility and service provision over the last several years. I have presented theoretical underpinnings and a conceptual framework to help readers better understand pathways to adverse health outcomes among LGBT elders and multiple points of intervention in which providers can improve on those outcomes. I have attempted to help the reader understand the nursing perspective *as it should be* with regard to LGBT senior health and the many nursing education, research, and care challenges that are yet to be confronted adequately. Finally, I identified several exemplar LGBT elder outreach programs in the United States that we can all learn from. Though achievements have been realized, our challenges remain and are great with respect to LGBT seniors. A formula for confronting the many challenges is simple. First, more high-quality research about LGBT elders will result in better education about them. More and better education regarding LGBT seniors will result in well-informed, culturally competent providers. Though research regarding LGBT elders should increase exponentially and immediately, current faculty, providers, and students should not wait for the trickle down. There are plenty of resources for us to improve our knowledge and competence with respect to this population. Though LGBT civil rights are on the move with marriage equality and the like, and it will one day be a better, safer world for LGBT seniors, there are current LGBT seniors who are still struggling and in need. They require care, services, and support that is affirming and that they can trust. We are all challenged to take more action to improve the lives of this important and vulnerable sub-group of older adults.

References

Ben-Shlomo, Y., & Kuh, D. (2002). A life course approach to chronic disease epidemiology: Conceptual models, empirical challenges and interdisciplinary perspectives. *International Journal of Epidemiology*, 31(2), 285–293. DOI: 10.1093/ije/31.2.285.

Blau, P.M. (1964). *Exchange and power in social life.* New Brunswick, Canada: Transaction Publishers.

Blane, D. (2006). The life course, the social gradient and health. In M. Marmot & R.G. Wilkinson (Eds.), *The social determinants of health* (pp. 54–77). New York: Oxford University Press.

Bradford, J., & Mayer, K. (2007). Demography and the LGBT Population: What we know, don't know, and how the information helps to inform clinical practice. In H. Makadon, K. Mayer, J. Potter, & H. Goldhammer (Eds.), *The Fenway guide to lesbian, gay, bisexual, and transgender health* (pp 25–44). Philadelphia, PA: American College of Physicians.

Brennan, A., Walsh, M., Barnsteiner, J., de Leon Siantz, M.L., Cotter, V.T., & Everett, J. (2012). Lesbian, gay, bisexual, transgendered, or intersexed content for nursing curricula. *Journal of Professional Nursing*, 28(2), 96–104. DOI: 10.1016/j.profnurs.2011.11.004.

108 Marcena Gabrielson

Cahill, S., Ellen, M., & Tobias, S. (2002). *Family policy: Issues affecting gay, lesbian, bisexual and transgender families.* New York: The National Gay and Lesbian Task Force Policy Institute.

Cahill, S., & South, K. (2002). Policy issues affecting lesbian, gay, bisexual, and transgender people in retirement. *Generations*, 26(2), 49.

Cahill, S., South, K., & Spade, J. (2000). *Outing age: Public policy issues affecting gay, lesbian, bisexual and transgender elders.* Washington, DC: The Policy Institute of the National Gay and Lesbian Task Force Foundation.

Carper, B. (1978). Fundamental patterns of knowing in nursing. *Advances in Nursing Science*, 1(1), 13–23.

Chen, Z., Williams, K.D., Fitness, J., & Newton, N.C. (2008). When hurt will not heal: Exploring the capacity to relive social and physical pain. *Psychological Science*, 19(8), 789–795. DOI: 10.1111/j.1467–9280.2008.02158.x.

Chinn, P.L., & Kramer, M.K. (2008). *Integrated theory and knowledge development in nursing* (7th ed.). St. Louis, MS: Mosby Elsevier.

Chinn, P.L., & Kramer, M.K. (2011). Integrated theory and knowledge development in nursing (8th ed.). St. Louis, MS: Mosby Elsevier.

Comerford, S.A., Henson-Stroud, M.M., Sionainn, C., & Wheeler, E. (2004). Crone songs: Voices of lesbian elders on aging in a rural environment. *Affilia: Journal of Women and Social Work*, 19(4), 418–436.

Diamant, A.L., & Wold, C. (2003). Sexual orientation and variation in physical and mental health status among women. *Journal of Women's Health*, 12(1), 41–49. DOI: 10.1089/154099903321154130.

Dibble, S.L., & Roberts, S.A. (2003). Improving cancer screening among lesbians over 50: Results of a pilot study. *Oncology Nursing Forum*, 30(4), E71–E79, 1p. DOI: 10.1188/03.ONF.E71-E79.

Dohrenwend, B.P. (2000). The role of adversity and stress in psychopathology: Some evidence and its implications for theory and research. *Journal of Health & Social Behavior*, 41(1), 1–19.

Dupre, M.E. (2008). Educational differences in health risks and illness over the life course: A test of cumulative disadvantage theory. *Social Science Research*, 37(4), 1253–1266.

Eisenberger, M., & Lieberman, M. (2005). Why it hurts to be left out: The neurocognitive overlap between physical and social pain. In K.D. Williams, J.P. Forgas, & W. van Hippel (Eds.), *The social outcast: Ostracism, social exclusion, rejection, and bullying* (pp. 109–127). New York: Cambridge University Press.

Eisenberger, N.I., Lieberman, M.D., & Williams, K.D. (2003). Does rejection hurt? An FMRI study of social exclusion. *Science*, 302(5643), 290–292. DOI: 10.1126/science.1089134.

Eliason, M.J., Dibble, S., & DeJoseph, J. (2010). Nursing's silence on lesbian, gay, bisexual, and transgender issues: The need for emancipatory efforts. *Advances in Nursing Science*, 33(3), 206–128, 13p. DOI: 10.1097/ANS.0b013e3181e63e49.

Fredriksen-Goldsen, K.I., Kim, H.J., Barkan, S.E., Muraco, A., & Hoy-Ellis, C.P. (2013). Health Disparities among lesbian, gay, and bisexual older adults: Results from a population-based study. *American Journal of Public Health*, 103(10), 1802–1809. DOI: 10.2105/AJPH.2012.301110.

Fredriksen-Goldsen, K.I., Kim, H.J., Emlet, C.A., Muraco, A., Erosheva, E.A., Hoy-Ellis, C.P., et al. (2011). *The aging and health report: Disparities and resilience among lesbian, gay, bisexual, and transgender older adults.* Seattle, Washington, DC: Institute for Multigenerational Health.

Gabrielson, M. (2009). *The long term care decision making of older lesbians: A narrative analysis*. PhD Dissertation. University of Iowa, Iowa City, IA.

Gabrielson, M.L. (2011a). 'I will not be discriminated against': Older lesbians creating new communities. *Advances in Nursing Science*, 34(4), 357–373.

Gabrielson, M.L. (2011b). 'We have to create family': Aging support issues and needs among older lesbians. *Journal of Gay & Lesbian Social Services*, 23(3), 322–334.

Gabrielson, M.L., & Holston, E.C. (2014). Broadening definitions of family for older lesbians: Modifying the Lubben Social Network Scale. *Journal of Gerontological Social Work*, 57(2–4), 198–217.

Godley, J., & Mclaren, L. (2010). Socioeconomic status and body mass index in Canada: Exploring measures and mechanisms. *Canadian Review of Sociology*, 47(4), 381–403.

Goldberg, S., Sickler, J., & Dibble, S.L. (2005). Lesbians over sixty: The consistency of findings from twenty years of survey data. *Journal of Lesbian Studies*, 9(1–2), 195–213. DOI: 10.1300/J155v09n01_18.

Gruskin, E.P., Greenwood, G.L., Matevia, M., Pollack, L.M., Bye, L.L., & Albright, V. (2007). Cigar and smokeless tobacco use in the lesbian, gay, and bisexual population. *Nicotine & Tobacco Research: Official Journal of the Society for Research on Nicotine and Tobacco*, 9(9), 937–940. DOI: 10.1080/14622200701488426.

Haas, S. (2008). Trajectories of functional health: The 'long arm' of childhood health and socioeconomic factors. *Social Science & Medicine*, 66(4), 849–861.

Hatzenbuehler, M.L., Nolen-Hoeksema, S., & Erickson, S.J. (2008). Minority stress predictors of HIV risk behavior, substance use, and depressive symptoms: Results from a prospective study of bereaved gay men. *Health Psychology*, 27(4), 455–462. DOI: 10.1037/0278–6133.27.4.455.

Hughes, T.L., & Eliason, M. (2002). Substance use and abuse in lesbian, gay, bisexual and transgender populations. *The Journal of Primary Prevention*, 22(3), 263–298. DOI: 10.1023/A:1013669705086.

Institute of Medicine (IOM). (2011). *The health of lesbian, gay, bisexual, and transgender people: Building a foundation for better understanding*. Washington, DC: The National Academies Press.

Johnson, M.J., Jackson, N.C., Arnette, J.K., & Koffman, S.D. (2005). Gay and lesbian perceptions of discrimination in retirement care facilities. *Journal of Homosexuality*, 49(2), 83–102. DOI: 10.1300/J082v49n02_05.

Joint Commission. (2011). *Advancing effective communication, cultural competence, and patient- and family-centered care for the lesbian, gay, bisexual, and transgender (LGBT) community: A field guide*. Oak Brook, IL: The Joint Commission.

Kehoe, M. (1988). Lesbians over 60 speak for themselves. *Journal of Homosexuality*, 16(3–4), 1–111.

Koh, A.S., & Ross, L.K. (2006). Mental health issues: A comparison of lesbian, bisexual and heterosexual women. *Journal of Homosexuality*, 51(1), 33–57. DOI: 10.1300/J082v51n01_03.

Lehavot, K., & Simoni, J.M. (2011). The impact of minority stress on mental health and substance use among sexual minority women. *Journal of Consulting and Clinical Psychology*, 79(2), 159–170.

Lesbian and Gay Aging Issues Network, American Society on Aging (LGAIN, ASA). (2010). *Still out, still aging: The MetLife study of lesbian and gay baby boomers*. San Francisco, CA: American Society on Aging.

Lim, F.A., & Bernstein, I. (2012). Promoting awareness of LGBT issues in aging in a baccalaureate nursing program. *Nursing Education Perspectives*, 33(3), 170–175.

110 *Marcena Gabrielson*

LGBT Movement Advancement Project and Services and Advocacy for Gay, Lesbian, Bisexual and Transgender Elders. (2010). *Improving the lives of LGBT older adults*. Denver, CO: Movement Advancement Project.

Lubben, J., & Gironda, M. (2003). Centrality of social ties to the health and well-being of older adults. In B. Berkman & L.K. Harooytan (Eds.), *Social work and health care in an aging world* (pp. 319–350). New York: Springer.

McCabe, S.E., Bostwick, W.B., Hughes, T.L., West, B.T., & Boyd, C.J. (2010). The relationship between discrimination and substance use disorders among lesbian, gay, and bisexual adults in the United States. *American Journal of Public Health*, 100(10), 1946–1952. DOI: 10.2105/AJPH.2009.163147.

McCabe, S.E., Hughes, T.L., Bostwick, W.B., West, B.T., & Boyd, C.J. (2009). Sexual orientation, substance use behaviors and substance dependence in the United States. *Addiction*, 104(8), 1333–1345. DOI: 10.1111/j.1360–0443.2009.02596.x.

MacDonald, G., Kingsbury, R., & Shaw, S. (2005). Adding insult to injury: Social pain theory and response to social exclusion. In K.D. Williams, J.P. Forgas, & W. von Hipple (Eds.), *The social outcast: Ostracism, social exclusion, rejection, and bullying* (pp. 77–90). Sydney Symposium of Social Psychology Series. New York: Psychology Press.

MacDonald, G., & Leary, M.R. (2005). Why does social exclusion hurt? The relationship between social and physical pain. *Psychological Bulletin*, 131(2), 202–223. DOI: 10.1037/0033–2909.131.2.202.

McEwen, B.S. (2006). Protective and damaging effects of stress mediators: Central role of the brain. *Dialogues in Clinical Neuroscience*, 8(4), 367–381.

McEwen, B.S., & Gianaros, P.J. (2010). Central role of the brain in stress and adaptation: Links to socioeconomic status, health, and disease. *Annals of the New York Academy of Sciences*, 1186, 190–222.

Maddux, S. (2011). *Gen Silent*. Novato, CA: Interrobang Productions.

Marmot, M. (2004). Status syndrome. *Significance*, 1(4), 50–54.

Marmot, M.G. (2006). *Social determinants of health* (2nd ed.). Oxford: Oxford University Press.

Mendoza-Denton, R., Downey, G., Purdie, V.J., Davis, A., & Pietrzak, J. (2002). Sensitivity to status-based rejection: Implications for African American students' college experience. *Journal of Personality and Social Psychology*, 83(4), 896–918. DOI: 10.1037/0022–3514.83.4.896.

Meyer, I.H. (2003). Prejudice, social stress, and mental health in lesbian, gay, and bisexual populations: Conceptual issues and research evidence. *Psychological Bulletin*, 129(5), 674–697. DOI: 10.1037/0033–2909.129.5.674.

Oetjen, H., & Rothblum, E.D. (2000). When lesbians aren't gay: Factors affecting depression among lesbians. *Journal of Homosexuality*, 39(1), 49–73. DOI: 10.1300/J082v39n01_04.

O'Hanlan, K.A., Dibble, S.L., Jennifer, H., Hagan, J., & Davids, R. (2004). Advocacy for women's health should include lesbian health. *Journal of Women's Health*, 13(2), 227–234.

Pachankis, J.E., Goldfried, M.R., & Ramrattan, M.E. (2008). Extension of the rejection sensitivity construct to the interpersonal functioning of gay men. *Journal of Consulting and Clinical Psychology*, 76(2), 306–317. DOI: 10.1037/0022–006X.76.2.306.

Phelan, J.C., Link, B.G., & Tehranifar, P. (2010). Social conditions as fundamental causes of health inequalities: Theory, evidence, and policy implications. *Journal of Health & Social Behavior*, 51(1), S28–S40. DOI: 10.1177/0022146510383498.

Saunders, J.M. (1999). Health problems of lesbian women. *Nursing Clinics of North America*, 34(2), 381–391, 11p.

Seabrook, J.A., & Avison, W.R. (2012). Socioeconomic status and cumulative disadvantage processes across the life course: Implications for health outcomes. *Canadian Review of Sociology/Revue Canadienne de Sociologie*, 49(1), 50–68. DOI: 10.1111/j.1755–618X.2011.01280.x.

Seeman, T.E., Singer, B.H., Ryff, C.D., Love, G.D., & Levy-Storms, L. (2002). Social relationships, gender, and allostatic load across two age cohorts. *Psychosomatic Medicine*, 64(3), 395–406.

Singh-Manoux, A., Adler, N.E., & Marmot, M.G. (2003). Subjective social status: Its determinants and its association with measures of ill-health in the Whitehall II study. *Social Science & Medicine*, 56(6), 1321–1333.

Singh-Manoux, A., Marmot, M.G., & Adler, N.E. (2005). Does subjective social status predict health and change in health status better than objective status? *Psychosomatic Medicine*, 67(6), 855–861. DOI: 10.1097/01.psy.0000188434.52941.a0.

Sullivan, M. (2004). *The family of woman lesbian mothers, their children, and the undoing of gender*. Berkeley, CA: University of California Press.

Thoits, P.A. (2006). Personal agency in the stress process. *Journal of Health and Social Behavior*, 47(4), 309–323. DOI: 10.1177/002214650604700401.

United States Department of Health and Human Services (USDHHS). (2011). *Lesbian, gay, bisexual and transgender health. Healthy People 2020*. Retrieved November 10, 2015, from www.healthypeople.gov/2020/topicsobjectives2020/overview.aspx?topicid=25.

Valanis, B.G., Bowen, G.D., Bassford, T., Whitlock, E., Charney, P., & Carter, R.A. (2000). Sexual orientation and health: Comparisons in the women's health initiative sample. *Archives of Family Medicine*, 9(9), 843–853.

Wilkinson, R., & Marmot, M. (2003). *Social determinants of health: The solid facts*. Copenhagen, Denmark: World Health Organization.

Yancey, A.K., Cochran, S.D., Corliss, H.L,, & Mays, V.M. (2003). Correlates of overweight and obesity among lesbian and bisexual women. *Preventive Medicine: An International Journal Devoted to Practice and Theory*, 36(6), 676–683. DOI: 10.1016/S0091–7435(03)00020–3.

CHAPTER **8**

Paid Caregiving for Older Adults with Serious or Chronic Illness: Ethnographic Perspectives, Evidence, and Implications for Training

Chris Wellin

Care involves a constant tension between attachment and loss, pleasing and caring, seeking to preserve an older person's dignity and exerting unaccustomed authority, overcoming resistance to care and fulfilling extravagant demands, reviving a relationship and transforming it.

(Abel, 1990, pp. 204–205)

The preceding statement contains the crux of what I wish to convey in this chapter regarding the challenge and skill required to care for disabled older adults. As it happens, the quote concerns *family care*: adult children caring for parents. However, it captures equally and vividly the subtle and poignant relational sub-text that underlies *paid care* for delicate selves and bodies. In principle, one might expect the public to recognize and value care for relative strangers as virtuous, even heroic, as compared to that which we provide in the context of lifelong familial ties. Such is not the case. Moreover, in shifting attention to care from the private to the public sphere, many people—policy analysts no less than lay people—contract a form of blindness to the skill, empathy, and moral commitment such work demands.

The costs of this blindness are steep—for paid caregivers, those for whom they care, and for family members and friends who have a stake in the availability of humane, consistent, and skilled care for those who are chronically ill or disabled. The premise of this chapter is that, while we have an abundance of academic and policy research on the severity and financial pressures of the growing need for paid caregiving, too little attention has been paid to the processes and relations of care, and to the occupational skills and demands of caregivers. But, in recent years, we have seen a flowering of research on this topic, which I undertake below to summarize, synthesize, and connect to emerging policy issues bearing on occupational skills and rewards in this large and fast-growing segment of the service sector of the economy.

What is the larger context for this effort? Given demographic changes in the United States, which portend higher rates of chronic illness and disability in the years to come, and growing pressure to contain health care costs (which are

Paid Caregiving for Older Adults 113

highest in medically oriented settings such as nursing homes, and met by public sources via Medicare and Medicaid), the need to address the caregiving dilemma has become acute. Moreover, labor projections reveal that over the next decade, service-sector occupations—especially in paraprofessional or "direct care" jobs such as nurses' and home health aides—will be among the fastest growing in the United States (Dawson, 2007; Hecker, 2005; Paraprofessional Healthcare Institute, 2003a, 2003b; Sommers, 2007). There are wide-ranging economic, political, and moral implications of consigning such a large and growing segment of the labor force to poor wages and unstable career conditions. As Stone (2000b) argues, the quality of life enjoyed by the aged and disabled, over-burdened family care providers, and direct care workers are inextricably intertwined.

My agenda in this chapter: After describing the research background and approach I bring to this topic, I summarize demographic and labor market trends that have propelled issues of low-wage care workers (LWCWs) to the forefront of policy concern in the United States. Then, we discuss distinctive conceptual and empirical issues that have informed ethnographic research on care work. Of particular importance in this review is how one defines and documents *skill* as a key referent in the study of work. Next, I identify and discuss recurring themes in ethnographic research on care work, with special attention to the (often subtle or neglected) skills that characterize competent and exemplary practice. Then, after addressing how skill demands vary, within particular work settings and in response to the needs of particular kinds of care recipients, I summarize contemporary perspectives and strategies, within groups that represent and/or advocate for LWCWs, aimed at enhancing the recruitment, retention, performance, and public recognition of care workers. Finally, I offer suggestive implications of the argument for education and training initiatives designed to enhance recruitment, practice, and retention of LWCWs.

A Focus on Low-Wage Care Workers

Our focus is on the lowest-paid and ostensibly least skilled personnel within this sector of the health care workforce—those "frontline" workers who provide direct care in nursing homes, rehabilitation centers, residential care facilities, and in the community through "home health" agencies. Whether termed nurses' aides, CNAs, or personal care assistants, these LWCWs share many common challenges, as well as rewards, in their efforts to enhance the independence, dignity, and morale of the large and growing numbers of people who live with chronic illness or disability (Atchley, 1996; Dawson, 2007; Paraprofessional Healthcare Institute, 2003b). Indeed, Whitebrook (1999) showed similar dynamics of the labor market for and experiences of *childcare* workers.

Who are these workers? What is their socio-demographic and economic profile? A report by the Institute of Medicine (2001, p. 181), citing data from the Bureau of Labor Statistics, indicates that, "in 1998, nursing homes, personal care facilities, residential care and home health and home care agencies accounted for nearly 3.2 million jobs. Of these jobs, 1.18 million, or 37 percent, were paraprofessional

114   *Chris Wellin*

(including nursing assistants, personal care aides, and home health aides) . . . Approximately 57 percent were employed by nursing facilities, 28 percent by home care agencies, and 15 percent by residential care facilities or programs in 1998." Potter, Churilla, and Smith (2006) enhanced the portrait by drawing on two waves of national survey data, comparing full-time direct care workers and female workers generally. They concluded that over one-third are African-American (who comprise about 12% of the larger group); fewer are married than is true of women workers in general (42 vs. 56%); 67% have a high school degree or less (vs. 38% in the larger group); and 25% (vs. 18%) have at least one child aged 5 or younger. Roughly one-third of direct care workers are also poorer than female workers generally (one-third have family incomes below 150% of the poverty level), and only 40% receive employment-based health insurance.

Demographic and Labor Market Trends Propelling Interest in Care Work

Research and policy interest in LWCW has been propelled by well-known and well-documented demographic and labor market trends: the conjunction of falling birth and death rates in recent decades has produced dramatic growth in the aging population in the United States. In little more than a single life span—that is, between the mid-twentieth century and the year 2025—the proportion of those older than 60 years will roughly quadruple, from about 5% to more than 20% (Quadagno, 2014). The fastest-growing group of elders is the "old-old," those aged 85 and above, who by 2040 are predicted to number nearly 14 million (Quadagno, 2014, p. 79). Improvements in diagnostic, pharmaceutical, and therapeutic medicine—especially in the treatment of cancers, heart disease, diabetes, and other chronic conditions that continue to be leading causes of mortality—have extended life substantially. However, even though the current "baby boomer" cohorts are, in the aggregate, healthier than those of the past, we can still expect a "compression of morbidity" at the end of life (Quadagno, 2014, p. 251), which will place enormous economic and logistical demands on the long-term care (LTC) system.

That system, broadly defined, encompasses a continuum of care, which spans (1) family/kin support in the community, (2) the growing world of assisted living/residential care, and (3) medically intensive institutional care. Movement through this continuum is neither linear nor unidirectional, and arrangements and relationships within these "points" on the continuum are not mutually exclusive (Kane, 1995). In fact, a combination of funding pressures and patient preferences is driving a compositional shift, in which a substantial percentage of nursing home residents return to community settings after rehabilitative care. Still, in our fragmented or "disaggregated" LTC system, there are "disparate programs, each with its own segregated funding 'silo.' In this vertical design, nursing home services are funded separately from home care services, which in turn are funded separately from assisted living and residential care settings" (Paraprofessional Healthcare Institute, 2001, p. 15). This has important implications for recruiting

Paid Caregiving for Older Adults 115

and training care workers, inasmuch as core aspects of work—including the nature of supervision, staffing ratios, and the primacy of residents' preferences—differ across care settings, and the fragmented nature of the system undermines continuity of care that is central to achieving quality.

Historically, family care for the aged has been both a cultural ideal and an historical norm, a pattern that persists. Barker (2001, pp. 6–7) claimed, in this connection, that most studies of non-kin care have assumed family care to be the ideal, and assessed alternatives in terms of a "deficit model." Kaye, Chapman, Newcomer, and Harrington (2006, p. 1113) estimated that, currently, only 16% of "personal assistance care" is provided by paid caregivers. However, lower fertility rates have curtailed the availability of family caregivers, to say nothing of the higher proportion of those in current cohorts who are single or childless. In this connection, Potter et al. (2006, p. 358) reported that "the supply of women aged 18–45 (the direct care worker pool) is decreasing relative to the exponential growth in the number of elderly Americans." Nonetheless, family members continue to provide the vast majority of care to the extent (and beyond) that they are capable. At the same time, intensifying work demands have placed ever greater stress on family/kin caregivers—typically women—many of whom jeopardize their own present and future economic security in order to provide care in the final years of their parents' lives.

Ironically, a prime legacy of the success of our acute-care medical system is an increase in the prevalence of chronic conditions of late life, which often leave elders with multiple health problems.[1] This profile of age and disability is driving the expansion of demand for long-term, non-medical care. Too often discussed in terms of instrumental "activities of daily living," such care (assisting with bathing, dressing, transportation, shopping, and housekeeping) is essential to the maintenance of independent, fulfilling adult life in the community. Projections of future demand are that "The number of people needing these services will more than double, from thirteen million in 2000 to some twenty-seven million in 2050" (Potter at al., p. 1113). Compounding the challenge will be increasing rates of dementias, which require not only medical and practical supports but also "identity support"—complex socio-emotional care to maximize quality of life (Wellin & Jaffe, 2004).

Thus, the serious nature of the current shortage of frontline LWCWs (Atchley, 1996; Paraprofessional Healthcare Institute, 2003a, 2003b, 2001) pales in comparison with that we will face in the years to come. Gatta, Boushey, and Applebaum (2007, p. 35) cited data from the *Monthly Labor Review* predicting that between 2005 and 2014, home health aides and nursing aides/orderlies/ attendants would be among the top ten occupations with the greatest job growth (approaching 50%) during the period. Within this labor force, there is also a compositional shift in terms of work settings—increasingly toward home and community-based options which are both less costly, and more responsive to the preferences of care recipients (e.g., Kitchener, Ng, Miller, & Harrington, 2005).

The ethnographic evidence (e.g., Karner, 1998; Piercy, 2000; Rivas, 2003) reveals that there are important social/interactional and skill-related implications of this

116   *Chris Wellin*

shift in the work locales in which care workers are likely to be found: it is truer in-home care and small residential settings, than in nursing homes, that LWCWs must adapt care tasks to individual circumstances, preferences, and schedules of care-recipients. The character of this contrast, and related assumptions about power and autonomy, are suggested by comparing the terms "patient" or "resident" with "client." Though home-health workers may have a significant number of clients, they work with them one at a time and in clients' territory, so to speak. We will find below that there are trade-offs in this arrangement for care workers. But the salient point here is that inter-personal skills and rapport, that may be marginal or even penalized in more medically oriented and bureaucratic nursing home settings, are expected and even required in home and community-based care.

Key Assumptions and Empirical Themes in Ethnographies of Care Work

Stated broadly, ethnographic research methods seek to provide richly detailed descriptions of work processes and interactions, and according to Friedman and McDaniel (1998, pp. 113–114), "a sensitivity to perceptions, and an opportunity to discover important new issues, (discoveries) that cannot be achieved through *a priori* theorizing." They note further that "Naturalism also allows the researcher to see the cumulative effect of multiple forces on people's actions." Although the ethnographic perspective has long been central to the field of cultural anthropology, it is now applied across a wide range of disciplinary and policy fields. In ethnography, the prime research instrument is the field researcher, who draws upon interviews, observation, and documents in order create a rich portrait that, ideally, is both informed by and generative of theory.

Though ethnography stresses internal validity and attention to conjunctions of factors in particular settings, there is growing interest in combining and interpreting findings across studies of a particular topic, which Noblit and Hare (1988) discussed as *meta-ethnography*. In this approach, which I take here, one seeks to confirm, integrate, and refine themes and findings from multiple studies, often to shed light on a theoretical or policy question that may have been tangential to the original research.

In reviewing ethnographies of care work, there are three critical issues that, in my view, cut across and inform the literature and thus warrant brief mention here: 1) defining and studying skill; 2) the gendered nature of care work, and its effect on the social appreciation and rewards of such labor; and 3) the legacy of the biomedical model in shaping the culture and distribution of professional authority in LTC institutions and policies.

Defining and Studying Skill

Theoretical and empirical approaches to studying workplace skills vary considerably (see Gatta et al., 2007 and Vallas, 1990, for a review of approaches in sociological research). Ethnographic research on care work asserts and reveals the value of assessing "skill" (and related issues bearing on worker recruitment, selection, and training) in the context of situational and interactional *contexts* in which work occurs. Kusterer (1978) developed an argument, based on industrial workers, which has clear relevance in the present case: many of the skills employees possess are "tacit," that is, exercised without conscious or public acknowledgement, and in contradiction to formal, managerial accounts of the work process. This insight underscores the importance of excavating workers' own perceptions and practices, via ethnography, and of skepticism regarding more abstract "top-down" conceptions of workers and work-skills (see Shortell, 1998).

Following Attewell (1990), there are especially sharp contrasts between *objectivist* and *positivist* approaches to skill, and others which are *constructivist* or *ethnomethodological*. While terminology varies across time and disciplines, Attewell argued that the former approach is taken by "those who treat skill as an attribute that is amenable to quantitative measurement and believe that this attribute or quality has an objective character independent of the observer." This conception of work skills, central to "human capital" models, is found in research on industrial and clerical work, and has provided powerful leverage in addressing such questions as the role of technological change in accounting for wage inequality (Fernandez, 2001). Attewell explained that "Human capital is typically measured as the sum of years of vocational or formal education plus years of on-the-job experience" (p. 425). However, as Gatta et al. (2007, pp. 9–10) point out, many of the fastest-growing service occupations require skills such as active listening, instructing others, speaking effectively, promoting a service orientation, and social perceptiveness. These skills—contextual and relational in nature—are difficult to assess outside of the practical sphere of work, and are seldom the focus of formal training. Moreover, when these skills are expressed in care work, linked to gendered assumptions about women's instinctual capacities for nurturance (Cancian & Oliker, 2000; Gatta et al., 2007, pp. 24–29), they tend to be all the more obscure or devalued.

Ethnographic research elaborates conceptions of skill that combine or contrast two other schools which Attewell reviews: ethnomethodological and neo-Marxist approaches (1990, pp. 429–443). The first, as noted, emphasizes "the fine texture, the many steps and contingencies, of activities that are normally thought of as simple" (p. 430). Despite its distinctive insights, ethnomethodological research is vulnerable to the critique that it reduces social processes to micro-level dynamics and fails to engage constraints of social structure, power differentials, and formal organizations. In turn, neo-Marxist perspectives have been fruitfully integrated with fine-grained ethnography, in order to analyze how and why particular labor processes are fragmented, coerced, and intensified in the name of efficiency and profit (e.g., Burawoy, 1979). Integrating these analytic stances also allows for inclusion of cultural/ideological rankings in assessing the work status and rewards. For Attewell (1990), "What is striking about this literature is the frequency and centrality of the social constructionist aspect of skill within Marxism, the idea that the social standing and perceived skill of an occupation stems in large part from the power of those workers rather than from intrinsic complexity of the work itself" (p. 440).

118   *Chris Wellin*

Care work certainly involves tasks that appear at first glance to be mundane or *un-skilled*, such as dressing, bathing, feeding, and comforting people. However, these tasks require complex, empathic, and embodied practices, which must be adapted both to the normative expectations of social relationships in which they are carried out (e.g., parenting or teaching children vs. caring for an older person following a stroke) as well as to the immediate practical and temporal division of labor.

Gendered and Racialized Assumptions and Inequalities Regarding Care Work

Integrating ethnographic insights into the practice of care work with critical attention to managerial strategy and coercion (aimed at "de-skilling" work) sharpened qualitative analyses of care work. What was missing, to achieve the explanatory power of the strongest contemporary research, was an explicit analysis of gender as a fundamental status system in which work is defined and remunerated (see Cancian & Oliker, 2000; England, 2005; Glenn, 2000; Steinberg, 1990) and of how tasks and qualities usually associated with women are perceived and rewarded more generally in occupations. These considerations become central in any analysis of care work because of the gendered, familial meanings that are—whether explicitly or subtly—attached to caring labor. As England, Budig, and Folbre (2002, p. 456) argued, caring work should be distinguished from the larger domain of interactive service work (e.g., in retail, food service, or customer service). They pointed out that, while there are structural similarities between the two (such as low wages and flat career lines), they involve different, if not opposing, skills and demands. Whereas interactive service work typically requires *routinization* of tasks, to promote efficiency and inter-changeability of labor in the provision of a service (see Leidner, 1993), care work ideally involves *personalization* of tasks in order to help maintain or enhance recipients' independence and quality of life. This commitment is clearly salient for workers and recipients, if not always for employers, a tension that is central to recurring dilemmas in care work.

The "helping/nurturing" dimension of care work has repeatedly been found to be a powerful lure in drawing people to such jobs (e.g., Aronson & Neysmith, 1996; England, 2005; Foner, 1994; Kopiec, 2000; Stacey, 2005; Wellin & Jaffe, 2004). Kopiec (2000), who conducted individual interviews and focus groups with LWCWs in New Hampshire, writes,

> The most common overarching reason for becoming a Certified Nursing Assistant (CNA) is the desire to help others. As one participant explains, 'It just started as a helping thing . . . I think because I like to chit chat and the fact that I can involve myself in somebody else's life.' Several women have personal experience caring for an ill family member, which they found rewarding and led them to this type of work . . . Joanne explains: 'I have a big heart and don't like to see people be by themselves, to suffer. I took care of

my first husband; when we were 24 he got cancer and later died . . . It's a talent I have inside of me'.

(p. 4)

In a similar spirit, an online CNA forum hosted by *Nursing Assistant Central* features personal, consciousness/pride raising statements such as: "I am the one, in many people's lives, who provides them with their basic human needs. What others take for granted—dressing, bathing, eating—some people are unable to perform for themselves anymore, and they depend on me. I am the one who goes to great lengths to maintain their privacy and dignity . . . Yet I am also the one they rage at, venting their frustration, anger, confusion and fear. I am the one who performs care, even though doing so will often put me at risk of physical or verbal abuse at the hands of those I care for."

The Legacy of the Biomedical Model

Public perceptions and professional problems of LWCWs cannot be understood without awareness of their historical role in the dominant, acute-care biomedical system (Henderson, 1995; Freidson, 1970/1988). Until recent decades, most of these workers were employed by hospitals, nursing homes, or rehabilitation centers, where they were regarded as menial and transient underlings in a hierarchical division of labor. Clearly, there are strong rationales for this organization of medical care, in the context of curative techno-medicine: in that case, there need to be clear lines of authority and responsibility, along with smooth intermeshing of administrative, laboratory, and clinical work. In this context, the patient is expected to comply with medical advice and to accept impersonal detachment on the part of members of the medical team, in exchange for timely and expert treatment (Parsons, 1951, pp. 428–479). As Morgan and Kunkel (2007) explained (pp. 270–273), the "medical model" carries cultural meanings that extend beyond discrete care settings. It also enshrines a dichotomy between mind and body, and a narrow reduction of illness to somatic causes and manifestations (the "doctrine of specific etiology"), to the exclusion of broader socio-cultural factors. To the extent that care for the person *qua* person is addressed in the acute-care setting, it typically is provided by nurses or by social workers or clergy for whom this mission is central and bolstered by professional training and status.[2]

Themes and Findings Regarding LWCWs in the Ethnographic Literature

In ethnographic studies of nursing home and elder care, only rarely have the roles (still less the perspectives) of LWCWs taken center stage. More often we have had mere glimpses of these workers and their impact on the quality of care and life. Rather than begin with descriptive vignettes and build up to broader themes and findings, I have chosen to develop the themes up front, in order to frame the

120   *Chris Wellin*

meaning and implications of the sources I review now in greater detail. It will be instructive throughout to bear in mind a set of recurring, work-a-day dilemmas that plague LWCWs, laid out in a discerning essay by Stone (2000a); these serve to link the broad conceptual themes discussed earlier, and the ethnographic stories and perspectives: *talk versus tasks, love versus detachment, specialness versus fairness, patience versus schedules, family relations versus work relations,* and *relationships versus rules.*

Nursing Home Ethnography

I begin with the tradition of *Nursing Home Ethnography*, which has a longer and more extensive history than does research on LWCW in other settings. Several sketches from a couple of important studies will help show the nature and development of knowledge of LWCW.

The contemporary nursing home sector is poised between ever greater consolidation and intensification of labor, on the one hand, and innovative programs to humanize care, on the other (see www.pioneernetwork.net/; Thomas, 1996). Eaton (1999) reported that "Today, 75% of nursing homes are owned by private, for-profit firms, 20% by private nonprofit institutions, and 5% are public. Public funds pay for the majority of nursing home care; 15% of all revenues go to the top six nursing home corporations . . . whose operating profits increased by 122 percent on a revenue increase of 19% between 1996–1997 . . . More than 1.7 million people live in nursing homes, a number that will double in the next twenty five years. Between 50–70% of residents suffer from some kind of dementia; more than 80% of residents are women, as are more than 90% of nursing home workers" (pp. 75–76). Eaton observed that as nursing homes seek to maintain profits in a more competitive managed-care atmosphere and with more seriously ill residents, they turn with increasing ardor to cutting labor costs, which account for roughly 60% of costs: "This increases the pressure on front-line workers, many of whom complain of understaffing, lack of training and support, inadequate supplies, and unresponsive management" (p. 77). The current political economy of long-term care shapes the issues that are central to critical ethnographies, and sets limits on the range of plausible remedies to recurring problems of staff recruitment and turnover, which varies widely, from roughly 30% for nurses, to more than 100% for aides (Castle & Engberg, 2006).

Gubrium's (1975) *Living and Dying at Murray Manor* is a widely cited ethnographic study (based on months of fieldwork and varied field roles) which revealed the deep *segmentation* between various "worlds" within the nursing home. He elaborated the rather self-contained domains of the "top staff," the "floor staff," and the world of residents—including their experience of time passing, friendships, and the nearness and reality of death. A crucial insight of *Murray Manor*, with implications for LWCWs, is that their labors are little known or appreciated by administrators, and thus are not integrated into larger goals. Principal among these is creating a "home-like" atmosphere conducive to "total patient care" (1975, p. 48). This fragile ideal took shape largely through an invidious

Paid Caregiving for Older Adults 121

comparison with hospital care, which most of the top staff had fled for Murray Manor. Nurses, too, found nursing homes to be "more personally satisfying" than hospitals as work locales, though they conceded that they had had little training for addressing residents' personal and emotional problems. Gubrium suggested that the floor staff members are potentially critical in enacting "total care." However, his portrait shows how rushed and physically grueling is their daily routine (pp. 124–157). Also, in *Murray Manor*, aides are presented as heedless of privacy, resistant to innovation or to any interactional digression as annoying barriers to getting through their round of "bed and body work." "Aides believe that the fact they're working for the patients, and working hard at that, is good enough reason to 'get 'em goin.' Thus, aides may enter rooms and urge patients along to their scheduled destinations with obvious exasperation or patronizing indulgence. Typical statements on these occasions express their sentiments: 'What *are* we going to do with you, Cora?' . . . Let's get moving now" (p. 129). Ultimately, the book shows how aides can be viewed, by residents, as intrusive and instrumental; there are few vignettes that reveal a warm or intimate quality to caring encounters. However, in concluding the section describing their work, Gubrium observed that:

> Floor staff, more than top staff or clientele, experience the social complexities that arise when [sense of] place is not well-insulated. As members of the floor staff enter and depart certain places as part of their work, they tacitly raise doubt about whether these places are private or public . . . Floor staff conciliates both top staff and clientele in order to guard what it considers normal work routine. This is a highly precarious working policy.
>
> (p. 157)

So, in the fragmented world of the nursing home, aides play a critical—albeit "precarious"—role in mediating the mission of total care. Still, to their arduous physical and emotional tasks is added the burden of simultaneously enforcing and buffering the most intrusive aspects of institutional life. Ideally, this role-conflict could be acknowledged and explored in the orientation and training of such workers, as a constructive step in retaining and supporting LWCWs in such settings. (See Gubrium [1993] for an important narrative study of residents' perspectives on nursing home life.)

Shield's (1988) *Uneasy Endings* is another rich ethnographic study of nursing home life, in which there are only glimpses of the circumstances and roles of LWCWs. An anthropologist, Shield is comparative in assessing distinctions between nursing home life and that in other "total institutions" as defined by Goffman (1961). She is also attentive to the significance—by their absence—of ritual and reciprocity in the lives of people who, after all, are collectively facing the existential crisis of death. For Shield, the puzzle is that a group facing the ultimate *rite of passage* should be denied the sense of togetherness (*communitas*) which would afford greater meaning and sustenance to the ordeal (pp. 205–209). The author also develops the themes of exchange and reciprocity, as generic qualities of

122　*Chris Wellin*

relationships that promote interdependence and a sense of control. The bane of nursing home life, from this vantage point, is not illness or institutional residency, per se; rather it is the asymmetrical nature of relationships—in particular between care workers and residents—that cast the latter always in the role of supplicant and dependent. Shield (1988) explained,

> Because residents have little power and must receive, they must be grateful. The responsibility that staff members exhibit toward residents is also reduced by the constraints on reciprocity. When one can repay nice staff members or visitors, one is able to rely on the other person's mutual sense of responsibility. A person who is unable to tap the other's sense of responsibility attempts to induce guilt, and with time guilt is resented. There is little reason for staff members to feel responsible toward the resident because staff members' obligations are to their bureaucratic duties.
>
> (pp. 158–159)

Shield (1988) lamented that residents are "de-cultured . . . misunderstood as children, as people with no pasts, as recipients with no legitimate input into the factors that determine their lives. Treated alike by staff, they recognize no bonds with each other—instead they splinter into their heterogeneous identities because there are no rituals to bind them together as separate individuals undergoing the passage from life in the community to death" (p. 216). Apart from barriers to *communitas* posed by cognitive illness, which is increasingly prevalent in nursing homes, Shield's account also contains seeds of insight about, and implications for staff development among LWCWs. If rituals are to be constructed and observed in the nursing home setting, it would seem to require the support and involvement of direct care workers. Given sufficient tenure in the particular setting, it is they who are uniquely possessed of the ongoing, personal knowledge about residents that would be required; also, it is they who are chronically starved for casual time with residents and, often, search out opportunities to step out of the formal routine and celebrate that which can be celebrated. An important caveat concerns the need for administrators and organizational routines to be oriented toward residents' quality of life.

Wellin and Jaffe (2004), in their study of residential care for older people with dementia, found that staff members often had detailed biographical knowledge about residents. However, they typically invoked and shared this knowledge in punitive ways—to criticize or pathologize residents' behavior—rather than with empathy or a desire to lend comfort. This process, which we term *appropriation of biography*, was rooted in the combination of a functionally diffuse division of labor (involving domestic labor, cooking, and field trips, as well as instrumental care), and the taxing nature of some behaviors associated with dementia (Jaffe & Wellin, 2008; Wellin & Jaffe, 2004, p. 286).

There is abundant evidence throughout nursing home ethnographies that staff members are kept in the dark about such issues as resident transfers and discharges,

Paid Caregiving for Older Adults 123

changes in health status, and, especially, death and dying. This reflects the more general concealment and "management" of death that prevails in the larger society (Shield, 1988, pp. 69–71).

A relevant study (Castle & Engberg, 2006) of staff turnover in nursing homes found the highest rates among Certified Aides (56.4%), with between 35 and 40% for licensed practical nurses (LPNs) and registered nurses (RNs), respectively. Organizational variables that were clearly associated with higher turnover include lower staffing ratios, for-profit ownership, and higher number of beds (and see Seavey, 2004). The authors also confirm the importance of mediating factors shaping job satisfaction, including pay and benefits, autonomy/lack of intensive supervision, loyalty to the setting, and the quality of relationships with residents and fellow staff members. Variables of facility structure and scale would appear to be necessary, but not sufficient, explanations for this core problem. Beyond this, initiatives such as the *Eden Alternative* and *Greenhouse Model* (nationally prominent models of nursing home reform), which promote more flexible, team-oriented work arrangements, appear to further enhance worker morale and reduce turnover (Kemper et al., 2008). A further incentive for moving toward these employment conditions, noted by an advocate for *Eden*, is the roughly $2000 savings (in recruitment and training costs) for every nurses' aid retained on staff (Thomas, 1996, pp. 73–75).

Before concluding the discussion of LWCW in nursing homes, it is important to highlight findings and implications from two other, critical and innovative ethnographies of nursing home life, Diamond's (1992) *Making Gray Gold* and Nancy Foner's (1994) book *The Caregiving Dilemma*. The analytic and stylistic qualities of *Making Gray Gold* convey, perhaps more fully than had any prior source, the perspectives and challenges of LWCWs, in connection with the organization and funding of nursing home care. This source is also unique in having connected the daily struggles and routines of care, directly to the bureaucratic categories and demands of Medicaid and Medicare, in reflecting the project of institutional ethnography (e.g., Smith, 2005). Moreover, Diamond— the protagonist who, as a male, tended to elicit especially candid responses from field informants—also deals with the training, skills, work culture, and the emotional tenor of life among nursing assistants (Wellin, 2012). His account of the training process reveals the dominance of basic scientific and medical material (e.g., first aid training, anatomy and physiology, and medical terminology). Trainees, many of whom had modest formal schooling, language barriers, and children to support were encouraged to continue on for degrees as LPNs, a goal that was beyond the reach of most. In turn, little of the practical, challenging human contact involved in the work found its way into the training. He notes that one day, after a rote memory exam and the completion of supervised clinical rounds, students asked the teacher what to do next. The reply: "Why don't you go back and do some psycho-social stuff," is a comical request to the students who had haltingly been trying to get to know residents all day. Reviewing the 2004 version of the National Nursing Assistant Assessment Program practice

124   *Chris Wellin*

exam reflects that little has changed in the composition of the test. Out of sixty multiple-choice questions, half concern physical care skills, twenty-three concern the role of the nurse aid (e.g., communication, client rights, legal, and ethical behavior), and only eight are devoted to "psychosocial care skills" ("emotional and mental health needs," "spiritual and cultural needs"). Another resonant theme in the book is that of "Mother's wit," a folk term among Diamond's colleagues that connotes the intuitive, deft handling of the physical and emotional vicissitudes of the work (see also Hochschild, 1983):

> Mother's wit requires a host of unwritten emotional, physical, and interpersonal skills. But it also involves working with residents under a specific set of rules and regulations; trying to make sense of them and make them livable; trying to bridge everyday needs and external control. Take away Mother's wit and the industry is left without the women and the work that hold the building up, mediating between its base in everyday caretaking, and the superstructure of ownership that has been built upon it.
>
> (p. 237)

Foner's (1994) *The Caregiving Dilemma* extends Diamond's book in several important respects. Foner's is a more conventional ethnography, in the sense that her field role—as a volunteer and observer—enabled but did not commit her, as Diamond's did, to a distinctive perspective or participant voice. A woman, she was also less conspicuous, and was permitted to float more freely and thus paints a panoramic view of "Crescent View," a 200-bed, non-profit nursing home near New York City. A cultural anthropologist, with special expertise in ethnicity and immigration, Foner was naturally drawn to the Jamaican, Latina, and other ethnic groups in the very diverse LWCW staff. Where Diamond made mention of the great diversity of the LWC workforces in Chicago, there was little sense of ethnic traditions in caregiving as sources of meaning or support for workers. In fact, in some parts of the United States, one sees striking examples of ethnic employment *niches:* in the Bay area of San Francisco, for example, a majority of LWCWs in assisted living/residential care are Filipina; in cities such as Chicago, Detroit, and Milwaukee, African-Americans are preponderant in care work; Latinas are likely to be especially numerous in Texas, Florida, and southern California. There is suggestive evidence that recruitment and retention of such workers is strengthened when there are chains of referrals, to which those hiring give preference. In addition, in Foner's account, ethnic solidarity among LWCWs fosters more light-hearted, informal social gatherings and rituals than one finds in other accounts, and there is little evidence of racial/ethnic animosity, since the day shift care staff is divided between English-speaking Carribeans and Latinas, with African-Americans comprising only 20% (p. 18).[3] Foner's case suggests the utility of exploring ethnic cultures (which, in turn may shape views and norms of kinship) as mediators, which may promote interdependence at work and collective responses to grievances. Foner concludes that LWCWs are more help than hindrance to one

Paid Caregiving for Older Adults 125

another, and this solidarity and morale seem on balance to enhance the quality of care. In fact, the attempt to link staff working conditions with resident quality of life has become a theme for reform in nursing home care, and Foner provides clues and encouragement in this direction. Other of Foner's suggestions to enhance quality of care and life for all concerned are to include aides in care conferences (where they can play vital roles in reaching medical as well as socio-emotional goals); another is to hold in-service training outside of the work shift (so as not to disrupt the routines of care dyads), and be led by neutral trainers who are outside of the facility's authority structure; still another is to designate "primary assignments: each day and evening shift aide would become the facility expert on one or more residents—medically, psychologically, and socially—and represent the resident's interests with other staff" (p. 160; also see Paraprofessional Health Institute, 2003).

Trade-Offs for Care Workers in Home and Community-Based Settings

Before concluding with implications of the argument for training and education, we turn to LWCW in home and community-based settings. There are more than one million home health workers in the United States (Sommers, 2007), reflecting growth in numbers driven by combined effects of societal aging, the impact of the Olmstead Decision,[4] and efforts by state governments to reduce LTC expenditures (Foner, 1994, pp. 153–155). Trade-offs for LWCWs, in terms of relative work conditions and rewards in hospitals/nursing home and community-based care, can be severe. Demographically, as Montgomery, Holley, Deichert, and Kosloski (2005) showed, home care workers are more likely to be urban/suburban than rural; to be Latino or foreign born, rather than African-American (roughly half are white); to be older, with a mean age of 46 (vs. 36 among nursing home aides); and to earn less than hospital or nursing home aides (averaging some $12,000 per year as of 1999 for full-time, year-round workers, with higher hourly wages for part-time employees). It is hard to reckon what the average time and gasoline investment are for those traveling widely to serve multiple clients, but this investment is typically uncompensated. Thus, because they often work longer than 40 hours per week, the compensation for home health workers is even worse than is immediately apparent.

A sharp dilemma for home care workers is that, in resisting the more rigid, bureaucratic constraints of institutional care and seeking to provide care that is tailored for individuals, they pay a heavy price: in addition to the logistical and financial costs, they submerge their own quasi-professional status and identities more deeply, since they labor in isolation, without peers, within clients' social spaces. Rivas (2002), quoting a home health aide, sharpened the point:

> It's being able to put yourself in a situation where you are almost not seen . . . where the recipient of care is so able to do what he wants . . . it almost feels like, "I'm doing this," and you [the aide] are not even in the picture in

126 *Chris Wellin*

his mind . . . When the person's so in tune with what they're doing, what he wants to do and feels really good, and you're almost non-existent and yet you're there but somehow not there . . . [When they can do something] without even realizing that they're doing it because you're there, that's quality work right there.

(p. 175)

A distinction worth making is that, while workers such as the informant have rejected bureaucratic rules, schedules, and supervision, they have not necessarily forsaken *medical or technical* components of work. As Aronson and Neysmith (1996, p. 61) made clear, "Home health care services encompass a wide array of health and social services and employ a variety of care providers. Services may cover acute, rehabilitative, supportive, and palliative types of medical care, may be provided on long- or short-term bases, and are staffed by a range of professional providers (e.g., nurses, physiotherapists, nutritionists, social workers, and medical technicians)." This category of employment also involves "personal care" or "personal assistant services" that require less training and aim to maintain people at a functional plateau, in-line with the "independent living" model usually associated with younger disabled adults. So, whether/how home care workers can embrace techno-medical skills and knowledge, as a vehicle for mobility and other collective goals, is an important question. As hospitals discharge people more quickly; as more people receive care in the community, via private pay or waiver programs; and as disability rights/independent living agendas increasingly dovetail with government pressures to cut costs (especially sharp under the Affordable Care Act), systemic distinctions between care work processes and demands in varied settings are eroding (Kane, 1996).

Implications of Ethnographic Research on LWCW for Education and Training

In concluding, we draw together some of the implications of the foregoing for recruitment, training, and retention of LWCWs. There is a disparate but substantial literature in the area of training recommendations for LWCWs, much of which is distributed online or locally, by groups such as the *Direct Care Alliance* and the *National Network of Career Nursing Assistants*. My remarks draw on discussions with directors of these organizations, as well as on published material. It may be helpful to organize the discussion so as to address three key questions: (1) *What does the review of ethnographic research suggest are especially important challenges and objectives in the area of worker education and training?* (2) *How do the broader, structural labor and policy conditions of LWCW limit adoption of successful approaches to education and training?* and (3) *To what extent and how do skill demands in LWCW reflect broader changes in the service economy? If there are common trends or objectives—for workers and employers alike—what appear to be promising alliances or policies for enhancing quality of care and work life?*

Paid Caregiving for Older Adults   127

What Does the Review of Ethnographic Research Suggest are Especially Important Challenges and Objectives in the Area of Worker Education and Training?

LWCWs will not maximize educational and training benefits, of whatever quality, until we address the poor job quality that continues to be endemic (Dawson, 2007). The median hourly wage for LWCWs was just under $12 in 2017 (according to the Bureau of Labor Statistics), "significantly less than the median wage of $19 for all U.S. workers." If we assume full-time, year-round employment, average annual incomes in 2017 were $22,000 for home health and personal care aides; and $27,650 per year for nursing assistants, based on a median hourly wage of $13.29. Yet these figures overstate what many workers earn, since more than half of the home-care workforce is employed part time . . . "A typical home health aide in New York City works 30 hours per week and earns approximately $13,000 per year" (Dawson, 2007, p. 3). In addition, these workers have among the highest rates of occupational injury in the nation.

Direct care staff in elder care are also seeing increasingly frail residents, especially in nursing homes, and such care requires integration of technical/medical tasks, quasi-medical knowledge (of areas such as dementia care, nutrition, and effects of prescription drugs), with a "person-centered" philosophy and practice of caring (e.g., Folkemer & Coleman, 2006; Rahman & Schnelle, 2008; Sloane, Zimmerman, & Ory, 2001). There is substantial convergence between these needs and motivations and preferences of direct care workers. It has been noted (e.g., Gipson, 2007; Wellin & Jaffe, 2004) that many LWCWs have family care experiences, with grandparents or others, through which they are "called" to care and discover personal fulfillment. Supporting the provision of such care requires a shift in training orientations, from the instrumental, task-driven approach described by Diamond (1992) and others, to one focused more on sensitive communication (with residents as well as other members of residents' social and clinical networks), team-building, critical thinking and problem-solving, and health related knowledge—in addition to personal/bodily care skills. This is precisely the agenda laid out by advocacy and public policy groups that work closely with the direct care workforce (Paraprofessional Healthcare Institute, 2003b).

The same professional/advocacy groups promote modes of teaching and learning that depart from conventional classrooms, in favor of *Adult Learner-Centered Education*. In this approach, trainers acknowledge and tap students' practical life experiences, and locate the learning process, and focal problems, in the practical work situation rather than in more detached classroom settings (Paraprofessional Healthcare Institute, 2003b, pp. 6–7). Such training, if offered in the learner's work site (often but not always by nurses), can help solidify mutual respect between staff and administration, and enhances workers' sense of safety and support in the work organization. For this reason, innovative approaches to training direct care workers often forge a close linkage between staff recruitment, training, and retention, in order to create what are termed *Employers of Choice* (Paraprofessional Healthcare Institute, 2003a).

128   *Chris Wellin*

How do the Broader, Structural Labor and Policy Conditions of LWCW Limit Adoption of Successful Approaches to Education and Training?

Even the most enlightened approaches to education and training will fail unless conditions—in the labor market and in employing organizations—that undermine continuity and quality of care are addressed. There is an acute need to approach a living wage for such workers and to attach employment to basic fringe benefits such as health insurance and supplementary pensions, which a majority of workers now lack. There is every reason to expect that, were these goals achieved, many LWCWs would be able to achieve the tenure required for sensitive, competent, and fulfilling work. To some extent, greater compensation and career stability would check the downward social estimation of the work, especially in the eyes of clients and family members who, despite mistrust of paid care, have compelling reasons to make common cause with LWCWs. It is also increasingly clear (Kemper et al, 2008) that concerted efforts at *culture change* in nursing homes (such as the Eden Alternative and Greenhouse Models, mentioned above), which aim to create a more collaborative, team-orientation in which direct care staff enjoy greater affirmation of their knowledge and ongoing professional development, are essential complements to enhancing economic compensation if we are to reduce turnover.

Unfortunately, however, efforts to increase wages for such workers are blocked by powerful public policy constraints that override the interests and wishes of employing organizations, no less than those of direct care workers themselves. Conventional assumptions about labor demand and costs do not apply to LWCW, given that "primary financiers" distort and undercut "effective demands" for care work (Paraprofessional Healthcare Institute, 2001). Federal and state "third-party" payers (i.e., Medicaid and Medicare) effectively set wages by virtue of their reimbursement rates, and they have strong pressures to limit costs. As of the year 2000, "long-term care expenditures for the elderly alone totaled $123 billion—60 percent from public sources (primarily Medicaid and Medicare), 4 percent by private insurance, and 36 percent by out-of-pocket and other sources" (Paraprofessional Healthcare Institute, 2001, p. 2). Moreover, despite the massive profits in the LTC system, "the financial viability of the entire industry is currently endangered, in part by passage of the Balanced Budget Act 1997. [Between 1999 and 2001], 20 percent of all Medicare-funded home care agencies closed, and five of the ten largest for-profit nursing home chains entered Chapter 11 bankruptcy" (Paraprofessional Healthcare Institute, 2001, p. 2). In sum, the current structure and funding of LTC in the United States create enormous barriers in addressing recurring labor conditions in LWCW.

Apart from these macro-level funding and policy constraints, there are more proximate, "meso-level" obstacles to wide-spread adoption of better education and training programs. Though it would be ideal—both for policymakers and advocates for LWCWs—to define and promote universal goals or "best practices" in this area, such a goal is, for several reasons, elusive. Identifying and assessing training approaches and practices is made difficult by wide state-level variations, both in licensure and other requirements for employment, and in mandates regarding continuing education and training. Although there are "registries" of LWCWs in, and reciprocity agreements between, many states, there are many departures from the basic federal standard, and a lack of consistency across care settings. The standard for direct care staff in *nursing facilities* was established in 1987, as part of the Omnibus Budget Reconciliation Act passed during the Reagan Administration. It requires 75 hours of training, and 12 hours of in-service training per year, and passage of a "competency test" within 4 months of employment (Institute of Medicine, 2001, p. 197).

Inadequate or ad hoc standards regarding who provides training (e.g., employers, the Red Cross, community colleges) and wide-state-level variations in training only exacerbate these problems. Moreover, training requirements and policies in *residential care/assisted living* are set by states, rather than federally, and these vary widely. Hawes and colleagues (cited in Institute of Medicine, 2001, p. 204) "found that 20 percent of licensed board and care homes and 33 percent of unlicensed homes did not require *any* staff training. Of the facilities that required training, most did not require training to be completed before staff began providing care."

Clearly, as vital as formal education and training efforts are, there are issues of labor politics and collective action that cannot be ignored if we are to gain traction on this problem. For example, the ethnographic literature supports the contention that *tenure* in particular care positions and relationships is a key mechanism in achieving a high quality of care, and staffing ratios are clearly another. Some states and labor organizations have attempted to establish job ladders/wage premiums based on tenure, as well as mandated staffing ratios, attempts that vary independently from particular training or licensing requirements. We need to work toward consensus, across states and in connection with distinctive care settings and groups of care recipients, regarding these standards.

To What Extent and How do Skill Demands in LWCW Reflect Broader Changes in the Service Economy?

An implication of the ethnographic research is that providing instrumental/bodily care, with knowledge and skill, is a necessary but not sufficient criterion for excellence in working with the chronically ill or disabled, of whatever age. Instead (reflecting the disillusion that has followed the advent of Managed Care in recent decades), we see greater demand for collaborative, person-centered, holistic treatment—a social model—throughout the health care system.

Human resource consultants (e.g., Houston & Ferstl, 2007), analyzing the job skills that will increasingly be in demand in the years to come, note the importance of sensitive communication skills, independent problem-solving capacity, and comfort with social/cultural diversity in the workplace. Other key competencies include adaptability—the ability and willingness to cope with uncertainty—and self-management. These traits are clearly relevant to paid care work, and very often present—especially where supportive supervision, staffing ratios, and job tenure are favorable. This analysis suggests that while formal educational skills

130   *Chris Wellin*

and credentials (literacy and numeracy) will continue to be important factors in training and rewarding care workers, they are unlikely to be decisive in framing and pursuing policy agendas in the years ahead.

Acknowledgements

An earlier draft of this chapter was presented to the Panel on Skill Demands in Growing Service Sector Jobs at the National Academies Center in Washington, DC. The author gratefully acknowledges help and guidance in preparing this chapter from Margaret Hilton of the National Research Council of the National Academies. For invaluable support and contributions to my understanding of care work, I thank Carroll L. Estes, Institute for Health & Aging, Univeristy of California, San Francisco; Arlie R. Hochschild and Barrie Thorne, Department of Sociology and former co-directors of the Center for Working Families, an Alfred P. Sloan Center, at the University of California, Berkeley. Finally, I appreciate research assistance from Karisha Wilcox and comments by Peter Kemper,, my workshop discussant, and Edward Wellin. Special thanks to Clare Stacey for detailed discussions, suggestions, and additional sources from the literature.

Notes

1 For example, drawing on data from the National Center for Health Statistics, Quadagno (2005, p. 315) noted that "among those age 75 and over, 52 % suffer from arthritis, 42 % from hypertension, and 36% from heart disease. Alzheimer's and other dementias afflict nearly 9% of those between 80–84, 15% of those 85–89, and 29% of people age 90 and above" (p. 156).
2 See the U.S. Department of Health & Human Services report (2006) on the challenge and necessity of recruiting and retaining more social workers in LTC.
3 See Berdes and Eckert (2001) and Lepore (2007) for important discussions of race relations in caring relationships.
4 The decision mandates that, "states are required to place persons with disabilities . . . in community settings rather than in institutions when the State's treatment professionals have determined that community placement is appropriate, the transfer from institutional care to a less restrictive setting is not opposed by the affected individual, and the placement can be reasonably accommodated, taking into account the resources available to the State and the needs of others with . . . disabilities."

References

Abel, E.K. (1990). Daughters caring for elderly parents. In J.F. Gubrium & A. Sankar (Eds.), *The home care experience* (pp. 189–208). Newbury Park, CA: Sage.

Aronson, J., & Neysmith, S.M. (1996). You're not just in there to do the work: Depersonalizing policies and the exploitation of home care workers' labor. *Gender and Society*, 10(1), 59–77.

Atchley, R.C. (1996). *Frontline workers in long-term care: Recruitment, retention, and turnover in an era of rapid growth.* Report of the Scripps Gerontology Center. Oxford, OH: Miami University.

Paid Caregiving for Older Adults   131

Attewell, P. (1990). What is skill? *Work and Occupations,* 17(4), 422–448.

Barker, J.C. (2001). *The anthropology of care-giving: A 25-year review.* Paper presented at the Annual Meetings of the Gerontological Society of America, Chicago, IL.

Berdes, C., & Eckert, J.M. (2001). Race relations and caregiving relationships. *Research on Aging,* 23(1), 109–126.

Burawoy, M. (1979). *Manufacturing consent.* Chicago, IL: University of Chicago Press.

Cancian, F.M., & Oliker, S.J. (2000). *Caring and gender.* Thousand Oaks, CA: Pine Forge Press.

Castle, N.G., & Engberg, J. (2006). Organizational characteristics associated with staff turnover in nursing homes. *The Gerontologist,* 46(1), 62–73.

Dawson, S.L. (2007). *Recruitment and retention of paraprofessionals.* A presentation to the Institute of Medicine's committee on the future health care workforce for older Americans. New York: Paraprofessional Healthcare Institute.

Diamond, T. (1992). *Making gray gold.* Chicago, IL: University of Chicago Press.

Eaton, S.C. (1999). *Changing labor-management relations in nursing homes.* Proceedings of the 51st annual meeting of the Industrial Relations Research Association, Vol. 1, pp. 75–86.

England, P. (2005). Emerging Theories of Care Work. *Annual Review of Sociology,* 31, 381–399.

England, P., Budig, M., & Folbre, N. (2002). Wages of virtue: The relative pay of care work. *Social Problems,* 49(4), 455–473.

Fernandez, R.M. (2001). Skill-biased technological change and wage inequality: Evidence from a plant re-tooling. *American Journal of Sociology,* 107(2), 273–320.

Folkemer, D., & Coleman, B. (2006). *Home care quality: Emerging state strategies to deliver person-centered services.* Washington, DC: AARP Public Policy Institute.

Foner, N. (1994). *The caregiving dilemma.* Berkeley, CA: University of California Press.

Freidson, E. (1970/1988). *Profession of medicine.* Chicago, IL: University of Chicago Press.

Friedman, R.A., & McDaniel, D.C. (1998). In the eye of the beholder: Ethnography in the study of work. In K. Whitfield & G. Strauss (Eds.), *Researching the world of work* (pp. 113–126). Ithaca, NY: ILR/Cornell University Press.

Gatta, M., Boushey, H., and Applebaum, E. (2007). *High-touch and here-to-stay: Future Skill Demands in low wage service occupations.* Paper commissioned by the National Acadmies Center for Education on Research Evidence Related to Future Skill Demands. Washington, DC, May 31 to June 1.

Gipson, G. (1999). Building a network of stayers: Fix your staffing woes by giving good CNAs reason to stay. *Contemporary Long Term Care,* 22(5).

Glenn, E.N. (2000). Creating a caring society. *Contemporary Sociology,* 29(1), 84–94.

Goffman, E. (1961). *Asylums.* Garden City, NY: Doubleday/Anchor.

Gubrium, J.F. (1975). *Living and dying at murray manor.* New York: St. Martins.

Gubrium, J.F. (1993). *Speaking of life: Horizons of meaning for nursing home residents.* New York: Aldine de Gruyter.

Hecker, D.E. (2005). Occupational employments projections to 2014. *Monthly Labor Review* (November), 70–101.

Henderson, J.N. (1995). The culture of care in a nursing home: Effects of a Medical-ized model of long-term care. In J.N. Henderson & M.D. Vesperi (Eds.), *The culture of long term care: Nursing home ethnography* (pp. 37–54). Westport, CT: Bergin & Garvey.

Hochschild, A.R. (1983). *The managed heart.* Berkeley, CA: University of California Press.

132   Chris Wellin

Houston, J.S., & Ferstl, K.L. (2007). Future skill demands, from a corporate consultant perspective. Presented at the National Academies Workshop on Research Evidence related to Future Skill Demands.

Institute of Medicine. (2001). *Improving the quality of long-term care.* Washington, DC: National Academy Press.

Jaffe, D.J., & Wellin, C. (2008). June's troubled transition: Adjustment to residential care for older adults with dementia. *Care Management Journals,* 9(3), 128–137.

Kane, R.A. (1995). Expanding the home care concept: Blurring distinctions among home care, institutional care, and other long-term care services. *The Millbank Quarterly,* 73(2), 161–186.

Karner, T.X. (1998). Professional caring: Homecare workers as fictive kin. *Journal of Aging Studies,* 12(1), 69–83.

Kaye, S., Chapman, S., Newcomer, R.J., & Harrington, C. (2006). The personal assistant workforce: Trends in supply and demand. *Health Affairs,* 25(4), 1113–1120.

Kemper, P.,, Heier, B., Barry, T., Brannon, D., & Angelelli, J. (2008). What do direct care workers say would improve their jobs? Differences across settings. *The Gerontologist,* 48(1), 17–25.

Kitchener, M., Ng, T., Miller, N., & Harrington, C. (2005). Medicaid Home and Community-Based Services: National Program Trends. *Health Affairs,* 24(1), 206–212.

Kopiec, K. (2000). *The work experiences of certified nursing assistants in New Hampshire.* Report submitted to the New Hampshire Community Loan Fund.

Kusterer, K.C. (1978). *Know-how on the job: The important working knowledge of "unskilled" workers.* Boulder, CO: Westview Press.

Leidner, R. (1993). *Fast food, fast talk.* Berkeley, CA: University of California Press.

Lepore, M. (2007). *High retention direct care workers' experience and views of racism among assisted-living residents with dementia.* Paper read at the Annual Meetings of the Society for the Study of Social Problems (August), New York City.

Montgomery, R.J., Holley, L., Deichert, J., & Kosloski, K. (2005). A profile of home care workers from the 2000 census: How it changes what we know. *The Gerontologist,* 45(5), 593–600.

Morgan, L., & Kunkel, S. (2007). *Aging: the social context* (3rd ed.). New York: Springer.

Noblit, G.W., & Hare, R.D. (1988). *Meta-ethnography: Synthesizing qualitative studies.* Newbury Park, CA: Sage.

Paraprofessional Healthcare Institute. (2001). *Direct care health workers: The unnecessary crisis in long-term care.* A report submitted to the Domestic Strategy Group of the Aspen Institute. Washington, DC: The Aspen Institute.

Paraprofessional Healthcare Institute. (2003a). *Finding and keeping direct care staff.* A report in partnership with the Catholic Health Association. New York: PHI.

Paraprofessional Healthcare Institute. (2003b). *Training quality home care workers.* A technical report from the National Clearinghouse on the Direct Care Workforce. New York: PHI.

Parsons, T. (1951). *The social system.* Glencoe, IL: Free Press.

Piercy, K.W. (2000). When it is more than a job: Close relationships between home health aides and older clients. *Journal of Aging and Health,* 12(3), 362–387.

Potter, S.J., Churilla, A., & Smith, K. (2006). An examination of full-time employment in the direct care workforce. *Journal of Applied Gerontology,* 25(5), 356–374.

Quadagno, J. (2014). *Aging and the life course* (6th ed.). New York: McGraw-Hill.

Rahman, A.N., & Schnelle, J.F. (2008). The nursing home culture change movement: Recent past, present, and future directions for research. *The Gerontologist,* 48(2), 142–148.

Paid Caregiving for Older Adults   133

Rivas, L.M. (2002). Invisible labors: Caring for the independent person. In B. Ehrenreich & A.R. Hochschild (Eds.), *Global woman* (pp. 70–84). New York: Metropolitan Books.

Seavey, D. (2004). *The cost of frontline turnover in long-term care.* A report published by Better Jobs Better Care, a national research and demonstration project funded by the Atlantic Philanthropies and the Robert Wood Johnson Foundation. http://www.bjbc.org.

Shield, R.R. (1988). *Uneasy endings.* Ithaca, NY: Cornell University Press.

Shortell, S.M. (1998). The emergence of qualitative methods in health services research. *Health Services Research,* 34(5), 1083–1090.

Sloane, P.D., Zimmerman, S., & Ory, M.G. (2001). Care for persons with Dementia. In S. Zimmerman, P.D. Sloane, & J.K. Eckert (Eds.), *Assisted living: Needs, practices, and policies in residential care for the elderly* (pp. 242–270). Baltimore, MD: Johns Hopkins.

Smith, D.E. (2005). *Institutional ethnography: A sociology for people.* Lanham, MD: Alta Mira Press.

Sommers, D. (2007). "Overview of occupational projections to 2014: Evidence from the Bureau of Labor Statistics." Presentation to the National Acadamies Center for Education, Workshop on Research Evidence Related to Future Skill Demands, May 31 to June 1. Washington, DC.

Stacey, C.L. (2005). Finding dignity in dirty work: The constraints and rewards of low-wage home care labour. *Sociology of Health & Illness,* 27(6), 831–854.

Steinberg, R.J. (1990). Social construction of skill: Gender, power, and comparable worth. *Work and Occupations,* 17(4), 449–482.

Stone, D. (2000a). Caring by the book. In M.H. Meyer (Ed.), *Care work: Gender, labor and the welfare state* (pp. 89–111). New York, NY: Routledge.

Stone, D. (2000b). Why we need a care movement. *The Nation,* March 13.

Thomas, W.H. (1996). *Life worth living.* Acton, MA: VanderWyk & Burnham.

U.S. Department of Health and Human Services. (2006). *The supply and demand of professional social workers providing long-term care services.* Washington, DC: Office of the Assistant Secretary for Planning and Evaluation.

Vallas, S.P. (1990). The concept of skill: A critical review. *Work and Occupations,* 17(4), 379–398.

Wellin, C. (2012). "Making gray gold: A twenty-year retrospective" Paper presented at the Annual Meetings of the Society for the Study of Social Problems, Denver, CO.

Wellin, C., & Jaffe, D.J. (2004). In search of personal care: Barriers to identity support for cognitively impaired elders in residential facilities. *Journal of Aging Studies,* 18(3), 275–295.

Whitebrook, M. (1999). Child care workers: High demand, low wages. *Annals of the American Academy of Political and Social Science,* 563, 141–161.

CHAPTER **9**

Silver Alert: Societal Aging, Dementia, and Framing a Social Problem

Gina Petonito and Glenn W. Muschert

Silver Alert: A Program to Find Missing Adults with Cognitive Impairment

Silver Alert programs are designed to engage the public in helping locate missing adults and return them to their loved ones. In general, these policies are an adaptation or outgrowth of the AMBER (America's Missing: Broadcast Emergency Response) Alert system used to identify and return missing children to their parents or guardians. When an adult is reported missing, Silver Alert and related programs provide information to media outlets and the Department of Transportation to activate roadside signs and/or emergency alert systems through law enforcement agencies. Adults with significant cognitive impairments are most of these programs' central focus (Carr et al., 2009; Petonito, Muschert, Carr, Kinney, Robbins, & Brown, 2013).

Silver Alert legislation is lagging at the national level. Bills to establish a national Silver Alert policy were first introduced in Congress in 2008 (Silver Alert Bill to Help, 2009) and resurrected in 2013 (American Silver Alert Coalition, 2016). However, state Silver Alert programs exploded onto the local scene. Since the development of Georgia's Maddies Law in 2006, Silver Alert programs spread to 42 states as of 2014. The Silver Alert policy development trajectory is interesting in that the programs emerged as a fully formed "solution" to an ostensible problem marked by little prior claims making and little controversy regarding its passage. As such, Silver Alert became a "valence issue" (Nelson, 1984) that elicits a "strong, uniform emotional response and does not contain an adversarial quality" (p. 421). Utilizing a social constructionist approach (Loseke, 1999), this chapter will discuss how claims makers typified Silver Alert as such a policy, against a backdrop of apocalyptic demography (Gee & Gutman, 2000) with a focus on the harried caregiver.

Social Constructionism

Social problems constructionists study how claims makers argue that a particular condition, person, or group is problematic (Loseke, 1999) and in need of a specific

Silver Alert 135

remedy or solution. Claims makers use rhetorical and framing devices to convince their audiences that their arguments are credible. Constructionists call such strategies "social problems work" (Miller & Holstein, 1989), whereby claims makers *typify* social problems by constructing solution *packages* to ostensible social problems (Loseke, 1999). Constructionist analysts typically avoid taking a position on the truth of claims focusing instead on their development, typification, and proliferation. Although this position seems theoretically sound, practically many researchers privilege the existence of an objective condition while using constructionist tools to help unpack rhetorical arguments about social problems. This position, which we share, is called "contextual" constructionism (Best, 1989), which allows the analyst to analyze claims makers' rhetoric, while privileging the existence of a truth, which may be obscured by the claims.

Social Problems History

One of the maxims of the constructionist approach to social problems theorizing is that social problems move through a "natural history" of emergence, vigorous claims making, and the hammering out and implementation of a "solution." Rather than focus on the "objective" nature of the social problem, constructionists maintain that social problems emerge as a result of collective behavior (Blumer, 1971). Initial formulations centered on the emergence of social problems in a temporal sequence of stages. These stages include: initial awareness of the problem, the growing legitimization or delegitimization of the problem, the rise of constructed solutions to the problem or actions against it, the emergence of a salient policy, and the actual implementation of the policy (Blumer, 1971; Fuller & Myers, 1941; Kitsuse & Spector, 1973). Later developments explored the ways people construct and debate the merits of various policies within "policy domains" (Burstein, 1991). In the policy realm, Kingston (1984) identified three claims making streams: constructing the ostensible problem and getting it on the government agenda, debating and formulating alternative policies, and choosing the best strategy.

These seminal formulations of a "natural history" of social problems formation found their way into the early constructionist treatments of social problems, but nevertheless faced critique. Edwin Lemert (1951), one of the earlier users and critics of the approach, applied it to the post-war emergence of trailer camps, that drew unilateral critique from local city councils and planning and zoning committees independent of citizen outcry. Gabe and Bury's (1988) study of tranquilizer dependence suggests that a "natural history" of a social problem exists, but the model does not speak to the existence of a discourse that renders the problem legitimate in the larger cultural context. Additionally, Berger (2002) stated that social problems histories do not necessarily end with the implementation of social policy, as the Holocaust "solution" to the ostensible "Jewish problem" clearly reveals. In fact, Best's (2008) recent formulation suggests that the stage model is simply a heuristic device that helps model complex interactions between claims makers, media coverage, policymakers, social problems workers, and the

136   *Gina Petonito and Glenn W. Muschert*

public. In fact, he argues that there are many possibly pathways through the social problems process.

Indeed, the "valence issue" concept suggests that there are at least some social problems that do not move through typical "natural history" streams, because there are some issues upon which there is almost immediate public consensus, such as defining "abducted children" as a social problem (Gentry, 1988). However, as Beckett (1996) noted, even valence issues are subjects of debate. While no one is "pro-child abuse," claims regarding the causes and definitions of abuse are hotly contested and the ways the problem is framed shifts based upon sponsor activities, media practices, and dominant cultural discourses.

We study "Silver Alert" against this analytic backdrop. As was the case with child abduction and child abuse, the problem of cognitively impaired older adults going missing became yet another valence issue that challenges the existence of a "natural history" model. Yet, even valence issues are subject to claims making. Valence issues occupy a "policy domain" (Burstein, 1991), subject to claims making streams (Kingston, 1984). Claimants construct policy and get it on government agendas: they "discover" child abuse (Pfohl, 1977), or frame it in ways that resonate with dominant cultural themes (Beckett, 1996). Claimants also debate alternative solutions and choose the best one. Yet, even as a valence issue, the Silver Alert case remains exceptional. Silver Alert underwent Kingston's first stream, claims makers within the policy domain constructed the policy and got it on government agendas. But no policy debate of any consequence occurred. Rather, Silver Alert emerged as a fully formed "solution" to the missing adult problem and claims making was confined to *ex post facto* justifications for its necessity. We posit that one reason for the policy to emerge so fully formed is because it is a case of "domain expansion" from the popular AMBER Alert program.

Domain Expansion

Domain expansion (Best, 1990; Loseke, 1999) occurs when the problem's definition expands to include new cases or place more issues at contest. We argue that the main reason for Silver Alert programs' rise to prominence was because claims makers link them to the popular AMBER Alerts program designed to find missing children. This connection allows Silver Alert claims to plug into existing discourse surrounding AMBER Alerts. Domain expansion from AMBER Alerts results in two outcomes: claims makers call attention to similarities in policy, and they typify the clientele they will serve similarly. In the policy domain, Silver Alert becomes another form of AMBER Alert, transforming virtually everyone into an electronic posse. Plugging onto existing AMBER Alert infrastructure makes Silver Alert an inexpensive and simple "solution," enabling the policy to be a soft sell to a potentially frugal public and budget conscious legislators.

The similarities in claims between both cases also create profiles of the "people problem" involved (Loseke, 1993). Claimants typify both missing children and adults as sympathy worthy people problems separated from families and loved ones by forces outside of their control. And even though missing elders are adults, claims makers create childlike beings, what activist and scholar Maggie Kuhn called "wrinkled babies" (Estes & Portacolone, 2009), in need of our "protection." While condemnation-worthy adults strip missing children of agency, claims makers argue that Alzheimer's disease rips elders of personhood (Clarke, 2006). Finally, just like missing children stories involve frantic parents and legal guardians, Silver Alert claims center on worried caregivers. Claims makers endow caregivers, not elders, with voice. Silver Alert ensures the caregiver's peace of mind, not the person with Alzheimer's disease.

Apocalyptic Demography

While there are similarities between claims about missing children and adults, claims about missing children depart from the concerns raised about missing elders in that claims makers position the Silver Alert solution within "apocalyptic" demographic discourse, warning of dire societal consequences as society ages (Gee & Gutman, 2000; Longino, 2005). One consequence of such demographic change is that older retirees will outnumber and burden younger working people, resulting in an almost certain collapse of systems in place to secure health and other forms of well-being for the elderly (e.g., Medicare and Social Security). Contributing to this notion of system collapse is the specter of an "Alzheimer's Disease" apocalypse. According to the Alzheimer's Association website, more than five million Americans are living with Alzheimer's and one in three will die as a result of the disease or a related dementia. They project that, by 2050, the number of people with the disease will triple, fueled largely by the numbers of Baby Boomers reaching older ages (Alzheimer's Foundation of America, 2017). Prominently displayed is the statement "Alzheimer's is not a normal part of aging." Yet, as early as the late 1980s, researchers speculated how much of the organic and behavioral markers generally associated with the disease are distinct from normal aging (Gubrium, 1986a). Even then, claimants typified Alzheimer's as the "disease of the century" (Gubrium, 1986b).

Apocalyptic demography claimants extend their concerns over the caregiver's "burden" once the safety nets disappear. To them, elder care will fall squarely upon the shoulders of the younger generation of caregivers (Petonito & Muschert, 2015). This vision posits an ever-increasing number of wandering and missing elderly, resulting in potentially more "horror stories" of elders found dead if people do nothing. While missing children are victims of predatory adults which can potentially be controlled by laws and punishment, there is no shelter from Alzheimer's, which will only grow in prevalence as America ages. This apocalypse is solidified in the contrived "age wars" discourse (Gullette, 2004, p. 45), where the Boomers (i.e., those in the older generation) are "sucking up the oxygen" the younger generations need. The positioning of Silver Alert programs within this notion of discourse allows claims makers to rhetorically paint Silver Alert as a solution for everyone, not just those with dementia.

The Missing Person Problem

Missing persons exists as a social category both in public discourse and in academic scholarship. The best definition we have of a missing person is provided by Payne: someone who "appears to have gone missing when they do not fulfill their normal patterns of life and responsibilities because they are absent from where they are expected to be" (Payne, 1995, p. 335). Specifying such a definition, however, has proven to be difficult. Initial work on missing adults focused on healthy people who "choose," for a variety of reasons, to go missing. In fact, books aimed at assisting professionals in finding missing adults did not even include the category of missing adults with dementia or cognitive impairment (Rogers, 1986; Zoglio, 1980). Arguably, Koester and Stooksbury's (1993) study of missing persons, which included a section on persons with dementia, was among the first to shine a spotlight on the special needs of missing elders and persons with cognitive impairments. Most notably, they called for speedy recoveries of persons with dementia to avoid injury and death, a departure from the 24-hour waiting period required before a person was declared missing (Koester, 1998).

Even when narrowing down one's focus on elders or persons with cognitive impairment, defining the missing remains problematic, compounded by the fact that many elders with dementia wander away from caregiver's watchful eye, a phenomenon known as "critical wandering" (Algase, Moore, Vandeweerd, & Gavin-Dreschank, 2007). In this case, the elder "wanders away," subjecting him or herself to all matter of danger and perhaps death. Yet, even in this case, complexities abound. For example, in their study of ninety-nine caregivers of persons with dementia, McShane, Gelding, Kenward, Kenward, Hope, & Jacoby (1998) found that 44% of individuals with dementia went out on their own and 33% lived alone. Rowe and colleagues' (2011) review of 266 cases discovered that caregivers sometimes permitted persons with dementia to leave their homes or care facilities. Of these, 48% went missing during a planned independent activity in the community; 28% were driving and 20% were walking. Similarly, the interview styudy by Bowen, McKenzie, Steis, & Rowe (2011) with caregivers of veterans with dementia revealed that almost half of missing veterans (44%) were engaged in normal independent activity, such as walking around the yard or retrieving the mail. When they took too long to return, caregivers discovered they were missing, and in 46% of the cases, caregivers had seen the missing veteran less than 10 minutes prior.

Finally, this literature reveals that in some cases, elders are "found" even though no one reported them lost. McShane and colleagues' (1998) study of 99 cases of missing persons with dementia reported that passers-by found eight of these people by chance and reported them to the authorities. Similarly, Bass, Rowe, and Moreno's (2007) examination of the Alzheimer's Association's Safe Return program discovered two times as many Safe Return enrollees are found prior to being reported missing, given that Good Samaritans alert Safe Return by calling the number on an elder's bracelet or necklace prior to them ever being missed (Bass, Rowe, Moreno, & McKenzie, 2008). In fact, many of the studies on missing people with dementia are based on retrospective studies that examine newspaper reports (Hunt, Brown, & Gilman, 2010; Lai, Jenny, Chung, Wong, Faulkner, & Ng, 2003; Muschert, Petonito, Bhatta, & Manning, 2009; Rowe & Bennett, 2003) that essentially report cases where caregivers' initial searches failed, and the missing elder is reported to local authorities.

Conceivably, many more elders go missing than are reported as such by newspapers; yet there is no consensus on the problem's scope. Koester and Stooksbury discovered that 42 (15 percent) of the 295 missing adult cases recorded in Virginia between 1986 and 1992 involved missing persons with dementia (1995). Yet, Bowen at al. (2011) found that 61.5% (24) of 39 home-dwelling veterans with dementia went missing at some point during the year. Such a finding lends credence to Rowe and Glover's (2001) warning that due to the unpredictable nature of wandering behavior, all cognitively impaired persons "in all situations are at risk" (p. 315). Yet, while the *potential* of going missing due to wandering certainly exists, the actual percentage of missing elders who go missing in any given year remains in doubt.

Given the uncertain existence of an objectively widespread problem of missing elders, the rapid emergence of Silver Alert as a policy to deal with this social problem is surprising, but not without precedent. As Lemert's (1951) study of trailer park camps suggests, policymakers can create plans to deal with what they deem problematic separate from scholarly study or even widespread public outcry. What is unique about Silver Alert is how the policy underwent so little scrutiny in its planning stages, given its relatively swift passage through various legislatures. With these ideas in mind, this study will analyze the ways claims makers framed the problem of missing elders and how they advanced the Silver Alert "solution."

Data Collection and Method

Data were collected via Lexis-Nexis Search of major US newspapers, using the following search terms: "Missing" and "Alzheimer's" or "Missing" and "Dementia" or "Missing" and "Cognitive Impairment." The project's study period ran from January 1, 2006, to September 30, 2008. We identified 140 articles that covered 80 unique cases. Given these search criteria, Silver Alert claims are embedded within stories about searches for missing adults which include traditional search and rescue operations as well as other programs designed to recover older adults with dementia. These data provide rich information on Silver Alert in that it makes it possible to compare and contrast Silver Alert claims with claims about other search and rescue efforts. We supplemented these data with transcripts of House, Senate and state Silver Alert bills, information from State Silver Alert websites and sponsoring representatives and senators' websites. Data were analyzed using the constant comparative method.

Our analysis will open with claims regarding the problem's growing prevalence and how claimants use these claims of apocalyptic demography to justify Silver Alert. We will then show how claimants used already existing frames to advance their arguments attesting to the necessity of Silver Alert. First, we will discuss how Silver Alert policy fits into the discourse surrounding search and rescue operations.

140   *Gina Petonito and Glenn W. Muschert*

Next we will show how claims makers piggybacked Silver Alert onto the already existing AMBER Alerts model. Finally, we will discuss how domain expansion from AMBER Alerts creates a cheap, easy-to-implement solution for harried caregivers rather than the missing elder.

A Widespread Problem

Even though Silver Alert emerged as a fully formed policy, claims makers engaged in typical social problem gambits. A narrowly defined problem affecting only a fraction of people, which some of the research studies suggest is the case, would be problematic. Claims makers adopted the strategy of framing the condition as "widespread," with horrifying consequences if ignored. The focus was not on any existing problem of missing elders, but was on the *potential* problem that will result once the baby boomers reach old age. Akin to labeling theory's notion of "potential labeling" (Becker, 1973; Glassner & Corzine, 1978) where social actors label categories of people as potentially deviant regardless of action, claims makers are suggesting that a potential future problem exists, even when the existing problem may be currently a minor one. As noted, claims makers draw from the "apocalyptic demography" discourse which warns that once the Medicare and Medicaid safety nets collapse, the burden of caring for society's elders will fall to the young (Gee & Gutman, 2000; Longino, 2005).

For Silver Alert proponents, the pending catastrophe is the widespread increase in the numbers of people with Alzheimer's disease. Numerous claims about this concern exists in our data: 53,000 people in South Carolina according to an AP piece (Davenport, 2008) or "1 in 8 people over the age of 65," according to the Silver Alert Grant Program Act (2008). This population will only grow, claimants say: "Every 71 seconds another individual in the United States develops this disease" (Silver Alert Grant Program Act). In many cases, the current number of people with Alzheimer's disease is contrasted with some future and much larger number: "The state has more than 2.7 million residents older than 60, according to the Texas Department of Aging and Disability Services in Austin. Within 25 years, that number will be about 7.4 million" (State's "Silver Alert," 2008).

Plugging into this discourse, claims makers construct a "causal story" (Stone, 1989) about how catastrophic demography will result in higher rates of missing persons. The causal argument is as follows: an aging America will create greater numbers of people with dementia leading to more wandering behavior, resulting in a greater "caregiver burden" (Clarke, 2006). In this causal story, the problem is constructed as an accidental one—demented older people inadvertently wander away. However, the victims in these stories are not the missing person, but the harried family saddled with a more salient "burden." Claims makers project the emergence of a future catastrophic problem, but they ground their claims in present stories. They point to current instances of wandering elders and the impact their wandering has on the caregivers, all the while implying that greater numbers of caregivers will be saddled with these worries. Silver Alert, then, becomes a proactive solution, for the legions of future over-burdened caregivers.

Wandering and the Caregiver Burden

Many claims makers refer to the statistic published by the Alzheimer's association that "60%" of those suffering from the illness will wander (Silver Alert Grant Program Act; Alerts Sought, 2008). The scholarly literature on wandering seems to reinforce claims makers' concerns, presenting it as a problem to be controlled and ultimately prevented (see Dewing, 2006). However, there is an emerging literature that suggests a confusion between wandering off and going missing (Bowen et al., 2011; Rowe et al., 2011; Rowe, Greenblum, Boltz, & Galvin, 2012; Rowe, Greenblum, & D'Aoust, 2012). What several of these scholars note is that even elders with dementia may go missing when conducting their normal daily activities (Bowen et al., 2011; Rowe, Greenblum, Boltz, et al., 2012). Such findings could be due to the current fuzziness in the literature regarding definitions of wandering (Algase et al., 2007) and Alzheimer's disease (Silverstein, Flaherty, & Tobin, 2002). "Wandering" could range from purposeful meandering that may benefit the person with dementia, helping them fulfill an absent need or duty (Robinson et al., 2007), to "critical wandering" that may lead to dangerous consequences (Algase et al., 2007). Similarly, persons with cognitive impairment may not all have Alzheimer's disease, nor may they be in advanced stages (Gubrium, 1986a; Silverstein et. al, 2002). Silver Alert claimants ignore these nuances, and in any case, they do not typify wandering a problem for the wanderer, but for the over-burdened caregivers and the family. Consider this newspaper account:

> Renee Trent, an Ooltewah resident, said she was lucky when her husband, who suffers from Alzheimer's disease, roamed from their home because he had more than a milelong walk before reaching the closest highway. But every time he walked away, she panicked. He now lives in an assisted living center.
>
> (Alerts Sought, 2008)

Note how Trent is "lucky" because "he" had a milelong walk to the nearest highway, so he could, presumably, be further away from danger. Nevertheless, his wandering was a source of *her* panic, relieved only by moving him to an assistance center. This stripping of agency of the older wanderer is a recurring theme in Silver Alert claims.

> "The thing that concerned me most, I learned as a caregiver is that she could be manipulative and that she could hide her dementia," said Kathy Simpson. "The most stressful thing as a caregiver was my mother hurting herself or her getting out and me not being able to find her."
>
> (Mattie's Call, 2006)

Simpson's mother is not only a wanderer but also a "manipulative" one, "hiding" her dementia from others. Consistent with other scholarly analysis on typification of people with Alzheimer's, Simpson's mother, Lee, is voiceless, her world and personality described by her daughter (Clarke, 2006). Removing voice also removes agency. Wandering is not stressful to Lee but is to her daughter Kathy. Silver Alert,

142 *Gina Petonito and Glenn W. Muschert*

or in this case "Mattie's Call," is aimed at Kathy, relieving her of her caregiver's burden: "Now, there's a bill that should prohibit fears like Kathy Simpson's from becoming true throughout the state" (Mattie's Call, 2006). Although blameless, the wandering elder becomes the "troublesome person" (Loseke, 1993), creating a problem for the equally blameless caregiver. The claims suggest that the villain in this case is the formidable disease that has cruelly stolen Renee's husband and Kathy's mother from them (see Clarke, 2006).

Accounts dealing with wandering are punctuated by "horror stories," where everyone's nightmares have come true. While many go missing, as was the case with Sumpter, South Carolina resident Barbara Ellen Brunson, a 66-year-old woman who wandered away from her care facility (Davenport, 2008), some experience worse, as in the case of a Pinellas County, Florida woman who went missing and was later found dead (West Fla. Community, 2008). Claims makers frame Silver Alert as a way of preventing these horrific consequences from occurring. For example, Sumter Police Chief Patty Patterson posits that Silver Alert would have helped find Barbara Ellen Brunson, a 66-year-old woman "known for wandering away before," by getting the "word out faster" (Davenport, 2008).

Reading story after story of harried families and their worries renders the person with dementia invisible, subsumed under the trope of "burden." As Longino notes (2005, p. 81), depicting older people this way objectifies them. They become merely "the burden," stripped of agency, incapable of constructing creative solutions to meet their own needs. Silver Alert then emerges as a "one program fits all" policy for this objectified group.

Silver Alert as Domain Expansion

As noted, Silver Alert exists as a case of domain expansion of AMBER alerts and they position claims about the policy within that context. AMBER Alerts allows claims makers to place Silver Alert within an already existing popular frame, enabling them to present a new and commanding problem from a familiar standpoint (Loseke, 1999). Like AMBER Alerts, Silver Alert aides existing search and rescue operations, and is a definitive improvement over other programs.

The Already Existing Problem

Traditional methods exist for finding missing people. A "broken stick and a footprint," for example, "speak volumes" to the Vermillion County's Special Tactics Search and Rescue Team (Huchel, 2008). "First rate K-9 units" (West Virginia, 2008) helicopters and low flying planes and FBI resources are also mentioned (Search for missing, 2008). The bottom line, however, is that a missing person is found by other people, either by simply using their "eyes and ears" or by using methods that will amplify their capacities. And the more people looking, the better. For instance, police asked "farmers and ranchers" to check "their land and buildings" for a missing man (Police, CAP search, 2008). Reports of missing people include identifying data and requests for people with information to call specific numbers or alert appropriate authorities. For example, Russell Kilen, a Battle of the Bulge veteran, told his family about "seeking out abandoned buildings and haystacks as an infantryman to escape the cold" (Sheriff says, 2007), suggesting that people should inspect such places. Tracking the individual stories reveals that these appeals work in about a quarter of the cases. In 27.5% cases, the individual was found, and an unrelated individual found several missing persons. Unforeseen circumstances that prevent people from looking, such as inclement weather or other factors, are deemed problematic. As one official lamented, a person who went missing one day after hunting season ended deprived them of the "many more eyes and ears in the field" (Search for missing, 2008).

Other existing programs were discussed in our data. One claimant referred to them as a "mini-industry of technologies" that "promise to find lost Alzheimer's patients" (Neergaard, 2007), also called "gerontechnologies" (see Mahmood, Yamamoto, Lee, & Steggell, 2008) designed to help older adults "age in place." These technologies range from simple identification bracelet or tag with a number linked to a database, the hallmark of the Alzheimer's Association's Safe Return Program, to radio frequency tags worn by residents of an assisted living facility to a full-scale tracking system, the mainstay of Project Lifesaver (see Neergaard, 2007). The scholarly literature suggests that elderly people can choose such devices (Mahmood et al., 2008; Robinson, Brittain, Lindsay, Jackson, & Oliver, 2009) and there were depictions of such agency within our data. In one instance, readers are introduced to a bracelet wearer's response to the device: "'I'm a marked man,' joked Melnick, of Hainesport, N.J. 'The police can pick me up anywhere'" (Neergaard, 2007), suggesting that Melnick chose to wear it. This characterization is not typical, however. Immediately afterwards, Melnick's wife is depicted as receiving "peace of mind" from the device, implying that the device is for her, rather than for him.

Similar to the claims made about Silver Alert, claims making regarding Project Lifesaver in newspapers focuses on ways in which other search and rescuers and family members can find a person. In fact, Project Lifesaver can track anyone or anything. While the article's focus was on finding wayward elderly (Cherokee, 2006) or cognitively impaired adults (W. Va. Hiker, 2007), the device was attached to 11-year-old children (Missing persons, 2007), lost hikers, and autistic children (Virginia search and rescue, 2007), even wildlife and hunting dogs, for which the system was first designed (Missing persons, 2007).

"Piggybacking" off of Amber Alerts

Even though part of the search and rescue discourse, Silver Alert, as implied by its name, fashioned itself as an extension of the AMBER alert program, designed to find missing children. For example, the text of the North Carolina Silver Alert brochure says that their program "builds off the success of the state's AMBER alerts system," and the House Bill 5898 text introduced by Florida Rep. Bilirakis similarly refers to AMBER alerts (Silver Alert Grant Program, 2008). As a comprehensive high-tech notification system, Silver Alert was the premier plan,

144   *Gina Petonito and Glenn W. Muschert*

according to claims makers, with the others existing as adjunct or supplement to it (see Proposal would create, 2007). In some cases, policymakers associated with other programs extolled the virtues of Silver Alert. For example, Alice Hoffman, coordinator of the state Safe Return, says: "This is giving families a sense of hope . . . Satisfaction and trust in their county because they are setting a precedent to get this alert program started" (Mattie's Call, 2006).

The main benefit for installing Silver Alert is what claims makers refer to as "the need for speed." Silver Alert would create an alarm system that would "quickly" find missing elderly (Davenport, 2008; Della Santi, 2008). Ross County Sheriff Dale Gilette defends the proposed Ohio Silver Alert plan, apparently cognizant of the Koester's (1998) recommendations: "If you don't find a missing adult that has Alzheimer's within the first 24 hours, the chances of finding that person alive and well goes down dramatically" (Proposal would create, 2007). Claimants argue similarly about speed in relation to Project Lifesaver, tracking people from an average of 30 minutes (W. Va hiker, 2007) to as little as 9 minutes in a demonstration (Clark County, 2006). Just how much more quickly Silver Alert would actually work is not specified.

Perhaps the most compelling argument that Silver Alert claims makers pose is that it is relatively cheap solution. Project Lifesaver is expensive. It "costs $275 per person to enroll in the Clark County Program, . . . a $10 monthly fee for maintenance of the wrist transmitters" and $5,500 for training and equipment came from the sheriff department budget (Clark County, 2006), but "it is considerably cheaper than launching a large-scale search" (Ore. County plans, 2007). Silver Alert is considerably cheaper than both of them, according to claimants, due to its use of preexisting AMBER alert technology (see Della Santi, 2008). As West Virginia Delegate Cliff Moore noted:

> 'It's just like the Amber Alert,' Moore said. 'But it's for the elderly people and people with mental disabilities. I just thought it would be something good we can be doing in West Virginia. We can plug right into the Amber Alert system and it's not going to cost the state any more money. But what a great thing to do for seniors and people with mental disabilities'.

Rhetorically, then, what claims makers accomplish by linking Silver Alert to the popular AMBER alerts policy is to create what constructionist scholars have suggested is the "ideal" or most adoptable solution to an ostensible social problem (Loseke, 1999): understandable, quick, easy, and cheap—a "no brainer." As the an editorial in the West Virginia Bluefield Daily Telegraph queries: "If West Virginia can implement a system to help quickly locate Alzheimer's patients or others suffering from mental disabilities without extra charge to taxpayers why not do it?" (West Virginia newspapers, 2008).

Discussion

Despite the lack of public debate on its efficacy, Silver Alert stands as a socially constructed solution within the policy domain dealing with missing adults. The

Silver Alert case challenges the existing constructionist notion of a "natural history" of social problem. Rather than undergo a robust claims making process, where the problem was brought to public attention and various solutions debated in the halls of policy-making, Silver Alert emerged on the scene as a fully formed solution to the ostensible problem of missing adults. Debates about its efficacy, how it would complement existing programs such as Safe Return and Project Lifesaver, were notably missing. Except for some mild critique levied by two newspaper reporters (Davenport, 2008, and Neergaard, 2007) (and summarily deflected), Silver Alert burst onto the scene as the best and most comprehensive solution to the problem. Just like Lemert noted nearly 50 years earlier, fully formed policies can emerge and be implemented with little prior claims making. Given these findings, we suggest, along with Lemert (1951), that any natural history or stage model of social problems need empirical support. While written years before, Lemert's work presaged the later concern with "ontological gerrymandering" (Woolgar & Pawluch, 1985), privileging the existence of a model that can explain claims making processes while examining the relativity of those very processes. Our research, along with Lemert's, suggests that natural history and stage models in all their forms remain a true heuristic tool, enabling researchers to systematically map social problems claims making in most, but not all instances.

The Silver Alert case also demonstrates how claims are shaped when positioned with another existing and ostensibly "successful" social problems solution. As an expansion of AMBER Alerts, Silver Alert claim makers are able to use rhetoric that places wandering elders in a similar discourse of helplessness as children. Stripped of agency, elders become an object of the policy, while the caregivers are given voice. Elders become children, or what Maggie Kuhn called "wrinkled babies" (Estes & Portacolone, 2009) in need of the larger society's protective care. Moreover, both cases emerge out of a discourse of fear that we are at risk of having bad things happen (Beck, 1999). Both AMBER and Silver Alert evoke altruistic fear, which Warr described as the fear that individuals have for the safety of others, which often means one's children (Warr, 1992), but can also be extended to one's elderly parents (Snedker, 2006).

Given the societal pervasiveness of fear, programs like AMBER and Silver Alert present a societal solution to an individual trouble. As Griffen and Miller (2008) suggested with regard to AMBER alerts, Silver Alert can be a type of theater that generate the appearance rather than the fact of a solution to a missing person problem. While Griffen and Miller's (2008) concept, "crime control theater," relates specifically to crime, we are extending the notion here to the missing adult case where the "people problem" is confined to unintentional victims. In both cases, the policies advertise "official commitment" to people's safety; safely returned individuals are used to "reinforce the public's faith in law enforcement"; and potentially the entire society becomes part of an "electronic posse" dedicated to finding a loved one, reinforcing our reliance on cutting-edge electronic technology (Griffen & Miller, 2008, p. 167; Petonito & Muschert, 2015).

While there is certainly nothing wrong with promoting public concern with missing people, however symbolically, we warn, as Griffen and Miller (2008) do,

146 *Gina Petonito and Glenn W. Muschert*

the risks of overselling such programs. In particular, we worry about the increasing "surveillance creep" into our everyday lives. While gerotechnology may have many actual and perceived benefits to help older adults "age in place" (Mahmood et al., 2008), the impact of structural ageism cannot be ignored. As Quadagno (2008) noted, earlier forms of ageism, defined as perceived discrimination against people due to age (Butler, 1969), have been replaced by a "new ageism," characterized by a patronizing and overly solicitous attitude toward older adults. Incorporating ageism into the Silver Alert equation lays bare the existence of power relations and the unequal relations that infuse the incorporation of technology. Yet, as Kenner notes (2008), ageism and its implications are often absent in discussions about gerotechnologies. Silver Alert and other high-tech solutions to the problem of missing adults promise the freedom to age in place, but at the cost of "securing the elderly body" (Kenner, 2008). Hence, any discussion of Silver Alert should include a parallel discourse addressing issues of privacy and the relative powerlessness of the elderly in relation to their caregivers and the rest of society. As the above data reveal, claims about Silver Alert focus on relieving caregivers of their burden, absolving them of any guilt regarding their cognitively impaired and wandering loved one. In framing the claims this way, claims makers strip elders' of agency and voice.

Silver Alert then walks a fine line between caring and control. Silver Alert and associated programs empower older people allowing them "age in place." Elders can choose from an array of gerotechnologies (Mahmood et al., 2008) that can help them feel secure at home, while Silver Alert can provide the same peace of mind when away from home. In the specific case of Silver Alert, however, public rhetoric does not address these issues. Instead, caregivers occupy the center of this caring discourse. Silver Alert becomes a program designed to provide peace of mind for the more valued caregiver struggling to monitor a loved one controlled by a powerful, fearsome disease (Clarke, 2006) that renders an elder incapable of speaking for him or herself. The Silver Alert solution, then, constructed as a solution to manage individuals with disease never questioned why elders even need to be empowered. As Kenner (2008, p. 267) noted, such technologies "reentrench and reinforce the norms, hierarchies, and oppression of ageism by rendering them invisible." "Aging in place," with its discourse of caring and choice, is transformed to "ageism in place" (Kenner, 2008), with its reproduction of power and control. What we are left with are theatrical "solutions" that emerge and are implemented with little debate regarding their efficacy, much less their morality, that extend a discourse of control to all of us.

Acknowledgments

The authors would like to acknowledge the collaboration of the following colleagues in the Miami University Silver Alert Project: Tirth Bhatta, J. Scott Brown, Dawn Carr, Jennifer Kinney, Emily Robbins. We would also like to thank C. Lee Harrington for her review of an earlier version of this manuscript.

References

Alerts Sought in Tennessee for dementia patients. (2008, August 23). *The Associated Press State & Local Wire.*

Algase, D.L., Moore, D.H., Vanderweerd, C., & Gavin-Dreschank, D.J. (2007). Mapping the maze of terms and definitions in dementia-related wandering. *Aging & Mental Health*, 11, 686–698. DOI: 10.1080/ 13607860701366434.

Alzheimer's Foundation of America. (2017). *Alzheimer's disease facts and figures.* Retrieved October 30, 2017 from www.alz.org/facts/overview.asp#prevalence.

American Silver Alert Coalition. (2016). *Silver Alert legislation.* Retrieved January 4, 2016, from http://silveralertbill.com.

Bass, E., Rowe, M.A., & Moreno, M. (2007). The Alzheimer's Association's Safe Return program for persons who wander. In A. Nelson & D.L. Algase (Eds.), *Evidence-based protocols for managing wandering behaviors* (pp. 251–258). New York: Springer.

Bass, E., Rowe, M.A., Moreno, M., & McKenzie, B. (2008). Expanding participation in Alzheimer's Association Safe Return(r) by improving enrollment. *American Journal of Alzheimer's Disease and Other Dementias*, 23, 447–450. DOI: 10.1177/1533317508320974.

Beck, U. (1999). *World Risk Society.* Malden, MA: Polity Press.

Becker, H. (1973). *Outsiders: Studies in the sociology of deviance.* New York: Free Press.

Beckett, K. (1996). Culture and the politics of significance: The case of child sexual abuse. *Social Problems*, 42, 57–76.

Berger, R. (2002). *Fathoming the Holocaust: A social problems approach.* New York: Aldine de Gruyter.

Best, J. (1989). Extending the constructionist perspective: A conclusion and an introduction. In J. Best (Ed.), *Images of issues: Typifying contemporary social problems* (pp. 243–253). New York: Aldine de Gruyter.

Best, J. (1990). *Threatened children: Rhetoric and concern about child victims.* Chicago, IL: University of Chicago Press.

Best, J. (2008). *Social problems.* New York: W.W. Norton.

Blumer, H. (1971). Social problems as collective behavior. *Social Problems*, 18, 298–306.

Bowen, M.E., McKenzie, B., Steis, M., & Rowe, M. (2011). Prevalence of and antecedents to dementia-related missing incidents in the community. *Dementia and Geriatric Cognitive Disorders*, 6, 406–412. DOI: 10.1159/000329792.

Burstein, P. (1991). Policy domains: Organization, culture and policy outcomes. *Annual Review of Sociology*, 17, 327–350.

Butler, R. (1969). Age-ism: Another form of bigotry. *The Gerontologist*, 9, 243–246.

Carr, D., Muschert, G.W., Kinney, J., Robbins, E., Petonito, G., Manning, L., et al. (2010). Silver Alerts and the problem of missing adults with dementia. *The Gerontologist*, 50, 149–157. DOI: 10.1093/ geront/gnp102.

Cherokee County Programs Tracks Down Wayward Elderly. (2006, September 10). *The Associated Press State & Local Wire.*

Clark County Program Electronically Tracks Missing People. (2006, March 26). *The Associated Press State & Local Wire.*

Clarke, J.N. (2006). The case of the missing person: Alzheimer's disease in mass print magazines 1991–2001. *Health Communication*, 19, 269–276.

Davenport, J. (2008, September 23). Police create senior wandering warning system. *The Associated Press State & Local Wire.*

Della Santi, A., (2008, September 15). NJ advances 'Silver Alert' to find lost seniors. *The Associated Press State & Local Wire.*

148 *Gina Petonito and Glenn W. Muschert*

Dewing, J. (2006). Wandering into the future: Reconceptualizing wandering 'a natural and good thing.' *International Journal of Older People Nursing, 14*, 239–249.

Estes, C., & Portacolone, E. (2009). Maggie Kuhn: Social theorists of radical gerontology. *International Journal of Sociology and Social Policy, 20*, 15–25.

Fuller, R.C., & Myers, R.R. (1941). The natural history of a social problem. *American Sociological Review, 6*, 320–328.

Gabe, J., & Bury, M. (1988). Tranquilizers as a social problem. *Sociological Review, 36*, 320–352.

Gee, E.M., & Gutman, G. (Eds.). (2000). *The overselling of population aging: Apocalyptic demography, intergenerational challenges, and social policy*. New York: Oxford University Press.

Gentry, C.S. (1988). The social construction of abducted children as a social problem. *Sociological Inquiry, 58*, 413–425.

Glassner, B., & Corzine, J. (1978). Can labeling theory be saved? *Symbolic Interaction, 1*, 74–89.

Griffen, T., & Miller, M.K. (2008). Child abduction, AMBER Alert, and crime control theater. *Criminal Justice Review, 33*, 159–176.

Gubrium, J. (1986a). *Oldtimers and Alzheimer's: The descriptive organization of senility*. Greenwich, CT: JAI Press.

Gubrium, J. (1986b). The social preservation of the mind: The Alzheimer's disease experience. *Symbolic Interaction, 9*, 37–51. Retrieved Apr. 4, 2017 from www.jstor.org/stable/10.1525/si.1986.9.1.37.

Gullette, M. (2004). *Aged by Culture*. Chicago, IL: University of Chicago Press.

Huchel, B. (2008, August 27). Illinois style: The world of the search and rescue team. *The Associated Press State & Local Wire*.

Hunt, L.A., Brown, A.E., & Gilman, I. (2010). Drivers with dementia and outcomes of becoming lost while driving. *American Journal of Occupational Therapy, 64*, 225–232. DOI: 10.5014/ajot.64.2.225.

Kenner, A.M. (2008). Securing the elderly body: Dementia, surveillance, and the politics of 'aging in place.' *Surveillance and Inequality, 5*, 252–269.

Kingston, J.W. (1984). *Agendas, alternatives and public policies*. Boston, MA: Little Brown.

Kitsuse, J.I., & Spector, M. (1973). Toward a sociology of social problems: Social conditions, value judgments, and social problems. *Social Problems, 20*, 407–419.

Koester, R.J. (1998). The lost Alzheimer's and related disorders subject: New research and perspectives. Response 98 NASR Proceedings. National Association of Search and Rescue, Chantilly, Virginia, pp. 165–181.

Koester, R.J., & Stooksbury, D.E. (1992). Lost Alzheimer's subjects-profiles and statistics. *Response*, 11, 20–26. Retrieved from http://dbs-sar.com/SAR_Research/Response.htm.

Lai, C., Jenny, K.Y., Chung, C.C., Wong, T., Faulkner, L.W., & Ng, L. (2003). Missing older persons with dementia—A Hong Kong view. *Hong Kong Journal of Social Work, 37*, 239–245. DOI: 10.1142/S0219 246203000214.

Lemert, E. (1951). Is there a natural history of social problems? *American Sociological Review, 16*, 217–223.

Longino, C.F. Jr. (2005). The future of ageism: Baby boomers at the doorstep. *Generations* (Fall), 79–83.

Loseke, D. (1993). Constructing conditions, people, morality, and emotion. In J.A. Holstein & G. Miller (Eds.), *Constructionist Controversies* (pp. 207–216). New York: Aldine de Gruyter.

Loseke, D. (1999). *Thinking about social problems*. New York: Aldine de Gruyter.

McShane, R., Gelding, K., Kenward, B., Kenward, R., Hope, T., & Jacoby, R. (1998). The feasibility of electronic tracking devices in dementia: A telephone survey and case series. *International Journal of Geriatric Psychiatry*, 13, 556–563. DOI: 10.1002/(SICI)1099–1166 (199808) 13:8<556::AID-GPS834>3.0.CO;2–6.

Mahmood, A., Yamamoto, T., Lee, M., & Steggell, C. (2008). Perceptions and use of gerotechnology: Implications for aging in place. *Journal of Housing for the Elderly*, 22, 104–126.

Mattie's call becomes useful technique throughout Georgia. (2006, February 20). *Associated Press State & Local Wire*.

Miller, G., & Holstein, J.A. (1989). On the sociology of social problems. In J.A. Holstein & G. Miller (Eds.), *Perspectives on social problems* (Vol. 1, pp. 1–16). Greenwich, CT: JAI.

Missing persons tracking program could go statewide by 2012. (2007, July 24). *Associated Press State & Local Wire*.

Muschert, G.W., Petonito, G., Bhatta, T., & Manning, L. (2009, August). "Missing older adults with dementia: A study of news coverage of incidents and policy developments, 2006–2008." Paper presented at the Society for the Study of Social Problems Meetings, San Francisco, California.

Nelson, B.J. (1984). *Making an issue of child abuse: Political agenda setting for social problems*. Chicago, IL: University of Chicago Press.

Neergaard, L. (2007, August 13). GPS, other technology tracks lost Alzheimer's patients. *The Associated Press State & Local Wire*.

Ore. County plans devices to find missing persons. (2007, May 13). *The Associated Press State & Local Wire*.

Payne, M. (1995). Understanding 'going missing': Issues for social work and social services. *British Journal of Social Work*, 25, 333–348.

Petonito, G., & Muschert, G.W. (2015). Silver Alert Programs: An exploration of community sentiment regarding a policy solution to address the problem of critical wandering in an aging population. In M.K. Miller, J.A. Blumenthal, & J. Chamberlain, (Eds.), *Handbook of Community Sentiment* (pp. 253–266), New York: Springer.

Petonito, G., Muschert, G.W., Carr, D.C., Kinney, J., Robbins, E.J. & Brown, J.S. (2013). Programs to locate missing and critically wandering elders: A critical review and a call for multiphasic evaluation. *The Gerontologist*, 53, 17–25.

Pfohl, S.J. (1977). The 'discovery' of child abuse. *Social Problems*, 24, 310–323.

Police, CAP search for Bismarck man. (2008, August 25). *The Associated Press State & Local Wire*.

Proposal would create alert program for missing elderly. (2007, December 27). *Associated Press State & Local Wire*.

Quadagno, J. (2008). *Aging and the life course: An introduction to social gerontology*. New York: McGraw Hill.

Robinson, L., Brittain, K., Lindsay, S., Jackson, D., & Oliver, P. (2009). Keeping in touch everyday (KITE) project: Developing assistive technologies with people with dementia and their carers to promote independence. *International Psychogeriatrics*, 21, 494–502. DOI: 10.1017/S104161020 9008448.

Robinson, L., Hutchings, D., Corner, L., Finch, T., Hughes, J., Brittain, K., et al. (2007). Balancing rights and risks: Conflicting perspectives in the management of wandering in dementia. *Health, Risk & Society*, 9, 389–406. DOI: 10.1080/13698570701612774.

Rogers, C.D. (1986). *Tracing missing persons: An introduction to agencies, methods, and sources in England and Wales*. Manchester, UK: Manchester University Press.

150 *Gina Petonito and Glenn W. Muschert*

Rowe, M.A., & Bennett, V. (2003). A look at deaths occurring in persons with dementia lost in the community. *American Journal of Alzheimer's Disease and Other Dementias*, 18, 343–348. DOI: 10.1177/ 153331750301800612.

Rowe, M.A., & Glover, J.C. (2001). Antecedents, descriptions and con-sequences of wandering in cognitively-impaired adults and the Safe Return (SR) program. *American Journal of Alzheimer's Disease and Other Dementias*, 16, 344–352. DOI: 10.1177/ 153331750101600610.

Rowe, M.A., Greenblum, C.A., Boltz, M., & Galvin, J.E. (2012). Missing drivers with dementia: Antecedents and recovery. *Journal of the American Geriatric Society*, 60, 2063–2069. DOI: 10.1111/j.1532–5415.2012.04159.x.

Rowe, M.A., Greenblum, C.A., & D'Aoust, R.F. (2012). Missing incidents in community dwelling people with dementia. *American Journal of Nursing*, 12, 30–35. DOI: 10.1097/ 01.NAJ.0000423503.53640.32.

Rowe, M.A., Vandeveer, S.S., Greenblum, C.A., List, C.N., Fernandez, R.M., Mixson, N.E., et al. (2011). Persons with dementia missing in the community: Is it wandering or something unique? *BMC Geriatrics*, 11, 28. Retreived Apr. 4, 2017 from www.biomedicentral.com/1471–2318/11/28. DOI: 10.1186/1471–2318–11–28.

Search for missing Stanley man downsized. (2008, January 5). *The Associated Press State & Local Wire.*

Sheriff says missing man might have driven east. (2007, December 1). *The Associated Press State & Local Wire.*

Silver Alert Bill to Help Find Lost Dementia Victims Reintroduced in U.S. Senate. (2009, March 17). Senior Journal.com. Retrieved from http://seniorjournal.com/NEWS/Politics/2009/20090217-SilverAlertBill.htm.

Silver Alert Grant Program Act of 2008, H.R. 5898, 110th Cong. (2008). *The Orator.* Retrieved January 4, 2016 from www.theorator.com/bills110/text/hr5898.html.

Silverstein, N.M., Flaherty, G., & Tobin, T.S. (2002). *Dementia and wandering behavior: Concern for the lost elder.* New York: Springer.

Snedker, K. (2006). Altruistic and vicarious fear of crime: Fear for others and gendered social roles. *Sociological Forum*, 212, 163–195.

State's 'Silver Alert' program successfully finds seniors. (2008, May 3). *The Associated Press State & Local Wire.*

Stone, D. (1989). Causal stories and the formation of policy agendas. *Political Science Quarterly*, 104, 281–300.

Virginia search-and-rescue group says radio transmitters could save missing hikers. (2007, January 16). *The Associated Press State & Local Wire.*

Warr, M. (1992). Altruistic fear of victimization in households. *Social Science Quarterly*, 734, 723–736.

West Fla. Community Enacts Silver Alert Program. (2008, September 30). *The Associated Press State & Local Wire.*

West Virginia newspapers speak. (2008, February 24). *The Associated Press State & Local Wire.*

W.Va. hiker who was lost 4 days receives radio locator. (2007, November 2). *The Associated Press State & Local Wire.*

Woolgar, S., & Pawluch, D. (1985). Ontological gerrymandering: The anatomy of social problems explanations. *Social Problems*, 32, 214–227.

Zoglio, M.J. (1980). *Tracing missing persons: A professional's guide to techniques and resources.* Doylestown, PA: Tower Hill Press.

CHAPTER **10**

Aging in Places

Stacy Torres

A generation ago, when anthropologist Barbara Myerhoff studied the lives of older adults, she discovered a resilient community of elderly Eastern European Jews struggling against the tide of gentrification in Venice Beach, California. They faced poverty, scarce affordable housing, displacement, and rising rents due to urban development that ignited property values (Myerhoff, 1978). Today a new generation of poor and moderate-income urban elders struggles to grow old in gentrifying cities like New York, Los Angeles, San Francisco, and other urban areas around the country whose residents are graying as the municipalities where they live absorb affluent new arrivals in search of urban amenities.

They face the traditional challenges associated with old age, such as declining physical mobility; difficulties performing activities of daily living; and the loss of friends, relatives, and other social connections, sometimes in the absence of strong or nearby familial support, in an urban context that offers many advantages for older people who wished to stay independent but also special hurdles for those that remain in some of the most valuable, coveted, and increasingly expensive real estate in the country. Unlike previous generations, as these older people enter their later years, they are not retreating into the family homestead or moving to a far-away retirement community but staying put in their present neighborhoods and living spaces for as long as possible.

While elderly poverty rates have dropped over the past half century, older adults remain vulnerable economically, especially as they move further away from the traditional retirement age. With their entrance into deep old age, they must also cobble together a means of supporting themselves financially on dwindling savings, if any, and fixed incomes. Even those elders who had enjoyed comfortable middle-class incomes in their younger years are not immune to the fallout of economic shocks, such as the most recent Great Recession.

While overall poverty rates for older adults have declined from 35% in 1959 to 8.7% in 2011 (Torres, 2014), this picture worsens when using alternate poverty measures such the Census Bureau's Supplemental Poverty Measure, which factors in regional cost-of-living differences and medical expenses. Using the Senior Financial Stability Index, the Institute on Assets and Social Policy at Brandeis University found that more than a third of older adults in 2010 were economically

152 *Stacy Torres*

insecure and in danger of outliving their financial resources (Meschede, Bercaw, Sullivan, & Cronin, 2015). And UCLA's Center for Health Policy Research has found using the "Elder Index" that a half million California elders living alone did not have enough income to pay for basic expenses such as housing, food, health care, and transportation (Wallace & Smith, 2009).

Securing affordable housing also poses a steep hurdle for seniors living on fixed incomes and a growing concern even for older adults with more resources, who in another era likely would have experienced greater housing support. But across the country, elders face the continued effects of the Great Recession and high housing costs. Since 2004, the number of elderly households that spent more than 30% of their income on housing has increased. Brandeis's Institute on Assets and Social Policy cited growing housing costs as a "significant policy concern" (Meschede et al., 2015), given the desire of older adults to age in place, combined with proposals to cut Social Security and Medicare benefits. Housing costs in expensive urban areas take an even greater bite out of many seniors' household budgets. For example, in Los Angeles, rent accounts for more than half the expenses of an older person living on her own, and 70% of these older California renters struggle to make ends meet (Wallace & Smith, 2009).

"I'd rather die than go to a nursing home" became a common refrain among the older adults with whom I spent 5 years conducting participant observations in New York City. Their outspokenness about wanting to die before entering a nursing home was more than hyperbolic natter, and in most cases, they passed away before ever having to move to an institutional setting. But some faced a longer period of illness, a few weeks to a few months, and spent time in a nursing facility before dying.

Their aversion to institutional care reflects a broader desire among older Americans to age in place despite rising economic vulnerability. In 2005, 89% of adults aged 50 and above surveyed by the American Association of Retired Persons (AARP) wished to remain in their homes (Klinenberg, Torres, & Portacolone, 2012). And as Eric Klinenberg's research in *Going Solo* has shown, the number of people living alone has risen significantly over the past half century and when people can afford solo living they choose this arrangement whenever possible, especially when the alternative is moving in with family at older ages (Klinenberg, 2012). Yet, the design and infrastructure of most cities and towns cater to families with young children and are ill equipped to meet the needs of an aging population (Scharlach & Lehning, 2016). Despite the vast need and desire for home-based care, we lack sufficient funding for non-medical supportive services to aid aging in place. Proposed cuts to Medicaid and Medicare seem perpetually on the horizon, posing threats first to services that help elders remain in their homes. Our social policies reflect this institutional bias and incorrectly assume family can and will step in when elders' needs exceed available resources.

With growing numbers of elders, scholars, policymakers, and ordinary people have an interest in understanding the conditions that enable older people to thrive in their communities. Aging in place is popular among older people who want to remain in their communities and with policymakers, who see aging in place as

Aging in Places   153

a less costly and popular alternative to institutional options. At the same time, elders living alone in the community may face a sense of precariousness due to their difficulty or inability to access necessary resources and bewilderment in navigating a tangled web of social services (Portacolone, 2011). Less research has focused on capturing the lived experience of aging in place over time and understanding to what extent places and neighborhood relationships enable elders to remain in their homes. My longitudinal observations over 5 years of ethnographic study offer a glimpse into how elders navigated their neighborhoods in the face of aging-related challenges, such as health declines, mobility concerns, and gentrification, pointing to a more fundamental question of what home and place means for older adults growing old in their communities.

Ethnographies of Aging in Place: An Overview

Earlier ethnographic studies give us important insights into the lived experience of aging in place. But new challenges require updating in a time of unprecedented societal aging. In addition to looming economic insecurity for this generation of elders, older people confront the challenges of maintaining home, independence, and social connectivity in a context of weaker family, social, and housing support. As baby boomers continue to enter late life, a handful of qualitative studies, old and new, provide a useful roadmap for scholars and the public as we attempt to understand the present circumstances and future developments in this context of sweeping demographic change. As someone who has researched this area, I have found a handful of classic and more recent studies crucial to understanding the current moment, tracing an arch from Arlie Hochschild's glimpse into the daily life of a senior housing complex in _The Unexpected Community_ to Corey Abramson's (2015) recent study of old age and inequality in _The End Game_.

Forty-four years after its publication, Arlie Hochschild's (1973) slim volume about older adults on the fringes of work and family, "caught in this contradiction of a society in transition," remains essential reading for gerontologists and sociologists alike (xiii). Her work helped to form an important wave of critique against "disengagement theory," which posited that old people chose to withdraw from the social fabric and their social ties, sensing death on the near horizon. On the contrary, Hochschild's research participants reproduced work-like and family-like relations in a lower-income senior housing complex off the shore of the San Francisco Bay. They showed resilience and ingenuity in fashioning a new set of family-like ties outside of a traditional, nuclear family arrangement and created bonds in a communal living context. While old age affects the shape and size of social networks in different ways (Carstensen, 1992; Schnittker, 2007), Hochschild rightly argued that there is nothing "natural" about a process of increasing isolation for older adults. She sees value in age-separated housing and social spaces and argued that the senior complex she studied helped the low-income, old widows she spent time with guard against isolation and put them in closer proximity with same-aged peers. This type of housing also offered a place where the old could gather and worry less about ageism and "acting their age" in a society that devalues

154 *Stacy Torres*

the old and constrains acceptable behavior for elders. From the previous literature on social isolation and disengagement in old age, Hochschild expected to find alienation and estrangement among a marginalized group. Instead, she found an unexpected community and thriving old age subculture.

Following on the heels of *The Unexpected Community*, Barbara Myerhoff's much beloved *Number Our Days* sheds light on another community of older people, this time a senior center where a group of elderly Jews gathered daily to avoid isolation. They drew on the culture, religion, and ritual, which had helped them to sustain against atrocities like the Holocaust and the hardship of shtetl life in Eastern Europe, to face their present adversities of aging in place, including poverty, loneliness, substandard housing, burgeoning physical limitations, and distant relationships with their socially mobile children. At the center, Myerhoff discovers a tight-knit collective, even when tensions and rivalries flared. Contrary to her training and prior research as an anthropologist, she finds that she does not need to travel to a far-flung "exotic" locale to study a disappearing culture, and through the relationships she forms with regular center attendees she offers a glimpse into their urgent need to share and bear witness. Myerhoff beautifully and sensitively shows through ethnographic vignettes and interactions the importance of reminiscence and storytelling that undergird their shared history as "Center people," Jews, and survivors.

Like Hochschild, Myerhoff anticipates a changing world for older people, in terms of their connection to family. Her research participants are largely on their own, in some cases by choice. For example, married couple, Shmuel and Rebekah, have a successful son with a PhD in sociology, who lives in Philadelphia with his four sons. While Rebekah tells Myerhoff that she aches for her grandchildren and longs to be closer ("It's like the heart is cut out of me"), she also says that she and her husband would not move closer to family for various reasons, including the cold weather and the lack of connections and daily routine accumulated over 32 years of living in Venice Beach. "Here is our life, our friends, our home, and the ocean," she says resolutely (Myerhoff, 1978, p. 48).

The Miracle of Intervale Avenue is the direct descendant of Barbara Myerhoff's work, also focusing on a community of elderly Jews embedded in a South Bronx synagogue in "one of the world's most famous slums" in the early 1980s (Kugelmass, 1986, p. 7). The book more closely examines aging in place with regards to changing neighborhood contexts, in this case a formerly Jewish neighborhood that had changed to a predominantly Puerto Rican area with pockets of black residents and a few Jewish holdout residents. At the time of Kugelmass's study, the Bronx held ominous associations with murder, arson, and crime. He found a changed neighborhood, once home to a thriving Jewish life and community, stripped of its former glory, lovely buildings, and inexpensive housing, now filled block after block with empty and abandoned buildings. That older, well-kept Bronx disappeared due to the social mobility of its residents, who moved up and out, and white flight led an "exodus from the urban core" (Kugelmass, 1986, p. 15). The Cross Bronx Expressway cut a path of destruction

Aging in Places 155

through neighborhoods, gutting them and setting the stage for blight that metastasized through the borough.

In this context, Kugelmass highlights the strength of the old Jewish congregants in the face of adversity and urban blight. They have a much different perspective on the Bronx than the media reports of devastation had suggested, and these elders experience this place not as a symbol of urban decay and destruction but as home. Surviving in an environment that most found inhospitable gives them some compensatory power over the devaluation and battles of old age. Aging in place is not just a matter of survival but a triumph over the dangers that threatened all residents left behind in this distressed area and bestows a special pride at managing and overcoming these additional challenges, such as muggers and harassing people on the street. Like Myerhoff's study, Kugelmass elevates this case beyond simply a study of survival and helps us understand how people give meaning to their survival and make sense of it.

Slim's Table, Mitchell Duneier's (1992) ethnography of relationships between older, mostly black working-class men is an "accidental" study of aging in place, insofar as he had not set out to study the aged when he stumbled upon this group of frequent patrons at the Valois cafeteria in Chicago. These men, ranging in age from their 50s to 80s, develop caring relationships in a neighborhood place that provides an important source of social support, which encompasses both emotional and practical aid when a problem arises. With these affecting portraits of African-American inner city life, Duneier shoots down harmful and inaccurate stereotypes of black men and challenges prevailing negative depictions with his careful observations of the cafeteria regulars. Over the years, they form a caretaking community, looking out for each other and demonstrating themselves as worthy role models, revealing through action their moral values of respect and concern for others and the premium they place on hard work and responsibility.

As a study of aging and masculinity, Duneier's embeddedness in the field provides an important lens into the value of work for these older black men and work as a means of safeguarding independence. The men also value face-to-face interaction and discussion, and Duneier's study helps us understand the importance of neighborhood places to foster this kind of civility. In the men's eyes, they and their way of life, in the form of daily gathering, hail from another age and sensibility. Duneier's focus on race also anticipates the necessity of understanding how communities of color age, something we will need to better understand given the swelling numbers of minority elders with diverse needs and circumstances.

Sociologist Katherine Newman's (2003) work, *A Different Shade of Grey*, picks up this line of inquiry and focuses our attention on the intersection of race, ethnicity, and poverty in the lives of vulnerable older adults left behind in challenging inner-city environments. As she shows in this study of black and Latino elders in New York City, aging is an inherently unequal process and the greater vulnerability of women, minority, and immigrant elders reflects the long-term effect of gender and racial discrimination in the labor market, the wage gap, singlehood, and more limited educational and employment opportunities.

156 *Stacy Torres*

Newman's work reminds us that despite the many strides we have made in alleviating poverty and disadvantage in old age, many African-American and Latino elders are aging in troubled, urban places, growing sick and dying earlier than their white counterparts.

Corey Abramson's *The End Game* directs our attention once again to how inequality shapes late life, circling back to a discussion Arlie Hochschild's book raised as a core concern in sociology. Abramson's multisited comparative ethnography examines how different groups of old people across racial, ethnic, and socioeconomic lines face common age-related challenges like physical decline and illness, some with few supports and some with abundant resources to cushion the journey at every step. He argues that aging is a "stratified process" and socioeconomic, racial, and gender differences remain salient for outcomes in late life. His effort to bridge the study of old age with a deep analysis of social inequality is timely and necessary, given the differences and disparities that exist in old age and growing diversity among people living longer than ever.

Finally, Meika Loe's study of the oldest old, *Aging Our Way*, provides insight into the strategies that the very eldest use to maintain their independence and live in the community. She offers a counter-narrative to prevailing doomsday predictions about old age as a major social problem. In the course of her qualitative study, she follows thirty "oldest old" people older than 85 years, the fastest growing age group in the United States (Loe, 2011). Over a period of 3 years, she spends time with and interviews the oldest-old in suburban upstate New York, many of them living on their own. Loe organizes her findings around the shared lessons octo- and non-agenarians have learned over eight and nine decades of living. Her sensitive portrayal highlights elders' agency in building vibrant lives. They demonstrate creativity and resilience in drawing on traditional and non-traditional sources of social support, such as family, friends, roommates, housekeepers, and home health aides (Loe, 2011 p. 30). As they patch together alternate and supplementary support networks, they reinvent the notion of family and create intergenerational bonds that allow them to "continue to do what you did" and sustain their preferred ways of living, with necessary but comfortable modifications.

Each of the qualitative works discussed in this chapter grapple with essential themes of belonging and touch on the potential for isolation among the old as they find themselves, to varying degrees, on the fringes of central organizing institutions such as work and family. Some older adults fare better than others, but even those with more privilege still face challenges to their survival. The earliest qualitative studies spotlighted in this chapter emerged from an era when older people more commonly lived with or closer to family, in contrast to the present day in which geographic mobility spreads family members across the country and the globe. Even older adults with close family ties resist moving in with relatives or prefer to live alone. As we look to the future of old age and use these studies as a guide to understanding how different cohorts of older adults reworked anchoring structures like work, family, and neighborhood, researchers, policymakers, and the wider public can no longer assume a caretaking model where the family absorbed the old.

Aging in Place in New York City Today

Given the sweeping demographic changes in the United States and the graying of countries around the world, such as Japan and most of Western Europe, the findings of recent qualitative work are more timely and relevant than ever. The research participants in my study of aging in place in New York City represent several key demographic trends that will shape the experience of growing old for generations to come, and thus offer another glimpse into the future of urban aging in twenty-first-century America. Most of them lived alone by choice and were single, due to a combination of widowhood, divorce, and having never married. Many never had children. The majority were women, who continued to face significant economic disadvantages in old age and higher poverty rates than their same-aged male counterparts (Torres, 2014). While elders in New York City may not be representative of older people in other parts of the country, they stand on the cusp of future trends that subsequent baby boom cohorts will further, such as having fewer children and multiple committed relationships during their lifetimes, along with rising economic pressures and higher retirement ages. In this context, it is even more crucial that we understand how elders forge supports and grapple with the blessings and burdens of increased longevity.

Rather than offer a prescription for how to age "well" or framing aging in America as a "crisis," my study provides an in-depth ethnographic account of how people attempted to age meaningfully and with dignity in communities where they had lived for decades or their entire lives. Many found social support in "third places" in the absence of kin yet struggled to balance the need for connection with the desire for autonomy (Oldenburg, 1989; see also Ben Noon & Ayalon, 2017 for more recent discussion of older adults gathering in public spaces such as parks). And growing discrepancies between people's constricted mobility and the neighborhood's changing retail landscape threatened their social ties and the larger possibilities for belonging to a community.

Like many in old age, my research participants have had to act as unwitting pioneers, forging alternate communities as they embarked on an uncertain process that tested people's strength, resilience, and creativity. In-line with the fluid nature of time and daily routine after retirement, the older adults I encountered during the course of my study often eschewed institutionalized spaces such as senior centers. Thus, their choices provide one possible blueprint for reimagining late life in this time of unprecedented demographic change with the aging of baby boomers. For example, despite the critical role centers play in the lives of elders, especially for low-income, vulnerable older adults, research has revealed baby boomers' reluctance about this option and dislike of the centers in their current incarnation, which suffer from an image problem (i.e., "not sexy") (Weil, 2014). Given the flurry of late-life opportunities and constraints, my ethnographic research suggests that aging scholarship across a range of disciplines should devote greater attention to the neighborhood contexts where these informal bonds blossom. They are more important than ever for older people living in urban areas and perhaps of growing importance in suburban and rural areas, where people

158   Stacy Torres

may know their neighbors and live closer to family but still crave intergenerational ties with people beyond the home and less formalized bonds that allow for more privacy and lower obligation. Alternative social ties stand alongside, and in some cases rival, other structures critical to well-being in old age, such as family and home.

I began observing social life at La Marjolaine Patisserie,[1] a mom-and-pop bakery in a gentrified Manhattan neighborhood. Over time, I noticed that this nondescript establishment not only evoked an earlier era in New York City history but also attracted its fair share of old New Yorkers, men and women predominately in their seventies and eighties, who were the bakery's most loyal customers and spent the most time there. For retirees on fixed incomes with plenty of time but who often could not walk more than a few city blocks, La Marjolaine served as a convenient gathering spot with reasonable prices and few restrictions on how long customers could linger. Most had lived in the neighborhood for multiple decades, and several had lived there for their entire lives.

Unlike the fictional bar in the television show *Cheers*, at La Marjolaine, everyone may not have known your name but usually offered a friendly hello. People checked on each other, asked about a neighbor's whereabouts, and waved to passersby. This place served as a clearing house of neighborhood information, and older customers caught up on news both good and somber, sharing pictures of grandchildren, updates on neighbors in nursing homes, and notices of wakes.

This remnant of a pre-gentrified neighborhood sat nestled among three main residential swathes—a union-built, low-equity co-op; public housing projects; and a large rental complex. These buildings housed many long-time tenants, a number of whom frequented the bakery. The rental protections afforded to them in the housing projects and co-op, or through rent control and stabilization programs in the rental buildings, meant that many long-time, lower-to-middle income residents had remained in a neighborhood now home to upscale restaurants and million-dollar condominiums. Many co-op and project residents had aged in place and lived independently in buildings classified as Naturally Occurring Retirement Community (NORCs), which Federal law defines as "a community with a concentrated population of older individuals" (Niesz, 2007). New York City has twenty-seven NORCs in four boroughs (D'Oca, et al., 2010). The concentration of older adults in these residential settings often facilitates a more cost-effective and efficient delivery of services to residents with multiple needs in late life.

As a customer at La Marjolaine, I came to know the bakery regulars—a fluid group of women and men older than 60 years, which skewed female, Puerto Rican, Jewish, ethnic white (Italian, Greek, Irish descent), and low-to-middle income, reflecting neighborhood demographics prior to gentrification. After the bakery closed, I followed former customers as they scattered across the neighborhood and gathered in other places within the surrounding blocks, including a McDonald's and Pete's Delicatessen. I also visited participants in their homes, hospitals, and nursing homes; attended wakes and funerals; and accompanied them to other neighborhood places such as park benches.

During the course of my study, I discovered how a nondescript mom-and-pop bakery on Manhattan's West Side satisfied much more than its older customers' craving for sweets and helped meet their desire for company in the face of loneliness, support when struggling, and perhaps most importantly a sympathetic ear to bear witness to the greater and more mundane struggles of late life. What may have appeared to the outsider a shabby bakery with worn tablecloths and hamantaschen was a bubbling hub of neighborhood life, the center of an invisible world of older people hiding in plain sight. The local McDonald's served not just burgers and fries but as a refuge when this group became displaced from their neighborhood gathering spot.

Neighborhood places not only allowed old people to socialize together but also offered a mix of companions in these intergenerational and diverse public spaces. They offered the possibility of alternate caretaking opportunities that differed from the more typical position of older adults in their families, where contact often involves receiving care and crisis management when a problem arises. Even when older adults take on roles as involved grandparents who provide significant financial and childcare assistance, this bond is a complicated family relationship overlaid with obligation and responsibility.

Public and neighborhood places in my study proved as important as home. Outside ties cultivated in nearby gathering spots helped enable many of my research participants to remain in their homes more comfortably as people formed ties with those who could help with smaller tasks, such as assistance with fixing a remote control or computer, which could otherwise feel overwhelming. In more extreme situations, such as a health crisis, connections to others saved lives, such as when someone had fallen or collapsed in their home and a neighborhood acquaintance went to check on them after noticing their absence. Outside help, usually unpaid and informal, freed people from over-reliance on family and health care institutions. But this form of assistance could also prove less reliable, not bound by pay or the obligation that more unconditional family ties impose.

Discovering this vital type of urban place for elders in my study raises the question of the meaning and contour of home to my research participants: what was the home that they wanted to return to after a bout with illness, a hospitalization, even a visit of a few days with relatives, and never leave? Their apartment residences of several decades formed a central component of their aging in place experience, but they aged in *places*. And the neighborhood places that ringed their residences in a radius of walkability served as crucial venues to develop connections with others, effectively serving as extensions of their living rooms.

For example, Dottie's circumstances toward the end of her life reflect many challenges my older research participants faced as they struggled to remain independent and dealt with health declines that threatened their ability to live on their own. After suffering a heart attack, Dottie, 83, landed in the hospital indefinitely. She and her family, along with an extended network of friends and neighborhood acquaintances, wrestled with tough medical questions about her future treatment and living arrangements. Faced with this crossroads, Dottie

160 *Stacy Torres*

confronted major, life-altering losses of physical ability. Her feeble condition worsened in the following weeks, in the hospital, and later a nursing home. In this rarer case of a permanent move to institutional care, Dottie and her family had to confront three searing realities while grappling with great uncertainty along the way. Physical consequences of the health crisis and the specter of death loomed first, followed by adjustment to institutional living with its concurrent loss of privacy and control, and finally the loss of home and neighborhood.

Months before she entered the nursing home, Dottie had great difficulty accessing the neighborhood places where friends and other familiar faces gathered daily. During an arduous walk with her one day from McDonald's to her home, a distance of approximately three and a half city blocks, I saw the difficulty she faced walking as she hunched over her metal shopping cart for support, sweating and breathing hard. The walk lasted 45 minutes. Her heartache and distress at the prospect of losing her apartment while in the nursing home stood as the final step in a more protracted process of loss that had started in earnest with the disappearance of the bakery. Once that gathering spot, affordable and less than a block from her building, shuttered, she fell further away from the group of regulars that had anchored her. In the months that followed the closing, she admitted feeling depressed about losing contact with people she used to see there. In the nursing home, her daughter Liz taped a picture to the armoire I had taken of Dottie and the bakery crowd alongside a treasured World Series photo of Yankees baseball player Derek Jeter clipped from the local newspaper. "I always knew where I could find Mom," Liz said, referring to the bakery.

The affection that Dottie developed for the bakery is representative of many former patrons' feelings for that establishment and other places where they gathered throughout the neighborhood. They often joked about the bakery's shabby, outdated décor; the worn table cloths; and the wobbly chairs, but the older adults who frequented this space daily revealed great sadness when the store closed after losing its lease. In the years after its shuttering, former customers spoke of this business as fondly and vividly as people in their lives whom they had also lost. Their attachment to this place reveals how much the bakery had for many become the center of their daily rounds and routines, echoing the observations of urban scholars such as Lyn Lofland (1998) on the transformation of public spaces into "home territories" that anchor people in neighborhoods and provide opportunities for repeated interactions over time (p. 70). For example, one older man who ate dinner alone every evening at a nearby diner never lacked for company. He sat by himself at the same booth near the kitchen, beneath a flat-screen television ideal for viewing the baseball and basketball games he enjoyed. He chatted with the waiters as they dashed past to pick up orders, and they honored his nightly "reservation" by setting out a placard that read RESERVED to save his booth. For urban-dwelling older adults facing multiple vulnerabilities, the accessibility of these public venues and the ability to make them their own provided crucial opportunities to connect. My research participants cultivated genuine affinity for the staff and other regulars at these establishments, reflected in their continual

Aging in Places 161

"sightings" of former bakery patrons they spotted in the neighborhood and reflections about how much they missed the characters who went there.

Sweeping demographic change will shape society and institutions for decades to come, bringing forth new challenges and new ways of living in old age. With this societal aging comes new vulnerabilities for older adults, due to our lack of preparedness and growing precariousness in many realms of social life. We no longer live in a society where we can count on one lifelong employer, intimate partner, or place of residence to sustain our needs. But the erosion of these traditional arrangements does not necessarily mean cause for alarm, if we take a proactive approach to shaping and implementing policies grounded in lessons learned from a wealth of existing scholarship. Previous qualitative studies provide a core foundation for understanding the array of changes and needs in late life and new challenges leave room for expansion of our knowledge and updating for a new century. The refashioning of old age will continue with new generations of elders, and as my research suggests, subsequent cohorts will adapt to their newfound freedoms and the necessity of forging new social bonds based less around family and formal community institutions.

My participants, the majority of them single and living alone while aging in place, represent larger demographic trends which will grow with future elderly cohorts. Higher rates of divorce and lifelong singlehood, coupled with increased longevity and the lengthening period that elders can expect to live independently, will compel greater numbers of older adults to construct support networks that enable them to thrive in their communities. Accordingly, more will draw these connections from unconventional venues such as informal public places and develop ties with people such as neighbors and acquaintances, which become more central in their lives over time and may prove hard to define but important nonetheless. For example, my participants managed to supplement their own living spaces by using a private business's openness to fit their needs. Qualitative research stands as an important counterweight to existing large-scale survey research into older adults' social lives, such as the National Social Life, Health, and Aging Project (NHSHAP, 2011); Survey of Health, Ageing, and Retirement in Europe (SHARE, 2015); and Longitudinal Aging Study Amsterdam (LASA, 2017). While these surveys offer an important cross-sectional portrait of the elders in the United States and abroad, sustained ethnographic observation offers rich insights into how people build supportive networks over the life course and a window into the interactions that buffered these older adults against cascading challenges related to aging and neighborhood change.

As more people discover the advantages of urban living across the country, seniors who live in expensive urban areas undergoing "revitalization" face the additional hurdle of fighting to remain in their communities. Urban areas are ideal places for people to grow old due to their greater walkability, public transportation options, and a denser infrastructure of social services. With growing constraints on finances and mobility, coupled with an increase in surplus time, the rising importance of neighborhood for elders aging in place complicates a simpler narrative of aging at home. The advantages that make them attractive

162 *Stacy Torres*

for older adults often draw younger, more affluent professionals who can afford to pay higher rents and desire upscale amenities and businesses. In burgeoning downtowns across America, vulnerable elders in the poorest stretches now face the added threat of gentrification, risk of wrongful evictions, and danger of ending up on the street. The buildings where my research participants lived represent some of the last large-tract affordable housing left in New York City, a great urban center that once had sufficient protections to enable the current generation to age in place but no longer provides a solid base for many future elders to grow old comfortably. They will face housing insecurity and dwindling access to the neighborhood spaces that transform a collection of buildings, sidewalks, and storefronts into home.

Note

1 For confidentiality reasons, I have changed the names of most sites and people.

References

Abramson, C.M. (2015). *The end game: How inequality shapes our final years.* Cambridge, MA: Harvard University Press.

Ben Noon, R., & Ayalon, L. (2017). Older adults in open public spaces: Age and gender segregation. *The Gerontologist,* 58(1), 149–158.

Carstensen, L.L. (1992). Social and emotional patterns in adulthood: Support for socioemotional selectivity theory. *Psychology and Aging,* 7(3), 331–338.

D'Oca, D., Theodore, G., & Armborst, T. (2010, March 17). *NORCs in NYC.* Urban Omnibus: The Culture of Citymaking. Retrieved March 17, 2010. New York: Architecture League of New York from http://urbanomnibus.net/2010/03/norcs-in-nyc/.

Duneier, M. (1992). *Slim's table: Race, respectability, and masculinity.* Chicago, IL: University of Chicago Press.

Hochschild, A.R. (1973). *The unexpected community: Portrait of an old age subculture.* Englewood Cliffs, NJ: Prentice-Hall.

Klinenberg, E. (2012). *Going solo: The extraordinary rise and surprising appeal of living alone.* New York: Penguin Press.

Klinenberg, E., Torres, S., & Portacolone, E. (2012, May). *Aging alone in America.* New York: Council on Contemporary Families Briefing Paper.

Kugelmass, J. (1986). *Miracle of Intervale Avenue: The story of a Jewish congregation in the South Bronx.* New York: Columbia University Press.

LASA. (2017). *Longitudinal aging study.* Amsterdam, the Netherlands: Vrije Universiteit Amsterdam. Retrieved July 14, 2017 from www.lasa-vu.nl/index.htm.

Loe, M. (2011). *Aging our way: Lessons for living from 85 and beyond.* New York: Oxford University Press.

Lofland, L.H. (1998). *The public realm: Exploring the city's quintessential social territory.* New York: Aldine de Gruyter.

Meschede, T., Bercaw, L., Sullivan, L., & Cronin, M. (2015). *Living longer on less: Post-recession senior in-security remains high.* Institute on Assets and Social Policy, Heller School for Social Policy and Management, Brandeis University, Waltham, MA. Retrieved May 19, 2015, from http://iasp.brandeis.edu/pdfs/2015/LLOL7.pdf.

Aging in Places 163

Myerhoff, B. (1978). *Number our days*. New York: Simon & Schuster.

Newman, K. (2003). *A different shade of grey: Midlife and beyond in the inner city*. New York: New Press.

Niesz, H. (2007). *Naturally occurring retirement communities*. OLR (Office of Legislative Research) Research Report. Hartford, CT: Connecticut General Assembly. Retrieved December 21, 2009, from www.cga.ct.gov/2007/rpt/2007-R-0148.htm.

NSHAP. (2011). *National social life, health, and aging project*. NORC at the University of Chicago. Retrieved July 14, 2017 from www.norc.org/Research/Projects/Pages/national-social-life-health-and-aging-project.aspx.

Oldenburg, R. (1999). *The great good place: Cafes, coffee shops, bookstores, bars, hair salons and other hangouts at the heart of a community*. New York: Marlowe. (Original work published 1989).

Portacolone, E. (2013). The notion of precariousness among older adults living alone in the U.S. *Journal of Aging Studies*, 27, 166–174.

Scharlach, A.E., & Lehning, A.J. (2016). *Creating aging-friendly communities*. New York: Oxford University Press.

Schnittker, J. (2007). Look (closely) at all the lonely people: Age and the social psychology of social support. *Journal of Aging and Health*, 19(4), 659–682.

SHARE. (2015). *Survey of health, ageing, and retirement in Europe*. Retrieved July 14, 2017 from www.share-project.org.

Torres, S. (2014). Aging women, living poorer. *Contexts*, 13, 72–74.

Wallace, S.P., & Smith, S.E. (2009). *Half a million older Californians living alone unable to make ends meet*. Los Angeles, CA: UCLA Center for Health Policy Research.

Weil, J. (2014). *The new neighborhood senior center: Redefining social and service roles for the baby boom generation*. New Brunswick, NJ: Rutgers University Press.

CHAPTER 11

Meanings of Age and Aging among Older, Incarcerated Women: Implications for Adaptation and Policy Reform

Leah M. Janssen

Introduction

It is evident that the population of older adults in the United States is growing rapidly. According to the United States Census Bureau (USCB), there were more than 41 million people aged 65 and above in 2012 (USCB, 2012a), with almost 73 million projected by the year 2030 (USCB, 2012b). As such, this demographic pattern also emerges in the "graying" of the prison populations (Auerhahn, 2002; Booker, 2016; Lemieux, Dyeson, & Castiglione, 2002; Moore & Unwin, 2002; Ollove, 2016; Ritter, 2006; Smith, 2004). It has been noted that tougher and longer prison sentences, such as three strikes mandatory sentencing laws, and the aging of the "baby boomers" is expected to bring about a dramatic increase in the growing numbers of increased older prisoners (Auerhahn, 2002; King & Mauer, 2001; Kratcoski & Babb, 1990; Moore & Unwin, 2002). A report from the American Civil Liberties Union (ACLU) describes the United States as the largest incarcerator in the world, with 2.3 million people behind bars, 124,900 of whom are aged 55 and older, with projections that this number will be more than 400,000 by 2030, which accounts for over a third of prisoners in the United States (ACLU, 2012). Within this growing segment of the population, women constitute a growing subgroup of the prison population. For instance, the US Department of Justice reports a recent increase particularly in female prisoners, from 108,800 in 2012 to 111,300 in 2013 (Carson, 2014).

In bringing the focus to state-level data, the Ohio Department of Rehabilitation and Correction (ODRC) annual census report states that the total 2016 Ohio inmate population was 50,515, and 8,900 (17.6%) of whom were inmates aged 50 and older (ODRC, 2016a). Table 11.1 illustrates that these numbers are growing. In fact, the 2016 ODRC census revealed that since this research was originally conducted in 2007, the number of all inmates aged 50 and above has increased by 66.5% (ODRC, 2016a). As prisoners age, there are many challenges that develop in response to the growth of this population—both for individual prisoners and prison staff and administrators. Older prisoners are often referred to as a "special population" because they present such different systemic demands, when compared to the rest of the population of inmates (Aday, 1994; Moore & Unwin, 2002;

164

Age and Aging among Older, Incarcerated Women   165

Table 11.1 Ohio's Aging Prison Population (2006—2016)

Ohio Inmate Population	2006	2016	Change (%)
Total (men & women, all ages)	46,871	50,515	3,644 (7.8%)
Total women (% of total population)	3,444 (7.3%)	4,219 (8.4%)	775 (22.5%)
Total men & women aged 50+ (% of total population)	5,346 (11.4%)	8,900 (17.6%)	3,554 (66.5%)
Women aged 50+ (% of total 50+)	265 (5.0%)	477 (5.4%)	212 (80.0%)

Note: Data for 2006 was taken from the ODRC Institution Census Report (2006) and data for 2016 was taken from the Census of ODRC Institutional Population, Demographic, and Offense Summary (2016).

Stojkovic, 2007). For example, some of the documented challenges associated with the stresses of this special population deal with the management of medical and mental health resources (Aday, 1994; Aday & Farney, 2014; Chaiklin, 1998; Lemieux et al., 2002; Moore & Unwin, 2002; Morton, 1992, 2004; Ross & Richards, 2003; Stojkovic, 2007); communication between staff and older prisoners (Moore & Unwin, 2002; Ross & Richards, 2003); programs and services (Aday, 1994; Lemieux et al., 2002; Moore & Unwin, 2002; Morton, 1992; Ross & Richards, 2003; Stojkovic, 2007); housing (Lemieux et al., 2002; Moore & Unwin, 2002; Stojkovic, 2007); and adjustment to life within, and after release from, prison (Aday, 1994; Leahy, 1998; Lemieux et al., 2002; Morton, 1992, 2004; Stojkovic, 2007).

Aging Female Inmates

Within the growing population of older inmates, a sub-group of the inmate population that has received little research attention is that of older female prisoners (Aday, 1994; Aday & Farney, 2014; Kratcoski & Babb, 1990; Wahidin, 2002, 2004). Considering the longer life expectancies and the high incidence of chronic health conditions in the general population of older females, the population of incarcerated older females demonstrates similar systemic and programmatic demands that will likely increase over time (Codd, 1996; Lemieux et al., 2002; Morton, 1992, 2004). Furthermore, there is evidence that the needs of older imprisoned women are notably different than those of their younger counterparts *and* those of older male prisoners (Codd, 1996; Morton, 2004; Ross & Richards, 2003; Wahidin, 2002). For example, Maschi, Kwak, Ko, and Morrissey (2012) addressed the growing prevalence of dementia among inmates, and the inadequate services and programs that currently exist.

Research on health care utilization is important in understanding the quality of life for older prisoners, and their likelihood of imposing greater financial

166   *Leah M. Janssen*

demands on the health care system when compared to younger inmates (Enders, Paterniti, & Meyers, 2005; Fearn & Parker, 2005; Lemieux et al., 2002; Lindquist & Lindquist, 1999; Moore & Unwin, 2002). A "geriatric" prisoner is predicted to develop disability and comorbid conditions earlier than persons in the general population, and costs on average of $70,000 per year, which is two to three times the cost of a younger prisoner (Williams, Lindquist, Sudore, Strupp, Wilmott, & Walker, 2006). Regarding the present and future management of health care in correctional facilities, it should be recognized that gender and age have been shown to be the most consistent demographic predictors of health status and medical care utilization (Aday & Farney, 2014; Enders et al., 2005; Lemieux et al., 2002; Lindquist & Lindquist, 1999; Moore & Unwin, 2002).

Although most prison research conducted on older offenders is on men, older women currently constitute a small but increasing percentage of the prison population. For instance, in Ohio, the number of women in prison aged 50 and older increased from 265 inmates in 2006 to 477 inmates in 2016, which is an increase of 80% (ODRC, 2006, 2016a). As this population steadily grows, it is ever more important to expand what little research has been conducted. Additional research would contribute to the cumulative knowledge and understanding of this minority population. Older incarcerated women might benefit from such research as well, in terms of identifying and fulfilling their unique needs, both currently and for future successful reintegration in the community. Recognizing the importance of research and furthering our knowledge of older women would also prove useful for prison staff and policymakers, who create programs for and work directly with this population.

Investigating the Lives of Older Inmates

There has been little qualitative research addressing the lives, social relationships, and modes of adaptation that are specific to older imprisoned women. In the next subsections, I examine some of the relevant literature available on life in prison on topics such as social relationships, modes of adaptation, and programming in prison.

Social Relationships in Prison

Research concerning mechanisms of adaptation and coping in prison populations has been somewhat prevalent in the literature examining the culture and social structure of the prison environment. Giallombardo's (1966) classic study, *Society of Women: A Study of a Women's Prison*, focuses on the significance of the larger macro social culture in the prison environment, particularly on how male and female roles are defined and how prisoners influence and give meaning to the creation of these roles. A related concept is the formation of organized *prison families* or *play families* (Ross & Richards, 2003), similar to *pseudo families* (Heffernan, 1972), which play an important part in the development of women's relationships in prison. Ross and Richards (2003) found that personal relationships

Age and Aging among Older, Incarcerated Women   167

with other prisoners, connections to family and loved ones in the free community, and the commitment to pre-prison identities continue to shape the core of the female prison culture. Furthermore, it is indicated that women organize their time and create a social world that is markedly different from the world of contemporary male prisoners.

The empirical literature on the social status of older inmates within the prison hierarchy provides a somewhat contradictory picture. Goetting (1983) and Rubenstein (1984) suggest that younger inmates respect older inmates for their knowledge of prison life. This enables older inmates to establish behavioral norms and occupy leadership roles, thus creating a sense of prestige and respect. Conversely, Kratcoski and Babb (1990) found that older inmates are vulnerable to and fearful of predatory younger inmates. Additionally, Leahy's (1998) research concluded that there was very little solidarity among inmates, which was illustrated through minimal contact with other inmates.

Kratcoski and Babb (1990) found that older women were less likely than older men to be involved in various forms of recreational activities within the institution. Investigating the social worlds of older inmates, the study reveals that 74% of males and only 53% of females indicated positive or neutral attitudes toward other inmates. Furthermore, older females were less likely to have interaction with other inmates. Older female inmates were much more likely to see other inmates as being aggressive and violent than were older male inmates. Older male and female inmates perceived young inmates as troublesome, and *both* groups expressed a preference for living with other inmates around their same age. Due to the reclusive characteristics of older female inmates, Kratcoski and Babb (1990) note that older women experience a greater degree of isolation than men, which is exacerbated by the lack of social support systems inside *and* outside the prison.

Adaptation in Prison

Lemieux et al. (2002) suggested that there are numerous individual and institutional factors that contribute to older inmates' adjustment to incarceration. Rubenstein (1984) and Goetting (1983) both concluded that inmate adjustment is related to various individual (e.g., educational level, health status) and institutional characteristics (e.g., security level, degree of mainstreaming). Therefore, it is important to consider adaptation as a multifaceted concept, which can be observed and described in a number of social, emotional, and physical contexts.

Leahy (1998) investigated the psychological adjustment to prison life and discovered that emergent coping strategies converged around three distinct aggregates referred to as *minimals, optimals,* and *utilitarians.* Each group is defined and characterized by the varying perceptions of inmate's self-concepts and participation within the prison culture. *Minimals* cope with prison life by maintaining a fatalistic view on life and have a low motivation to work or participate in the prison environment. *Optimals* adapt by striving to be the best in terms of participating in prison life as preparation for release into society, they follow the rules, are highly motivated, and have high self-esteem. *Utilitarians* are characterized

168   *Leah M. Janssen*

as being concerned only with their own happiness, blame is placed on society for criminal acts, and are primarily interested in opportunities for personal gain and benefit.

Azrini Wahidin's (2002) research also explores psychological adaptation, specifically for older women in prison. Informants describe their identities as being "caught" within the movement of time and space, both in terms of *real time* referring to time on the outside and within prison time. Wahidin refers to this as *carceral time,* an in-between space within which women live and negotiate. Further findings reveal that older incarcerated women adapt to prison life by protecting their sense of self-worth through the creation of *prison performances,* which involve mentally withdrawing oneself from a physically coercive institution, thereby regaining greater subjective control as they move to the periphery of the prison environment.

Studying adaptation to institutional life in terms of physical health, Aday (1994) found that older offender's health problems and limited access to medical care served as barriers to adaptation, as many informants suffered from multiple chronic health problems and a general deterioration of health. Aday and Farney (2014) examined the perceived experiences of health care utilization by older women in prison, and found that many endure high levels of mental distress (depression and anxiety), as well as chronic physical health issues (arthritis, hypertension, issues related to menopause, digestive issues/ulcers, and heart conditions). Kratcoski and Babb (1990) found that twice as many older women than men reported heart, respiratory, and degenerative illnesses. Further, a significantly larger proportion of older female inmates than older male inmates claimed that their health was "poor" or "terrible." Lemieux et al. (2002) suggests that older inmates are more likely to demand health care services than are their younger counterparts, and that the prison environment, housing, and availability of specialized programs influence the extent to which older inmates consume services.

Programming for Older Inmates

There appears to be tremendous variability in the extent to which correctional systems provide older and other special needs inmates with formal provisions, such as housing accommodations and specialized educational, vocational, medical, and recreational programming (Aday, 1994; Lemieux et al., 2002; Moore & Unwin, 2002; Morton, 1992; Ross & Richards, 2003). In a report published for the ODRC produced by the Bureau of Research, Moore and Unwin (2002) described two distinct goals of programming in prison. First, that it helps inmates cope with the prison environment and work toward self-rehabilitation. Second, such programming enables the individual, regardless of age, to prepare for life after release. Older inmates in Ohio are able to participate in a multitude of programs, some of which are offered to the general inmate population, while other less common programs focus on the needs of older adults. Since the programming at each institution varies, as do the needs of this special population, not all prisons are able to provide the same aging-related programs and services.

Research Design: An In-Depth Interview Project

This section describes the research design and methodology used in the current research project, which warrants the use of a qualitative research approach in expanding our understanding of adaptation among older women in prison. Consistent with the *interpretive constructionist paradigm*, the goal of this research is to explore, describe, and understand a multitude of meanings (Rubin & Rubin, 2012). The construction of meaning is discovered through language and is derived from patterns and themes related to interpersonal relationships and adaptation strategies that are rooted in the *subjective* perspective of older women in prison (Gubrium & Holstein, 1999). An essential part of the qualitative research design is using a type of methodology that recognizes the importance of understanding people's thoughts and feelings, as well as the cognitive categories in which they organize the meanings of age in discrete settings.

In this study, aging refers both to *chronological age*, and related expectations regarding roles and behavior, and to *tenure*—time passing—which takes on distinctive and vivid meanings behind bars. Qualitative in-depth interviews, administered one-on-one, offer a method of data collection that enables the focus to be on the informant's personal experience and allows the researcher to take on the human-as-instrument role and accept the responsibility of collecting and drawing meaning from the data. In an attempt to avoid potential researcher bias, Dr Christopher Wellin served as a *peer debriefer*, to assist in reviewing the data and analysis (Maykut & Morehouse, 1994).

Methods: Sample

In-depth one-on-one interviews were conducted with eleven women in their mid-fifties to mid-seventies, who were incarcerated through the ODRC in Ohio in 2007. Sampling female inmates older than 50 years was chosen because correctional agencies nationwide typically use the age of 50 as a chronological starting point to define "older prisoners," which is based on a number of factors including socioeconomic status, access to medical care, and the lifestyle of prisoners (Morton, 1992). The sample population and setting have been selected so that diversity is maximized in the data with variation in age, race, and prison tenure (8–20 years). Six of the women were identified as Caucasian and five identified as African-American. Interviews were audiotape-recorded and transcribed, with an average length of 2 hours each. Additionally, research informants were asked to fill out background information sheets that captured basic demographic characteristics. Informants' tenure in prison was 5–10 years for three informants; and 11–20 years for the remaining eight.

Description of Prison and Informants

The ODRC currently oversees twenty-seven institutions (ODRC, 2016c) that house prisoners convicted of a range of crimes, with a total inmate population of 50,515 (ODRC, 2016a). The identity of the prison in which the research was

170 *Leah M. Janssen*

completed is protected, but it is noted that this is a multi-security correctional facility located in Ohio. At the time this research was conducted, the facility had more than 2,300 incarcerated women in varying levels of security and the racial breakdown of this prison was about two-thirds Caucasian and one-third African-American. The identities of informants were protected through the use of pseudonyms, which have not been paired with ages, prison tenures, and other identifying information when referencing direct quotes, as a means to further safeguard informants' identities.

Data Analysis Procedures

Once collected, data were analyzed through a process of multiple readings, open and thematic coding of responses, and attempts to document and relate central explanatory themes. Thus, it will be appropriate to use the *constant comparative method* in the data analysis procedures (Maykut & Morehouse, 1994). This method of analyzing qualitative data combines inductive category coding with a simultaneous comparison of all units of meaning obtained, thereby allowing salient themes or patterns to emerge from the interviews.

Dimension One: Day-To-Day Life

The first dimension briefly discusses key aspects of day-to-day life for older women in prison, which are explored in terms of housing, daily schedules, autonomy, and daily challenges. In the book *Asylums*, Erving Goffman (1961) refers to this type of environment as a *total institution*, which is a social establishment or institution where all aspects of life are controlled and surveilled by the authorities of the organization. Each institution creates a specific world by which its inmates reside, thereby imposing its own rules, regularities, and barriers to the outside world.

Housing

Housing for each interviewee varied in terms of location and the ages and number of cellmates or "bunkies." For instance, some women have between one and four cellmates; others live in large dorm-style cottages, while a smaller group live in a medical dorm of up to eight women. Unlike older male inmates incarcerated in Ohio, there is not an age-segregated unit specifically designed for older female inmates, although some informants described living among other older inmates. The location of the inmate's cottage is important in understanding their access and maneuverability to other facilities and programs across the compound. The variation in housing also impacts one's primary source of social interaction within the confines of the prescribed living arrangement, which is further explored in Dimension two.

Schedules

A typical schedule varies depending on one's job and the security status of the individual. Since all informants were held in medium security status, they were permitted to travel to work stations and other scheduled appointments alone with an approved pass. On a daily basis, doors are unlocked when Central Food Services serves breakfast at 6:30 am; attendance to this meal, as well as others during the day is not required. Informants reported low attendance to these formal meals, due to overcrowding and a higher incidence of conflict among inmates. Instead, whenever possible, many choose to purchase their food through the commissary, which can only be purchased through an inmate's personal financial account.

Regardless of age, if an inmate is medically able, they are required to maintain a job within the institution. Inmates are called at 8:00 am to report to their job stations and work for much of the day, with the exception of inmate counts (five times throughout the day), meals, and scheduled meetings. In the evening hours following dinner, women have a window of personal free time until their cell doors are locked for the night at 11:00 pm. Informants acknowledged that they look forward to evening hours, in which they are allowed to wear their own personal clothing, and many spend their time socializing, knitting, reading, watching television, or working on community service projects.

Autonomy

Experiencing a loss of power within one's environment is particularly important in considering adaptation to prison life. The above description of a daily schedule illustrates significant strict temporal regimentation, which is monitored through 24-hour surveillance. Goffman's (1961) *total institutions* place a great emphasis on the management of time, in that there is an expectation of efficiency and predictability in the operations of the facility. This results in a limited amount of freedom and choice for inmates, who may experience what has been termed the *miniaturization of satisfaction* with their environment (Rubinstein, Killbride, & Nagy, 1992). This concept introduces the notion that decisions inmates make about satisfaction in their daily lives are not based "in the realm of big choices or possibilities, but in the realm of small events" (Rubinstein et al., 1992, p. 143). From the inmate perspective, time is an important and abundant commodity in which they take pride, and over which they seek some modicum of control.

The maintenance of autonomy in everyday prison life proved to be critical to the adaptation of each of the women interviewed, and was experienced in many different ways. Some women explained that they found autonomy through mentoring, sharing resources, and teaching new skills to younger inmates. Other women described the connection between autonomy and privacy, which proved to be a very important resource for adaptation. Some women found privacy and solitude in the quiet of the early mornings before other inmates were awake, spending their time alone reading, journaling, or in meditation or prayer. While daily activities varied, all women expressed a sense of satisfaction in maintaining some level of control and autonomy over their daily lives, no matter how minute it might seem to an outsider.

172 *Leah M. Janssen*

Another adaptation promoting a sense of autonomy was the creation of parallel biographies—a sense of continuity between life inside and outside the prison. "Colonization" is an adaptive process described by Goffman (1961, p. 62), in which one reduces the tension of either world by integrating the two. This does not seem uncommon for an inmate in a total institution, as the differences between the two worlds are reduced, thereby helping the inmate come to terms with adapting to her environment. For example, women interviewed referred to establishing similar norms between present and former worlds, such as through maintaining employment and heavy involvement in community service activities. These norms were not described as the simple passing of time in a mechanical or withdrawn sense, but rather in a productive and altruistic manner, allowing for reciprocation with the outside community.

Daily Challenges

Overwhelmingly, responses to challenges faced by women on a daily basis centered on issues pertaining to personal physical mobility and inmate crowding. Several of the informants used assistive devices, such as canes or wheelchairs, to maneuver the grounds of the institution. However, even women who did not use such devices expressed frustration about not being able to get around on a timely basis. Women expressed that they recognized the change in their physical bodies as they negotiate the prison environment. This change seems to be met with anxiety about being able to care for oneself while keeping up with the many younger inmates. For example, since the institution functions on such a structured schedule, women are only given 15 minutes to get to and from their work stations to report for inmate counts. Informants voiced that this was not enough time for people with different abilities. This results in feelings of forced adjustment in that they overexert themselves at an uncomfortable and unsustainable rate, which is driven by the fear of sanctions imposed for being late. As I witnessed in my interviews, women were expected to transfer from their wheelchair on their own and climb the stairs by themselves, with hope that someone might be considerate enough to help them carry their wheelchair up the stairs. Therefore, unfortunately, this means that an assistive device, such as a wheelchair, actually becomes more of a barrier in this environment, due to the lack of supportive infrastructure.

Dimension Two: Interpersonal Relationships

The second dimension explores interpersonal relationships and connections created and maintained by older women inside and outside the confines of prison walls. This examined informants' sources of support, which helped determine how important and meaningful their relationships were for adaptation to prison life. There were found to be varying degrees of contact that women had inside and outside the prison. Social contacts are identified and defined according to the sociological terms of *primary* and *secondary groups* (Cooley as cited in Anderson

Age and Aging among Older, Incarcerated Women 173

& Taylor, 2004). Interpersonal connections can be built on strong values of social support and companionship that provide a sense of security, safety, and comfort throughout life (Krause, 2006). However, relationships can also waver through negative social encounters and *weak social ties* that lack intimacy and frequency of interaction (Granovetter as cited in Krause, 2006). Important social relationships are established and maintained throughout our lives, which create interactions and realities that shape and influence each other and the larger society. As relationships continue into late life, their nature and significance often affect one's health and overall well-being. For instance, when stressful life events arise, it is the members of one's social network that are called upon to help confront difficulties, provide advice and guidance, and help identify and negotiate effective coping strategies, which facilitates adaptation (Krause, 2006).

Inside Prison Social Contacts

Contacts that inmates maintain within the prison are primarily based on social interactions in three main arenas: housing, work, and involvement in programs and/or groups. While inmates have very little control over whom they are surrounded by, it was apparent that the most consistent factor shaping social contacts was security status, since inmates are separated according to maximum, medium, minimum, juvenile, and death row security levels. According to informants, social contact among inmates generally remains minimal, with a low level of emotional investment. Informants note the lack of close friends inside, and refer to social interactions with "acquaintances" or "associates" who appear to be distanced and detached from one another. The following are examples of how informants characterize their interactions with other inmates inside prison:

> Mostly I keep these people away from me, I don't want anything to do with most of them. I'll smile and be friendly and say hello to be polite, but I don't want to be friends because you'll walk up behind them and hear them gossiping about you or something, and it's just—I just gave up. It's more peaceful to be alone; I have to deal with extreme loneliness, but at least it's more peaceful that way.—*Ms Burt*

> I have associates here, but no friends, none—I don't want to attach myself to nobody.—*Ms Fry*

> Prison is full of people that are slick players, gamers, liars, and thieves. They just don't have any friend ethics. They don't know how to be a friend. It's always me, me, me. Some of these people I can't even carry on a conversation with. I don't want to get into it. I don't want that around me. I don't want to pick that up, so I really don't say too much.—*Ms Homme*

Informants are straightforward in relaying that most of their social interactions are approached cautiously. They express a preference and tendency to seek support

174　*Leah M. Janssen*

through outside social networks, if and when they are available. Social disconnection seems further exacerbated by the heavy congestion and cycling of inmates in and out of the institution, as well as the constant transferring of inmates from one cottage to another. Informants attributed the difficulty in maintaining steady relationships within prison to the fluctuation of inmates at any given time. Therefore, it is likely that the formation of affiliations or bonds is partly dependent on proximity and opportunities for contact, which are controlled by the institution.

However, this social phenomenon of distancing oneself from other inmates is not to be generalized to all informants. Some women expressed having strong support within her social community of inmates. Often, this finding was associated with the lack of outside support, when the social ties established prior to incarceration no longer exist. The following quotes illustrate the establishment of a more optimistic perception of social connections inside prison, some reflecting a kind of *fictive kinship* (Stack, 1974).

> It's like I don't have that family outside anymore, so I have family in here. You know how it is when one thing is taken away something else comes up and covers it.—*Ms Thompson*

> I love some of the ladies that live down stairs with me, and some of them I don't. I've been adopted quite a few times (laughs), because I move from different places, and I got to know some of these women, the young ladies especially that come here. The young ones, some of them have adopted me as a grandma, and some as a mom.—*Ms Shannon*

> Well, I usually talk to my friends in here because my family's never been in prison, so they really don't know what I'm going through . . . they go through the same thing I do. I mean we have the same emotional ups and downs . . . and you can relate.—*Ms Parker*

As the quotes demonstrate, there are many trade-offs to friendship in prison which can elicit feelings of cohesion and companionship that are critical to one's social adaptation and understanding of the prison culture and environment. Still, interviews revealed that a sense of collective identity is rare. Even in this brief glimpse into what appears to be an emotionally detached, sterile world, informants display the importance of friendship and community and the slow, but present, exchange of emotional intimacy in their social environment.

Generational Gap

As in broader society, meanings of age are often relational rather than intrinsic to individual experience. Intergenerational social contacts in prison gave way to what informants referred to as a "generational gap" in inmate interactions. This gap creates a source of great tension between younger and older inmates, which is further intensified by the growing population of young offenders in prison.

In Ohio, incarcerated females in the age group 15–49 compose 88.7% of the female prison population, while 11.3% are aged 50 and older (ODRC, 2016a). Informants expressed a strong sense of stress and anxiety when referring to the chaos they associated with newer and younger populations of inmates. Primarily, the negativity associated with younger inmates centers on the lack of respect and trust exhibited to older inmates, and also to staff.

Despite the overall negativity associated with young inmates, informants were careful not to draw overgeneralizations purely based on age. In a few interviews, women even described taking on mother and grandmother roles for younger inmates by sharing life stories, wisdom, and advice on survival in prison. The reciprocity between generations involves physical assistance from younger inmates, such as helping push wheelchairs or cleaning difficult to access areas. Ms Shannon, for example, relays her opinion on younger inmates by saying, "We need the young to enhance our ability to still be part of this world, part of what's going on, and to keep us motivated."

Outside Social Contacts

The types of personal contacts that informants revealed having with the outside were strongly connected with the depth of relationships maintained since being incarcerated. Social networks typically consisted of family, friends, ex-convicts, and members of prison ministries. Communication with one's outside social network consisted of letter writing, phone calls, and monthly visits. Outside of the more personal form of contact, connections to the outside world are sought out through different forms of media, such as watching television and reading newspapers and magazines.

Sending and receiving letters was found to be the most common form of personal interaction, most likely because it is the least expensive and obtrusive. Phone calls occurred less often, simply due to the fact that only collect calls were permitted, and the high cost. Regarding visits, medium security status inmates are typically allowed to have two visits per month, but the procedures for scheduling and attending these visits seems to inhibit visitation. For example, informants expressed feelings of humiliation and degradation by being subjected to full body searches, which are conducted before and after visits to prevent any illegal exchange of contraband. Informants who have visitors look forward to their monthly visits, and put a lot of thought and preparation into these important events. More recently, the ODRC has contracted with outside vendors, who operate online portals in which inmates can pay to communicate with their friends and family outside of prison. While these services were not available when the original research was conducted, it provides a convenient and secure way to send money, email, video visitation, music, and facilitate some probation and parole services (JPay, n.d.). While these advancements are attractive at first glance, they are often cost-prohibitive to many inmates, and those found in the digital divide may have less familiarity in using such technologies.

176 *Leah M. Janssen*

Establishing and managing links to the outside world occupy a significant place in the lives of informants and their adaptation to prison life, where there is a sharp separation of inside and outside worlds. Informants expressed finding themselves living vicariously through their outside connections, such as in the images or reminiscence of significant moments their friends and family speak of: births, weddings, traveling, cooking, etc. However, in times of crisis, informants relayed feelings of helplessness and distance from their outside social networks, such as not being able to attend funerals and not being able to provide care for ill or aging loved ones. These turning points echo the *generational reminders* that Karp (1988) argued mediate perceptions of aging more generally: these events and rituals are crucial for marking age and maturation, and perhaps the rites of passage throughout one's life.

The following quotes depict informants' relationships with outside social contacts:

> I am thankful, first, that in the __ years I've been here my family has maintained, they have continued in the way that I raised them . . . I am happy and pleased and proud and hopefully not conceited and arrogant about it, that the only thing I've lost is my freedom; I still have my home, I still have my family. If it's possible for us to be any closer than we were before I came here—then certainly that has happened. I haven't lost that closeness, that cohesiveness, that love and caring and support from my family, that I was getting before I came here. That's why I consider myself very fortunate because I know there are hundreds of women here that have lost all of those things— *Ms Norris*

> I have the best family in the world. I couldn't have done it without them. I get visits, letters, calls three times a week. You'd be surprised what people will remember you by keeping in touch. So, I spend a couple hours a day writing letters. Saturday, I received 7 or 8 letters from brothers and sisters, and those contain money and pictures. They remember the holiday, and they remember me, and that—that is what makes me get through this.—*Ms Shelley*

The above-mentioned quotes reflect the pride and appreciation many informants feel for their families and friends, many of whom have worked hard to continue these relationships over years, and even decades. Relying on the support of an external social structure helps inmates cope with the instability of the internal environment. This also fosters the belief that they will have someone and somewhere to turn if and when they are released. It is clear then, that many informants seek emotional, and some even financial, support from members of their outside networks. This, however, is shaped by the availability and willingness of outside members to reciprocate these exchanges.

Investing in these close relationships with the outside comes at a price: the frustration of balancing the demands of both inside and outside worlds:

You can't live in two worlds. If you know you're going to be in an institutional situation for a long period of time, just to keep your sanity, you have to adjust to the situation you're living in that day. You can't say, "well tomorrow I'm going home and I'm going to do this and this," because you're not guaranteed that. And someone in my situation that is pretty much going to finish my life here—I know this is it, so I have to do the best with what I can. I can't wait for tomorrow.—*Ms Boncquet*

It's hard being separated from your family. I don't care what anybody says, you know, but it's the traveling between two worlds. You're trying to live in this world, but you're still trying to live out in the world on the street. You can't live out in the world out in the street, you've got to learn to cope with this world. But yet you keep in contact, and know what's happening out there, through newspapers, through TV, through your family. Once that you can do that, you're going to sail through this stuff.—*Ms Thompson*

Informants convey that this balancing act is difficult because they have to be careful not be swept away in the special attention and excitement paid to outside events. Getting too caught up in what happens "out there" deepens the gap between the two worlds. Instead, they try to maintain a more present-tense orientation, which enables them to deal and adapt with the here and now, and the harsh realities of prison life. For the most part, the inside and outside relationships and lives of informants are kept separate from one another. This oscillation between the two life-narratives, clashing and yet co-existing worlds, requires attention to different formal and informal rule systems that are not always easy to discern.

Primary and Secondary Social Networks

Defining and determining primary and secondary social networks are dependent on the level of interaction we have with particular individuals, each having specific gradations of intimacy or distance. The Chicago School sociologist, Charles Horton Cooley, introduced the concept of the *primary group*, which is defined as a group consisting of intimate, face-to-face interaction and relatively long-lasting relationships, which typically includes one's family and peer groups (as cited in Anderson & Taylor, 2004). These primary groups have a powerful influence on an individual's personality and self-identity, and provide companionship and emotional support. In contrast, there are *secondary groups*, which are larger in membership, less intimate, and less long-lasting (Anderson & Taylor, 2004). These primary and secondary groups fulfill different needs of the individual, and are differentiated by how strongly the participants depend and identify with one another. In applying these conceptual distinctions to the social lives of older female inmates, we are presented with interestingly inverted social groupings, which is illustrated in Figure 11.1.

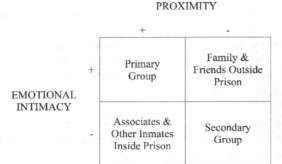

Figure 11.1 Emotional Intimacy and Proximity in Social Relationships

Interviews revealed that the majority of social interactions and relationships typical of primary groups were found in informants' outside social networks. The emphasis is on seeking emotional intimacy and support from family and friends, which occurs without the regular face-to-face contact that characterizes primary groups. Conversely, a common theme of the secondary group shows that given the limited control inmates have over their daily in-person social interactions, they are cautious to minimally invest socially and emotionally, thereby accentuating the detachment from one another.

Dimension Three: The Relevance of Age in Adaptation

In the third dimension, I explored the relevance of age in adapting to prison life for older women, with a focus on sources of adaptive techniques in informants' lives. I explore what appears to be the most salient mode of adaptation as voiced by informants, which generally centers on the maintenance of a positive mindset. This was described with the integration of life experience and prison tenure (sentence length) as being inseparable and thus informing their overall mode of adaptation to prison life.

Adaptation: "There's Always Hope"

In a broad sense, informants relied on a common philosophy that appeared to be strategic to surviving prison life, which was the importance of maintaining a positive mindset. This belief was also tied to maintaining a positive self-concept, which manifested in different ways, and included many facets. For instance, informants very often expressed keeping a positive attitude by maintaining a relatively high level of meaningful activity, which helped to pass the time in a purposeful way, particularly when adjusting to the realization of serving a life sentence. This narrative orientation exists on a continuum with other darker views, much as Gubrium (1993) found with the informants he interviewed regarding adaptation to life in a nursing home.

Age and Aging among Older, Incarcerated Women 179

Some of the more individual-level modes of adaptation include reading (books, magazines, newspapers, etc.), participating in religious or spiritual activities, listening to music, and staying physically active. Within these activities, there is a clear emphasis on the ability to learn new things, to educate oneself, and to take advantage of what resources are available. This introduces avenues through which women maintain some sense of control regarding how they invest their time in a meaningful way. The following two quotes truly exemplify ways in which informants use their time in pursuing activities that help them pass—and enjoy—the time, which helps in keeping a positive attitude.

> Yes, I love to read. I utilize the library in our cottage and also the main library. I read anywhere from 4–5 novels a week. I also get a newspaper every day, and have since I've been here. I get at least six magazines through the mail, and I read them cover-to-cover. Most of my time is spent reading. I don't crochet, knit, or embroider, none of that. My outlet is reading. And when I was able—walking. I would walk early in the mornings before it got crowded . . . But I can actually sit here and just observe, and it's very satisfying. I have a very vivid imagination, and if you have that imagination, you can take yourself wherever you want to go. I don't live in here, as far as my mind is, my body is in here, but I'm interested in what's going on out there.—*Ms Norris*

> A lot of people sit out there all day play cards, and I feel that's kind of a waste of time to do all day, when you can further your knowledge with different things. You can get a book, and there's a lot of different things in the book, we have a big library over here and then we have a library in the cottage. You can read about places you've never been and different things. I do the music, the books, and the community service, and write letters, read newspapers . . . That's how you keep up with what's going on out there. I probably wouldn't do this if I was out in the free world, but in here you have a whole new way to adapt. Just like in the free world, you would have things to keep you busy, to keep your mind occupied, that's what it's all about—keeping your mind occupied.—*Ms Sanders*

Religion and spirituality did not arise in all interviews, but for a few, it played a significant role in adaptation and keeping a positive mindset. Similar to the free world, informants relayed that it is not necessary to participate in formal or organized religious gatherings in order to connect with a particular faith. Informants' connections with their beliefs were held on a deeply personal level, as demonstrated by Ms Shelley:

> My adaptation is combination of growth, programs, and spirituality of being able to go to spiritual meetings and listening to what God has to say, because he plays a very important part in my life, and I only go to church 3 times a year. I don't have to go, for real. I am very peaceful, and being at peace is very

180 Leah M. Janssen

important. Most of all, my daughters are talking to me, and me having the contact with the outside world speaks volumes as to why I am this calm and this gentle today. Staying in a calm place as much as possible is important—walkmans with headphones are essential in here.—*Ms Shelley*

Another aspect of keeping a positive outlook is maintaining a laid back, "go-with-the-flow" attitude. The source of this adaptive technique appeared to be significantly rooted in informants' prison tenure, as they gained experience with the prison culture. Women who used this type of approach described remaining calm during times of intense inmate conflict and having the ability to take a step back and remove themselves from the situation. In addition to keeping a calm demeanor, there is a strong emphasis placed on abiding by the rules of the institution. The following quotes depict informants' experiences in maintaining a positive mindset through a go-with-the-flow attitude:

If I can't think them out, I'll just say, 'ok there's another day, just let it roll, just let it go.' Just let it go and the news rules, you just try to follow them. I keep telling the girls, it's not a lot of new rules, it's the old rules that they're just re-implementing or changing. Because I've been here since _____, come on now, I started out an orange shirt, which is the badest of the bad. When the new kids start, I say yea I was an orange shirt, so what, you just don't get it do you? Everything is the same, it's just a different day, no matter what they say, what they do, it's the same it's just a different day. We just got a new sheriff in town that we've got to deal with it, so you might as well just kick back. That's the whole key to everything, just kicking back and letting it roll, and not getting in the mix. You stay out of the mix—and you can cruise, you know.—*Ms Thompson*

You learn not to take things quite as seriously as you would maybe if you were younger, you don't take things as personally. Because there's nothing personal in here, it's just part of the process. I can only speak for myself, but I find that when there's a new rule imposed, a lot of people will get hyper . . . For as long as I'm concerned, oh go with the flow, you know. This is what we have today, it'll be something else tomorrow, it'll be something else next week, and then it'll change. And It'll come back right to where it was, so I think you learn to go with the flow a little more.—*Ms Boncquet*

You have to keep adjusting . . . I think if you're older and you're in prison, you're more mellowed out. You can tolerate and go with the changes better than you can say, if I was in my twenties, because you know when you're in your twenties you don't like all that. When you get older you'd be like ok, rules change every day, that's the only thing around here that is consistently different.—*Ms Shannon*

In addition to exhibiting a calm and positive mindset, the quotes given above recognize a contrast in how younger and older inmates cope with constant institutional change. The informal education of younger inmates, by older inmates, demonstrates the salience of age and tenure, which is influenced by the evolution of their adaptation techniques over time, and is dependent on life experience and prison tenure. Informants relay that they cannot dwell on the changes of the environment simply because they are inevitable and constant. Rather, the focus shifts to accepting those changes in order to move on and to continue to adapt.

Another part of maintaining a positive outlook on life comes with the reliance on hope, and an avoidance of negativity. Many informants conveyed hope for a better life beyond the prison walls, even despite a life sentence. As the following quotes depict, sources of hope stem from optimism about release, reflecting on the salience of relationships with family and friends, and an overall appreciation for life. Informants expressed the ability to look beyond their incarceration, and demonstrated a desire to recreate their lives.

> I'm going to get out of here someday. A lot of people give up—and I say you can't never give up. There's always hope. It's at the end of the rainbow—you got hope. As long as you have hope, you can conquer anything . . . You just can't never give up. I mean some people give up but, you know, giving up is not what it's all about, it's about adapting and go ahead and do what you have to do every day.—*Ms Sanders*

> So, you know just times when the attitudes of people when they're real negative, or sometimes you know you get sucked into that, and then you just have to regroup and just go in a positive thought . . . Freedom to me is not just being outside those gates, freedom to me is being able to get up in the morning and appreciate life. Life doesn't have to be full with a whole lot of stuff to be alright. You know as long as you have your inner peace, you can do it.—*Ms Parker*

Awareness of Age

Age awareness focused on whether and when inmates considered themselves to be "old," how they expressed a conscious awareness of their age, and in what situations their age proved to be a salient factor in their adaptation to the prison environment. Defining "old age" can be shaped in many different ways, and when informants were asked to describe an "older inmate," the focus was quickly drawn to physical attributes and functional abilities, rather than to chronological age. These included classifying inmates according to having overt physical characteristics, such as having a disability, using a wheelchair or walker, graying of the hair, and having wrinkles—what Karp (1988) termed *body reminders*. When asked if they considered themselves to be old, the majority of informants said that they did not feel old, despite evident physical disabilities that many informants associated with and classified as old age. Here again, informants reiterated the importance in being mentally alert and physically active as key components to healthy adaptation to prison life.

182 *Leah M. Janssen*

Age awareness emerged in what informants describe as two main scenarios. In the first scenario, informants relay that they are more aware of their age when they are in physically demanding situations. The following two quotes are examples of how many informants expressed an awareness of their age through issues of mobility, and how they associate old age with personal physical limitations.

> I feel old on those days when I literally can't move . . . I'm going to give you a perfect example. You know the ball field that has just come up in the last 6 months—I'm afraid to go to the field. It's a small area that we are made to go through to smoke, all 2,200 women. The most dangerous times are at 1:15 pm, and 6:15 pm when everybody comes through the yard at one time. And we have to stick us older people in back, for fear of being trampled. We have to stand off and wait for that crowd to get through because we're afraid to go through. As a person who has a hip replacement—I am afraid of being trampled.—*Ms Shelley*

> It's moving around and trying to get somewhere. Going to the store, thank god it's on the first floor now, because it used to be down in the basement. I can't live anywhere else but on that first floor with a wheelchair because you can't carry it. Nobody wants to be bothered with carrying it up and down. Makes my day easier. I try to walk, but sometimes it's just too difficult.—*Ms Homme*

In the second scenario of age awareness, informants conveyed consciousness of their age through social interactions with other inmates, which were classified as being either positive or challenging in nature: positive in the sense that there is an informational and mentoring exchange between the generations, where older inmates pass on advice to younger inmates, as was discussed in *Dimension Two*. Informants also expressed awareness of their age in a positive sense through increased feelings of pride and self-confidence, such as through their work responsibilities and perceived mental and emotional strength gained over time.

> Like at work I can sew up a storm. My hands, my mind, my eyesight is good, I'm one of the top sewers there's no body yet to beat me, to do as many as I do a day. Oh yea, they try it. I say, 'come on girls,' and it's challenging but I stay up there.—*Ms Homme*

> I am comfortable in my own skin, and I like who I am right now. Whether its old, young or indifferent or what. . .I don't feel old when I'm walking in the sunshine and the day is nice and you feel alive and vibrant inside, that part of you never changes. I'm never any older on the inside then I was when I was 10—that part of you does not change. It doesn't. This is the only thing that changes.—*Ms Boncquet*

Social encounters also have the capacity to create frustrating experiences of age, particularly those occurring with younger inmates. In the following two instances,

Age and Aging among Older, Incarcerated Women 183

Ms Doyle and Ms Burt describe difficult situations in which they find that they are most aware of their age while interacting with younger inmates. These portrayals illustrate the more challenging perceptions that informants have regarding their age.

> When I see all the foolish activity, all the irresponsible ways the women in here conduct themselves. But, I feel more out of the loop then I feel old, we just have nothing in common. I mean I had an entirely normal lifestyle and now I'm set into an environment where 95% or more of the women were used and lived in a whole different way, more of a street way. What really brings my age to mind is I think it's I'm of an era where values were different.—*Ms Doyle*

> Now, I'm old now. I realize that . . . I feel old compared to them, but we have nothing in common anyway, so even if I was on the other side of the fence, I'd still feel old compared to them. I feel old when they start with all the foul language and all the sexual graphic sexual talk and reading sexual letters from other people, other guys in prison. Then I feel old, but I don't know if that's an age difference, or a culture difference, or what or both or . . . I just don't get it.—*Ms Burt*

As could be interpreted in these quotes, it is quite possible that it is not solely age that presents such differences in these social interactions. Rather, as some informants admit, their age awareness stems from more than just generational differences. Cultural and lifestyle differences between younger and older inmates can contribute to one's consciousness and perception of their age in relation to others around them.

Old Age in Prison: An Advantage or Disadvantage?

In this section, responses are explored regarding whether or not informants perceive older inmates as having particular advantages or disadvantages in prison. Similar to the discussion above entitled, "There's Always Hope," informants illustrate the benefits of age through maintaining a positive attitude and self-concept, which helps in the evolution of personal adaptive techniques.

> The number one thing that has helped me is my age, because prison is not for older people. Prison is for young people. I think the number one advantage is, for me, nobody bothers me. I can go out in the rec room and sit at a table, and I can sit there all day and nobody comes over.—*Ms Norris*

> If you are an older lady and you act in that account, they give you that respect, as an elder. I think all elders need respect, because they've been through things that I haven't yet, and they might be able to guide me . . . I think being older helps me realize what my needs are and what my wants are.—*Ms Shannon*

184 *Leah M. Janssen*

> You will find that if you talk to most of us, especially if we're 50 and over, life gets a little easier, you don't take things quite the same way you do when you're younger. As you get older there's not the social pressures that you have when you're younger, especially in a correctional institution. The younger people are more worried about the peer pressure things going on around them. Older inmates don't get that. We're either ignored or respected. Depending on how you hold yourself and how you react. If you have to be an inmate, it's best to be an older inmate because you're treated better. Not by staff so much, it's how you're treated by the younger inmates. They either stay away from you or they treat you as they would a family member that's older.—*Ms Boncquet*

Some informants believe that with old age comes ease with which one navigates the prison system, which is supported by the knowledge and experience gained through prison tenure. Knowing how and when to exhibit appropriate behavior for specific situations is important in establishing one's status as an older inmate. Therefore, attitude and reputation are clearly influential components in this process. Acting with dignity and having respect for oneself and others influences the likelihood of having a relatively favorable prison experience.

Conversely, informants respond to the disadvantages and more challenging aspects of being an older inmate:

> There are no advantages to being older there are more disadvantages—like when you get harassed by the younger ones. You know how many times I've been called an old [expletive]—all the time!—*Ms Burt*

> I have been called ugly names like, you old [expletive], move your old [expletive] . . . I don't think there's any advantage to being older here. You have to be able to take care of yourself.—*Ms Shelley*

> Oh my god, oh—there's no advantages to being older here. No, because they don't do anything for us.—*Ms Homme*

It could be inferred through these quotes that these negative experiences may impact their overall perception of age and adaptation. Living in a harsh and ever-changing environment, the demands can easily begin to stretch the capacity of the individual. However, informants proved that there are ways of negotiating such an intense atmosphere and emphasize the importance of not becoming too overwhelmed by issues that are out of one's direct control.

Dimension Four: Programming for an Aging Prison Population

The fourth dimension aims to give voice to older female inmate's awareness, use, and needs of programming, which is important to further understand aspects of adaptation to internal prison life. A common aim in many penal institutions is to maintain a controlled and supervised rehabilitative environment, one which works with inmates in dealing with issues related to their crime. Often, this goal is founded on the provision of intensive programming that attempts to tap into the varying needs of inmates. For instance, some programs aim at preparing inmates for reentry into society by providing educational, vocational, and recreational programs (ODRC, n.d.). Other programming may be implemented to address behavioral and addiction issues, while some programs have more therapeutic goals. The availability and utilization of programs impact an inmates' acclimation to the prison environment, as well as possible reentry into the community.

Utilization of Programs

The utilization of programs is linked to inmates' awareness and knowledge of what is offered within the institution, which is likely connected to the communication by staff to inmates. Many informants explained that programs appear to have a general focus on young, "short-timers" nearing their parole board hearing. Perhaps this has become a broader focus of institutions since there is an increasingly large number of young women being incarcerated for petty crimes. From the perspectives of informants, programs specifically targeting older inmates are rare and thus do not seem to be widely utilized. Informants did not claim to currently participate in any age-related programs. It is not inferred here that older offenders in general do not use programs or that programs do not exist. Rather, the reasons for participating vary and include influential factors such as one's access to the program area, personal interests, and prerequisites associated with particular programs. In reference to informants' experiences, it seems that one's health status, mobility, and physical distance to the program area have a lot to do with inmate participation. Several informants said that they would be more likely to take part in programs that were located within their cottage because their concerns with mobility would not hinder their participation.

Since there are a variety of programs offered to the general population of inmates, informants expressed enjoyment in discovering both familiar activities and newfound personal interests. Learning a new trade and gaining work experience will help inmates find a job when released back into the community. The rehabilitative elements of many programs offered create personal and psychological benefits that help inmates understand and cope with the stress and anxiety behind their crime. Additionally, all informants conveyed compassionate involvement in community service opportunities, and many described the positive feelings they experience when they are able to give back to others. On a statewide scale, the ODRC reports that the total year-to-date number of community service hours completed by all inmates as reported in December 2016 for all of 2016 was 5,194,772 hours (ODRC, 2016b).

Needs of Older Inmates

Informants expressed that while the needs of older inmates vary, their primary area of concern centers on health-related issues, for example, challenges with

186   Leah M. Janssen

accessing limited medical services, meeting dietary needs, and mobility throughout the institution. Recall that many of these issues are heavily impacted by over-crowding and personal physical mobility, which surfaced throughout interviews. Among the most common needs of older female inmates, informants noted that better attention must be given to the health concerns of older women and that medical processes are much too slow. Even with guaranteed prison health care, the issues of overcrowding create a heavy flow of inmates in and out of the infirmary on a regular basis. This creates frustration in the inability to seek prompt medical care, especially when age may exacerbate what appear to be more common afflictions. Further, they believe that the available programming does *not* meet the needs of older inmates and appears to be designed for the general inmate population, irrespective of age.

Program and Housing Suggestions

This section explores information pertaining to program and housing suggestions as indicated by informants. While there were a small number of aging-focused programs available at different times in the past, informants voiced that they did not know of any aging-focused programming currently available. According to the perspectives of informants, the most successful programs available to older women in past programming had an aging-specific focus. For example, some program topics had a medical focus (exercise, osteoporosis, arthritis, diabetes, menopause, etc.), while other programs focused on social and mental health topics (team-building games and intergenerational programs). Informants explained that the more common general programs offered to all inmates do not recognize aging-related issues and is therefore less relevant and accessible for older inmates. Due to the lack of response from the institution, the availability of aging-focused programs could not be fully determined. However, discontinuation of these programs could likely be linked to lack of funding or participation issues.

> They used to have a group, Older Resourceful Women, but they cut that out. We were all in it, out at the camp, yea we used to pay $1 a month to buy materials. We made quilts and all kinds of stuff . . . and then they done away with it, anything productive it's passed [by]. Yea, I'd like to see that back; that was really nice.—*Ms Fry*

Housing preferences were found to be another area of contention that fueled suggestions addressing the needs of older inmates. Informants adamantly voiced their opinions and concerns about their current housing arrangements. This topic brought up the reoccurring challenges and tension between older and younger inmates, accessibility and mobility issues, and institutional overcrowding. The majority of informants expressed that they would like to have a segregated housing unit just for older inmates:

> If you put the older offenders together, we're not only going to be well behaved, but we are going to participate in programs and we are going to look

out and take care of each other. That's what we're going to do. We're going to do that. It needs to be done. And we wouldn't be so afraid to walk this farm because sometimes I'm afraid.—*Ms Shelley*

The concept of age-segregated and age-integrated prison housing is a very complex issue. The Hocking Correctional Facility is an age-segregated institution for older male inmates in Ohio; however, a comparable facility does not exist for older female inmates. Since not all informants agreed that this would be a universal solution, it is important to review the potential advantages and disadvantages of implementing an optional housing unit designed for older women.

Advantages of an age-integrated environment would likely promote social interaction and an exchange of resources between different ages and generations. For instance, younger and older inmates could exchange valuable resources through conversation about sharing advice and insights on adaptation to life in prison. This creates a positive experience for both contributing parties. Conversely, as demon-strated by many informants, the disadvantages of an age-integrated environment can weigh heavily upon the life satisfaction of many older women, due to generational and cultural differences as discussed previously. The higher demands of an environment and the lower the resources of the individual, the less likely the person is to experience a high level of life satisfaction and morale (Gubrium, 1972).

A primary advantage of age-segregated settings involves a sense of support and protection that these secure communities could provide, just as informants have illustrated throughout interviews. Collective reciprocity helps in lessening the fear that many older inmates associate with younger inmates. Inmates living in an age-segregated setting may have similar lifestyles and use similar goods, programs, and services. Services can be delivered more effectively and efficiently, and at a lower cost, for instance, with architectural/environmental design features and delivery of medical care services. Older adults in age-segregated environments consistently report high levels of satisfaction with their residences, which could allow for ease of adaptation to the prison environment (Golant, 1985). In contrast, it is believed that age-segregated environments physically and socially isolate older adults from the rest of the population. When older adults are kept separate from the rest of society, they are prevented from sharing their insight and life experiences with younger generations. Few informants voice this concern; however, those who do, share their appreciation for the mentorships they have created with younger inmates.

Overview of Findings

This research sought to explore the lives of older incarcerated women, with an emphasis on understanding areas of adaptation. This was described through four interrelated dimensions: day-to-day life, interpersonal relationships, the relevance of age in adaptation, and available programming for older inmates. Findings suggest that adaptations made within each of these dimensions have an important

188 *Leah M. Janssen*

impact on the overall adaptation to prison life. In this section, I will address these findings through major emergent themes relevant in each dimension.

In the first dimension, the day-to-day lives are explored for older incarcerated women. This includes a description of informant's schedules, activities, and daily routines, as well as what they consider to be the positive and negative aspects of a typical day. Findings reveal that while schedules remain regimented, women are able to maintain some control over how they spend (or pass) their time. Informants demonstrate that even the smallest decisions made are meaningful and are taken with great pride. This reflects the importance of creating and maintaining avenues of personal control. This finding is speculated to positively contribute to one's perception of autonomy and satisfaction, which thus eases adaptation to prison life.

The second dimension investigated the interpersonal relationships of older incarcerated women, whose social networks inside and outside prison are explored in terms of breadth of contact and depth of meaning and support. Generally, most informants convey a sense of emotional detachment from other inmates. This results in feelings of withdrawal and distrust, which appears to leave informants without immediate avenues for seeking social support. This was especially evident in the cultural and generational gap of social exchanges with younger inmates, where particularly negative associations are formed. Furthermore, informants are most likely to rely on the support of their outside social networks, that is, if they are available. The majority of informants claim that maintaining meaningful outside social ties plays an important role in their ability to adapt to the harsh realities of prison life. Lastly, informants voiced anxiety and stress in the tension between inside and outside social worlds, and the inability to fully relate or belong to either side.

In the third dimension, relevance of age in adapting to prison life for older women was discussed, which is clearly influenced by a combination of knowledge and experience gained from life prior to incarceration as well as one's prison tenure. Informants illustrated the importance in maintaining a positive attitude and self-concept, which aids in the evolution of personal adaptive techniques. Here, informants reveal ways of negotiating the intense prison environment and emphasize the importance of not becoming overwhelmed by issues that are out of one's direct control. Instead, informants focus on maintaining some sense of control over activities they find joy and interest in, thereby channeling their energy toward a positive outlook. Informants spoke to their personal experiences and associations regarding their awareness of old age in prison, thereby revealing great insights into how their age is often perceived as an advantage *and* a disadvantage.

The fourth dimension investigated several aspects of programming as voiced by older inmates. Use of these programs and reasons for enrollment varies widely by individual. Informants did not express a general awareness or participation in current programs designed for older inmates, despite the ODRC's effort to provide such programming. Moreover, informants gave their opinions on what they deemed the needs of older inmates' to be, which were largely focused on housing, health, and medical concerns. Informants asserted that their needs were not being met by the institution, and were asked to voice their suggestions as to what

Age and Aging among Older, Incarcerated Women   189

they believe to be beneficial for older inmates and their adaptation to prison life. Suggestions centered on improving the health and medical care for older inmates, re-implementing previously successful aging-related programs, and most of all, the creation of an older inmate housing unit.

Implications for the Future

This chapter has described many contextual factors and broader policies that militate against more fulfilling adaptation to everyday life for older, incarcerated women. In the decade since I undertook this research, the dramatic expansion of incarceration in the United States only sharpens the sense of public alarm about the inadequacies of extant policies. Growing inmate populations and rising costs of incarceration have led to overcrowded and overspent prisons, which have also brought about an ill-advised push for lawmakers to privatize prisons (Brickner & Diaz, 2011). In an Ohio budget report, newly elected Governor John Kasich supported the auction of public prisons to private corporate ownership, which was denounced for creating further barriers to prison regulation and tax-payer transparency (Bischoff & Magan, 2011). For-profit prisons are often criticized for their inability to provide effective rehabilitative programming, due to the fact that they are incentivized to increase, rather than decrease, their populations (Brickner & Diaz, 2011). It can be inferred that the lack of adequate programming has long-term impacts on education and employment training, which ripple out into communities upon inmate release—for those who reenter the community. Meanwhile, funding support for educational programs, which has been shown to reduce recidivism and diminish inmate housing costs (Esperian, 2010), has been slashed in many states.

Additionally, individuals entering prison generally have been subject to poor nutrition, more chronic health problems, fewer resources, and higher rates of drug and alcohol use than is true in the population at large. Layering these risk factors upon incarceration and advanced age, there exists a process of *cumulative advantage or disadvantage (CAD)* (Dannefer, 2003), in which relatively small risk factors or health conditions, in earlier years, compound their harmful effects later in life. (Quadagno, 2014, p. 39). Further, CAD is "concerned with the existence and sources of age-specific individual differences and with questions of fairness in the distribution of opportunities and resources" (Dannefer, 2003, p. S327). This cumulative impact creates further inequality for those using health care resources and seeking to survive prison life as older inmates. Finally, in combining these systemic issues with overcrowding and overspending, it is important to consider the prudence of initiatives to release older "non-threatening" inmates into the community, where housing and medical care will be almost impossible to access. We are thus left with the realization that supportive programs—both for incarcerated and community-dwelling older women who are vulnerable to poverty—are woefully inadequate. We can only hope that the broad-based political backlash against mass incarceration will free up more funding to address these pressing needs.

Acknowledgments

I would like to thank Dr Christopher Wellin for his unconditional support as my advisor throughout my master's research, and in the process of revising and updating the scholarship for publication. I would also like to thank Dr Glenn Muschert and Dr Christine Caffrey for their guidance and support as thesis committee members. These three individuals provided the encouragement that was instrumental in giving voice to a population of older women who are often forgotten. Finally, I am grateful to the eleven women who were trusting enough to participate in this research; I am honored to tell their stories.

References

Aday, R. (1994). Aging in prison: A case study of new elderly offenders. *International Journal of Offender Therapy and Comparative Criminology*, 38(1), 79–91.

Aday, R., & Farney, L. (2014). Malign neglect: Assessing older women's health care experiences in prison. *Bioethical Inquiry*, 11, 359–372.

American Civil Liberties Union (ACLU). (2012, June). *At America's expense: The mass incarceration of the elderly*. Retrieved January 2, 2017 from www.aclu.org/files/assets/elderlyprisonreport_20120613_1.pdf.

Anderson, M.L., & Taylor, H.F. (2004). *Sociology, understanding a diverse society* (3rd ed.). Ontario, Canada: Wadsworth/Thomson Learning.

Auerhahn, K. (2002). Selective incapacitation, three strikes, and the problem of aging prison populations: Using simulation modeling to see the future. *Criminology & Public Policy*, 1(3), 353–388.

Bischoff, L.A., & Magan, C. (2011, March 16). *Deep cuts, privatization fill Kasich's first budget: He is reducing aid to cities and selling several state assets*. Springfield, News-Sun. Retrieved October 28, 2017 from www.springfieldnewssun.com.

Booker, M. (2016, May 19). *BJS data shows graying of prisons* [Blog post]. Prison Policy Initiative. Retrieved January 11, 2017 from www.prisonpolicy.org/blog/2016/05/19/bjsaging/.

Brickner, M., & Diaz, S. (2011). Prisons for profit: Incarceration for sale. *Human Rights*, 38(3), 13–16. Retrieved October 28, 2017 from www.jstor.org/stable/23375625.

Carson, E.A. (2014, September). *Prisoners in 2013*. United States Department of Justice, Office of Justice Programs, Bureau of Justice Statistics. Retrieved October 28, 2017 from www.bjs.gov/content/pub/pdf/p13.pdf.

Chaiklin, H. (1998). The elderly disturbed prisoner. *Clinical Gerontologist*, 20(1), 47–62.

Codd, H. (1996). Feminism, ageism and criminology: Towards an agenda for future research. *Feminist Legal Studies*, 4(2), 178–194.

Dannefer, D. (2003). Cumulative advantage/disadvantage and the life course: Cross-fertilizing age and social science theory. *Journal of Gerontology*, 58B(6), S327–S337.

Enders, S.R., Paterniti, D.A., & Meyers, F.J. (2005). An approach to develop effective health care decision making for women in prison. *Journal of Palliative Medicine*, 8(2), 432–439.

Esperian, J.H. (2010). The effect of prison education programs and recidivism. *The Journal of Correctional Education*, 61(4), 316–334.

Fearn, N.E., & Parker, K. (2005). Health care for women inmates: Issues, perceptions and policy considerations. *California Journal of Health Promotion*, 3(2), 1–22.

Giallombardo, R. (1966). *Society of women: A study of a women's prison*. New York: John Wiley & Sons.

Age and Aging among Older, Incarcerated Women   191

Goetting, A. (1983). The elderly in prison: Issues and perspectives. *Journal of Research in Crime and Delinquency*, 20(2), 291–309.

Goffman, E. (1961). *Asylums, essays on the social situation of mental patients and other inmates*. Garden City, NY: Anchor Books.

Golant, S.M. (1985). In defense of age-segregated housing. *Aging*, 348, 22–26.

Gubrium, J.F. (1972). Toward a socio-environmental theory of aging. *The Gerontologist*, 12(3), 281–284.

Gubrium, J.F. (1993). *Speaking of Life*. Hawthorne, NY: Aldine de Gruyter.

Gubrium, J.F., & Holstein, J.A. (1999). Constructionist perspectives on aging. In V.L. Bengston & K.W. Schaie (Eds.), *Handbook of theories of aging* (pp. 287–305). New York: Springer.

Heffernan, E. (1972). *Making it in prison: The square, the cool and the life*. New York: John Wiley & Sons.

JPay, Inc. (n.d.). *About JPay*. Retrieved October 28, 2017 from www.jpay.com/AboutUs.aspx.

Karp, D. (1988). A decade of reminders: Changing age consciousness between fifty and sixty years old. *The Gerontologist*, 6, 727–738.

King, R.S., & Mauer, M. (2001). *Aging behind bars: "Three strikes" seven years later*. Sentencing Project. Retrieved February 2, 2007 from http://public.soros.org/initiatives/justice/articles_publications/publications/agingbehindbars_20010801/agingbehindbars.pdf.

Kratcoski, P.C., & Babb, S. (1990). Adjustment of older inmates: An analysis by institutional structure and gender. *Journal of Contemporary Criminal Justice*, 6(4), 264–281.

Krause, N. (2006). Social relationships in late life. In R.H. Binstock & L.K. George (Eds.), *Handbook of aging and the social sciences* (6th ed., pp. 181–200). New York: Academic Press.

Leahy, J.P. (1998). Coping strategies of prisoners in a maximum security prison: Minimals, optimals and utilitarians. *Social Thought & Research*, 21(1–2), 279–290.

Lemieux, C.M., Dyeson, T.B., & Castiglione, B. (2002). Revisiting the literature on prisoners who are older: Are we wiser? *The Prison Journal*, 82(4), 440–458.

Lindquist, C.H., & Lindquist, C.A. (1999). Health behind bars: Utilization and evaluation of medical care among jail inmates. *Journal of Community Health*, 24(4), 285–303.

Maschi, T., Kwak, J., Ko, E., & Morrissey, M.B. (2012). Forget me not: Dementia in prison. *The Gerontologist*, 52(4), 441–451.

Maykut, P., & Morehouse, R. (1994). *Beginning qualitative research*. London, UK: RoutledgeFalmer Press.

Moore, E., & Unwin, T. (2002). Ohio's older inmates. In M. Black (Ed.), *Ohio Corrections Research Compendium 1* (pp. 36–44). Columbus, OH: Ohio Department of Rehabilitation and Correction, Bureau of Research.

Morton, J.B. (1992). *An administrative overview of the older inmate*. Washington, DC: U.S. Department of Justice, National Institute of Corrections.

Morton, J.B. (2004). *Working with women offenders in correctional institutions*. Alexandria, VA: American Correctional Association.

Ohio Department of Rehabilitation & Correction (ODRC), Bureau of Research/Office of Policy and Offender Reentry. (2006, July). *Institution census report*. Retrieved Janurary 2, 2017 from www.drc.ohio.gov/LinkClick.aspx?fileticket=gNMLpNW-eWg%3d&portalid=0.

Ohio Department of Rehabilitation & Correction (ODRC), Bureau of Research and Evaluation. (2016a, January). *Census of ODRC institutional population, demographic, and offense summary*. Retrieved January 4, 2017 from www.drc.ohio.gov/LinkClick.aspx?fileticket=ArGu7dKNUpQ%3D&portalid=0.

192   *Leah M. Janssen*

Ohio Department of Rehabilitation & Correction (ODRC). (2016b, December). *ODRC monthly fact sheet.* Retrieved January 4, 2017 from www.drc.ohio.gov/Portals/0/Reentry/Reports/Monthly/2016/Dec%202016%20Fact%20Sheet.pdf?ver=2016–12–15–110423–520.

Ohio Department of Rehabilitation & Correction (ODRC), Bureau of Research and Evaluation. (2016c, December). *Prison community service monthly report.* Retrieved January 4, 2017 from www.drc.ohio.gov/Portals/0/Reentry/Reports/Community%20Service/COMMUNITY%20SERVICE%20REPORT_ENDING%20DECEMBER%202016.pdf?ver=2017–02–21–084005–053.

Ohio Department of Rehabilitation & Correction (ODRC). (n.d.). *ODRC programs.* Retrieved October 28, 2017 from www.drc.ohio.gov/programs.

Ollove, M. (2016, March 17). *Elderly inmates burden state prisons* [Blog post]. The Pew Charitable Trusts. Retrieved January 11, 2017 from www.pewtrusts.org/en/research-and-analysis/blogs/stateline/2016/03/17/elderly-inmates-burden-state-prisons.

Quadagno, J. (2014). *Aging and the life course* (6th ed.). New York: McGraw-Hill.

Ritter, N.M. (2006). Preparing for the future: Criminal justice in 2040. *National Institute of Justice Journal,* (255), 8–11.

Ross, J.I., & Richards, S.C. (2003). *Convict criminology.* Belmont, CA: Wadsworth/Thomson Learning.

Rubenstein, D. (1984). The elderly in prison: A review of the literature. In E.S. Newman, D.J. Newman, & M.L. Gewirtz (Eds.), *Elderly criminals* (pp. 153–168). Cambridge, MA: Oelgeschlager, Gunn & Hain.

Rubin, H., & Rubin, I. (2012). Research philosophy and qualitative interviews. In *Qualitative interviewing: The art of hearing data* (3rd ed., pp. 13–24). Los Angeles, CA: Sage.[WC1]

Rubinstein, R.L., Killbride, J.C., & Nagy, S. (1992). *Elders living alone: Frailty and perception of choice.* New York: Aldine de Gruyter.

Smith, S. (2004, November 7). *U.S. prison population approaches 1.5 million* [Press Release]. Washington, DC: Department of Justice's Bureau of Justice Statistics.

Stack, C.B. (1974). *All our kin.* New York: Harper & Row.

Stojkovic, S. (2007). Elderly prisoners: A growing and forgotten group within correctional systems vulnerable to elder abuse. *Journal of Elder Abuse & Neglect,* 19(3–4), 97–117. Retrieved October 26, 2017 from www.tandfonline.com/doi/abs/10.1300/J084v19n03_06.

United States Census Bureau (USCB), Annual Social and Economic Supplement. (2012a). *Current population survey.* Retrieved January 12, 2017 from www.census.gov/population/age/data/2012.html.

United States Census Bureau (USCB), Population Division. (2012b). *Table 2. Projections of the population by selected age groups and sex for the United States: 2015 to 2060.* Retrieved January 12, 2017 from www.census.gov/population/projections/data/national/2012/summarytables. Html.

Wahidin, A. (2002). Reconfiguring older bodies in the prison time machine. *Journal of Aging and Identity,* 7(3), 177–193.

Wahidin, A. (2004). *Older women in the criminal justice system: Running out of time.* London, UK: Jessica Kingsley.

Williams, B.A., Lindquist, K., Sudore, R.L., Strupp, H.M., Wilmott, D.J., & Walter, L.G. (2006). Being old and doing time: Functional impairment and adverse experiences of geriatric female prisoners. *Journal of American Geriatrics Society,* 54, 702–707.

CHAPTER 12

How Thinking about Children from a Global Perspective Can Fortify Social Gerontology

Maria Schmeeckle

Introduction and Overview

The other day, I pulled out my "Aging Qual" notebook to show a student. This was a 3-inch binder put together in 1997, a repository of all that I had learned in preparation for doctoral "qualifying" exams in Gerontology. Looking back at this notebook almost 20 years later, and reflecting on highlights I have taken with me, I continue to be grateful for the insights learned. Yet there are ways in which I would now challenge and query the field.

In this chapter, I will first describe my academic trajectory and research interests. Then, I will share concepts from my training in gerontology that have helped me think about children, including age-period-cohort-generation distinctions, heterogeneity, cumulative disadvantage, the life course perspective, and the latent kin matrix. Following this, I offer some questions for a critical social gerontology which are inspired by a consideration of children from a global perspective. By inquiring about "missing elders," gerontocracies, life pathways in a global context, the impact of cumulative disadvantage in childhood, and world megatrends, I intend to challenge the field of social gerontology to transcend its age and geographic limitations, and in the process to consider new issues related to power and inequality.

Academic Trajectory

It was my interest in family relationships that brought me to gerontology. Coming from a large, complex, troubled family, I was eager to learn more about family boundary complexity and other family topics. When I arrived at the University of Southern California in the graduate program in sociology in 1993, I was assigned to a faculty mentor, who turned out to be Vern Bengtson. "Become a research apprentice," he advised me, "and draw upon the strengths of the department." Recognizing this wisdom, I immediately became a volunteer on the Longitudinal Study of Generations (LSOG), which was founded and overseen by Vern. The LSOG was a study of more than 300 four-generation families that began in 1971. It originated with a multistage stratified sample of grandfathers enrolled in southern California's first large health maintenance organization. Their spouses, adult

194 *Maria Schmeeckle*

children, adult grandchildren, and (eventually, starting in 1991) young adult great-grandchildren were invited to participate (Bengtson, 1996). At the time when I joined the project team, mail-back questionnaires were sent out every 3–4 years, and I was able to work on the entire survey cycle of questionnaire development, mailing, "nagging" of survey respondents, coding, data entry, data cleaning, and analysis. I found the LSOG to be an inviting and enriching work and learning environment, and spent many hours at its headquarters during my 8 years of graduate school. Vern's additional advice to draw upon the strengths of the department served me well, too. I chose to study families through the specialties of "aging" and "gender studies," both being rich, complementary areas of concentration at my university.

For my dissertation, Vern and the LSOG project director, Roseann Giarrusso, allowed me to submit original questions into the Time 6 (1997) wave of the study, and to interview a subset of survey participants who were adult stepchildren. I finished my dissertation in 2001, and was fortunate to find a sociology position at Illinois State University, where there was a great fit between my interests and the needs of the department. At ISU, I was asked to teach a general education course called *American Family*, which focused on the diversity of family life across historical time in America. I still enjoy teaching that class regularly, but after teaching a global social problems course and becoming fascinated (and concerned about) global issues, I gravitated toward teaching courses from a more global perspective. I took my *Marriage and Family* elective class in a global direction, and eventually created a new course—*Children in Global Perspective*. Recently, I have been teaching our department's senior research capstone courses. In 2015, my students and I took a team approach to studying "Cosmopolitan Students at Illinois State University." The following year, another cohort of students worked with me on another globally focused report: "Acquiring Global Competencies at Illinois State University." In addition to teaching about global issues, I have also expanded my knowledge of global learning and global pedagogy through service roles at my university, and it has been a pleasure to contribute to ISU's "comprehensive campus internationalization" efforts. So here I am, in Bloomington-Normal, Illinois, with interests now focused on children and global knowledge.

Research Interests

In graduate school, I became curious about subjective perceptions of family boundaries, and on the LSOG was able to study these from the point of view of adult children in stepfamilies. I was very interested in complex family structures and their increasing prevalence in the population. At the time, I found the gerontological literature to give only cursory attention to trends in divorce, remarriage, and cohabitation. Empirical studies in gerontology often portrayed parent-child relations in a way that disconnected them from the family structure contexts in which they were embedded. I set out to explore one domain of complex family structures—stepfamily relationships. The relevant literatures in this area overlapped with the study of kinship, and later I had opportunities to write about extended family and social networks with my ISU colleague, Susan Sprecher (Schmeeckle & Sprecher, 2004, 2013). As my interests became more globally focused, I developed an interest in "children in especially difficult circumstances." Before I knew this particular UNICEF phrase, I framed them in my mind as "the world's throwaway children." I am still passionate about these children, and spent several years exploring what recent global data can tell us about children's inequality worldwide (Schmeeckle & Gran, 2015a). I am also interested in speaking to multiple publics, as has been endorsed in sociology (Burawoy, 2005). With Brian Gran and other collaborators, I worked on a web resource called Worldwide Outlook for Children. Our goal was not only to expand comprehensive global awareness about children within academic circles, but to inform policymakers, the media, the public, and young people across the world (Schmeeckle & Gran, 2014a, 2014b). Due to the complexities of global data, technology, and available time, we have put this project on hold for now and I have turned my attention to a less daunting but very fascinating area of study: children's rebellion against parents. I use the topic of rebellion to examine the interplay between children's ability to have some control over the direction of their lives and their marginalization due to age and other intersecting identities. I will examine this through retrospective interviews with adults reflecting on their actual and desired rebellions against parents prior to age 18.

Aspects of my Training in Gerontology that Inform my Research and Teaching about Children

Age-Period-Cohort-Generation

Learning to distinguish between age-period-cohort-generation issues was important in my training, and it remains so today. We learned about this in classes and readings by Bengtson (1993) and others. With classmates, I thought about these distinctions as we considered research questions for *LSOG* analyses. I learned to think with more precision about whether timing, historical period, age group/cohort, or family lineage generation were applicable in various situations. For instance, the generational-sequential design of the LSOG lent itself somewhat to a cohort analysis (i.e., Bengtson, Biblarz, & Roberts, 2002) and yet age spacing between generations on the LSOG and the population at large is far from uniform, and made even messier when we consider the age gaps (or lack thereof) between stepparents and stepchildren.

Despite the rough way of approximating cohort differences through family lineage generations, I have found family generation comparisons to be a useful way to help students recognize the magnitude of social change and cohort change. In my *American Family* class, I have had students explore changes and similarities in attitudes and experiences across three generations of their own family, with a focus on changing historical contexts around gender relations, race relations, gay rights, and immigration. I can usually count on there to be enough of an age

196   *Maria Schmeeckle*

gap between my students and their grandparents so that changes in social norms and values are evident. Many students report increased acceptance of same-sex and interracial partnerships across their family generations, and expanded roles for women. These intergenerational changes parallel our readings about diversity and change in American families.

I also recognized the importance of historical period in my recent focus on global children. Not until the recent past have we been able to say we have global knowledge about children's well-being and human rights. The United Nations, individual governments, and non-profit organizations have, for some time, gathered evidence of experiences of young people with an eye to improving their lives. With the development of the internet, UN statistics began to be released through a UN Common Database in 1999 (United Nations Statistical Commission, 2007). In collaboration with sociologist Brian Gran, I compiled usable indicators from the UN and other sources, working to assess where we are with our global knowledge about children, and conceptualizing a way to share that information with the public (Schmeeckle & Gran, 2014a, 2014b, 2015a, 2015b). I am mindful that our work reflects the particular historical moment.

Heterogeneity

Sociologist George Maddox spoke at my university's Multidisciplinary Research Colloquium Series in Aging in 1998. By then, I was in my fifth year of graduate school and had been well socialized into the field of gerontology. My multidisciplinary classmates at the Andrus Gerontology School and I were entranced with Maddox, our Kesten Memorial lecturer, and to this day I have kept not only my summary of his talk but the summaries of five classmates. What delighted me the most was his emphasis on the diversity of human experience. Rather than focusing on "negative regression lines in statuses with age" (his phrase, recorded in my notes) (Maddox, 1998), Maddox (1987) encouraged us to examine age/period/cohort variations across sex, ethnicity, education, income, and other factors.

> "The pervasiveness and persistence of heterogeneity we observe are significant gerontological facts documenting the potential for modification of aging processes; and . . . once the potential for modifiability is established, choosing among realistic alternatives for older adults becomes a responsibility as well as an opportunity for gerontologists," he wrote in his earlier Kleemeier Lecture, published in *The Gerontologist*.
>
> (p. 557)

This message deeply resonated with me. I must have internalized a curiosity about the diversity of lives and life choices, because I see now that I have made the study and teaching of diversity a priority.

Some examples from my dissertation research demonstrate my focus on diversity. The co-chair of my dissertation committee, Roseann Giarrrusso, helped

Thinking about Children 197

me to explore heterogeneity in adult-children's relationships with stepparents in terms of subjective perceptions of family membership. "We can't assume that adult children perceive their *biological/adoptive* parents as family members and parents," she counseled me. "It's an empirical question." (I've since used the phrase, "It's an empirical question" many times with students who are tempted to overreach in what they know based on available information.) With Roseann's help, I fashioned survey questions for the 1997 LSOG study that asked about subjective perceptions toward *biological/adoptive parents* as well as stepparents, former stepparents, cohabiting partners of parents, and former cohabiting partners of parents. The findings revealed slight but understandable heterogeneity in adult children's subjective perceptions of whether biological/adoptive parents were family members. The great majority of adult children in the sample perceived biological/adoptive parents to be "fully" family members, but 9% of these parents were perceived to be family at lower levels or "not at all" (often biological/adoptive fathers who were divorced from the childrens' mothers early in the children's lives, and with whom the children did not live for very long) (Schmeeckle, 2001).

Later, I supplemented my survey analysis of adult children's family perceptions of stepparents with a purposive interview design that highlighted not just common scenarios (such as perceiving stepparents acquired in childhood as partial or full family members) but less common ones (perceiving stepparents acquired in childhood as "fully" family but "not at all" a parent, or as "not at all" family or parent). My design allowed me to explore the diversity of stepfamily relationships and to make comparisons across perception groups, participants' gender, and stepparents' gender, all from adult children's point of view. Making visible the variety of relationships in a context of increasing family diversity remains very important, I believe, and eliciting (adult) children's views is very in-line with a growing focus on children's agency in childhood studies (James, 2004). Exploring less common cases helped to build understanding about the full range of stepfamily relationships, and led me to hear some fascinating stories such as the story of "Travis" whose father had not informed his teenage son that his "roommate" had become his wife. Or "Catherine," who saw herself as one who had broken the "rules of family inclusion," and went from perceiving her stepmother as a complete mother figure to being estranged and no longer invested in the relationship (Schmeeckle, 2001).

My examination of subjective perceptions of family in biological and stepfamilies in a large sample showed me that *very* diverse perceptions were evident toward current stepparents and that much less diverse perceptions were evident toward biological parents (who tended to be viewed as family members) and former stepparents (who tended not to be viewed as family members). Survey participants had no trouble selecting perception categories that reflected a partial family or parent status for their stepparents. In interviews, they were readily able to explain their particular levels of family and parent perceptions that they had indicated in their surveys, and how these perceptions had evolved across time. Like Johnson and Barer's (1987) study of the kinship networks of grandmothers following a child's divorce, I was able to discover that perceptions of family in

198 *Maria Schmeeckle*

stepfamilies were diverse, complicated, but understandable when explored in greater detail.

My interest in heterogeneity has translated into an exploration of the range of children's inequalities across the world using global data. I have also reviewed literature on the global diversity of orphans, foster children, and children in street situations (Schmeeckle, 2016a, 2016b, 2016c). Currently, I am studying the range of reasons why children rebel against parents, ways they go about it, and perspectives about the benefits and costs of such rebellions. I doubt if I will ever stop taking an interest in the heterogeneity of social phenomena.

Cumulative Advantage/Disadvantage

Angela O'Rand, another symposium presenter from my graduate school days, continues to inform me about children. I have returned to her work on "cumulative disadvantage" over time. O'Rand (2006) wrote, "Unequal parental (and societal) investment in the early life course contributes significantly to unequal fortunes across the life course. The processes by which this occurs are complex and cumulative . . ." (p. 148). In her examples, she highlighted how a lack of parental resources could affect mortality even for neonates. Interest in this theory led me to a related theory in gerontology, that of "cumulative inequality theory" (Ferraro & Shippee, 2009). The authors list axioms and propositions, theorizing, for example, that "disadvantage increases exposure to risk, but advantage increases exposure to opportunity" (p. 337).

The concepts of cumulative disadvantage and cumulative inequality theory apply very well to children and have been insightfully used (as "cumulative vulnerability") in recent longitudinal work by Fothergill and Peek (2015) on children's trajectories following the 2005 disaster of Hurricane Katrina in New Orleans, Louisiana. The longitudinal design of their *Children of Katrina* study enabled Fothergill and Peek to trace the trajectories of their focal children across seven years. Three longitudinal trajectories emerged from analysis of the lives of seven focal children: a *declining trajectory*, in which children's lives following the disaster were characterized by "serious and ongoing instability" (p. 37); a *finding-equilibrium* trajectory, in which the disruption of the hurricane was followed by "a return to or a newfound type of stability" (p. 97); and a *fluctuating trajectory*, in which a lack of comprehensive recovery or rapid fluctuations in well-being characterized the children's experiences. Though they may not have intended it as such, Fothergill and Peek's book contributes beautifully to the literature on cumulative disadvantage and provides a rare glimpse into how the dramatic event of a major disaster may play out very differently in the trajectories of children who are differently situated in the social structure. (For a review of this book, see Schmeeckle, 2015.)

Although I admire the concept of cumulative disadvantage and teach about it, I do not see how the currently available global comparative data lends itself to studying children's cumulative disadvantage across countries. *Compounded* disadvantage might be another story. With compounded disadvantage, one might

Thinking about Children 199

analyze multiple inequalities that occur simultaneously. Comparative global indicators are often portrayed one at a time, inhibiting our ability to see the simultaneous disadvantages experienced by children in particular regions and countries. But these data can be organized together in tandem. Indexes such as the *State of the World's Mothers Report* (2015) or the *Children's Rights Index* (Gran, 2010) provide useful examples of compounded disadvantage (and advantage) as reflected in mother and child indicators, and children's rights. Repeated indexes give a sense of how ratings and rankings of countries change over time. Gran plans to extend the Children's Rights Index to later years, and the State of the World's Mother's Report has been created annually since 2000 (Save the Children International, 2015).

Life Course Perspective

This framework is truly useful for understanding lives at any point along the life span. Key principles of *time and place, timing, linked lives, life span development* and *agency* help explain human transitions and trajectories, and are commonly used to organize life course findings (Elder, Kirkpatrick Johnson, & Crosnoe, 2003). The life course perspective reminds us that lives are dynamic and that change can occur on many levels—historically, within extended families, within individuals. Long-term trajectories are affected by choices, social networks, levels of tolerance in society, and a multitude of turning points. Some of these turning points are very positive. For instance, a hopeful area of transition is when relationships can improve across time. Ingrid Connidis (2001) argued in her Multidisciplinary Symposium on Aging presentation at USC that perhaps the greatest implication of increased longevity of life is the renegotiation that can take place between adult children and their parents as they get older. I have seen this relationship repair in my family and in others' families. I saw it in the data when my interview participants reported reconnecting with their fathers and stepmothers as they progressed through adulthood (Schmeeckle, 2007). Longitudinal research allows us to see changes in relationships over time, and in follow-up interviews, I noticed important changes that took place across only three years. "Percy" decided to claim his stepfather as his father (demonstrating agency), and this development seemed not only related to his growing maturity (demonstrating life span development) but also related to the recognition that his stepfather was a role model for parenting as he anticipated the birth of his first child (demonstrating linked lives).

The life course perspective has been helpful in explaining quantitative findings as well. In survey research conducted with colleagues, we found that measures of life course principles helped explain why adult children considered some stepparents to be family members and parents. We found that adult children's very diverse family perceptions of stepparents were associated with the life course transitions of biological parents (such as whether they married or were still living with the stepparent), the timing of these transitions in the lives of children, and long-term opportunities for interaction through co-residence (Schmeeckle, Giarrusso, Feng, & Bengtson, 2006). These life course factors helped

200   *Maria Schmeeckle*

explain whether adult children perceived stepparents as "fully," "quite a bit," "a little," or "not at all" family members and parents.

The Latent Kin Matrix

I remember valuing anything that Matilda White Riley wrote, but a particular piece she wrote with John Riley during the 1990s really inspired me. At the time, they were two of the only gerontologists I could find who were writing about the complexity of family boundaries in the aftermath of divorce, remarriage, and cohabitation. The Rileys argued that divorce, cohabitation, and substitute kin, combined with persistent traditional ties, were increasingly creating larger networks of potentially significant relationships across the life course. They coined the term "latent kin matrix" to refer to the "latent web of continually shifting linkages that provide the potential for activating and intensifying close kin relationships" (Riley & Riley, 1993, p. 173). These latent matrix relationships could be complex in structure, prolonged throughout the life course, and characterized by flexibility of choice rather than obligation. When I ran into the Rileys at a conference one time, I asked them about this term, the "latent kin matrix," and whether they meant to imply dormancy in the matrix. They assured me that it need not be dormant, and in fact what I found in my research was examples of adult children's vibrantly active kin extension with step-relatives and sometimes even the step-relatives of step-relatives (Schmeeckle, 2001). Some family systems fostered particularly inclusive attitudes toward stepfamily members, which were conducive to flexible family boundaries and expanded perceptions of family. The impact on children? Larger networks in which to find belonging, affirmation, and affiliation.

Questions for the Field of Social Gerontology, Inspired by my Teaching and Research Experiences Related to Children in a Global Perspective

My interests and experiences have led me to identify some questions that might be useful to students and educators in social gerontology. They are worth wrestling with in the classroom, and some of the questions might even give rise to new research agendas. What follows are five questions that I would pose to the field of social gerontology.

Which Groups of Children Worldwide Never Make it to Adulthood, Much Less Later Life?

This is a question I have been curious about for years. There may be global estimates, but I have not found them. Answering this question would complement a preoccupation in gerontology, that of the trend of longer life expectancy. While this trend is prevalent in the West, not every country is experiencing an extension of the life course for the majority. Although we might not be able to comprehensively answer the question of which groups of children die before adulthood, we can answer about some groups of children. The United Nations Millennium Development Goals, 2000–2015, focused attention on countries with the highest rates of child mortality in children younger than 5 years. Much progress has been made, but huge disparities still exist across countries. A look at recent data reveals countries in which lives are often cut short, such as Angola, Sierra Leone, Chad, and Somalia, where more than 14% of children in 2013 died before the age of 5. In comparison, the US rate is less than 1% (World Bank, 2013).

We might call the children who never make it to adulthood or later life *missing elders*. Another way in which these *missing elders* are visible is through ethnographic research on groups of children at particular risk of early death, such as children in street situations. In a follow-up to his book *At Home in the Street: Street Children of Northeast Brazil*, Tobias Hecht (1998, 2008) wrote 10 years later that most of the children he had originally studied were deceased. One of the survivors informed him that many of them had been murdered.

Quantitatively, there are globally comparative data on children who are killed prior to age 19. The numbers are higher in Latin America, with 2% or more of young people dying due to homicide in El Salvador, Guatemala, and Venezuela, and more than 1% in Brazil, Panama, Colombia, and Honduras in 2012. By way of contrast, although its rate was not the lowest, the percentage in the United States was 0.4 (UNICEF, 2012).

The term *missing girls* has been used to refer to girls who were never born due to high rates of female feticide in countries such as India, China, and Korea (Park, 2011; Schmeeckle, 2013). Investigative journalism alerts us to emerging ways of preventing the birth of certain types of children. In the United States, it is possible that we might be writing about the *missing boys* in the future, if evidence of a preference for girls continues. As writer Mara Hvistendahl (2011) puts it, the latest in vitro fertilization techniques allow sex selection to occur in the petri dish. The concept of *missing elders* could draw attention to those who never become old because they die much earlier in life, or are never born in the first place.

Thus, child mortality, child and youth homicide, and sex-selective abortion combine to contribute to missing adults and elders in our societies. Considering these groups adds nuance to the often-cited statistics on longer life expectancy. Other demographic topics connect to this discussion as well. Has Westernized gerontology adequately considered the implications across the life course for societies with unbalanced sex ratios? In countries with many more men than women due to significantly imbalanced sex ratios at birth, there are implications for marriage opportunities, later life care, and elder participation.

How do Power Structures Favor Older People in Some Parts of the World?

I never learned about *gerontocracies* in my study of gerontology, but wish I had. Simply put, a gerontocracy is a society in which power is consolidated in the hands of older people. From a global perspective, gerontocratic dynamics are important to know about, and they challenge many Western assumptions that older people

202 *Maria Schmeeckle*

are disproportionately needy, stigmatized, and in danger of being denied basic rights. The proportion of young people is very high in sub-Saharan Africa, but particularly in rural areas, political structures are dominated by the elderly (Argenti, 2002; De Waal, 2002). It can take a very long time for young people to achieve full status, rights, and responsibilities in gerontocratic societies. Young adults are often viewed with suspicion and framed as delinquents or criminals. The education of youth during post-colonial eras led to frustration, as young people were not given meaningful job opportunities. With few outlets to advance or achieve meaningful participation, many youth turned to empowerment in religious movements or militant groups (Argenti, 2002). With long-standing rituals and reverence for elders fueling gerontocracies, it is not clear how a better social balance can be achieved. It would be beneficial for gerontology educators to grapple with such alternative forms of arranging power. The relative power of young and old has been discussed in the intergenerational equity debate, but perhaps that debate could be broadened. I wonder what Carroll Estes, whose writings give such careful attention to power relations and their impact on older people's lives, would say about gerontocracies across the world.

How do Very Different Life Pathways across the World Correspond with Diverse Forms of Inequality in Later Life?

In the United States, people are marrying later and having fewer children compared to the past (Coontz, 2010). Only 2.8% of 15- to 19-year-old females in the United States were married in 2009; yet, in Bangladesh, Mali, and Mozambique in recent years, more than 40% were married by the age of 19. In Western Sahara and Niger, it was more than 60% (United Nations, 2013) Teenagers are giving birth to children at very different rates across the world. While only 3% of US teenage girls had given birth by age 19 in 2013, 19% of girls in Niger had done so (Population Reference Bureau, 2013). Studies have shown that early marriage and childbearing are associated with lower education levels and higher health complications for young women (Nugent, 2006). How might these situations affect them in later life?

Another issue, birth registration, virtually universal within the United States, is significantly absent in some countries. The percentage of children registered by age 5 is estimated to be as low as 3% in Somalia and 7% in Ethiopia (UNICEF, 2013). What are the citizenship and mobility effects of having no official identity? What happens to older people with no birth certificates? The diversity of common life course pathways is an important area for research and social change in our globalized world.

How Might a Greater Focus on Cumulative Disadvantage Starting in Childhood Reveal Deterrents to Healthy Aging?

A look beyond the borders of high resource countries enables us to see areas of cumulative disadvantage that are not typically discussed at gerontology conferences.

Thinking about Children 203

A dramatic example comes from Christopher Kovat-Bernat's (2006) ethnographic research on children in street situations in Port-au-Prince, Haiti. Kovats-Bernat found that children fought with each other for optimal work spaces in the streets. One method children used to reduce the economic threat of another child was to drop concrete blocks on a rival child's legs while he slept. The intent was to maim rather than to kill, but a surviving child might become seriously debilitated after such an encounter. This example shows how the marginalization of children working in city streets, in a context of scarce resources, can lead to severe attacks on the mobility and health of fellow children, exacerbating the disadvantage of the children involved.

A more common example of how cumulative disadvantage starting in childhood might deter healthy aging involves those without strong economic support in families. Larson (2002) notes the worldwide trend of taking more time to transition to adulthood. Families with greater financial resources are better situated to help their children prepare for the challenges of adulthood in an increasingly complex and globalized world. Those who lack family support as young adults must become independent before they are fully prepared. Settersten and Ray (2010) have considered the implications within the United States, but we would do well to consider this within a global context as well, and to ask what healthy aging means for those whose trajectories lead them to greater vulnerability while they are still young.

How are World Megatrends Shaping the Aging Landscape of the Future?

Demographic megatrends provide a start for this discussion. When we compare the age structures of different societies and the corresponding social dynamics that go with different proportions of younger and older people, we can see that social changes in fertility and mortality are having a strong effect on lived lives. Zinnecker (2001) wrote about how social experiences are drastically different when the proportions of children in countries are low versus high. Children are likely to receive more attention from adults in aging societies where the young are relatively scarce. Exploring how this operates across the world challenges common assumptions about status and norms of living for people of different ages.

Researchers also use world megatrends to imagine large-scale scenarios that could emerge in the future. The National Intelligence Council (NIC, 2012) of the United States predicts future scenarios with very different outcomes for all human beings. Their *Global Trends 2030* report emphasizes four megatrends: individual empowerment, diffusion of power, demographic patterns (urbanization, migration, and aging societies), and increased demands for food/water/energy. Each of these megatrends could have considerable effects on all age groups. The NIC identifies "game-changing" factors such as economic and political volatility, conflict and instability, new technologies, and the uncertain role of the United States. It describes four possible future scenarios, ranging from a world of increased interstate conflict to one of enhanced global cooperation. These global trends, factors, and hypothetical scenarios are worth pondering in gerontology as well as

204 *Maria Schmeeckle*

in childhood studies, as our futures will be bound up with the futures of people of all ages across the planet.

Other organizations also do global forecasting and scenario projection. The Great Transitions Initiative has conceptualized six possible future scenarios, including "eco-communalism," "fortress world," and "policy reform"(Great Transitions Initiative, 2015). How will older and younger people experience global trends differently depending on the country context, region of the world, and different timing of global developments in political, economic, demographic, and human rights realms? Drawing upon the concept of "structural lag" (Riley, Khan, & Foner, 1994), will there be a global "structural lag" in opportunities for young people?

Conclusion

At a *Gerontological Society of America* conference one year in the later 1990s, I was at a session in which established scholars poked fun at the field. One made the case that two types of people go into gerontology: the "gerophiles" (those who love older people) and the "gerophobes" (those who are afraid of the aging process). I remember being amused, but thinking that I did not particularly fall into either of these camps. My interests were not driven by a particular age group. I was interested in linked lives and complex contemporary relationships, and my study of gerontology encouraged me to consider these across a wide age span.

Two decades later, although I study children, my primary motivation is still not driven by an interest in an age group. I have become interested in human rights and social justice, in inequality and avenues to equality. I have become interested in the range of social situations surrounding children and families worldwide. For me, broadening the age and geographic scope of the questions I ask enables me to better understand the range of human behavior, the importance of which George Maddox spoke so positively. My study of social gerontology has served me well and I am grateful for it. I believe it serves a critical social gerontology to explore the broader questions I have offered here. With this chapter, I have tried to encourage the expansion of gerontology beyond the unintentional age-limited and geographically-limited assumptions embedded in the field.

References

Argenti, N. (2002). Youth in Africa: A major resource for change. In A. De Waal & N. Argenti (Eds.), *Young Africa: Realising the rights of children and youth* (pp. 123–154). Trenton, NJ: Africa World Press.

Bengtson, V. (1993). Is the "contract across generations" changing? Effects of population aging on obligations and expectations across age groups. In V.L. Bengtson & W.A. Achenbaum (Eds.), *The changing contract across generations* (pp. 3–42). Hawthorne, NY: Aldine de Gruyter.

Bengtson, V. (1996). Continuities and discontinuities in intergenerational relationships over time. In V.L. Bengtson (Ed.), *Adulthood and aging: Research on continuities and discontinuities* (pp. 271–303). New York: Springer.

Thinking about Children 205

Bengtson, V.L., Biblarz, T.J., & Roberts, R.E. (2002). *How families still matter: A longitudinal study of youth in two generations.* New York: Cambridge University Press.

Burawoy, M. (2005). For public sociology. *American Sociological Review,* 70(1), 4–28.

Connidis, I.A. (2001, April). *Stability and change across three generations.* Presentation at the Ethel Percy Andrus Gerontology Center, University of Southern California, Multidisciplinary Research Colloquium Series in Aging.

Coontz, S. (2010). The evolution of American families. In B. Risman (Ed.), *Families as they really are.* New York: W.W. Norton.

De Waal, A. (2002). Realising child rights in Africa: Children, young people and leadership. In A. De Waal & N. Argenti (Eds.), *Young Africa: Realising the rights of children and youth* (pp. 1–28). Trenton, NJ: Africa World Press.

Elder, G.H. Jr., Kirkpatrick Johnson, M., & Crosnoe, R. (2003). The emergence and development of life course theory. In J.T. Mortimer & M.J. Shanahan (Eds.), *Handbook of the life course* (pp. 3–19). New York: Kluwer Academic/Plenum.

Ferraro, K., & Shippee, T.P. (2009). Aging and cumulative inequality: How does inequality get under the skin? *The Gerontologist,* 49(3), 333–343.

Fothergill, A., & Peek, L. (2015). *Children of Katrina.* Austin, TX: University of Texas Press.

Gran, B. (2010.) Comparing children's rights: Introducing the Children's Rights Index. *International Journal of Children's Rights,* 18, 1–17.

Great Transition Initiative. (2015). *Great transition ideas: Introductory video.* Retrieved November 14, 2015 from www.greattransition.org/.

Hecht, T. (1998). *At home in the street: Street children of northeast Brazil.* New York: Cambridge University Press.

Hecht, T. (2008). Globalization from way below: Brazilian streets, a youth, and world society. In J. Cole & D. Durham (Eds.), *Figuring the future: Globalization and the temporalities of children and youth* (pp. 223–243). Santa Fe, NM: School for Advanced Research Press.

Hvistendahl, M. (2011). *Unnatural selection: Choosing boys over girls, and the consequences of a world full of men.* New York: Public Affairs.

James, A. (2004). Understanding childhood from an interdisciplinary perspective: Problems and potentials. In P.B. Pufall & R.P. Unsworth (Eds.), *Rethinking childhood* (pp. 25–37). New Brunswick, NJ: Rutgers University Press.

Johnson, C.L., & Barer, B.M. (1987). Marital instability and the changing kinship networks of grandparents. *The Gerontologist,* 27(3), 330–335.

Kovats-Bernat, J.C. (2006). *Sleeping rough in Port-au-Prince: An ethnography of street children and violence in Haiti.* Gainesville, FL: University Press of Florida.

Larson, R.W. (2002). Globalization, societal change, and new technologies: What they mean for the future of adolescence. *Journal of Research on Adolescence,* 12(1), 1–30.

Maddox, G. (1987). Aging differently. *The Gerontologist,* 27(5), 557–564.

Maddox, G. (1998, April). *The future of aging: What can we expect and what can we do?* Presentation at the Ethel Percy Andrus Gerontology Center, University of Southern California, Multidisciplinary Research Colloquium Series in Aging.

National Intelligence Council. (2012). *Global trends 2030: Alternative worlds.* Retrieved November 14, 2015 from www.dni.gov/nic/globaltrends. ISBN 978-1-929667-215.

Nugent, R. (2006). *Youth in a global world.* Washington, DC: Population Reference Bureau.

O'Rand, A. (2006). Stratification and the life course: Life course capital, life course risks, and social inequality. In R.H. Binstock & L.K. George (Eds.), *Handbook of aging and the social sciences* (6th ed., pp. 146–162). New York: Academic Press.

206 *Maria Schmeeckle*

Park, S. (2011). Korean multiculturalism and the marriage squeeze. *Contexts,* 10(3), 64–65.

Population Reference Bureau. (2013). *Adolescent fertility rate: Births per 1,000 women ages 15–19.* Retrieved November 14, 2015 from www.prb.org/DataFinder/Topic/Rankings. aspx?ind=304.

Riley, M.W., Kahn, R.L., & Foner, A. (1994). *Age and structural lag: society's failure to provide meaningful opportunities in work, family, and leisure.* New York: Wiley.

Riley, M.W., & Riley, J.W. (1993). Connections: Kin and cohort. In V.L. Bengtson & W.A. Achenbaum (Eds.), *The changing contract across generations* (pp. 169–189). New York: Aldine De Gruyter.

Save the Children International. (2015). *State of the world's mothers report.* Retrieved November 14, 2015 from www.savethechildren.net/state-worlds-mothers-2015.

Schmeeckle, M. (2001). *Rethinking the ties that bind: Adult children's perceptions of step, ex-step, and biological parents.* Doctoral dissertation. University of Southern California. *Dissertation Abstracts International,* 63(9).

Schmeeckle, M. (2007). Gender dynamics in stepfamilies: Adult children's views. *Journal of Marriage and Family,* 69, 174–189.

Schmeeckle, M. (2013). [Review of the TV episode *Female Foeticide: Daughters are Precious*]. *Humanity and Society,* 37(3), 265–268. DOI: 10.1177/0160597613493742.

Schmeeckle, M. (2015). [Review of the book *Children of Katrina,* by A. Fothergill & L. Peek.]. *Children, Youth, and Environments,* 25(3): 204–208. Retrieved November 14, 2015 from www.jstor.org/stable/10.7721/chilyoutenvi.25.3.0204.

Schmeeckle, M. (2016a). Foster care. In C.L. Shehan (Ed.), *The Wiley-Blackwell encyclopedia of family studies,* pp. 1–4. Hoboken, NJ: John Wiley & Sons. DOI: 10.1002/ 9781119085621.wbefs167.

Schmeeckle, M. (2016b). OrphansIn C.L. Shehan (Ed.), *The Wiley-Blackwell encyclopedia of family studies,* pp.1–6. Hoboken, NJ: John Wiley & Sons. DOI: 10.1002/9781 119085621.wbefs296.

Schmeeckle, M. (2016c). Street children. In C.L. Shehan (Ed.), *The Wiley-Blackwell encyclopedia of family studies,* pp. 1–4. Hoboken, NJ: John Wiley & Sons. DOI: 10.1002/ 9781119085621.wbefs057.

Schmeeckle, M., Giarrusso, R., Feng, D., & Bengtson, V. (2006). What makes someone family? Adult children's perceptions of current and former stepparents. *Journal of Marriage and Family,* 68, 595–610.

Schmeeckle, M., & Gran, B.K. (2014a, July). *The Worldwide Outlook for Children (WOC): A web resource of young people's wellbeing, rights, and interests.* Presentation at the World Congress of Sociology: Facing an Unequal World: Challenges for Global Sociology, Research Committee on Sociology of Childhood. International Sociological Association, Yokohama, Japan.

Schmeeckle, M., & Gran, B.K. (2014b, April). *Worldwide Outlook for Children (WOC): A web resource offering global perspectives of young people's experiences.* 4th Annual Joint Area Studies Conference: Children and Globalization: Issues, Policies, and Initiatives, University of Illinois at Urbana-Champaign. Champaign, IL.

Schmeeckle, M., & Gran, B.K. (2015a, August). *The global state of children's inequality: Introducing Worldwide Outlook for Children.* 110th Annual Meeting of the American Sociological Association, Session on Children/Youth/Adolescents. Hilton, Chicago.

Schmeeckle, M., & Gran, B.K. (2015b, January). *The international geography of children's inequality.* 4th International Conference for the Geographies of Children, Youth, and Families, Session on Sociology and the Intersection of Space and Place among Children and Youth. Wyndam San Diego Bayside.

Thinking about Children 207

Schmeeckle, M., & Sprecher, S. (2004). Extended family and social networks. In A. Vangelisti (Ed.), *Handbook of family communication* (pp. 349–375). Hillsdale, NJ: Lawrence Erlbaum Associates.

Schmeeckle, M., & Sprecher, S. (2013). Widening circles: Interactive connections between immediate family and larger social networks. In A. Vangelisti (Ed.), *Routledge handbook of family communication* (2nd ed., pp. 302–317). New York: Routledge.

Settersten, R., & Ray, B.E. (2010). *Not quite adults: Why 20-somethings are choosing a slower path to adulthood, and why it's good for everyone.* New York: Bantam Books.

UNICEF. (2012). Homicide Rate: Number of homicide victims among children and adolescents aged 0 to 19 years per 100,000 population. Retrieved from http://files.unicef. org/publications/files/Hidden_in_plain_sight_statistical_analysis_EN_3_Sept_2014.pdf.

UNICEF. (2013). *Birth Registration (% total registration)* (Data From UNICEF Global Data Bases). Retrieved November 14, 2015 from http://data.unicef.org/child-protection/birth-registration.

United Nations. (2013). *Child Marriage [Population aged 15–19 ever married (%)]* (1970–1999 data removed; 2000–2011 Data from UN World Marriage Data). Retrieved November 14, 2015 from http://unstats.un.org/unsd/demographic/products/indwm/June%202013/3b.xls).

United Nations Statistical Commission. (2007). *United Nations statistical commission: sixty years of leadership and professionalism in building a global statistical system, 1947–2007.* New York: United Nations.

World Bank. (2013). *Infant mortality rate.* World Bank data. Retrieved November 14, 2015 from http://data.worldbank.org/indicator/SP.DYN.IMRT.IN.

Zinnecker, J. (2001). Children in young and aging societies: The order of generations and models of childhood in comparative perspective. In S.L. Hofferth & T.J. Owens (Eds.), *Children at the Millennium: Where have we come from, where are we going? Advances in Life Course Research* (Vol. 6, pp. 11–52). New York: Elsevier Science.

CHAPTER **13**

Lost in the "Big World"?: Korean College Students Coming of Age in the United States

Kirsten Younghee Song

Introduction

In 2009, Gina took one year off from college in Korea and came to the United States to "learn English and broaden [her] perspectives." She enrolled in an "English as a Second Language (ESL)" program at a large state university. She had been ready to embark on an adventure away from the people, language, food, and culture in which she had been born and raised. On the first day of school, however, the presence of "too many Korean students" on campus disappointed her. Gina's observation was perhaps not completely her subjective impression. Rather, it mirrored the remarkable rates of young Koreans studying abroad nowadays.[1]

When it comes to international students, their cultural and academic adjustment to new college life has been a central focus of scholars, policymakers, school administrators, and educators. More globalization-focused studies have examined this young population as new leading actors of transnational migration (e.g., see Fong, 2011; Lee, 2006). The latter approach takes educational migration as a research site to examine how the influence of globalization is manifested on a micro-level and how it changes ways of living and belonging. I diverge from these two common approaches, which reduce subjectivity of these young individuals to their "primary status" of being *either* students *or* migrants. Instead, I rely on the life course perspective, which theorizes the life course as a holistic experience, involving taking and leaving multiple roles and statuses, each of which intersects with one another and constitutes one's life trajectory (Riley, 1987). Emphasizing how individual biographies are embedded in larger contexts, the life course perspectives also situate life stage transitions, which are ostensibly personal experiences, in social, cultural, and historical realms. Considering that college is a stepping stone on the way to adulthood for international students, the relevance of the life course perspective on educational migration/international student studies seems self-evident. Yet, theoretical/empirical conversations between the two studies have rarely occurred in the existing literature.

In my study, I conceptualize Korean college students in the United States as young individuals who are making their entry into adulthood in the context of accelerated global integration. As will be clear throughout this chapter, Korean college students' experiences are not very dissimilar from any other young individuals in post-industrial countries who undergo the lengthening time of the adulthood transition, often described as "emerging adulthood" (Arnett, 2000) or "prolonged adolescence" (Settersten, Ottusch, & Schneider, 2015). Nonetheless, the life stories of Korean college students also make a clear case that there are challenging conditions unique to educational migrants as they navigate the transitory stage thousands of miles away from their families and communities. My study identifies three distinct but interrelated issues: (1) insufficient guidance from older adults, (2) a lack of local resources, and (3) institutional constraints. Each of these issues worked to limit the young individuals' freedom to explore life opportunities and develop a sense of autonomy. Through an intimate account of the Korean college students' lives in the United States, this chapter shows how larger forces like globalization, a high demand for cultural and linguistic competency in the labor market, and migration policies shape young individuals' transition to adulthood.

Research Methods

For the current study, I used multiple research methods including ethnographic fieldwork (2009–2012) at one Korean educational migrant community called the College and Young Adult group (CYA), a small survey ($N = 118$), and conversational and semi-structured interviews ($N = 60$). CYA was a sub-group of one of the biggest Korean churches in central New Jersey.[2] For the entire research period, I attended their official activities every Friday as a member and a researcher. During my fieldwork, I met approximately 150 Korean college students and recent graduates between ages 18 and 25. Most of them self-identified as educational migrants who came to the United States with or without family primarily for their educational opportunities. Their age at migration varied from 8 to 18. At the time of my fieldwork, most of them were college students with varied migration statuses, including international students, permanent migrants, or US citizens. Beyond the official CYA activities, I joined the members for informal social activities outside of the church. My study also included those who sporadically participated and who stopped coming at all for various reasons, such as returning to Korea, moving out of the area, or other personal reasons. I continued my relationship with them through email, instant text messages, conversations over the phone, and in-person meetings. For 3 years of my fieldwork, I followed my informants while they were growing into college seniors, recent graduates, and first-time employees as well as newly wedded husbands and wives. I also witnessed many dark moments when they experienced academic probation, unemployment, loss of legal immigrant residency, returning to Korea against their own will, and more.

Growing up with "Global" Dreams

We cannot understand how and why educational migrants live their lives the way they do without knowing what drove them to the United States in the first place. My informants expressed a desire to live in the "big world." They often used the

210 *Kirsten Younghee Song*

phrase "big world" when discussing their ultimate migration goal. Most sociologists will agree that personal desires and aspirations are largely socially constructed. As such, the CYA members' quest for the "big world" was driven by external forces, in particular aggressive globalization projects taking place inside and outside of Korea.

Since the late 1990s when globalization began sweeping Asian countries, the Korean government has zealously implemented globalization policies on a national level through restructuring political, economic, and educational systems in both private and public domains. Business sectors and mass media have also eagerly promoted Korea's global integration as a national mission and demanded the entire country to be better equipped to respond to the changing world. "Global" discourses have occupied Koreans' public and private lives in the name of a "global leadership," a "global mindset," and "global standards," just to name a few. Since then, adaptability to the highly globalized world—the "big world"—has become a matter of survival in Korean society. While such discourses have developed rapidly without sufficient discussion about what it actually means to be "global," linguistic competency in English—a means of international communication—has become a primary qualification of "global" competitiveness (Song, 2010).

The national fervor for "becoming global" stirred up middle-class families' anxiety to secure their class position. English education was one of the strategic choices they made in response. Depicted as "English education fever" (Chung, 2008), Korean families spend about $15 billion a year on extracurricular English lessons through cram schools, private tutoring, English camps, or overseas ESL programs (Chun & Choi, 2006). Such a large investment in English education, however, has never yet satisfied Korean parents and their children (Park, 2009). Thus, in combination with their long-lasting dissatisfaction with the brutally competitive Korean educational system, the cost-benefit calculation of English education began pushing parents to send their children to English-speaking countries for schooling. In the parents' calculation, English proficiency and a US college degree would lead their children to upward mobility in Korean domestic and/or global class structure. That would pay off a large financial and emotional investment they were willing to make. The birth cohorts born in the early- and mid-1990s reached their school age during this globalization fervor in Korea and made up the first wave of the so-called "Korean education exodus" (Lo, Abelmann, Kwon, & Okazaki, 2015). The CYA members were at the forefront of that wave.

English Fluency is Key to the "Big World"

Unlike parents' calculating and strategic motives for migration documented in many prior studies, my study suggests that children's understanding of their migration can be very different. In-depth interviews with my informants began with a question asking why they came to the United States at first. Most of them put their answers largely in developmental frameworks such as to "see the big world," to "experience cultural diversities," to "learn communication skills with people from all over the world," or to "broaden world views." These are important conditions to become "global citizens." What the parents mean by a "better life in the big world" often implies better life chances in materialistic terms, as well as in personal development or self-actualization. Throughout my fieldwork, however, it became evident that the parents did not necessarily make it clear that those global qualifications would be necessary for them to get a job at a company with a good national or international reputation, as well as decent income and benefits which could enable them to lead middle- to upper-middle-class lifestyles.

A college freshman, Joon, shared his migration story. At the age of 8, he first came to the United States alone. He recalled the day his mother asked if he would like to "go to the United States to learn English." A few days later, he would find she had already picked a school for him, finished a visa application, appointed a guardian to take care of him, and purchased a round-trip airplane ticket. Joon reflected:

> I was attending English *hagwons*[3] anyway. So, when I thought of going to the United States to learn English, it felt like going to a new English *hagwon*. That was my first thought. The next thing was, "Wow, I will get on a plane," which sounded so cool to me at that time.
>
> (Joon Interview, December 12, 2011)

His recollection shows he took the idea of moving to the United States precisely as going to a new English *hagwon* in Korea. The primary difference was that it would be further from home than his current *hagwons*, but he also thought it would be more fun, like "going to a summer English camp or adventure." One month later, his parents took him to an airport. Before letting him get on a plane, they said, "Do not worry about doing well in school. If you can speak good English by the time you return home, that would be enough." Considering the significant pressure on children to do well in all school subjects in Korea, it is no wonder he felt that having to study one subject, English, was the same as having a vacation.

My informants' recollections of the beginning of their migration were starkly similar to Joon's. Other informants stated:

> My family moved here for me to have "better" education and more life opportunities. You know, to experience the "big world." If it were not for my education, they would have not had any reasons to come to the U.S. They were pretty successful in their career in Korea. My parents chose to sacrifice their lives for me.
>
> (Chanwoo Interview, September 12, 2011)

> My parents sent me. I didn't even want to come. They said I would be better off in the U.S. I would learn English faster. School would be easier and more fun.
>
> (Yoonjae Interview, September 13, 2011)

212 *Kirsten Younghee Song*

In the beginning of migration, my informants' parents justified their highly instrumental goals of migration with liberal educational values such as broadening worldviews, experiencing diverse culture, or cultivating a global mindset. Furthermore, the parents often simplified all those values into "better," "easier," "more fun" school, and "learning English faster" in the United States to make it easier for their young children to understand why they would have to leave their school, teachers, and friends behind. The CYA members often did not realize the underlying meaning of "speaking English well" until they reached their junior or senior year in college when they were expected to show their parents the results of their migration. Instead, such a strong emphasis on English fluency grew into their central focus, and it often even overshadowed their reasons for needing English proficiency.

The Quest to "Speak English like a Native"

The pressure and desire to "speak English well" was so strong that it lurked in my informants' minds and abruptly sprang out even when English was the least relevant issue at a given moment. On my first day at CYA in 2009, I introduced myself as a PhD student. Immediately, Chanho exclaimed, "Wow, you must speak English very well!" Later, I found this was not a coincidence on that particular day. The CYA members often asked the question, "Do you speak English well?", half-jokingly and half seriously when a new member joined them. The question almost always prompted a conversation in which other members commented on their own English in comparison to each other. The comparisons were often accompanied with self-criticism about their English and envious feelings about others whose English was better than their own. The seemingly blunt question did not seem to bother them. Even the new members reacted to it as if they were familiar with such a question.

The question implied more than a simple curiosity. As English fluency was the most instant goal of their migration, it was also indicative of success in migration. In the longer term, it was a proxy for assessing the potential to achieve "broader world views," "more life opportunities," and "better futures." The presumed link between English fluency and "better" futures speaks to the notion of "linguistic capital" which could make language speakers more marketable commodities (Heller, 2003). When language fluency carries a value as capital, who has more of it becomes a central concern among the same market participants. The question "Do you speak English well?" was then my informants' way of measuring this capital. Interestingly, in CYA, their English fluency was always measured in comparison *within* the group and never to those speaking English as a first language. This observation resonates with other studies' claim that young Koreans' quest for English fluency is driven by their desire to get ahead in the competition *among* the same Korean nationals who imagine their future in the same "bigger world." In this respect, young Korean communities abroad are an extension of the Korean local system of class competition (Park & Lo, 2012). CYA was one of these communities.

Once English fluency is perceived as capital, its *quality* becomes an important issue. "Fluent English" of course requires functional capability as a means of communication. And yet, a more immediate concern regarding English fluency in CYA was whether one's English *sounded* like a native speaker in terms of pronunciation, accent, or intonation (e.g., see Kang, 2012; Shin, 2012; Song, 2012). The following excerpt of my field notes illustrates the CYA members' high interests in "speaking English like a native-speaker." The excerpt was taken from a conversation during dinner at the church. The minister and a female member, Jinhee, were sitting at the same table and talking about the college radio show on which Jinhee was working as a DJ for her extracurricular activity:

> *Minister:* I listened to your radio show this weekend. Your English is excellent. You were not born in the U.S., were you? I was impressed.

> *Jinhee:* Well . . ., th . . . ank you. [being shy]. I should work harder to improve my English. . . . There are so many people speaking English very well.

> *Minister:* I wonder if it is ever going to be possible that I speak English well enough so I don't get stressed out because of English . . .

> *Jinhee:* Your English is really good, too. I know you are just saying that to make me feel better.

Jinhee devoted her time and efforts to developing programs for her show: she read all the messages from the audience and picked some of them to read on the show. She paid attention to news and events on campus and shared them with her audience. Jinhee's English fluency should have been the least substantial component of her show, and yet her "excellent" English was the first thing that caught the minister's attention and it was the only topic throughout the entire conversation about the radio show. The minister's question of whether Jinhee was born in the United States was an indirect way to acknowledge her English without a Korean accent and further to compliment her "excellent" English.

Here, it is noteworthy that the notion of "good" English is highly racialized in that it tacitly refers to white American English without particular accents of the Southern or Eastern regions; this presumably unaccented English is often further regarded as "standard" or "authentic" English. The CYA members' desire to "speak English well" was thus inseparable from their desire to have "foreigner" friends, more precisely "White American." My interview with Joon, a freshman in the Fall of 2011, showed the centrality of English fluency in my informants' lives. The interview started with a simple question: "Are you living in a dormitory?" Joon replied, "Yes. I have a roommate. He is White, in ROTC. I think I am very lucky." When I asked why he was "lucky," Joon explained:

> I was so worried about what if I got assigned a weird one. You know, drinking, doing drugs, bringing girls to the dorm room . . . My roommate seems to be

214 *Kirsten Younghee Song*

a good guy. As I said, he is in ROTC. Also, I can speak English while living with him. All my friends are envious of me. None of them has an American roommate.

Under the intense desire and pressure to "speak English well," Joon was anxiously looking for opportunities to practice English as much as possible. His anxiety was also seen in his comments on his friends. Most of them were living with Koreans or people from other non-English-speaking countries. According to Joon, they "ended up" speaking all Korean or "broken" English. In comparison to them, he presumably could learn "authentic" English in a natural setting. Clearly, Joon's white American roommate was objectified as a good English conversation partner rather than being viewed as a person with whom to develop a good friendship. Moreover, Joon was the only one among his friends who had such an ideal condition for learning English. He said it was difficult to get such a roommate, describing it as being "like hitting the lottery."

"Speaking English well" was in fact *the* reason why my informants traveled thousands of miles away to the United States. In their expectation, fluent English would lead them to the "big world." Their almost-obsessive quest for English fluency, however, entailed unanticipated consequences. Being away from their families and friends, it was very difficult for my informants to expand their social boundaries and in turn CYA took a central place in members' everyday lives. Their primary reference group mostly consisted of the CYA members and other Korean college students connected through their rather limited social networks. Since they were all college students with similarly limited work and social experiences, they shared common interests related to college life. They were conscious about their relative position within their small communities with very narrowly focused interests such as English fluency, academic performance, social life, or summer internship opportunities. This in turn resulted in directing these young individuals' attention inward to their small local boundaries as opposed to expanding their horizon toward the "bigger world" as they and their parents originally had intended.

Lost in Global Dreams

It is understandable that my informants viewed their migration with such narrowly defined goals as attending "better" schools and "learning English faster" in light of their young age at migration. However, when I met them as college students and asked about *their own* migration goals, they often repeated the same answers that their parents had furnished years earlier: better education, English fluency, global mindset, more life opportunities, and better future. Those answers were too generic and ambiguous to suggest a direction for their future in any tangible way. They commonly commented that the interview with me was their first chance to sit and reflect on their migratory lives. Upon their arrival in the United States, they had been caught up with more immediate tasks such as learning

English and adjusting to a new school, friends, and teachers. In the meantime, they grew up as young adults without having had time to dream about their new lives in the "big world" on their own terms. If English competency was the key to a successful career, which would ostensibly enable them to enjoy a middle-class, cosmopolitan lifestyle, they would have to know how to connect the two dots. In other words, a processual understanding of how to meet the ends with the means would be a determinant of their success. Yet, understanding how to use their fluent English to actualize other goals was starkly absent in my informants' lives before and after migration. Instead, they had rules and strategies for how to improve their English.

Admittedly, Korean educational migrants like the CYA members were not unique in that matter. As more middle-class occupations require higher education, college has become a rite of passage. Many students enter college in vague anticipation that a college degree will get them a "good job" after graduation. Regardless of citizenship/immigration status, young individuals in post-industrial society often experience this sort of ambiguity about the value and utility of a college education for their future. As many scholars have documented, the adulthood transition takes longer now than ever before due to the increasing demand for higher education and professional training for full-time employment (Arnett, 2000). While uncertainty or insecurity about the future is a universal feature of young adulthood, the experience of today's young individuals is different in that they undergo the transitory phase for an extended period and even the transition is often ambiguous. In this respect, the CYA members were a part of this large universe of young individuals in contemporary societies.

In fact, refining future goals and developing a clear direction are what young individuals do in college. They become self-sufficient adults through such processes. Yet, my informants' positions as transnational migrants added another layer to this developmental stage and made it more challenging. Most importantly, transnational migration often reduced oversight and guidance from parents, older relatives, and communities that are critical for young adults to develop attitudes, aspirations, and behaviors (Juarez, LeGrand, Lloyd, Singh, & Hertrich, 2013). A lack of parental guidance and social support became a more serious problem for my informants because they often did not have sufficient access to local resources to compensate for it. Lastly, because of their legal status as immigrants in the United States, federal immigration regulations significantly limited these young individuals' freedom and choices to explore their life opportunities. Those conditions can place young individuals with little social experience in vulnerable situations during migratory life, which is already full of risks such as psychological stress and a greater likelihood of abuse and exploitation (Zenteno, 2013). The following sections illustrate how all those above-mentioned conditions worked together in real life and created contexts in which my informants experienced a sharp contradiction between their global dreams and realities of life in small local communities.

Living Small in the "Big World"

Many studies have highlighted international students or Asian/Asian American students' voluntary or involuntary segregation on campus (e.g., Abelmann, 2009). In other words, these students aggregate themselves and do not try to go outside of their comfort zone. Typically, language barriers and cultural difference are the identified major reasons. Yet, the CYA members' stories reveal other reasons. For example, a lack of transportation and institutional constraints were critical factors that hindered my informants from going outside their "small world," even if they wished to.

The phrase "living in the small world" represented how my informants felt about their lives. The "small world" could mean many different things. Their social network was small in that it was composed of a limited number of age peers who graduated from the same high school or were from the same hometown, or who belonged to CYA. Their daily lives revolved around a small geographic boundary: school (classes, cafeterias, libraries, computer labs, and dorm rooms), restaurants and coffee shops near the campus, CYA, and occasionally nearby cities.

Most of my informants did not have a driver's license or a car. They had to rely on a few people in their social circle for rides. My informants' everyday lives were, therefore, largely confined within places they could reach on foot or by local public transportation or places where they could get a ride without having to cause too much inconvenience for the driver. Those constraints left them only a handful of places such as school, the church, or grocery stores. The limited mobility meant more than inconvenience. It significantly limited their opportunities to expand their horizons. When they found a part-time job, a summer internship, educational or cultural events, or social gatherings they wished to join, their first thought was, "How can I get there?" Many of them found it cumbersome to deal with the logistical issues. More importantly, it hurt their sense of independence and self-esteem to rely on other people for transportation all the time. As they continually experienced this problem, they developed methods to be self-sufficient. That is, they often limited themselves only to things available to and around them. CYA member Hanah's story illustrates how a lack of transportation and institutional constraints put her in a "small world."

The fall of 2011 was Hanah's first semester at her new school. She was living in a small rented room at a big townhouse owned by a Chinese-Korean woman, near her small college. Like many other international students, she did not have a car or family members who could help her get around. She felt lucky at first because there was a bus route between her house and school, so she did not have to completely rely on other people for a ride every day. According to Hanah, the first few weeks were fine. She was busy adjusting to her new life: school, classes, rules in her new house, bus schedules, and so on. Yet, it did not take long for her to settle down as it was not her first time living abroad alone for school. She went to high school in the Philippines and came to the United States for college right after graduation. Through her previous experience, she was already familiar with how to make herself comfortable in new environments. This time, however, she felt it was more difficult mostly because of the "ridiculous bus system" in the town: the bus ran only once every hour. Second, she found it hard to believe the town was called a "city." It was like the "countryside to her" as it lacked many qualities for a city. She expressed her frustration, saying, "Nobody walks on the street. Actually, there is nothing to go by walking. There is no place to buy food where I can go on foot! How can this be a city?" The cities where she had lived in Korea and the Philippines were busy all the time, with crowds walking down streets, shopping at stores, and running errands. Most of all, she could not understand why there was no night life in her new "city": "After seven in the evening, everything is closed and nobody is out. It is really strange."

The "strange" scene soon became unbearable. She vented her anguish: "I am going stir-crazy from getting stuck in my room and school." Hanah was not used to "living like a bird in a cage." She used to be free; she walked to schools, went out with her friends, walked down streets, shopped at stores, and enjoyed the city life. When she wanted to travel more widely in the town, she could easily take a bus or a taxi. In the United States, supposedly a "bigger world," her life was confined within the boundaries of the small bus route between her house and school, and the church van route going around her school and the church. Her feelings of being confined worsened when she met her friends at CYA. With a deep sigh, Hanah said, "I wish I had a part-time job like Joohee." Joohee was also an international student but lived with her immigrant aunt's family. Twice a week, she worked at her aunt's nail shop to make her allowance and "have life experience." At the Friday CYA meeting, Joohee often spoke about her demanding aunt and difficult customers. Yet, she usually ended her complaints with a constructive conclusion: She would "take the experience as learning moments about the real world and to become a better person." To Hanah, Joohee seemed to have a whole other world that she did not have.

When Hanah openly shared about her "prison-like" life, her friends suggested she find a part-time job and get out of her "little cage." When she tried, she ran into a wall. First, she learned from an Internet search that she would need a working permit from her school to be able to legally work on or off campus. When she went to get a working permit at school, the officer told her to come back with a Social Security card. She walked, took a bus, got on a train, walked further, and finally arrived at the Social Security office. Yet, they told her to come back with a working permit. She could not end a 6-hour long round trip in vain. She went back to her school office but heard the same thing: "come back with a Social Security card." Soon, however, she learned not everyone worked with a working permit, a green card, or any other official documents. Yet, she would need family members or close friends who could set her up for work as a tutor, a cashier, or a restaurant server in settings that would not ask her to bring official documents for the job. Such informal network connections are, of course, not always readily available to international students like Hanah.

Hanah and many other CYA members received tuition and living costs from their parents. It is certainly privilege that they did not have to work to support

218 *Kirsten Younghee Song*

themselves financially. Yet, the downside of this privilege was to cut off them from many important opportunities to "experience the real world" or "get a lesson to become a better person" as Joohee interpreted her part-time work. It could be like losing an entire "world," as Hanah expressed. As many studies have documented, educational, occupational, and familial domains are of greatest significance to young individuals' development (Kalakoski & Nurmi, 1998). Being apart from family, these young migrants' life boundaries were already much smaller than non-migrant young adults. Not having to or being unable to work thus could mean they were living in a world that was one-third the size of the world of a college student who had family nearby and a part-time job.

Navigating the "Big World" Alone

CYA and CYA-based friendships were at the center of the young individuals' lives in this chapter. Once they began joining CYA regularly, they often became loyal to their community. That was not necessarily because they were all very religious Christians or because they were always content with things happening in CYA. There were constantly voices among the members questioning the pastor's leadership. Conflicts among the members divided them into small groups. Some members rarely attended a worship on Friday but came for social gatherings afterward. Many of my informants struggled with time constraints while juggling schoolwork, volunteering at the church, a part-time job, or an internship or full-time job applications. Nonetheless, they wholeheartedly committed themselves to the CYA community life and rarely missed the official Friday meeting or formal/informal social events. Those active members were often self-defined international students. Being apart from family in Korea, they were most likely alone in the United States or had relatives in other states. CYA was their "entire world," and the CYA members were their family who spent all the important holidays together.

Wonjae was an international student, but he had an older brother living in a nearby city after graduating from a college in the United States He expressed his sympathy for other CYA members:

They hang out with each other. I mean, *only* with each other. It is a shame. Their parents sent them here to experience a bigger world. I don't blame them, though. It's not like Korea. There is no place we can go besides school and church. Nothing we can do for life experience. If we don't have a car, we get stuck. Especially, if you don't have family here, it is hard to get out of school and do something for experience. It is hard to meet new people. And you know, we [Korean students] are not very active in college activities either like clubs or volunteer groups. If you don't go out of your zone, you get behind. It's unfortunate.

Although my informants came to the United States for college, their school took up very little space in their daily lives. Most of them had never joined any clubs, groups, or organizations on campus. Many of them never participated in any occasional events on campus such as watching films or attending workshops, career fairs, or lecture series. Wonjae was different, but his case was rare. He was attentive to upcoming news in his academic department. His brother guided him to better use professors' office hours, talk to his academic advisor, and use school resources like student life/development and the writing center. Wonjae and his brother talked on the phone almost every day.

Wonjae's story reveals a gap between the CYA members with good guidance and those without. Such practical guidance or mentorship was not readily available to most of my informants. Almost half of my informants had migrated alone. While their parents in Korea offered their child full support financially and emotionally, they had little knowledge specific to migratory life such as language barriers, cultural differences, administrative works related to the US government, or careers in the US job market. Those who migrated with their parents were not necessarily better off. As new migrants themselves, their parents were also dealing with overwhelming life transitions. In many cases, my informants were aware that their parents had limited ability to guide them due to lack of English communication skills, a busy work schedule to make ends meet, and limited social experience in the United States.

Many of my informants confided that they suffered from not having sufficient guidance necessary to navigate their college and migratory lives. While their parents in Korea or in another state fully supported them financially and emotionally, the physical distance made it difficult for them to get involved in their adult child's life. My informants often heard from their parents over the phone, saying "I believe in you. You make a wise decision." The physical distance between my informants and their parents often worked as a buffer against potential conflicts between them, but it also served as a divider to separate these young individuals from better resourceful environments for adult socialization they could have had in Korea.

Ideally, the CYA members would need someone like Wonjae's brother who was close but also had authority over them and who was also knowledgeable about the US college system and migratory life. Wonjae would listen to his brother's advice even when it was uncomfortable or contrary to his opinions. He explained, "My brother went through what I am going through. I don't mean he is perfect, but he learned from his mistakes and he wants me not to make the same mistakes." In Wonjae's freshman year, his brother told him to join clubs belonging to his college major department. Wonjae was reluctant at first because he was not confident that he could meet all the obligations from classes and club memberships. Yet, his brother pushed him because he learned from his own experience that social skills and teamwork skills are critical elements for a career in the business world. Wonjae respected and followed his brother's advice because he knew his brother cared about him and wanted him to go outside of his comfort zone and be better prepared for his future dream to become a business consultant.

220 *Kirsten Younghee Song*

Stuck in the "Big World"

Another challenging condition for my informants was the US immigration regulations, which significantly limited their physical and cognitive horizons. In particular, student visa policies prohibit visa holders from a vast array of activities that are not directly related to schoolwork. A simple example is that international students are not allowed to work off campus during the semester.[4] Considering young individuals learn valuable social skills and build inter-personal relationships through work, not being able to work is a great loss for their development. Moreover, the student visa imposes strict rules on the holders' time: if they wish to stay in the United States, they must maintain full-time student status, meaning they cannot have part-time school registration or time off. Upon graduation, they must have full-time employment with a working visa sponsorship to stay in the United States. Otherwise, they must return to their home country.

Under these strict immigration rules, there is limited flexibility given to these young migrants for self-exploration or self-realization. They often met their college graduation without sufficient preparation for life after college. In this respect, whether to stay in the United States or to return to Korea was not always a fully voluntary choice made through well-informed decisions. Emerging circumstances often made the choice for them. Some "chose" to return to Korea with an expectation that their US college degree and English fluency would help them land a well-paid job in Korea. Soon, however, they would most likely to find out that the job market in Korea is not necessarily favorable to them. The first wave of early study-abroad students[5] have recently returned to Korea after college graduation. Many business consulting companies have reported that job applicants or newly hired employees with a US college degree do not always perform better (Kwon, 2014) while they lack social skills and networks necessary for working at Korea-based companies which could be gained only through life experiences in Korea.

Other CYA members were more aware that there were many young people just like them in Korea. Even so, their resumes were not necessarily better than others'. Thus, many of them "chose" not to return to Korea as long as they could maintain their legal resident status. Under the Optional Practical Training (OPT)[6] policy, they were given 9 months to look for a full-time job after graduation. While a full-time job with an employer's visa sponsorship was the only way these migrants could have their stay extended after the OPT period, the US job market was unfortunately not all that favorable to them either. They had a hard time finding a full-time job, not to mention an ideal job that would satisfy their own desire and their parents' expectations. Thus, when a company offered a job with a salary just enough for them to pay their rent and cost of living, they settled. While on OPT, they tried to get a full-time job and secure a working visa sponsorship while enduring poor working conditions to have their stay extended. Some of them even joked about or seriously considered getting married to someone with a green card or US citizenship. Male members entertained the idea of joining the US military to secure their US residency. Yet, the 9 months available on OPT went too quickly to actualize any of their plans or ideas. When their OPT ended without a working visa sponsorship, they had no choice but to return to Korea with knowing the harsh reality awaiting them. In extreme cases, some of them "chose" to remain in the United States and became "illegal."

My informants' parents sent them abroad to avoid the brutally competitive environment in Korea and hoped a US college degree would help them get ahead in the global job market. The unanticipated consequence was that they did not have a chance to fully develop the skills necessary to survive in Korean or American society. Unexpectedly and ironically, this made them less favorable job candidates in both countries. Those social and institutional barriers, unfortunately, never entered their or their parents' minds when they were preparing for educational migration. They came to learn of those challenging conditions only by living through them. As time went by, they realized that their life boundary was much smaller in the United States than what it could have been in Korea if they had stayed there. This is the very paradox of educational migration that had these young individuals "stuck" in the United States or left them nowhere.

Closing Remarks

In post-industrial society, more individuals now spend time in higher education and professional training before they step into the "real world." This in turn makes the transition to adulthood take longer than ever before and even makes the transition ambiguous. In addition, as shown in this chapter, the extensive and intensive influence of globalization complicates the adulthood transition as it brings paradoxical impacts on individual life trajectories. Advancements in communication and transportation technologies have increased individuals' transnational mobility in both an actual and a virtual sense. This consequently has expanded horizons of possible life opportunities beyond one's native country. However, the economic and cultural integration on a global scale poses challenges for young individuals as social norms and institutional regulations contain both global values and local particularities. The two often collide and create tension in everyday life, and further leave young individuals with increased uncertainty about future. The Korean educational migrants in this chapter are a part of this large universe of young individuals who live for protracted periods of young adulthood without anchoring in conventional notions of nationhood, citizenship, and borders. In this sense, while the subjects of my study were Korean educational migrants, the implications of their life stories in this chapter can be transcendent.

As a final point, my study also offers some insights for policy development for educational migrants. In recent years, there has been a strong emphasis on internationalization of colleges and curricula. Whereas the increasing number of international students serves as a growing revenue source, universities and colleges make little investments into better serving their international students. This is not to discount their continuing efforts to provide programs and services for students. Rather, I want to make a point that most of my informants or international students more generally tend to underutilize school resources available to them.

222   *Kirsten Younghee Song*

This is mostly because they find the services in their school less useful or relevant to them than they are to domestic students.

My informants often understood their migration as a long-term investment that their parents made for them to have "better" life opportunities. They often conceived of their life goals or migration goals with images of themselves living in the "big world" and being able to work internationally or to enjoy a lifestyle that would allow them to travel internationally.[7] These goals are undeniably impressionistic and lack articulation of their connection to tangible roles, positions, or statuses, or of how to achieve them in a practical sense through education, training, or skill sets. The loosely defined future works as two sides of the same coin: it gives them great freedom to explore possibilities yet leaves them without a clear sense of direction.

The Korean international/immigrant students in my study did not ask their schools to teach them how to adapt to "American culture," but that was usually all their schools offered. What universities do not seem to see is that international/immigrant students are similar to any other domestic students in that their primary concern is how they can discover their talents and skills, develop career and life goals, and find opportunities to realize them. Despite these similarities, international students have social and institutional barriers that make their entry into adulthood challenging in different ways from those of domestic students. The first and the most important step for universities and colleges to better serve their international/immigrant students is, then, to understand those unique constraints and offer them practical guidance for developing future goals while making efforts to mitigate the challenging conditions that obstruct their path to the "real" world after college. To that end, I hope this study of Korean educational migrants sheds light on this little known part of international students' lives in the United States.

Notes

1 About 27,350 Korean students at pre-college age migrated abroad for English study or school in 2008, which reflected a marked increase from 1,840 in 1999. Koreans make up 10% of the total international students in US higher education institutions (Institute of International Education [IIE], 2010). Korea is in third place among the top sending countries of study-abroad students to the United States following China and India, each of which has more than twenty-seven times the population of Korea.
2 The church held separating congregations for three different age groups for worship: older adult/married members, college students and young adult members (i.e., CYA) from ages 18 to 27, and youth/children members. Young adult individuals joined the church through the two most typical channels. First, religious Christian people would find the church through voluntary Internet searches or referral from family members or friends. Second, CYA recruited new non-Christian people through their partnership with Korean student associations affiliated with nearby universities and colleges. At the beginning of every semester, CYA helped new students settle into the town by offering them rides to stores, banks, or government offices. Once they established a relationship with new people, they invited them to the church for meals or social events. Some of the new people would continue participating in CYA with and without becoming Christian,

Lost in the "Big World"?   223

whereas many people stopped joining CYA after several occasional social gatherings. I first joined CYA through the second route as a new arrival to the town. Later, CYA became my research fieldwork site.

3 A *hagwon* is a for-profit institute, academy, or cram school (Korean: 학원).
4 United States Citizenship and Immigration Services (www.uscis.gov/working-united-states/students-and-exchange-visitors/students-and-employment).
5 Early study-abroad students are those who went to study abroad during their preteen or teenage years.
6 This work authorization by the US Citizenship and Immigration Services is given to international college students. Within this OPT period, a trainee must find an employer who can sponsor him or her for a working visa and have a visa application processed. If not, the trainee must leave the country when the OPT period ends.
7 IIE survey results show that a major contributing factor for international students' decision to study in the United States is to "enhance *career* opportunities and gain experience for *future employment* at home or internationally" (emphasis added, Report, p. 18).

References

Abelmann, N. (2009). *The Intimate university: Korean American students and the problems of segregation.* Durham, NC: Duke University Press.

Arnett, J. (2000). Emerging adulthood: A theory of development from the late teens through the twenties. *American Psychologist,* 55(5), 469–480.

Chun, H.C., & Choi, H.S. (2006). *Economics of English.* Samsung Economic Research Institute, CEO Information, 578.

Chung, K. (2008). *Korean English fever in the US: Temporary migrant parents' evolving beliefs about normal parenting practices and children's natural language learning.* Unpublished master's thesis. University of Illinois at Urbana-Champaign, IL.

Fong, V. (2011). *Paradise redefined: Transnational Chinese students and the quest for flexible citizenship in the developed world.* Stanford, CA: Stanford University Press.

Heller, M. (2003). Globalization, the new economy, and the commodification of language and identity. *Journal of Sociolinguistics,* 7, 473–492.

Juárez, F., LeGrand, T., Lloyd, C., Singh, S., & Hertrich, V. (2013). Youth migration and transitions to adulthood in developing countries. *The ANNALS of the American Academy of Political and Social Science Series,* 648, 6–15.

Institute of International Education, USA, (2010). *Open Doors.* Washington, D.C., USA.

Kalakoski, V., & Nurmi, J. (1998). Identity and educational transitions: Age differences in adolescent and commitment related to education, occupation, and family. *Journal of Research on Adolescence,* 8, 29–47.

Kang, Y. (2012). Singlish or Globish?: Multiple language ideologies and global identities among Korean educational migrants in Singapore. *Journal of Sociolinguistics,* 16(2), 165–183.

Kwon, E. (2014, December 2016). Big companies, unfavorable to applicants studied abroad. *Hankook Daily.* Retrieved January 6, 2016 from www.hankookilbo.com/v/ff4bf47f3db04e7390806026b8f171e2.

Lee, A.J. (2006). Asian American studies: Identity formation in Korean American parachute kids. *Scholarly Commons.* Retrieved December 15, 2015 from http://repository.upenn.edu/cgi/viewcontent.cgi?article=1011&context=curej.

Lo, A., Abelmann, N., Kwon, S.A., & Okazaki, S. (2015). *South Korea's education exodus: The life and times of study abroad*. Berkeley, CA: Center for Korean Studies Publications.

Park, J.S., & Lo, A. (2012). Transnational South Korea as a site for a sociolinguistics of globalization: Markets, timescales, neoliberalism. *Journal of Sociolinguistics*, 16(2), 147–164.

Park, J. (2009). 'English Fever' in South Korea: Its history and symptoms. *English Today*, 25(1), 57.

Riley, M. (1987). On the significance of age in sociology. *American Sociological Review*, 52, 1–14.

Settersten, R., Ottusch, T., & Schneider, B. (2015). Becoming adult: Meanings of markers to adulthood. in R.A. Scott & S.M. Kosslyn (Eds.), *Emerging Trends in the Social and Behavioral Sciences*, pp 1–16. Thousand Oaks, CA: Sage.

Shin, H. (2012). From FOB to cool: Transnational migrant students in Toronto and the styling of global linguistic capital. *Journal of Sociolinguistics*, 16(2), 184–200.

Song, M. (2010). *Choosing ethnic identity*. Malden, MA: Blackwell.

Zenteno, R. (2013). Mexican adolescent migration to the United States and transitions to adulthood. *ANNALS, SSPSS*, 648, 18–37.

CHAPTER **14**

Migration and Gendered Webs of Obligation: Caring for my Elderly Puerto Rican Mother in a Transnational Context

Maura I. Toro-Morn

Introduction

In the last three decades our awareness of how migration has become a way of life for families around the globe has grown exponentially (Castle & Miller, 2009; Hondagneu-Sotelo, 2003; Toro-Morn & Alicea, 2004). This has been called the era of global migrations due to the numbers of people who themselves uprooted around the world. We know that underlying the era of global migrations lie complex globalization processes responsible for the differential incorporation of men and women as immigrants, refugees, and migrants. Empirical research has exposed the way families manage migrations, the disruptions it has created, and how families reconstitute themselves across time and space (Abrego, 2014; Ehrenreich & Hochschild, 2003; Herrera, 2013; Parrenas, 2001). It is well known too that men and women migrate for different reasons and the social consequences of migration are felt around the world. Immigrant women, in particular, share a greater burden of the migration process as many are called to reconstitute emotional and reproductive tasks transnationally (Flores-Gonzalez, Guevarra, Toro-Morn & Chang, 2013; Alicea, 1997; Parrenas, 2005; Pessar & Mahler, 2002).

I have spent a good part of my career immersed in this vast body of work, theorizing the gendered dimension of global migrations, but also witnessing some of these processes in my own family. This essay grows out of a desire to capture an element of the migration stories that has not been studied: who cares for our elder parents when adult children leave to work and live abroad? Migration scholars have shattered the notion that immigrants break away from their families of origin. In fact, we know that immigrant families are reconstituted across transnational fields and that emotional and reproductive work gets done from afar. As sociologists Peggy Levitt, Josh De Wind, and Steven Vertove (2003) put it "the recognition that some migrants maintain strong, enduring ties to their homelands even as they are incorporated into countries of resettlement calls into question conventional assumptions about the direction and impacts of international migration" (p. 1).

226 *Maura I. Toro-Morn*

The migration of Puerto Ricans—the second largest Latino group in the United States—represents an important body of literature in the sociological study of migrations. The study of Puerto Rican migration has contributed to understanding how under the auspices of US colonialism men and women were deployed as a source of cheap labor to work in factories (Sanchez-Korrol, 1994; Whalen, 2001), farms (Findlay, 2014), and the emerging service sector in large urban centers (Perez, 2004; Whalen, 2001). Puerto Rican scholars have worked to recognize how gender obligations and gendered work shaped the migration of women (Toro-Morn, 1995, 1999) and the transnational work that women do on behalf of their families (Alicea, 1997; Aranda, 2003, 2006, 2007; Perez, 2004). Scholars in a variety of fields have studied the growth and development of Puerto Rican communities and the struggles Puerto Ricans have encountered as "immigrants" and as people of color (Perez, 2004; Whalen, 2001). Sociologist Marixsa Alicea (1997) made the case that while the transnational literature had helped to envision a new way of thinking about migration, studies had not explored the role that women play in sustaining links between families and communities. She argued that Puerto Ricans maintained ties to their communities in Puerto Rico as a way to cope with the prejudice and discrimination they face as migrants. Even more importantly, she also provided evidence of the important role that women played in the construction of a transnational community. She argued that the subsistence and kin work that Puerto Rican women carried out on behalf of their families was not equitably distributed, and it created contradictions in women's lives. Puerto Rican women met the physical and emotional needs of more than one household and in doing so created webs of obligation that frequently taxed them emotionally and physically.

More recently, sociologist Elizabeth Aranda (2003, 2007) offered new insights into how migration heightens the meaning of kinship and family for both Puerto Rican men and women. She provides empirical evidence of how men and women engaged in emotion work to address the dislocations that migration engendered. She documented how men were able to reconcile their gendered identities through migration. As she puts it, migration enhanced men's ability to do gender. For women, on the other hand, migration precluded them from doing gender in culturally prescribed ways. In other words, "migration leads to a separation of social life in which professional success is, in many cases, pitted against emotional fulfillment through care work; for women, specifically, work and family stand in opposition to each other" (2003, p. 624). Indeed, Aranda (2003) found that for women "constraints on global care work result not just in emotional dislocation but also carry the potential to alter settlement decisions, opening the door to further migration," (p. 624) in most cases returning to Puerto Rico. Aranda reported that women felt dislocation processes more acutely because migration limits their ability to do gender. Aranda concluded that the frustrations Puerto Rican women migrants encountered in trying to accomplish care work were indicative of how globalization processes tear at the fabric of intimate lives. She called for more research to examine how global actors and transnational families continue to deal with these new family situations. This essay attempts to respond

Migration and Gendered Webs of Obligation   227

to Aranda's call for more evidence on how middle-class professionals are dealing with the dislocations engendered by migration processes and how migration reconstitutes family obligations.

This chapter seeks to deepen these insights on the nature of the transnational gender work that sustains family life across communities by offering an auto-ethnographic account of how my family—primarily my younger brother, Jose Toro, and myself—cared for our mother during the last 3 years of her life. At the most basic level, to live a transnational life means to account for practices and relationships linking immigrants/migrants to their families in the home country. Transnational care refers to the work that women and men do to care for each other both materially and emotionally. Transnational care comes with its own emotional terrain and complexities, a process I hope to unravel in this chapter. Drawing on my experiences, I propose that caring for elderly parents in a transnational context challenges the gender obligations of sons and daughters. In the end, we met familial gendered expectations of care for our mother in the last stages of her life in the best way we could.

A few words about method are important here. I did not set out to write an auto-ethnography when my mother suffered a stroke that left her incapacitated and prompted a new set of family arrangements in order to care for her. I wrote in my journal as a way to deal with the stress and emotional issues I faced as a "transnational daughter," a term I use in this essay as a way to describe my experiences. In teaching and writing about the gendered dimensions of global migrants, I realized that there is very little work that addresses how families separated by migration care for each other at the end of life, thus my desire to write this essay. At the most basic level, this chapter offers a "personal story" (Mohanty, 2003). Chandra Mohanty (2003, p. 191) writes that the task for contemporary feminist theorists is to deploy the "personal story" not as "immediate feelings expressed confessionally" but "as something that is deeply historical and collective." She adds the meanings of the "personal (as in my story) are not static," but "they change through experience and with knowledge." As a Latina sociologist, my work is also informed by two foundational traditions: qualitative-ethnographic research and the practice of *testimonio*. It is in the larger context of qualitative-ethnographic research that I wish to place the current effort. This is not my first attempt writing auto-ethnographically about my life. In 2010, I wrote about my experiences as a woman of color teaching in a predominantly white institution (Toro-Morn, 2010). In 2013, I reflected upon my experiences as an academic mother by offering a *testimonio* to my mother's story as a working woman (Toro-Morn, 2013). In Latin America, the practice of testimonio has been used as a way to speak truth to power. However, more recently, the Latina Feminist Group (2001, p. 19) offered a way to deploy the practice of testimonio as a way to capture "Latinas' complex, layered lives." Thus, I call the current effort an auto-ethnographic *testimonio* as I seek to draw from two foundational traditions that have shaped my work. For this essay, I draw upon my journals, memories, family stories, and available sociological literature about aging, migration, and women's work experiences in Puerto Rico.

228   *Maura I. Toro-Morn*

This essay is organized in the following fashion: first, I offer a quick overview of the colonial context connecting Puerto Rico to the United States and what has come to be known Puerto Rico's modernization program, Operation Bootstrap, the export-processing model that shaped the incorporation of women into the labor force. Operation Bootstrap is also responsible for transforming Puerto Rico into a "nation on the move," a term coined by anthropologist Jorge Duany, to characterize how migration has become the most pervasive strategy for Puerto Ricans across social classes to deal with economic, familial, social, and cultural problems. My own family's story threads through those events in significant ways: my mother was a factory worker in the export-processing zone in Mayagüez. When I migrated to the United States in the 1980s, I too became a transnational daughter, a term I coined in this chapter. Through the years of separation, we provided transnational care for each other, but as her health declined, my brother in Puerto Rico and myself in Illinois collaborated to provide care for our mother in a transnational context: he was in Puerto Rico and I was in Illinois. This essay aims to capture the complexities of providing transnational care for my mother—an unanticipated gender role reversal that took place in our family: whereby my brother became the main provider of care for her in San German. From my home in Illinois, I cared for my mother by calling daily to the nursing home to speak to her and learn about her well-being. Transnational care also included buying and mailing toiletries and clothes; calling the nursing home to inquire about her daily care and routines; when she was well, I talked to her daily by phone; I consulted with her doctor, arranged and payed for her nursing home expenses. I also paid for additional care (someone to stay with her at the hospital) when needed during her many frequent hospitalizations. There were times when I flew home to care for her in the hospital. Unbeknown to me, the last visit I made proved to be in the final week of her life. Once the funeral was over, I flew back to Illinois with my family and was left to grieve her transnationally too. In the last part of this essay, I offer some concluding thoughts about the nature of transnational care work for elderly parents and the caveats within in my own story.

Overall, this essay seeks to contribute to the growing body of literature about how Latino families exist and take care of each other in a transnational context. It seeks to argue that Puerto Ricans continue to be relevant to understanding transnational migration processes. But, most importantly, this chapter seeks to engage the migration literature by calling for more research that recognizes how migration strategies also impact end-of-life stages. It also seeks to contribute to the body of work that recognizes that transnational work, like migration, is deeply gendered.

Modernization, Operation Bootstrap, and Migration: A Historical Overview

It is beyond the scope of this chapter to offer an exhaustive overview of Puerto Rico's history and industrialization program—Operation Bootstrap—that propelled the island to become "the showcase of the Caribbean," but the outlines

Migration and Gendered Webs of Obligation 229

of the story, alongside the migration that it engendered are relevant here. Historian, Eileen J. Suarez Findlay (2014) reminds us that modernizing tropes arrived in the island in the aftermath of the US invasion in 1898. She writes "the occupying power collaborated with liberal Puerto Rican elites to launch public health campaigns, build schools, and legalize divorce in Puerto Rico" (2014, p. 28). These policies implemented by the United States created severe disruptions among working-class families, thereby disrupting modernization goals. We had to wait for nearly half a century for a new version of modernity to fully realize itself in the middle decades of the twentieth century, under the economic development known as Operation Bootstrap. According to Findlay (2014, p. 35), Luis Munoz Marin, the political architect of the economic development model, spoke the language of science, technology, planning, and modernity to both Puerto Ricans and US economic interest. To US colonial and economic agents, he presented Puerto Rico as the poster child for Cold War modernity dreams. For Puerto Ricans, modernity included "the promise of social justice and national dignity, as well as access to new material objects and ideas. Land distribution, decent wages, a home of one's own, gender complementarity, an end of racial degradation and the shame of a past steeped in slavery, a political voice for all Puerto Ricans, regardless of wealth and gender" (Findlay, 2014, p. 35).

The motto of Munoz Marin's party—the Popular Democratic Party—"Pan, Tierra, y Libertad" (Bread, Land, and Freedom) packaged the dreams offered to Puerto Ricans at the time. At the broadest levels, the promise of modernity came with an attempt to redefine US colonial rule. Munoz Marin and the intellectual elite that supported him wanted to redefine US colonial rule as a partnership that would bring prosperity and dignity to Puerto Ricans. The plan was to modernize the island and bring to a job-starved nation work that would end misery and poverty. Indeed, Operation Bootstrap transformed Puerto Rico from an agricultural economy to a modern industrial society of consumption and dreams of upward mobility by attracting foreign investment. Export-processing zones appeared all over the island and offered low-wage employment to mostly working-class women. The "maquila model," the heart today's global assembly line, was first developed in Puerto Rico (Colon-Warren & Alegria-Ortega, 1998; Rios, 1990). Anthropologist, Gina Perez (2004, p. 55) notes that while it is clear that the success of the industrialization model depended on the low-wage work of Puerto Rican women, the modernization ideology underlying the program was decidedly masculinist. In other words, in theory, the industrialization model and its accompanying modernization ideology came with its own gender assumptions. First, factories were supposed to provide employment for mostly men who were displaced from agricultural work and in that way restore the traditional gender order in the family. The lived realities of Puerto Ricans then and today crushed the ideology of modernity and progress so cherished by the intellectuals of the industrialization model and policymakers. Modernization via industrialization was fraught with contradictions and unresolved tensions that continue today (Perez, 2004).

230   *Maura I. Toro-Morn*

My mother was part of the massive labor force of working class and poor women and men who became the backbone of the industrialization model. I have vivid memories of her life and struggles as a factory worker for a US manufacturing company that made uniforms for the US military. These memories—far too numerous to fully capture in this essay—are punctuated by pain, hers and my own. Daily and weekly struggles to meet production, frequent complaints and frustrations about management, and fears of being laid-off impacted our lives in profound ways. The summer of 2008 I reconnected with her friends from "la fabrica," (the factory), women that I knew by name from my childhood, but whose faces were now unrecognizable. They gathered at the hospital to help me care for her and they visited her at the nursing home as an act of friendship and solidarity. Some took it upon themselves to call me in Illinois to offer reports about her health and well-being. I learned a lot more about my mother, her friends, and their lives as working mothers as they gathered to visit my mom at the nursing home. Collectively, they belong to a generation of Puerto Rican women who found themselves as historical agents in the development of export industrialization in Puerto Rico.

It is also well known that as the modernization program failed to produce expected outcomes of lowering unemployment, declining poverty rates, and prosperity that was anticipated, migration became the safety valve to address failures of the program. The local intellectual elites promoted migration as a way to both address the failures of the industrialization program and promote the tropes of modernity. Again, this is a complicated story that transcends this essay, but it is important to point out that Puerto Ricans had a history of migration to New York and Hawaii, among other places, as a source of cheap labor. In the 1950s, the government promoted migration to New York, where there was a mounting backlash against Puerto Ricans who were seen as "problem people." To be sure, working-class dreams of modernity and prosperity inspired women to leave Puerto Rico to work as *domesticas* in the homes of upper-class Chicagoans (Toro-Morn, 1999), the steel mills of Chicago (Alicea, 2001), and the sugar beet fields of Michigan (Findlay, 2014), among other places. As a result, migration has become a way for Puerto Ricans across social classes to address the unresolved tensions of more than 100 years of colonialism and new neoliberal globalization policies. Today, Puerto Ricans are adding a new chapter to the migration diaspora as record numbers move to a new destination, Orlando Florida. As anthropologist Jorge Duany (2002) asserts, we are "a nation on the move."

Migration and Transnational Care: A Transnational Daughter Remembers

In the next pages, I describe and analyze the various ways that we cared for our mother, as we became a transnational family because of my migration to Illinois in the 1980s. In retrospect, transnational care work had become a characteristic of our family since my departure and it intensified over the years as my mother aged. Here, I first describe how care was reconstituted in the aftermath of my

Migration and Gendered Webs of Obligation   231

departure to pursue graduate studies; the intervening years as my commitment to staying permanently in the United States was evident; and then, I describe the last 3 years of her life when transnational care intensified for me. The structure may seem arbitrary, but in my view, these points serve as "magnified moments" that help me contextualize the shifting nature of our gendered obligations to our mother and how care intensified and shifted as my mom grew older. In keeping with Alicea's (1997) and Aranda's (2007) findings, caring for my mother from Illinois added stress and strained obligations to my nuclear family in Illinois. As a professional woman, I already struggle balancing work and family demands; now I had the added dimension of caring for my mother in Puerto Rico. Caring for our mother also strained my relationship with my brother and his family. It sharpened family divisions and exacerbated emotional issues that had been present but buried in our family history. A dimension of transnational care that has not been addressed by the current literature—with a few exceptions—is death and mourning.

A Daughter Migrates . . . A Son Stays Behind: Gender Tensions

In 1983, I added my own chapter to the family's migration story when I left Puerto Rico to pursue graduate work in Illinois. In retrospect, I realize now that we provided emotional transnational care for *each other* in the aftermath of my departure through letters and frequent phone calls. We communicated frequently and helped each other emotionally as we had done when we lived together. At the time she was still working at the factory and her letters were filled with stories about the problems she faced with management. I, in turn, shared my experiences as a graduate student and my struggles learning English and trying to maintain good grades. This is in keeping with Alicea's (1997) findings among Puerto Rican women migrants in Chicago (see also Padilla, 1987).

In the 1980s—pre-Internet era—letters and telephone calls constituted our most important forms of communication. I have copies of the letters she wrote me, they offer a glimpse of her days and what mattered to her at the time, her worries about my well-being, and her continued struggle to provide for me and my brother who was still living at home. After a while, letters were not enough and with the advent of cheap-long distance calling, phone calls kept us connected to each other in complicated ways. Sometimes the phone calls were too invasive as I tried to create my own space in the United States, but as a good daughter, I obliged. We called each other every day without fail and sometimes we would call each other more than once. Through these frequent phone calls, I felt as if I never left. I learned about who got married, who was sick, who was detained by the police, and about the developing political situation in the island. In an aging society, my mom's news shifted from marriages and births to who had Alzheimer's, was sick, or has passed away. I witnessed from afar the aging and emptying of my neighborhood. These absences were even more pronounced during my frequent visits in December. I am sure I was an oddity among my graduate school friends in terms of my strong attachment to my mother and our frequent phone calls to

232 Maura I. Toro-Morn

each other. It did not matter where I went in the world, I would always find a way to call her to inquire about her life and health. Similarly, my calls would let her know that I was well too.

Emotional care constitutes an important part of the work that immigrant women do for their families from abroad. Leisy Abrego's (2014) ethnography, *Sacrificing Families: Navigating Laws, Labor, and Love across Borders* captures in heartbreaking detail how Salvadorean families are separated by years due to immigration laws and the work that parents do to sustain those ties and support their families. Abrego (2014) stated, "it is clear that most transnational families seek migration and family separation as survival strategies that take advantage of global inequalities in wages. Mothers and fathers practice parenting from afar through remittances, gifts, and weekly phone calls; children play a role in supporting or challenging these arrangements; and the bulk of the care work in both sending and receiving regions falls on women" (p. 4).

As I stated before, the tropes of modernity arrived in the island in the 1950s, but traditional gendered expectations continue to shape men and women's lives today. Empirical evidence suggest that much has changed for Puerto Rican women in terms of their participation in politics, educational opportunities, and labor market experiences, but family demands and gendered expectations continue to permeate women's lives. Although both sons and daughters are expected to care for parents and grandparents, women continue to feel a greater obligation to provide care for family members. In my family's case, migration shattered those expectations as the moment I left to pursue graduate study, my brother, who was still living with my mother—in keeping with Puerto Rican custom—became responsible for her care and well-being. At the time, she was relatively healthy, active, and my brother was there for her when she needed him. She was a fiercely independent woman with a life of her own, outside of the home. There were times when she got sick—mild cold, flu, or something minor—and so my brother took care of her. This entailed taking her to the doctor and waiting for her and taking her back home. When he got married and left the house, things changed dramatically.

In keeping with the definition of transnational work provided at the beginning of this chapter, since my departure, I traveled to the island every December, first alone, then with my fiancé—who became my husband—and then when we had a family, with my son, Carlos. Christmas was a time to gather as a family, to reconnect, and to be with each other. Our family extended to relatives from my father's side of the family and my non-blood-related extended family, requiring us to make numerous trips to visit family members across town. Since we had transportation (a car rental), December was also her time to visit friends and to go out shopping. The availability of "carros publicos" allowed her to run errands on her own, but with some limitations. Our house was within walking distance to downtown Cabo Rojo, where my mother had her network of friends and bought her groceries. Walking to town constituted her daily exercise and source of distraction and social connection. She had her routine of eating breakfast, running errands, talking to her friends. Like other elderly people in the United States,

Migration and Gendered Webs of Obligation 233

she loved to go to the casinos with her friends. During our December visits, we took her with us as we toured around the island. We also indulged her delight to go to the casinos to play slot machines. After our son Carlos was born, our outings tended to be more organized around family visits and our favorite pastime, the beach.

Invariably, every December questions about her health and well-being were raised and the question of her care would be raised. We always tried to reassure her that we would care for her no matter what! She would not have demanded that I abandon my career and return to the island to care for her, but the expectation of her care was implicit in many of these family conversations. She wanted to live and die in her home, a place she had labored to create by herself as a working woman. At the time, the notion of placing a parent in a nursing home was tantamount to abandonment of filial obligations. Even when some of her close friends had to be placed in nursing homes, there was always a tinge of recrimination aired against sons and daughters. At some level, I understood her desire to live and die in her home, but I had no idea what that might entail if I was living in Illinois. Who would care for her 24/7?

I would never forget the year when the conversation changed and she tacitly gave us permission to put her in a nursing home. Did she recognize the complexities of her request to receive care at home? What had shifted for her? We lived in a poor, working-class neighborhood, and over the years, she herself witnessed the death of many neighbors and friends. She also witnessed the struggles of sons and daughters caring for aging parents. One family in our neighborhood provides a particularly relevant example of the struggles of prolonged care for aging parents. Theirs was a big family of several daughters and sons who had migrated to Chicago in the 1960s and they too constituted a transnational family of care and obligation. After many years of working in Chicago, the parents retired to Cabo Rojo. They also sought to escape the brutal winters in Chicago and enjoy their home in Puerto Rico, home that had been constructed with their hard work and remittances. Like us, the children shuffle back and forth between Chicago and Cabo Rojo to be with kin for Christmas, summers, and vacations. Eventually, their mother became bedridden and the father became the primary care provider for over a decade of her life. Suddenly, the father too fell ill and caring for bed-ridden parents intensified. They traveled back and forth to care for both aging parents, some daughters managed to stay for prolonged periods of time. When the father died, the question of care for the surviving yet bed-ridden mother was raised. To take her back to Chicago was for the family—and the inquiring neighbors—out of the question. Instead, they placed her in the care of a recently arrived immigrant woman from the Dominican Republic who moved into our neighborhood with her children. She did not have proper documentation to work but needed to work. The family in Chicago pooled their income and paid her the monthly wages for her care. Doctors visited her in the home. For over 15 years, they were able to sustain this level of care for their mother until she died. It was common knowledge, in the neighborhood, of the sacrifice that the family incurred to care for both aging parents. Researchers have found that immigrant women from the Philippines and

234   *Maura I. Toro-Morn*

Latin America also provide this kind of care work for aging Americans (Parrenas, 2001b). Many of the immigrant women are also in the United States without documents.

As the years passed, my commitment to my career and family in Illinois deepened, but the trips home continued. We flew to Puerto Rico in December like clockwork, no matter what conditions. In the intervening years, caring for her was not a source of concern. She was relatively healthy, active, and my brother was there to care for her. There were times when she got sick—mild cold, flu, or something minor—and so my brother took care of her. This entailed taking her to the doctor and waiting for her to be seen. Buying her medicines and checking on her once she was home. Sometimes, he spent the night with her at the emergency room if the situation warranted.

After my brother got married and formed a family of his own, providing care for her became more difficult for him. Now, he had growing obligations to his new family. In the past, marriage of sons and daughters expanded the web of care in the family, but in my brother's case this was not possible. Tensions between my mother and sister-in-law resulted in strained and volatile relations between our families, placing my brother in the middle of a horrible dilemma: Do your obligations to your family—in this case our mother—change once you are married? My mother believed that his obligations toward her were as important, if not more important, than his obligations to his wife and new family. I witnessed these issues many times during my December visits. He expressed to me a multitude of times the difficulties he faced in trying to balance his responsibilities to Mom and his new family. Nevertheless, there was nothing I could do; he was in Puerto Rico and I lived in Illinois!

My mother had been a fiercely independent and hard-working woman all her life. She defied gendered conventions—some may say she exemplified notions of the modern woman—by having us as a single woman and now in her old age she continued to be fiercely independent and self-reliant. Yet all of that crashed when she suffered a stroke on Father's Day in 2008, the topic I will address next. In the remaining pages, I will describe the most intense period of transnational care that took place for the last 3 years of her life. She died at the Metropolitan Hospital on September 23, 2011. She was 82 years old. For 3 years, my brother and I shared the responsibilities of her care. We made decisions about her care and health in collaboration with each other: he worked and lived in Puerto Rico and I worked and lived in Illinois. He visited her weekly in the nursing home and provided a lot of the most immediate emotional care. He spent many hours with her in the hospital, at the expense of sacrificing his family obligations. From Illinois, I consulted with the nursing staff and her doctor about her well-being and called my brother if necessary. My family traveled to Puerto Rico in December, like we had done in the past, to be with her and to spend Christmas together. I also traveled to Puerto Rico every 3 months to supervise her care and to be with her. During periods of sudden hospitalizations, I flew home to care for her as well. The last days of my mother's life were spent in the Metropolitan Hospital of San German.

Health Crisis and Nursing Home

My mother had suffered a stroke episode—clinically labeled a TIA—a few years before the big one that robbed her of her independence in 2008. I was in California visiting my husband's family when I got a phone call from my brother. I could not rush home, but more importantly, he did not think it necessary for me to do so. He cared for her while at the hospital. This entailed staying with her while the results of blood tests arrived, waiting for her physician to come to see her, and waiting many hours for the hospital to dismiss her; hospitals in Puerto Rico are incredibly slow to process patients in emergency care. He took her home and in 24 hours she was back to "normal." She recovered fairly rapidly from what the doctor called "an episode," but her primary physician alerted my brother that this could get more serious. My brother conveyed the message to me on the phone. I realized then that things were bound to get more complicated. As a result, I increased the number of times we visited in the ensuing years. In 2008, my son and I spent spring break with her. A few months later, we were faced with a new set of family arrangements and demands that transformed our lives and stretched our emotional capabilities and economic resources.

My mother was the first to call us on birthdays and important holidays like Father's Day. In keeping with her tradition, that morning she had called my husband to wish him a happy Father's Day and expressed to me on the phone that she was not feeling well. I told her to get something to eat before she headed to the cemetery to leave flowers for her father, a Puerto Rican custom that she rarely missed. I promised I would call upon her return to check on her. I called back at the agreed time but no response, very unusual for my mom. I called my brother and asked him to check on her. Within minutes he called back with the news that the ambulance was at home: mom had suffered a stroke. She was hospitalized and a few days after her stroke, I flew to Puerto Rico to care for her, unaware of what this meant for us and my family, the one I left in the United States and the one I was returning to in Puerto Rico. At that moment, I became aware that I too had become like the immigrant women I studied, transnational mothers, caring for families on both sides of the ocean (Alicea, 1997; Aranda, 2007). As a Puerto Rican woman living and working in the US Midwest, this meant that the physical and emotional work of caring for my mother continued to be done in a transnational space.

I spent that summer in Puerto Rico, devoted entirely to caring for her. My brother and my extended family wrestled to understand the repercussions of the stroke for her health and her future. She had suffered quite a bit of damage and would no longer have use of her left hand and leg. Since she could no longer live by herself, the questions arose of how we were going to care for her. The notion of taking her with me to live in Illinois was deemed unrealistic. How could you travel with someone who has lost the capacity to sit in a chair for an extended period of time? She could not physically make the trip in her weak condition. Also, uprooting her to a place that was foreign was egregious. Given the contentious relationship that existed between my sister-in-law and mom, the idea of moving

236 Maura I. Toro-Morn

her to my brother's house was also quickly dismissed. Who would help us care for her? Could I afford to hire someone to care for her at home? I gathered phone numbers, called people, crunched numbers, inquired with friends who had reached similar arrangements, but it was clear to me that it was extremely costly and out of our reach. We had only one option: a nursing home. We visited many nursing homes in the West Coast of Puerto Rico (CaboRojo, San German, Mayaguez, and Hormigueros) and each visit was filled with dread and revulsion at the conditions we witnessed. This opened my eyes to the crisis of care in an aging island like Puerto Rico.

A friend of my brother told us that there was a nursing home facility opening in San German (West Coast) owned by a local professional who also owned the ambulance services in the town. We met the owners and began to explore transitioning mom to the new facility, which opened a few days before mom was released from the hospital. It was a beautiful house nestled in the mountains of Santa Marta, San German, a colonial city in the West Coast. I figured that the house had once been a very nice comfortable home to a middle-class family. Now it had been restructured as a nursing home facility for more than 15 patients. The large cement home was airy, clean, and accessible to my brother. It was a short distance from my mom's house in Cabo Rojo, where I stayed during my visits. The nursing home had a nice big kitchen facility and parking. But most importantly, it had a rather large and competent team of staff, with whom I was instantly friendly. We came to know them and the new residents pretty closely. Over the years, there was a sense of familiarity that helped us deal with the stressors of my mom's deteriorating health. My mother's Social Security check of $500 per month covered a portion of the $1,100 monthly nursing home cost. I assumed the remaining $600 of her monthly fee. Her health care expenses were paid by Social Security benefits. My brother took responsibility for the co-pay for her medicines. He also provided her with diapers and other toiletries.

For the 3 years she lived in the nursing home, my brother alone bore the brunt of her care since he was nearby. There were many emergencies, days lost in the hospital with a fever and infection, and other ailments. There were frequent calls to address her needs and just the routine visits. I tried to help by calling every day, mobilizing my own resources, but he was the one who was there and was called whenever any issues arose. During period of prolonged hospitalizations, I mobilized the care work of several local women who for a fee cared for her at the hospital, a role that is frequently provided by a daughter or son. I had a list of local women—an unemployed neighbor, a college student, and a friend of a friend who also worked as a care worker—that I could hire on a moment's notice to care for my mother in the hospital, while my brother worked. For $25 to $50 (typically 2–4 hours), they would sit with my mother at the hospital and make sure that she was bathed, fed, and that someone was there to advocate for her. I had access to them on the phone and so could call them while they were at the hospital with her and inquire about her health. They freed my brother of some of the burden of being at the hospital during the time he had to work.

Migration and Gendered Webs of Obligation 237

I also mobilized my own resources at the nursing home. For example, when the doctor visited her at the nursing home, I would know immediately—even before my brother—if she needed a new prescription—or anything related to her care. I would call and inform my brother of the changes and ask him to secure her new medicines. In other cases, if she needed toiletries, I would send them directly to the nursing home. I also had frequent conversations with her physician about her health. He understood the predicament we faced in caring for her and gave me his personal cell number with instructions to call him anytime I had any questions or queries. Early September of 2011, she had yet another emergency hospitalization. When I talked to him on the phone, he instructed me to come home as soon as possible. Unbeknownst to me, it would be the last emergency trip for me. A week later she passed away at the Metropolitan Hospital in San German, Puerto Rico.

I arranged cover for my classes and administrative obligations and left for Puerto Rico assuming that I would be back in a few days. She was conscious all the way through and was happy to see me at her bedside, but somehow this was different. I found the following notes in my journal.

> She was actively dying, but I did not know it, or perhaps I did, but I did not want to face it. I told her—and believed it in my heart that—IF she made it through the night we could go back home. But, she did not make it through the night. After midnight, her heart gave up. I had imagined that moment in the worst and darkest moments of the three years that we spent shuffling her from the nursing home to the hospital, but nothing ever prepared me for it. Nothing in the world prepared me for the feeling of being alone in the world.

The last week of her life, my brother and I cared for her every day. Since he worked, he would come in and out of the hospital, bring me food, and leave. I spent day and night at her bedside. I bathed her every day and fussed to make her comfortable. In my diary notes, I wrote about her passing: "as a working-class woman, my mother labored through her death like she did through most of her life. But I do know that she faced it with valor and strength, qualities that characterized her. My mother was a very strong, resolute, fiercely independent, generous woman, who loved deeply and passionately." In what remains of this essay, I will turn to her passing, funeral, and mourning transnationally.

Death and Funeral

My mother died a few minutes after midnight on September 23, 2011, that day also happened to be my husband's birthday, and the first day of the Patron Saint Festivities (Fiestas Patronales a San Miguel De Arcangel) of my home town. I learned the night of her funeral that my father and mother fell in love during one such night at the Fiestas Patronales many years ago. Also, 3 days earlier (September 20) was the tenth anniversary of my father's death. I want to believe that my father came for her; he seduced her away from us like he did many years ago! So fitting because theirs—I have come to know—was a love story for the history books.

238 *Maura I. Toro-Morn*

More than 200 people came to the funeral and paid respects. The mayors of Cabo Rojo (our home town) and San German (my brother's place of residence) came as did our island wide senator and many of her co-workers from the factory where she worked for more than 30 years. Again, I turn to my journal notes to capture the last moments we were together.

> While at the hospital, I was alone with her in the room, something that I came to cherish. I changed her sleeping position from leaning on her left side (paralyzed side due to the stroke) to the right. I knew she slept better on that side. She fell asleep and seemed out of pain, giving me an opportunity to close my eyes and lay down for a while. At around 11:00 pm, the nurses came to take her vitals. I asked about her blood pressure and was told that it was very low. I commented to the nurses about her heavy breathing, but their reply suggested that I should not be concerned. In retrospect, they probably knew what was coming, but did not want to tell me. Exhausted, I closed my eyes again until the IV machine woke me up after midnight. The IV ran out and it was beeping. "I have to call the nurse," I told myself half asleep. I slowly opened my eyes and looked at the heart rate monitor. It had a flat line!! I rushed to her side. Her face was so warm, but no breath. I pressed the nurse's station call button but no response. I heard them in the hallway and I rushed to the door, "Marilyn, ven, ven, que mami esta mala." She took her pulse and just looked at me. I think I screamed; I know I cried, long and hard, and between tears and screams, kissed her face many times. "Mi reina, se acabo la lucha, mi reina, mi reina." I told her many times as I touched her body, her working hands, and told her often how much I loved her, and will continue to love her, for the rest of my life. The entire nursing staff of the floor surrounded her bed and cried with me. They all had come to know her too, due to her frequent hospitalizations. Eventually, my brother came. We cried in each other's arms, hugged, and comforted each other. A young Tejano attending, Dr Cooper pronounced her dead at 12:45. We did not leave the hospital until the funeral home came for her. I had imagined that moment many times before: would it be at the nursing home? Would it be at home? Would it be at the hospital? It did not matter where it took place because the pain swept me off my feet and left me breathless. It is so deep that I still struggle to find words in English and Spanish to describe it; neither language allows me to capture it.

Funeral and burial rituals have changed a lot in Puerto Rico. Gone are the days when funerals were held in people's homes and the family stayed up for days. The funeral took place at the Funerary Montalvo, in Cabo Rojo, on Saturday, September 24, 2011. From 8:00 am until midnight, people came to see her and pay respects. My husband Frank and Carlos arrived in San Juan that afternoon and our compadres, Luz and Emilio (Carlos' godparents), picked them up at the airport and drove them to Cabo Rojo. At 10:00 am, on Sunday, September 25, 2011, with a city police escort from Cabo Rojo and San German—organized by my brother's co-workers—a caravan of friends, family, and town people drove in a funeral procession toward our home in el Barrio El Coqui, Cabo Rojo. Her one wish during most of the 3 years and 3 months that she lived in the nursing home was: "take me home." We wanted our mom to have one last chance to be in her house and the neighborhood where she lived and we grew up. The funeral hearse backed up on to the small alley way and parked in front of our house. Neighbors, friends, and family quickly gathered around us. We placed her casket on a set of wheels provided by the funeral home and rolled her into the yard where we reaffirmed our love and celebrated her life. From there, we carried her onto the street and walked the neighborhood, a path she had taken many times during her walks into town. My husband called it "the soul's stroll." We walked with her like we did when we were growing up ... A procession of neighbors, family, and friends followed the casket on to the street. At the end of our walk, we placed her back on the hearse and then caravanned with a police escort through town to the cemetery where it is customary to have one small final program. She was buried under a hot tropical sun with her friends and family around her.

Discussion and Concluding Thoughts

In the preceding pages, I have provided a deeply personal account of how my brother and I cared for our aging mother as a transnational family split between Puerto Rico and Illinois. Since I left Puerto Rico nearly three decades ago, I have lived a transnational existence—I am here but I am there. During the last 3 years of her life that transnational existence became a "modus vivendi" for me. I worked with my brother, Jose, to care for our mother every single day. The tropes of modernity in Puerto Rico have not caught up with the implications of aging, death, and dying. A gender role reversal characterized our family experience, in which my brother endured the most of her care from the moment I left the island to pursue graduate studies. In the last stages of her life, we made decisions about her health and well-being but he was left to execute them. As a transnational daughter, I tried to provide both material and emotional care. I contracted people to care for her when she was hospitalized. I called the nursing home every day. I traveled every 3 months to see and care for her. I was with her when she died, something that I will cherish for the rest of my life. But there is an emotional residue of the whole experience which must be unpacked and addressed.

I will continue to live a transnational existence because my ties to home have not been broken; my brother and his family live there and my mother's house needs to be managed. Electricity, water, cleaning bills must be paid. I continue to live a transnational existence with different kinds of obligations. The life course has changed that. We continue to visit the island as we have done for the last three decades. Now, the island has become the place where my son learns about his heritage.

I cared for her in a transnational space, now I must learn to grieve her "*entre mundos*" (between worlds). Where do I put my grief? What do I do with myself? Where can I go to see her, to remember her? The cultural differences in how

240   *Maura I. Toro-Morn*

people grieve remain striking to me. Here, grief is private, personal, contained. There, grief is open, public, ritualized, and communal. Megan O'Rourke felt "the privatization of grief" did not allow her to mourn her mother adequately. Some speak and write, in this connection of disenfranchised grief. I too search for ways to mourn my mom. I realize that I must invent my own means of mourning.

As an *auto-ethnographic testimonio,* this account contains limitations of its form. For one, this is one story, my story. This point can be pressed further in that, this is my story, not my brother's. His account might differ, but there are threads of our story that would certainly overlap. Similarly, given the scholarly research cited here, one could also argue that, like us, there are other Puerto Rican and Latino families struggling to provide care for their aging parents. Unfortunately, there is very little research that addresses their experiences. Collectively, Latinos are demographically young and there is a tendency in the research to study other life stages, not late life. Yet, as a sociologist, I recognized that our family story is not that far off the mark as elements of our story resonated empirically and theoretically with current research about transnational working mothers and transnational families in the Americas. A literature that addresses caring for aging parents in a transnational context, to my knowledge, does not exist, thus my desire to pursue this project in future research with a larger sample and other research conventions connected to qualitative research.

I am also keenly aware that as a Puerto Rican family, there are social and cultural dimensions of this story that separate us from other Latino groups. For example, there is the issue of citizenship—however flawed it may be—and how it allows Puerto Ricans movement back and forth between island and mainland communities, thus making care during emergencies and attending funerals possible. Further, as a US citizen, my mother received health care protection and a small Social Security check that helped toward her expenses. In other words, for women and families without documentation, being able to fly back and forth to care for an aging mother or father is impossible. There are anecdotal accounts of people who have gone back to care for their families, but returning to the United States has proved to be difficult in the aftermath of current militarization of the border and difficulties crossing borders without documentation. Many undocumented workers pay into Social Security, yet they are never able to take advantage of those services.

Social class matters here too. As a middle-class Puerto Rican professional working at a prestigious university, I was able to afford paying for my mother's nursing home and the frequent travels to the island. My family accommodated my departures and frequent absences for the 3 years that I shuttled back and forth, not without emotional costs. I also was able to use my social class location as a space to gather information from other sources.

Historically, migration has split families and in doing so has exposed important tensions in what have been constituted as traditional gender arrangements across immigrant families. This account has exposed the tensions that remain from an incomplete modernity experiment. Now, as Puerto Rico ages and the island continues to send its young and educated citizens to new destinations in the

Migration and Gendered Webs of Obligation 241

United States, the question remains: Who will care for our aging families? In the era of neoliberal globalization, we know that an army of women from the Global South have been dislodged to care for aging people in the Global North. The question still begs to be asked: Who will care for the aging parents of the immigrant men and women who leave to work and care for others?

References

Abrego, L.J. (2014). *Sacrificing families: Navigating laws, labor, and love across borders.* Stanford, CA: Stanford University Press.

Alicea, M. (1997). A chambered nautilus: The contradictory nature of Puerto Rican women's roles in the social construction of a transnational community. *Gender and Society*, 11(5), 597–626.

Alicea, M. (2001). Cuando nostros vivíamos: Stories of displacement and settlement in Puerto Rican Chicago. *CENTRO: Journal of the Center for Puerto Rican Studies*, 13(2), 166–195.

Aranda, E. (2003). Global care work and gendered constraints: The case of Puerto Rican transmigrants. *Gender & Society*, 17(4), 609–626.

Aranda, E. (2006). *Emotional bridges to Puerto Rico: Migration, return migration, and the struggles of incorporation.* Lanham, MD: Rowan & Littlefield.

Aranda, E. (2007). Struggles of Incorporation among the Puerto Rican middle class. *The Sociological Quarterly*, 48(2), 199–228.

Aranda, E. (2008). Class origins, modes of incorporation, and pathways into the Puerto Rican transnational middle class. *American Behavioral Scientist* (November), 52(3), 426–456.

Castle, S., & Miller, M.J. (2009). *The age of migration: International population movements in the modern world* (4th ed.). New York: Guilford Press.

Colon-Warren, A., & Alegria-Ortega, I. (1998). Shattering the illusion of development: The changing status of women and challenges for the feminist movement in Puerto Rico. *Feminist Review*, 59(summer), 101–117.

Duany, J. (2002). *The Puerto Rican nation on the move: Identities on the island and in the United States* (1st ed.). Chapel Hill, NC: The University of North Carolina Press.

Ehrenreich, B., & Hochschild, A.R. (2002). *Global woman: Nannies, maids, and sex workers in the new economy.* New York: Metropolitan Books.

Findlay, E.J.S. (2014). *We are left without a father here: Masculinity, domesticity, and migration in postwar Puerto Rico.* Durham, NC: Duke University Press.

Flores-Gonzalez, N., Guevarra, A., Toro-Morn, M., & Chang, G. (2013). *Immigrant women in the neoliberal age.* Urbana, IL: University of Illinois Press.

Herrera, G. (2013). Gender and international migration: Contributions and cross-fertilizations. *Annual Review of Sociology*, 39, 471–489.

Hondagneu-Sotelo, P. (2003). *Gender and U.S. immigration: Contemporary trends.* Berkeley, CA: University of California Press.

The Latina Feminist Group. (2001). *Telling to live: Latina feminist testimonios.* Durham, NC: Duke University Press.

Levitt, P., DeWind, J., & Vertovec, S. (2003). International perspectives on transnational migration: An introduction. *International Migration Review*, 37 (3), 565–575.

Mohanty, C.T. (2003). *Feminism without borders: Decolonizing theory, practicing solidarity.* Durham, NC: Duke University Press.

242 *Maura I. Toro-Morn*

Padilla, F.M. (1987). *Puerto Rican Chicago*. Notre Dame, IN: University of Notre Dame Press.

Parrenas, R.S. (2001a). Mothering from a distance: Emotions, gender, and intergenerational relations in Filipino transnational families. *Feminist Studies*, 27(2), 361–390.

Parrenas, R.S. (2001b). *Servants of globalization: Women, migration, and domestic work*. Palo Alto, CA: Stanford University Press.

Parrenas, R.S. (2005). *Children of global migration: Transnational families and gendered woes*. Palo Alto, CA: Stanford University Press.

Pessar, P., & Mahler, S. (2003). Transnational migration: Bringing gender in. *International Migration Review*, 37(3), 282–298.

Perez, G.M. (2004). *The near northwest side story migration, displacement, and Puerto Rican families*. Berkeley, CA: University of California Press.

Rios, P. (1990). Export–oriente

Sánchez-Korrol, V.E. (1994). *From colonia to community: The history of Puerto Ricans in New York City (Upd. Sub ed.)*. Berkeley, CA: University of California Press.

Toro-Morn, M. (1995). Gender, class, family, and migration: Puerto Rican women in Chicago. *Gender and Soceity*, 9 (6), 706–720.

Toro-Morn, M. (1999). Género, trabajo y migración: las empleadas domésticas puertorriqueñas en Chicago. *Revista de Ciencias Sociales Río Piedras*, (7), 102–125.

Toro-Morn, M. (2010). Migrations through academia: Reflections of a tenured Latina professor. In C.C. Robinson & P. Clardy (Eds.), *Tedious journeys: Auto-ethnography by women of color in academe* (pp. 63–96). New York: Peter Lang.

Toro-Morn, M., & Alicea, M. (2004). *Migration and immigration: A global view*. Westport, CT: Greenwood Press.

Toro-Morn, M.I. (2013). Threads that bind: A testimonio to Puerto Rican working mothers. In M. Castaneda & K. Isgro (Eds.), *Mothers in academia* (pp. 100–110). New York: Columbia University Press.

Whalen, C.T. (2001). *From Puerto Rico to Philadelphia: Puerto Rican workers and postwar economies*. Philadelphia, PA: Temple University Press.

Index

Abramson, Corey 153, 156
Affordable Care Act 29
aging enterprise 5, 25, 26, 37–38, 40–42, 46–57; *see also* institutions and institutional care
aging: impacts of, in the U.S. and other developed nations 1; places, as context for 7–8; aging network 5, 46–58
Alzheimer's disease 52, 86, 130–146; *see also* dementia
auto-ethnography 12, 47, 227, 240
autonomy 11, 116, 123, 157, 170–172, 188, 209

baby boomers 1, 2, 38, 39, 114, 137, 140, 153, 157, 164
Becker, Gaylene 10
Becker, Howard S. 14
Bengston, Vern 193
bio-medicalization of aging 5, 53,116, 119
Birren, James 42
Burawoy, Michael 25
bureaucracy 36; *see also* institutions and institutional care
Butler, Robert 42

Cabin, William 4, 5
caregiving (familial/kin) 1, 10, 12, 225–241

caregiving (paid) 1, 74, 112–130
children 7, 11, 21, 30, 47, 50, 95, 112, 118, 122, 123, 134, 136, 137, 143, 145, 152, 154, 157, 193–204, 210, 211, 212, 225, 229, 232, 233
Crampton, Alexandra 6, 51, 53
critical gerontology: (defined) 3–4, 35–45; theoretical approaches in 24, 28; *see also* gerontology
Cruikshank, Barbara 51
cumulative advantage/disadvantage 27, 29, 66, 98, 100–101, 116, 189, 193, 198, 202–203

Dannefer, Dale 2, 39, 189
dementia 7, 14, 57, 86, 115, 120, 122, 127, 137, 138, 139, 140, 141, 142
Diamond, Timothy 4, 123, 124, 127
discourse on aging/aged 4, 7, 24, 27, 30, 41, 43, 47, 49, 51, 52–57, 65, 70–73, 135–139, 140, 143, 145–146, 201; *see also* social problems perspective
Duneier, Mitchell 55

Emerson, Robert 47
Estes, Carroll 4, 5, 6, 12, 14, 20–31, 202
ethnography 2, 4, 12, 52, 73, 116–130, 153–156, 232

244 *Index*

feminist perspectives 10, 20, 21, 22, 24, 26, 30, 31, 227; *see also* gender
Foucault, Michele 47, 53

Gabrielson, Marcena 6
gender 1, 7, 8, 10, 12, 13, 20, 21, 22, 25, 27, 30, 46, 57, 58, 92, 93, 101, 104, 116, 117, 118, 155, 156, 166, 194, 195, 197, 225, 226, 227, 228, 229, 231, 232, 234, 239, 240
gerontology 1–13, 19–31, 35–53, 46–58, 63, 75, 193–204; *see also* critical gerontology
global perspectives 2, 10, 11, 27, 29, 36, 49, 57, 193–204, 208–211, 214–215, 221, 226, 227, 229–232, 241; *see also* trans-national aging
Goffman, Erving 14, 28, 121, 170, 171, 172
Gouldner, Alvin 19–20
Gran, Brian 195, 196, 199
grandparents 9, 47, 63, 68, 72, 127, 159, 174, 175, 193, 196, 197, 232
Gubrium, Jaber 13, 50

Habermas, Jurgen 37,
Hendricks, Jon 5, 12
Hochschild, Arlie 56, 153–154, 156
Holstein, James 13, 50, 53
home health care 5, 67, 71, 79–89, 113, 114, 115, 116, 125, 126, 127, 156
Hudson, Robert 48
Hughes, Everett 14, 51, 52–56, 58
human service institutions 5, 6, 46–58

immigration 11, 12, 25, 38, 124, 195, 208–223, 225–241
institutional ethnography 73; *see also* ethnography
institutions and institutional care 1, 2, 4, 5, 6, 7, 11, 14, 15, 19, 20, 24, 29, 37, 40, 42, 43, 46–58, 66, 67, 73, 80, 93, 95, 102, 114, 116, 120, 121, 122, 123, 125, 130, 152, 156, 157, 159, 160, 161, 164–189, 209, 216, 221, 222; *see also* human service institutions; total institutions

Jaffe, Dale 57, 122,
Janssen, Leah 8

Klinenberg, Eric 152
Koreans 11, 208–223
Kugelmass, Jack 154–155
Kuhn, Maggie 22, 23, 62, 76, 137, 145

Lemert, Edwin 135, 139, 145
lesbians 92–107,
life course perspective 1–2, 8–12, 13, 27, 30, 35, 36, 41, 49, 98, 99, 101, 105, 161, 193, 198, 199–201, 208, 239

Mattingly, Cheryl 6,
McAdams, Dan 10,
meanings in/of aging 1, 6, 8, 23, 28, 46, 53–54, 96, 118–119, 121,124, 155, 157, 159, 164–189, 212, 220, 226, 227
Medicaid 4, 23, 26, 29, 69, 72, 74, 79, 80, 82, 88, 113, 123, 128, 140, 152
medical model/perspectives 5, 6, 14, 24, 25, 40, 46, 53, 54–56, 65–66, 69, 71, 74–75, 80, 82, 86, 88, 105, 113–116, 119, 123, 125–127, 151, 159, 165–166, 168, 170, 186–187, 189; *see also* bio-medicalization
Medicare 4, 23, 26, 29, 39, 62–76, 80–88, 113, 123, 128, 137, 140, 152
Meyerhoff, Barbara 13, 151, 154, 155
Miller, Gale 6, 18, 47, 50, 53
Moody, Harry R. 3, 4, 50
Muschert, Glenn 7, 190

narrative gerontology 4, 6, 7, 8, 12–13, 42, 65, 67, 69, 93, 121, 156, 161, 177, 178
Neugarten, Bernice 14
Newman, Katherine 155–156

nursing 22, 80, 92–107
nursing home residents, 1, 8, 40, 52, 53, 63, 64, 68, 69, 72, 74, 79, 80, 82, 88, 94, 113, 114, 116, 119, 120–125, 127, 128, 152, 158, 160, 178, 228, 230, 233, 234, 235, 236, 237, 238

Older Americans Act 5
Omnibus Budget Reconciliation Act (OBRA) of 1980 81

Petonito, Gina 7
Pithouse, Andrew 6
places (as contexts for aging) 7–8, 151–162
policy and policy-makers 2, 3, 4, 5, 7, 8, 10, 11, 14, 15, 23–27, 28, 29, 36, 38, 42, 46, 47, 50–52, 62–76,79–88, 112–114, 116, 121–128, 130, 134–146, 152, 156, 166, 195, 204, 208, 220–221, 229
political economy perspective 3, 4, 10, 25, 26, 30, 36, 120

Index   245

public sociology 4
Puerto Ricans 12, 154, 158, 225–241

race/ethnicity 1, 7, 20, 24, 25, 27, 30, 46, 57, 155, 169, 195
reflexivity 13, 19, 25, 30
Riley, John 9, 10
Riley, Matilda 9, 10, 14, 200

Quadagno, Jill 1, 7, 146

Sasser, Jennifer 4,
Schmeeckle, Maria 11,
Silver alert 7, 134–146
social class 1, 2, 7, 9, 10, 12, 24, 25, 27, 30, 46, 57–58, 151, 155, 210–212, 215, 222, 228–230, 233, 236, 237, 240; see also social inequality
social constructionism 13, 134–135
social inequality 1, 22, 30, 117, 153, 156,
189, 193, 195, 198, 202, 204; see also cumulative advantage/disadvantage
social problems perspective 7, 24, 48–49, 50–51, 53, 96, 134–146, 156, 194
Social Security 4, 21, 23, 26, 29, 38, 39, 49, 50, 63, 66, 73, 137, 152, 217, 236
Song, Kirsten Younghee 11
standpoint perspectives 68

theory in gerontology 3, 6, 12, 19, 20, 24, 25, 29, 30, 35, 36, 40, 63, 97, 116, 140, 153, 198, 229; see also life course perspective
Toro-Morn, Maura 12,
Torres, Stacy 8
total institutions 121, 170–172
Trump, Donald 16, 30, 38, 43

Wellin, Chris 14, 57, 122, 169, 190
Wellin, Edward 9